The European Union and Regionalism

Nijhoff Studies in European Union Law

Series Editors

VOLUME 27

The titles published in this series are listed at *brill.com/seul*

The European Union and Regionalism

Conceptual and Contextual Perspectives

Edited by

Eva Kassoti, Teresa Cabrita and Narin Idriz

BRILL | NIJHOFF

LEIDEN | BOSTON

The Library of Congress Cataloging-in-Publication Data is available online at https://catalog.loc.gov
LC record available at https://lccn.loc.gov/2025032136

Typeface for the Latin, Greek, and Cyrillic scripts: "Brill". See and download: brill.com/brill-typeface.

ISSN 2210-9765
ISBN 978-90-04-70064-2 (hardback)
ISBN 978-90-04-70065-9 (e-book)
DOI 10.1163/9789004700659

This book is printed on acid-free paper and produced in a sustainable manner.

Contents

Introduction: The EU as a Regional International Organization 1
Eva Kassoti, Teresa Cabrita and Narin Idriz

PART 1

Framing the EU as a Regional International Organization: Conceptual Issues

1 The Soft Phenomenology of the Regional International Organization 21
Jan Klabbers

2 The EU Is Not a Role Model! Why Other Regional Organizations around the World Do Not Follow the Path of European Integration 40
Sebastian Krapohl

3 Solving European Problems with Regional Solutions? Conceptualizing 'the Region' in EU Higher Education and Climate Change Policies 66
Andrew Telford and Anne van Wageningen

PART 2

EU Regionalism in Practice

4 Enhancing Global Health and Human Rights Law through Regionality?: The Case of EU International Cooperation for Pharmaceuticals 93
Katrina Perehudoff

5 Can the EU Not Promote Free Movement of Persons in the External Action on Migration? Neglecting Regional Mobility in EU–Africa Cooperation 118
Eleonora Frasca

6 The Notion of Regionalism in the Context of Sanctions Adopted by Regional International Organizations in the Defence of the General Interest 142
Maruša T. Veber

7 The EU Anti-coercion Mechanism: A Tool for Development or Fragmentation of International Law? 170
Petr Stejskal

PART 3
Identity and Outlook

8 Questioning the Regional Character of EU Citizenship 201
Victoria Hooton

9 'Geopoliticization through Law': The European Union and Beyond 227
Joris E. Larik

10 Latin America Regional International Organizations and Climate Change: Managerialism and Judicialization 251
Andrés Delgado Casteleiro

Index 277

Introduction: The EU as a Regional International Organization

Eva Kassoti, Teresa Cabrita and Narin Idriz[1]

Abstract

This introductory chapter canvasses out some general thoughts on the broader topic of 'the EU as a Regional International Organization (RIO)' thereby setting out the context and framework for the discussion that follows in the subsequent chapters. First, it highlights the relevance of employing the RIOs' analytical lens in international legal discourse. The chapter argues that the RIOs' angle offers unique insights that feed into a number of important debates in modern international (institutional) law. Against this backdrop, it continues by exploring the merits of using the 'regional perspective' in debates regarding the EU. It is shown that the regional framing offers a fresh vantage point of view from which to approach lingering questions of EU law. The chapter concludes by providing an overview of the contributions in the edited volume.

Keywords

European Union (EU) – Regional International Organizations (RIOs) – region – regionalism – accountability – international organizations – International Law Commission (ILC) – regional integration

1 Introduction: RIOs in International Law

The rise and proliferation of Regional International Organizations (RIOs) has been one of the most salient features of modern international law. Nowadays, RIOs play an active and important role in a wide range of global governance

1 Eva Kassoti, Senior Researcher in International and EU Law, academic co-ordinator of the Centre for the Law of EU External Relations (CLEER), T.M.C. Asser Institute; Teresa Cabrita, Assistant Professor of EU Law, UCLouvain Saint-Louis Brussels; and Narin Idriz, Senior Researcher at T.M.C. Asser Institute.

 | DOI:10.1163/9789004700659_002

fields, such as migration, security, health, or climate change mitigation. Despite their increasing significance as global governance actors, RIOs have largely remained at the margins of scholarly attention – at least as far as international legal literature is concerned.[2] By way of contrast, regions, regional actors and regionalism have long been a focal point in international relations research.[3] It is only recently that international legal scholarship has started tackling in earnest the multifaceted questions that regional ordering poses for international law. Acknowledging the relevant gap in international legal literature, a Study Group (SG) on the *International Law of Regional Organizations* was established under the auspices of the International Law Association (ILA) in 2020 with the explicit aim to explore the law and practice of RIOs with a view to understanding the relevance and impact of this practice on international law.[4] The SG issued its final report in 2024.[5] In parallel and as an academic companion to the SG's work, the co-chairs of the ILA SG edited a Special Issue on the topic of 'The International Law of Regional Organizations' addressing a number of further conceptual, normative, historical and institutional issues pertaining to RIOs.[6]

These developments attest to the need to study RIOs and to pay closer attention to their significance for international law. Finally, there are some inherent difficulties to doing so. First, one must contend with the fact that no widely accepted definition of RIOs exists. Often, these entities are simply defined negatively by reference to universal international organizations (IOs).[7] In lieu of a common definition, the existing discussion focuses on two central elements: (i) the nature of RIOs as international organizations; and (ii)

---

2 Notable exceptions are Laurence Boisson de Chazournes, *Interactions between Regional and Universal Organizations: A Legal Perspective* (Brill/Nijhoff, 2017); Damian Chalmers, 'Regional Organizations and the Reintegrating of International Law' (2019) 30 EJIL 163.

3 Tanja A. Börzel, 'Theorizing Regionalism: Co-operation, Integration, and Governance', in Tanja A. Börzel, Thomas Risse (eds.), *The Oxford Handbook of Comparative Regionalism* (Oxford University Press, 2016) 41–63. For an overview, see Samantha Besson, Eva Kassoti, 'Introduction to the Special Issue: The International Law of Regional Organizations – Mapping the Issues' (2024) 21 IOLR 1, 7–13.

4 https://www.ila-hq.org/en_GB/study-groups/international-law-of-regional-organisations.

5 Fernando Bordin, Jed Odermatt, Samantha Besson, Eva Kassoti, 'International Law Association Study Group on the International Law of Regional Organizations, Final Report' 2024, available at https://www.ila-hq.org/en_GB/documents/ila-study-group-regional-organisations-final-report-may-24-1, accessed on 15 January 2025.

6 Besson and Kassoti (n 3).

7 Harry G. Schermers, Niels M. Blokker, *International Institutional Law* (6th Rev. Ed., Brill, Nijhoff, 2018), 57; Christoph Schreuer, 'Regionalism v. Universalism' (1995) 6 EJIL 477.

the element of regionalism.[8] In the literature, regionalism is employed to connote: (i) geographical proximity; and (ii) a social element referring to proximity founded on various 'solidarity links' that reflect common interests and values and may have economic, religious, social, cultural and political dimensions.[9] Secondly, the diversity of RIOs complicates matters even further. Since RIOs are quite diverse in many respects, legal generalizations are not easily made in this context. What holds true for one RIO may not hold true for another taking into account the many differences that may exist among them in terms of their institutional structure, tasks, competences and relations with the outside world.

These are formidable difficulties and thus, they may also explain the reluctance with which international legal scholarship has, until quite recently at least, approached the regional phenomenon. This reluctance is also evident in this volume. Jan Klabbers, for instance, in his chapter on 'The Soft Phenomenology of the RIO', questions the value of having recourse to the concept of the RIO on the grounds that it 'is far too elusive to be of much practical use ... Second, the law does not attach legal consequences to the quality of being a regional international organisation.'[10]

Difficulties notwithstanding, this book argues, and attests to the need, for more research on the 'regional' dimension of RIOs. It is worth recalling that the existing work on the topic acknowledges the inherent difficulties and the complexity surrounding RIOs and a number of arguments highlighting the relevance of employing the RIOs' analytical lens have also been put for

8 Bordin, Odermatt, Besson, and Kassoti (n 5) 12.

9 According to Boisson de Chazournes: '[T]wo elements can be said to characterise the regional phenomenon behind the creation of a regional organization: geographical proximity and solidarity founded on common interests and shared values.' Boisson de Chazournes (n 2) 8; Samantha Besson, 'Du Droit de Civilisation Européen au Droit International des Civilisations: Instituer un Monde des Regions' (2021) 31 Swiss Review of International and European Law 396.

For instance, when asked to present its view on what it means to be 'European' and where the borders of Europe lie in 1992, the Commission provided that 'European' in Article 237 of the Rome Treaty (now Article 49 TEU) combines: '... geographical, historical and cultural elements which all contribute to the European identity. The shared experience of proximity, ideas, values, and historical interaction cannot be condensed into a simple formula, and is subject to review by each succeeding generation.' Commission of the European Communities, Europe and the Challenge of Enlargement, Brussels, 24 June 1992, para. 7, p. 11, available at https://op.europa.eu/en/publication-detail/-/publication/d94b400d-b92f-4d91-995e-5f0ad1b36abe, accessed on 15 January 2025.

10 Jan Klabbers, 'The Soft Phenomenology of the Regional International Organization', in this volume.

ward.[11] This introduction will only briefly sketch out a few of them. First, the sheer diversity of RIOs is not a reason precluding their examination as an analytical category in the same vein that the sheer diversity of international organizations (IOs) has not precluded their study as such.[12] After all, the nature of RIOs as IOs is taken as a point of departure in the relevant discussion.[13] Yet, merely treating them as IOs would be to ignore their specificity and their increasingly important role in global governance. Granted, positive international law may not directly vest 'regionalism' with normative effects, but this does not negate the fact that the RIOs' law and practice can offer unique insights feeding into a number of important debates in modern international (institutional) law. Second, while the term 'region' remains opaque,[14] RIOs' law plays a central role in the legal construction and articulation of the regional identity, namely describing what the region stands for in legal terms.[15] Thus, for instance, while the European Union (EU) has consistently portrayed itself as a legal formalist whose pursuit of interests goes hand in hand with its commitment to the ethos of multilateralism and respect for international law, the Association of Southeast Asian Nations (ASEAN) has prioritised sovereignty, the peaceful settlement of disputes and recourse to soft law as part of its mandate. Casting into legal terms the regional narrative provides a tangible yardstick against which to assess whether the RIO actually sticks to the story it has created for itself. This provides concrete tools for holding RIOs accountable as significant loci of power.[16] This is no mean feat – particularly in light of the 'serious accountability deficit' that plagues IOs' law.[17]

---

11 See, for example, Besson and Kassoti (n 3); Eva Kassoti, 'The European Union and Other Regional International Organizations: Tales of Solidarity' (2024) 21 IOLR 190, 192–199; Chalmers (n 2) 163–166.

12 On the diversity of IOs, see generally, Jan Klabbers, 'Unity, Diversity, Accountability: The Ambivalent Concept of International Organisation' (2013) 14 MJIL 1, 14.

13 Apollin Koagne Zouapet, 'States and Regional International Organizations' (2024) 21 IOLR 190.

14 Tanja A. Börzel, Thomas Risse, 'Introduction: Framework of the Handbook and Conceptual Clarifications', in Tanja A. Börzel, Thomas Risse (eds.), *The Oxford Handbook of Comparative Regionalism* (Oxford University Press, 2016) 6.

15 Damian Chalmers, The Distinctiveness of Regional Organizations Law (2016) 21 IOLR 43, 46.

16 On this, see further, Samantha Besson, 'The Politics of Regional Organizations: A New Dawn for the Political Legitimacy of International Law' (2024) 21 IOLR 87.

17 Jan Klabbers, Guy Fiti Sinclair, 'On Theorizing International Organizations Law: Editors' Introduction' (2020) EJIL 31, 491.

Furthermore, RIOs constitute sites where the contributions of non-Western peoples and legal traditions to international law come into sharp focus. Thus, the study of RIOs helps us to problematize what counts as 'international' in international law[18] and provides a rich trove of source material for answering pressing questions of inclusiveness and representation in international law-making.[19] In a similar vein, enquiring into the practice of RIOs provides concrete examples of the Global South's contribution to the development of international law.[20] As Orford has eloquently put it: 'Taking regional orders seriously might open up space for considering how other states and their peoples have tried to shape international law in a world in which hegemonic powers exist.'[21]

RIOs also bring into sharp relief the role of the individual in international law. A number of RIOs such as Mercosur, ASEAN, the EU and ECOWAS have developed notions of regional citizenship, a point discussed in Victoria Hooton's contribution to this book.[22] Moreover, it is no accident that regional human rights protection regimes constitute the main pillars of the international system for the protection of human rights. This reflects the privileged position of RIOs when it comes to law-making processes. As the International Law Commission (ILC) has highlighted, within a regional setting: 'The presence of a coherent cultural community better ensures that the regulations enjoy legitimacy and that they are understood and applied in a coherent way. This is probably the reason why human rights regimes … have always commenced in a regional context, despite the universalist claims of ideas about human rights …'.[23]

Occupying the intermediate level between States and IOs, RIOs challenge the traditional binary of territory/function, thereby posing awkward questions about the relevance and accuracy of the very tools through which interna-

18 Anthea Roberts, *Is International Law International?* (OUP, 2017) 254–256.

19 Besson and Kassoti (n 3) 193; Besson (n 16); Chalmers (n 2) 165; Kassoti (n 11) 193.

20 For example, the predecessor of the African Union, the Organization of African Unity played a prominent role in the formulation of the concept of the Exclusive Economic Zone in the law of the sea. Abdulqawi A. Yusuf, 'Pan-Africanism and International Law' (2014) 369 Recueil des cours 1, 141–148.

21 Anne Orford, 'Regional Orders, Geopolitics and the Future of International Law' (2021) 74 Current Legal Problems 149, 193.

22 Päivi J. Neuvonen, 'Transforming Membership? Citizenship, Identity and the Problem of Belonging in Regional Integration Organizations' (2019) 30 EJIL 229–255.

23 Report of the Study Group of the International Law Commission finalized by Mr M. Koskenniemi, Fragmentation of International Law: Difficulties arising from the Diversification and Expansion of International Law, 13 April 2006, UN Doc. A/CN.4/L.682 and Add. 1, para. 205.

tional lawyers cognise the social reality on the ground of practice.[24] RIOs invite us to rethink the geographies of international law and to explore alternate spatial arrangements therein. In this sense, enquiring into the regional can feed into broader debates regarding the meaning of 'territory' in international law. There is, for instance, a growing body of public international law literature that advocates in favour of abandoning the understanding of 'territory' as a physical, geographical space since it no longer reflects the complexities of modern-day global governance and the rise of non-State entities, such as IOs and RIOs, with a wide array of public powers traditionally exercised by States.[25] Instead, authors of this school of thought have re-imagined 'territory' as a 'socially and legally bounded space',[26] a construct that allows us to consider non-State entities as also creating legal space through their social practices.

Finally, one should remain alert to the fact that the unease towards RIOs could also be attributed to the fact that these entities call into question dominant narratives about the universalist nature of the international legal order as well as the vision of IOs as politically neutral bodies working towards the public good. This has been aptly captured by Brölmann, who notes that: 'Regional organizations by their very existence challenge certain ideological underpinnings of international law, notably those connected to the universality of the law and to the 'neutrality' of organizations … So it is the case that … in the ideology of international law RIOs do not fit'.[27] Klabbers has also noted that RIOs disrupt the vision of IOs as entities that essentially work in the public interest and perform public tasks.[28] These concerns should not lead us to shy away from scrutiny of these 'misfits'. Quite to the contrary. The RIOs' strain on the universalist paradigm as well as on the ideal of IOs as neutral, apolitical and essentially benevolent creatures, confirms that they are important reference points in the debate on the nature of the international (institutional) order.

---

24 Catherine Brölmann, 'Review of L. Boisson de Chazournes (2017) Interactions between regional and universal organizations: a legal perspective' (2020) 114 AJIL 335; Besson and Kassoti (n 3) 5–6.

25 See for example Gail Lythgoe, *The Rebirth of Territory* (CUP, 2024) 208; Saskia Sassen, 'When Territory Deborders Territoriality' (2013) 1 TerrPolGov 21.

26 Jure Vidmar, *Territorial Status in International Law* (Hart Publishing, 2024) 22–25.

27 Catherine Brölmann, 'Regional Organizations in International Law: Exploring the Function-Territory Divide' (2024) 21 IOLR 132, 144–145.

28 Klabbers (n 12) 18–22.

2 The EU as a RIO

Against this backdrop, the next question that needs to be addressed at this juncture is the value of using the 'regional lens' in debates regarding the EU – probably the most well-known (and well-studied) example of a RIO. The 'regional' perspective is largely absent in debates about the EU's identity and external posture, as are reflections about how this perspective relates to that of other RIOs. What does the 'regional' lens offer to the study of EU law and how is it weaved in the legal and political imaginary of the Union? How is the regional dimension reflected in EU policy-making and how does it impact norm production? How does this dimension interact with regional solutions found in other RIOs and in other regional orders? These are some of the overarching questions that this edited volume sets out to address.

The RIO label remains a relevant identity-descriptor for the EU on the international stage. The term RIO is a common topos in the EU's discursive practice. Not only are RIO or regional economic integration organization (REIO) clauses common in the EU's international treaty practice,[29] the term is still, to date, often perceived as 'a code-name for the EU'.[30]

One forum where such dynamics – and the relevance of the descriptor – can be witnessed is the UN Sixth Committee and the debates therein on the work of the International Law Commission (ILC).[31] Here, EU legal advisers seeking to vindicate the relevance of EU practice for the ILC's work of codification and progressive development of international law, have relied on the REIO or RIO descriptor both to distinguish the EU from other IOs but also, perhaps inadvertently, to promote and advocate for the recognition of (R)IOs as relevant actors in the fabric of international law.

Examples of such reliance are recurring in UN Sixth Committee ILC-related debates. The most emblematic of such examples concerns the well-known drafting history of the Articles on the Responsibility of International Organisations (ARIO), where EU legal advisers sought, to little avail, to see codified special rules of attribution of conduct or of responsibility for REIOs and their

29 Jed Odermatt, *International Law and the European Union* (CUP 2021), 70–74; Tamas Molnar, Ramses A. Wessel, *Interactions between EU Law and International Law: Juxtaposed Perspectives* (Edward Elgar, 2024) 150–151.

30 Esa Paasivirta and Pieter-Jan Kuijper, 'Does One Size Fit All? The European Community and the Responsibility of International Organizations' (2005) 36 Netherlands Yearbook of International Law 169, 211.

31 On this, see generally, Teresa Cabrita, 'The Integration Paradox: An ILC View on the EU Contribution to the codification and development of rules of general international law' (2021) 5 Europe and the World: A Law Review 1.

member states.[32] Special Rapporteur Gaja, initially open to the idea of establishing different rules for different types of organization, also advanced a proposal recognising the right of REIOs to adopt countermeasures on behalf of their members '[w]here an injured State or international organization has transferred competence over certain matters to a regional economic integration organization of which it is a member'.[33] Granted, all such attempts at carving out a special legal place for R(E)IOs were soon rejected either by States or ILC member or both,[34] who were against codifying rules which they perceived as tailored to the 'special case' of the EU.

At the same time, the importance of RIOs has significantly grown in codification efforts that move from classic topics of international law to emerging issues of global governance such as the protection of persons in the event of disasters and the protection of the environment. In this context, it is expected that the EU will have a greater role to play as a RIO with significant practice in such new and emerging fields.[35] At the same time, EU practice also draws attention to the relevance of IOs practice more broadly. Take, for instance, the ILC's work on the protection of persons in the event of disasters, where EU legal advisers repeatedly requested that RIOs be expressly mentioned in the draft.[36] This request was heeded by Special Rapporteur Valencia-Ospina in

32 ILC, 'Responsibility of international organizations: Comments and observations received from Governments and international organizations', 2005 (A/CN.4/556), 31; Paasivirta and Kuijper (n 30) 216; Jed Odermatt, *International Law and the European Union* (CUP 2021) 201–204.

33 ILC, 'Sixth report on responsibility of international organizations, by Mr Giorgio Gaja, Special Rapporteur', 2008 (A/CN.4/597) para 66. Two chapters of the present edited volume deal with countermeasures. See the contributions by M. Veber and P. Stejskal.

34 With respect to a rule on countermeasures by REIOs, for instance, Jamaican ILC member Vasciannie objected to the idea that 'an entity denominated a [REIO] should be given a special status'. Statement by Mr Vasciannie, ILC, Summary record of the 2964th meeting, 16 May 2008, YBILC 2008 vol I (A/CN.4/SER.A/2008) 53, para 42.

35 Molnar and Wessel (n 29) 163.

36 See Statement by Mr Gussetti (Observer for the European Union), Sixth Committee, Summary record of the 21st meeting, 27 October 2011 (A/C.6/66/SR.21) para 57: '... the reference in those draft articles to the United Nations, other competent intergovernmental organizations and relevant non-governmental organizations might raise the question as to whether the provisions also included regional integration organizations, such as the European Union. In order to dispel any doubts on that score, [the EU] suggested that regional integration organizations should be expressly mentioned in the draft articles or that their inclusion should be made clear in the commentaries'. See also, Statement by Mr Gussetti (Observer for the European Union), Sixth Committee, Summary record of the 18th meeting, 1 November 2012 (A/C.6/67/SR.18), para 73; Statement by Ms Cujo (Observer for the European Union), Sixth Committee, Summary record of the 23rd meeting, 4 November 2013 (A/C.6/68/SR.23), para 32.

the commentary to the articles' draft text.[37] As it has been stressed: 'Through its observations to the Commission's work, the EU has championed the cause of international (regional) organizations as actors in their own right and has left a small but not negligible mark on the final outcome of the discussions in a number of topics'.[38]

In this context, it is important to note that the term 'RIO' has arguably been used in legal discourse both to *exclude* and to *include*. At first sight, the use of the RIO descriptor, in the sense of regional *integration* organization, seems mostly aimed at distinguishing (by justifying special rules), excluding (by carving out exceptions), or emancipating (by promoting) the relevance of the EU, and of EU integration, to the codification and progressive development of international norms. In doing so, however, this process also emancipates and includes other RIOs, at differing degrees of integration, into international codification processes. RIO clauses create a space for treaty accession and membership, and the use of the RIO descriptor opens up the debate about the relevance of international organizations' practice to the identification of rules of custom, to the protection of persons in the event of natural or man-made disasters, or to the conclusion of treaties.

The regional framing also allows us to move beyond the analytically unhelpful label of the EU as a 'sui generis' entity since it encourages comparisons with other RIOs, thereby providing a useful background for assessing the EU's claim to specialness. Despite the EU-centrism in research on regional citizenship, for instance, many other regional entities have developed these regimes[39] – with regional citizenship in the Economic Community of West Africa States (ECOWAS) predating that of the EU.[40] Furthermore, the East African Community (EAC), the Andean Community and the Eurasian Economic Union (EAEU) have developed notions of 'supremacy' and 'direct

37 ILC, Draft articles on the protection of persons in the event of disasters, 2016 ILC Report (A/71/10) chapter IV, para 48, commentary to draft article 1, para 3.

38 Teresa Cabrita, The EU's Contribution to the Development of International Law at the UN International Law Commission: Little Effort or a Tough Crowd?, UACES Graduate Forum, 2018, 20, available at https://www.researchgate.net/publication/341214733_The_EU%27s_contribution_to_the_development_of_international_law_at_the_UN_International_Law_Commission_Little_Effort_or_a_Tough_Crowd_Uaces_Graduate_Forum, accessed 15 January 2025.

39 Amelie Weinrich, 'Varieties of Citizenship in Regional Organizations: A Cross-Regional Comparison of Rights, Access and Belonging' (2021) 24 International Area Studies Review 255.

40 ECOWAS, 'Protocol A-P.3-5-82 Relating to the Definition of Community Citizen', 1982, available at https://citizenshiprightsafrica.org/wp-content/uploads/2016/06/ecowas-Protocol-Relating-to-the-Definition-of-Community-Citizen.pdf accessed 15 January 2025.

effect' of their internal laws.[41] In a similar vein, a number of other RIOs have claimed autonomy from the international legal order – albeit in varying degrees.[42]

---

41 Bordin, Odermatt, Besson, and Kassoti (n 5) 25–27.

42 In relation to Mercosur law and international law for instance, a Mercosur ad hoc arbitration tribunal has stated: '[T]he aforementioned concurrence of elements ... justify the invocation of the [international] law principles of estoppel ... However, it should be noted that, ..., the fact that the issue in question arose within an integration process such as the one MERCOSUR intends to carry out, should facilitate the application of legal principles that promote trust and therefore prohibit 'venire contra factum propium' ... The application of the [international law] principle of estoppel theory to relations between States linked by economic integration treaties such as those that constitute and develop MERCOSUR cannot ignore the special relationship that such treaties create between their signatories. The existence of this relationship ... must be taken into account when considering the possibility of applying the estoppel theory to a particular situation ...' [Translation by the author]. Mercosur, ad hob arbitration panel, Arbitral Award of 9 January 2002, *Import Ban on Remolded Tires* (Uruguay v Brazil), available at https://jusmundi-com.translate.goog/en/document/decision/es-import-ban-on-remolded-tires-uruguay-v-brazil-laudo-arbitral-wednesday-9th-january-2002. Furthermore, the Mercosur Permanent Tribunal, for instance, has stressed that Mercosur law 'has and must have sufficient autonomy from other fields of law. Denying this always contributes, in a negative way, to the development of MERCOSUR normative institutions.' Mercosur, Permanent Review Tribunal, Award No. 1/2005 on the motion for review submitted by Uruguay against the 25 October 2005 arbitral award of the ad hoc Tribunal concerning the dispute 'Prohibition of the Remoulded Tires Imports from Uruguay', 20 December 2005, as quoted in Martha Lucia Olivar Jimenez, 'The Law of MERCOSUR and International Law: The Struggle for Independence' in Marcilio Toscano Franca Filho, Lucas Lixinski, María Belén Olmos Giupponi (eds.), *The Law of MERCOSUR* (Hart Publishing, 2010), 204–205. The Court of Justice of the Andean Community has also highlighted the autonomous nature of Andean Community Law vis-a-vis international law. 'By virtue of its autonomy, it is confirmed that the Community legal order, both primary and secondary, is neither subordinate to domestic law nor to the international sources of such countries.' Court of Justice of the Andean Community, Preliminary Ruling 158-IP-2006, part C, as quoted in Karen Alter, Laurence Helfer, *Transplanting International Courts: The Law and Politics of the Andean Tribunal of Justice* (OUP 2017), 107. On the emerging autonomous legal nature of the Eurasian Economic Union, see the Dissenting Opinion of Judge Chaika in the *Kaliningrad Transit* Judgment, Court of the Eurasian Economic Union, Case SE 1-1/1-16-BK *Russia v Belarus* (*Kaliningrad Transit*), judgment of 21 February 2007. 'By creating the Eurasian Economic Union of unlimited duration, which is an international organization of regional economic integration, vested with international legal personality according to Article 1(2) of the Treaty of the Union, and having its own system of institutions, Member States of the Union have transferred real powers, have limited their sovereign rights in strictly specified fields and created an autonomous totality of legal norms, which are binding upon all Member States.' As quoted in Maksim Karliuk, The Emerging Autonomous Legal Order of the Eurasian Economic Union (CUP, 2023), 154. In a similar vein, the Caribbean Court of Justice has stated in relation to the

In the same vein, the focus on the 'region' brings to the fore issues of collective identity. While, arguably, such issues have always mattered[43] – principally, in the fields of enlargement and European neighbourhood policy – recent developments such as Brexit and Russia's invasion of Ukraine have accentuated the importance and relevance of regional identity (narratives) in the EU's response thereto. Recourse to notions of collective identity and shared values is also part of the EU's response to internal challenges, such as the rule of law backsliding in Hungary and Poland.[44] Issues of identity are important in the context of other RIOs too. In her contribution to this volume, Eleonora Frasca underlines the importance of migration for the regional identity of Regional Economic Communities in Africa and African integration in general.

The intimate link between regional identity and the RIO shows that the RIO is essentially a relational concept.[45] The regional 'we' acquires its meaning when compared and juxtaposed to 'others' that do not share the same identity and values. In this sense, the RIOs' lens helps us not to lose sight of the complex, yet significant, questions of 'us' and 'otherness' that the construction of a European identity inevitably brings.[46] The triggering of the Temporary Protection Directive in relation to Ukrainian refugees[47] illus-

Caribbean Community (CARICOM) that: 'Implementation of the very idea and concept of a Community of States necessarily entails as an exercise of sovereignty the creation of a new legal order and certain self-imposed, albeit perhaps relatively modest, limits to particular areas of State sovereignty.' Caribbean Court of Justice, Shanique Myrie v Barbados and Jamaica [2013] CCJ (OJ), para. 69.

43 Daniel C Thomas, *The Limits of Europe: Membership Norms and the Contestation of Regional Integration* (OUP, 2021).

44 See, for example, Case C-157/21 *Poland v European Parliament and Council of the European Union*, ECLI:EU:C:2022:98, paras. 140–145; Case C-156/21 *Hungary v European Parliament and Council of the European Union*, ecli:EU:C:2022:97, paras. 124–127. On the role of values in the EU legal order more broadly see also the Opinion of Advocate General Ćapeta in Case C-769/22, *Commission v Hungary* (*Valeurs de l'Union*), ECLI:EU:C:2025:408, paras. 155–163.

45 Guy Fiti Sinclair, 'Between Functionalism and Hegemony: Regional International Organizations in the History of International Law' 21 IOLR 65 (2024).

46 Violeta Moreno-Lax, 'Solidarity's Reach: Meaning, Dimensions and Implications for EU (External) Asylum Policy', 24 *Maastricht J. Eur. Comp. L.* 740 (2017).

47 Council of the EU, Ukraine: Council Unanimously Introduces Temporary Protection for Persons Fleeing War, 4 March 2022, available at https://www.consilium.europa.eu/en/press/press-releases/2022/03/04/ukraine-council-introduces-temporary-protection-for-persons-fleeing-the-war/, accessed 02 May 2025.

trates this point well.[48] Arguably, the way in which the EU reacted towards Ukrainian refugees stands in stark contrast to other people fleeing war. There is evidence to suggest that the showing of solidarity towards Ukrainian people fleeing from their country in the aftermath of the Russian invasion is due to the fact that most Europeans view Ukraine as part of the 'European family'.[49] This could raise questions of double standards and selectivity.

The RIO perspective also offers a new vantage point from which to approach lingering questions of EU law. It has been argued in the literature that the concept of the 'EU territory' remains underexplored and undertheorized.[50] The regional framing could contribute to a deeper understanding of the EU's legal spatiality. For instance, in a recent article Toni Marzal explores the EU Court of Justice's case-law on the (extra)territorial scope of EU law from the point of view of the 'local community'.[51] Marzal argues that a principal consideration guiding the Court's exercise of drawing the boundaries of EU law is who belongs within that particular political community.[52] This perspective also allows us to reflect on how the 'region' is constructed and thus, lays bare sub-regional tensions within the EU and brings into sharp focus how the EU handles questions of social justice and re-distribution.[53] The migration and European debt crises have shown that internally, there are inequalities and asymmetric burdens which the Union does not necessarily have the tools to systematically deal with – thereby putting to the test the assumption that

48 Eva Kassoti, Narin Idriz, "The Kindness of Strangers' - Solidarity in International and EU Law: An Introduction' in Eva Kassoti, Narin Idriz (eds.), *The Principle of Solidarity: International and EU Law Perspectives* (Springer, T.M.C. Asser Press, 2023) 8–9.

49 European Commission, 'Eurobarometer: Europeans approve EU's Response to the war in Ukraine' May 2022, available at https://europa.eu/eurobarometer/surveys/detail/2772, accessed 02 May 2025.

50 Gail Lythgoe, 'Distinct Persons; Distinct Territories: Rethinking the Spaces of International Organizations' (2022)19 IOLR 365, 380. See also, generally, Eva Kassoti, 'The EU and Questions of 'Territory' under Public International Law' ASSER Research Paper 2025–02, forthcoming in Lucia Leontiev, Artur Simonyan (eds.), *Territory and Territoriality in Eurasia: Law and Geopolitics* (Edward Elgar, 2026) available at https://papers.ssrn.com/sol3/papers.cfm?abstract_id=5204973, accessed 2 May 2025. Floris De Witte, 'Here Be Dragons: Legal Geography and EU Law' (2022) 1 European Law Open 113, 116–118.

51 Toni Marzal, 'The Territorial Reach of EU Law: A Private International Law Enquiry into the European Union's Spatial identity' (2024) 73 ICLQ 29.

52 Ibid., 32.

53 Loïc Azoulai, 'Editorial Comments: A Jurisprudence of Distribution for the EU' (2022) 59 Common Market Law Review 963; Floris De Witte, 'Finding Space in EU Law, Transnational Legal Theory' (2024) 15 Transnational Legal Theory 543.

participation in the European project is, at the end of the day, beneficial to all.[54] While the RIOs' lens does not offer ready-made answers, it is a promising avenue for understanding how EU law affects people in different parts of Europe as well as distant strangers.

3 The Structure of This Volume and Overview of the Contributions

From the outset it is worth stressing that in this edited volume different views on 'regionalism' have been put forward. **Telford and van Wageningen** argue for a 'relational' understanding of regions, criticizing the notion of regions as static territorial units, in line with the work of human geographers advocating for a 'new regional geography'. In this context, regions are conceptualised as 'contingent bundles of geographical, political and historical relations' rather than being pre-defined spaces. They are socially constructed and feature porous and shifting boundaries. On the other hand, **Veber** calls for a revision of a primarily geographical, binary (regional-universal), and membership-oriented understanding of 'the regional' in favour of a co-constructed concept grounded on the mutual influence between the regional and the universal. **Delgado Casteleiro**, in turn, draws our attention to the limited value of inter-RIO comparative exercises, notably where regional features are pitted against EU integration, and focuses on the imminently political – rather than geographical – nature of the idea of region in Latin America and its impact on the volatile features of Latin American RIOs.

At the same time, a number of chapters manifest similarities in method, theme or approach towards the regional phenomenon. At least three contributions – **Klabbers, Krapohl and Delgado Casteleiro** – challenge the idea that the EU might operate as a valid model for regional integration or remain the archetypical prototype of a RIO. Beyond the colonial undertones of such assumptions, these authors either draw attention to the unique and non-replicable constellation of circumstances that explain EU regional integration (Krapohl) or underline how such comparative practice tends to obfuscate the unique legal and political dynamics that underpin other RIOs and other conceptualizations of RIOs (Delgado Casteleiro).

Perehudoff, Veber and Stejskal, in turn, all highlight the EU's potential, as a RIO, to shape international law, either by projecting its regional interests onto a co-constructed universal general interest or by contributing to (or

54 Azoulai (n 53), 958–959.

compromising) RIOs overall compliance with international rules on, for instance, countermeasures and international cooperation.

Turning to the structure of this volume, **Jan Klabbers**' contribution opens this book with a challenge. In his view, the RIO label is, at best, 'elusive' and useless – from it derive no specific rights nor obligations. Instead, this concept creates the *pretention* that the EU might work as a model, which is questionable at best. Beyond indicating that Member States share a set of common values or characteristics or interests and are geographically close, Klabbers considers that this category adds little to debates about the EU. In his view, what makes the EU 'unique' – its enforcement powers, supranational decision-making features, provisional application practices, disconnection clauses, multilateralism or other – stems from the fact that the EU *is* the EU and enjoys a broad breath of competences, not from any regional features of the EU's design.

Contesting less the concept but more its application, **Sebastian Kraphol** then pursues the inquiry into what the regional adds to an understanding of the EU (or the EU adds to the understanding of regionality) by challenging the idea that the EU is a credible model of regional integration. He argues that the dynamic of European integration can be ascribed to 'the interaction of two very specific conditions' that are not met by any other region in the world. These conditions are the existence of a high degree of intra-regional economic interdependence and the lack of a regional hegemon. No other region is able to come close to the EU's level of economic interdependence (40% in the early 1960s, and more than 60% at present). Similarly, even if replicated elsewhere, no other institutions of a RIO elsewhere in the world have acquired the strength and (supranational) powers the EU institutions have over the years. Kraphol explains that this unique development was possible due to the existing demand in Europe for economic integration and a strong regional market, coupled with the lack of a strong hegemon seeking to impose its own rules. Examining other examples of regional integration, from North America to South America, Africa and East and Southeast Asia, he demonstrates the validity of his argument, and concludes that 'the EU is more an exception than a role model for regional integration'.

Andrew Telford and Anne van Wageningen argue that to understand what the EU as a RIO means one needs to examine how the 'region' is utilized in EU policy-making and law. They claim that regions, as socially constructed, politically contested and relational constructs, play an important role in EU policy-making. They rely on two case studies to demonstrate their claim: the EU's Just Transition Mechanism (part of its broader 'European Green Deal'), and the European Higher Education Area. The examination of these two case studies provides insights into the EU's 'regional thinking', that is how the EU constructs 'regions' at different levels and across different policies.

The chapters that follow unpack some of the challenges raised in Part 1 of the book by turning our attention to the concrete application of 'the regional' in specific EU policy areas.

Katrina Perehudoff's contribution opens this section with an examination of examines the EU's practice of international cooperation with respect to pharmaceuticals and its impact on global health law. Relying on an analysis of three distinct EU instruments in this field – the Health Threats Regulation and Joint Procurement Agreement, the EU Trade Diversion Regulation, and the European and Developing Countries Clinical Trials Partnership – Perehudoff argues that the EU is able to leverage its regional market power to shape companies' extraterritorial trade activity, in line with international human rights standards and international law. Testing the practical application of this potential, Perehudoff concludes that while EU practice is generally aligned with international human rights law, it has at times waivered in its coherence when faced with global health emergencies such as the Covid-19 pandemic.

Eleonora Frasca takes one of the fundamental freedoms of the EU internal market, namely the right to free movement of persons, and investigates to what extent this integration objective is also promoted in EU cooperation in the area of migration with third countries members to other RIOs. The focus in this chapter is on policies and funding devoted to EU-Africa cooperation, and more specifically, Regional Economic Communities (RECs) with similar free movement ambitions. Frasca demonstrates how the EU, disregarding global developments pleading for 'advancing a common understanding of migration' and promoting regional mobility, focuses almost all its efforts on preventing irregular migration from Africa to the EU. By focusing on bolstering African states' border control and migration management capacities, the EU hinders the development of regional free movement objectives within African RECs. She characterizes EU policies in this area as 'counter-productive and short-sighted' and calls on the EU to live up to its commitments to facilitate mobility, as taken in the context of the Global Compact on Migration.

Building on the appraisal of EU practice and its potential to shape international practice and international law, **Maruša T. Veber** turns the focus to EU sanctions as an instrument through which the EU, much like other RIOs, projects its own regional interests externally, influencing the notion of 'general interest' under international law. In her view, 'when adopting sanctions against third States ... RIOs engage in the construction of the understanding of the generally posited interest in international law, that is, *erga omnes* obligations'. Through their sanctioning practices RIOs both 'project regional interests to the universal level' in a hegemonic fashion and contest or legitimise so-called universal interests. Veber therefore calls for a revised understanding of regionalism, wherein the regional and the universal are co-constructed realities instead of a static binary and hierarchically disposed categories.

Finally, **Petr Stejskal** also picks up on the EU's sanctioning practice and its broader impact – here not on international interests but instead on the rules of responsibility under international law. He examines the implications of the EU's toolbox against economic coercion – namely the EU's new Anti-Coercion Mechanism (ACI) – on the understanding of the principle of non-intervention and the prohibition of third-party countermeasures under international law. Stejskal approaches the ACI as a manifestation of the EU's operation as a regional block regulating its own interests against international economic threats, and argues that the EU's practice has the potential to shape how the legality of third-party countermeasures is understood in international law. He questions the compatibility of economic countermeasures with WTO rules and the legality of suspending EU obligations in response to economic coercion against individual EU Member States, positing that EU practice as a RIO has both the potential to develop but also to further fragment international law.

The aim of the contributions in the last part of the book varies from establishing whether or not the concept of Union citizenship denotes the existence of a cohesive regional identity, to establishing current trends in the context of the EU's response to current geopolitical realities and Latin American RIO's approach to climate change.

Victoria Hooton in her contribution looks at EU citizenship through the prism of regionalism. More concretely, she examines the extent to which Union citizenship as a legal construct aligns with the concept of regionalism. To that end, she explores the internal and external dimensions of this 'fundamental status' with a view to establishing the issues or obstacles that challenge its characterization as a 'regional' status. Internally, she establishes that in addition to its derivative nature, its link to free movement makes it irrelevant for large parts of the population of Member States, namely, immobile and economically inactive citizens and third-country nationals. Externally, citizenship-by-investment schemes and 'the inclusion of overseas territories in certain applications of EU citizenship law' are some of the obstacles in front of the concept being imbued with 'a cohesive regional identity'.

Joris Larik identifies an important trend, namely, the geopolitical awakening of the EU, and more interestingly, its 'geopliticization through law'. He acknowledges the existence of this trend prior to Russia's invasion of Ukraine but demonstrates how this event has amplified it further. He identifies the plethora of instruments adopted in this context as the EU's emerging *acquis* of 'geopolitical law' and clusters them in two categories: security and defence instruments, and foreign trade and investment instruments. He provides an overview of these instruments by placing them in context, discussing their legal basis as well as the institutional implications flowing from that choice. Next, to establish whether this trend goes beyond the EU, he examines the responses of two other RIOs, namely, the East African Community (EAC) and the Association of Southeast Asian Nations (ASEAN) to find out that the responses of the latter two do not go beyond acknowledging the current geopolitical realities in a few policy documents. After explaining the possible reasons underlying this stark contrast, Larik proposes a research agenda for the future study of RIOs, geopolitics and the law.

Finally, **Andrés Delgado Casteleiro** examines the specific case of Latin American RIOs' approach to climate change as an alternative approach to regional cooperation within the EU. He argues that this approach, the unique features of which stem from the imminently political – rather than geographic – idea of 'the region' in Latin America, combines managerial coordination based on the sharing of best practices with strategic litigation aimed at advancing common regional standards on climate change. Drawing attention to the heterogenous character of RIOs in general, and of Latin American RIOs, in particular, Delgado Casteleiro sheds light on both the strengths and weaknesses of regional integration in Latin America, notably in response to climate change. He argues that while the region's formalist tradition and sovereign concerns explain the reliance on informal coordination rather than legally binding cooperation among RIOs with respect to environmental threats, the reconceptualization of climate change as a human rights issue and its slow yet growing judicialization may gradually change the managerial paradigm of Latin American RIOs.

Acknowledgements

The idea for the edited volume arose in the context of a joint T.M.C. Asser Institute – Amsterdam Centre for European Studies (ACES) conference on 'The EU as a Regional International Organization' that took place at T.M.C. Asser Institute on 1st December 2023. We are indebted to ACES for their generous financial assistance in organizing the event. We would also like to thank Mx Lars van der Ent and Mr Santiago Dresen for their invaluable assistance in editing this volume.

PART 1

Framing the EU as a Regional International Organization: Conceptual Issues

CHAPTER 1

The Soft Phenomenology of the Regional International Organization

Jan Klabbers[1]

Abstract

This chapter investigates whether it is even possible meaningfully to think in terms of regional international organizations: the concept seems to have few clear boundaries, and is bound to remain elusive. As a result, anything that can be learned from studying specific regional organizations can be learned by virtue of the specific characteristics of those entities – the idea of the 'regional international organization' does little to no work here. That said, the chapter discusses a number of international organizations located in the geographical region Europe (itself already unstable!), and hopes to make clear that while one should not expect too much, taxonomies and classifications can be useful for some purposes.

Keywords

international organization – regional – phenomenology – European Union – Office Franco-Allemand pour la Jeunesse – Arctic Council

1 Introduction

We live in a social world that is constructed rather than made or discovered, and this holds true as much for international organizations as it holds true for states, among others.[2] It follows, that the only plausible approach to figuring out what a regional international organization is, is a phenomenological ap-

1 Jan Klabbers is affiliated with the University of Helsinki. This paper is written as part of the ERC-funded PRIVIGO project: International Organizations between Mission and Market, ERC Advanced Grant nr. 883417.

2 Seminal on the latter is Thomas Biersteker and Cynthia Weber (eds.), *State Sovereignty as Social Construct* (Cambridge University Press, 1996).

 | DOI:10.1163/9789004700659_003

proach: how do international organizations lawyers think of and speak of regional international organizations, and to the extent that they do so to begin with, does what they do make some sense?

Put differently, there is nothing 'out there' in the real world that will at some point unveil itself as the 'essence' of the regional international organization. There is no such thing that can be found or discovered if only observers look hard enough, stare long enough, study seriously enough or think deeply enough. It took a while for social scientists and philosophers to realize that the social world is a socially constructed world,[3] but once that realization took hold, it also became clear that there was no going back. As a result, the question of what regional international organizations are, can only meaningfully be approached by asking how that term, that concept, is used by particular groups, whether the media, the general public, in diplomacy, or by those who have made a profession out of the study of international organizations. This paper aims to do the latter: it aims to establish a phenomenology of regional international organizations under reference to the professional practices of (mostly) international lawyers. Doing so seems warranted by context: the conference where this paper is first presented is a conference among international lawyers and EU lawyers (the two groups overlap to some extent) geared at finding out what lessons can be learned from regional international organizations.

My argument will be, in a nutshell, that plenty of lessons can be learned, and can be learned from most international organizations, but that these owe little to whether an international organization can be called 'regional' or not. I will largely provide two, probably related, reasons. The first is that the concept of a 'regional international organization' is far too elusive to be of much practical use – hence the adjective 'soft' in the title. Second, the law does not attach legal consequences to the quality of being a regional international organization. Such concrete rights and obligations as any particular international organization may turn out to possess, result mostly from intense negotiations with host states, member states, and the world around the organization. There simply is no rule in international law suggesting that once an entity is a regional international organization, it can *ipso jure* claim or do X, Y or Z.

3 Milestones along that route include Peter Berger and Thomas Luckmann, *The Social Construction of Reality* (London: Penguin, 1966) and John Searle, *The Construction of Social Reality* (New York: Free Press, 1997). With respect to the study of international relations, seminal is Friedrich Kratochwil, *Rules, Norms, and Decisions* (Cambridge University Press, 1989).

It is customary, in the standard textbooks,[4] to provide a taxonomy of international organizations, and this taxonomy is usually based on two juxtapositions. First, there are the technical, functional international organizations, juxtaposed against the political international organizations. The latter are few and far between (during the interbellum the League of Nations, since 1945 the United Nations (UN)), and the juxtaposition is deeply misleading in suggesting that functional international organizations are not political, and in suggesting that regulating politics is somehow not functional. Second, the textbooks usually set universal against regional international organizations. This is also misleading, but for different reasons. While it is clear that universal international organizations can be either functional (World Meteorological Organization, World Health Organization) or political (UN), somehow this distinction is absent when thinking of regional international organizations – despite its general jurisdiction, the Council of Europe is rarely seen as the regional counterpart to the UN. Somehow, regional organizations are almost invariably associated with functional ones, but on the basis of a different notion of function than the one that informs conversations about universal counterparts – the 'function' of the regional organization comes much closer to being an 'interest group' on behalf of the region concerned.

These distinctions, misleading as they are, nonetheless have a certain value: they provide a snapshot of the discipline and its wide variety, and this can be useful, in much the same way in which all taxonomies have some use. Yet, these distinctions have also been subject to considerable criticism (again, as is usually the case with classifications and taxonomies), for different observers would come to different categorizations. The most fundamental critique is probably that taxonomies may start to lead a life of their own and create hierarchies and power structures that are difficult to counter: somehow, the 'political' organization is deemed more important than the 'technical' organization; somehow, the 'universal' beats the 'regional'. Some other critiques are well-known: there is, e.g., no shortage of 'politics' going on in so-called technical organizations; and it is not so much the case that the political organizations have no specific function, but perhaps rather that they have a broad variety of functions. Few international organizations are truly universal (the largest may be the WHO, still a handful of states short of universalism), and where to draw the line? Is the International Organization for Migration, with

4 The leading treatise does exactly this, and has done so since its first edition: See H.G. Schermers and Niels Blokker, *International Institutional Law: Unity within Diversity*, 6th edition (Leiden: Martinus Nijhoff, 2018).

175 member states, universal? Or is the World Trade Organization, with 164 members (the number includes Hong Kong, Macau, Taiwan and the European Union) universal? If not, they surely are not regional organizations either – so then what are they?

The term regional organization is often used without much precision: what does it mean to speak of a regional international organization? The convocation to this very conference unproblematically assumes that the EU is a regional organization – and assumes this is a meaningful label. It is not: there is little to be gained from viewing the EU as a regional international organization, and perhaps even less from calling it a 'regional economic integration organization', a term sometimes used in diplomatic practice and therewith having a different status from the classification 'regional international organization', which is an academic label but not a term used in diplomatic practice. This is not to deny that things can be learned from the EU – in much the same way as things can be learned from any exogenous actor: one can no doubt also learn from the International Labour Organization, or the Organization of Petroleum Exporting Countries, or the European Forest Institute. But the things that can be learned from the EU derive from the EU itself, not from the circumstance that it may happen to be a regional international organization – the concept of regional international organization does no work here.

2 An Overview of European Organizations

In 1963, two major states in Western Europe, having just normalized their political relations after World War II, established an international organization. The organization still exists, and has remained an organization of two states,[5] located adjacent to each other: the Office Franco-Allemand pour la Jeunesse. It is not the only example of two neighbouring states setting up an international organization: France and Germany possibly share another bilateral organization, although this entity suggests a large degree of informality (the Office France-Allemand pour la Transition Énergétique); South Africa and Lesotho set one up to manage the Lesotho Highland Waters Project,[6] and well-known from the ICJ's *Pulp Mills* case is the Comisión Administradora

5 For some reason, often left unspecified, scholarship in International Relations tends to hold that an international organization needs at least three member states to qualify.

6 Discussed in Jan Klabbers, 'Responsibility as Opportunism' in Samantha Besson (ed.), *Theories of International Responsibility Law* (Cambridge University Press, 2022), 119–142.

del Río Uruguay (CARU), set up between Argentina and Uruguay.[7] And if the net is cast a bit wider, there are organizations consisting of three neighbouring states: Benelux is a prime example. Are these to be seen as regional international organizations? Or would 'sub-regional' be more appropriate and if so, what on earth (sad pun intended) does that mean? The very term 'regional' probably suggests that members must be located in a definable part of the world.[8] This need not be a continent, presumably, but it should involve, one would think, some neighbouring countries. Put differently: an organization composed of Bulgaria, Botswana, Belize, Brazil, Bangladesh, Bahrain and Benin would make for a nice alliteration club, all starting with B (at least in English), but with members spread over Europe, Central America, South America, Asia, Africa and the Gulf area, it would do an injustice to the word 'regional', even in its most relational sense. Likewise, apart from whether it qualifies formally as an international organization (whatever that entails), few think of BRICS (Brazil, Russia, India China and South Africa, and a handful of others by now) as a regional international organization. And if all member states should somehow be located adjacent over land, then even the EU has a problem, with Greece being somewhat disconnected.[9]

Following the logic of neighbourliness, the Organization for Economic Cooperation and Development (OECD) is not a regional international organization, at least not anymore, as its membership has come to comprise not just European states and (more or less adjacent, with an ocean in-between but few other states[10]) the US and Canada, but nowadays also includes Japan, South Korea, Australia, New Zealand, Israel, Mexico and Chile – none of them located in or near Europe. Neither are OPEC and the Organization of Islamic Cooperation, both of them with membership in various corners of the globe.

Some international organizations are remnants of days gone by: their members used to be connected through colonial or imperial ties, and have seen fit

---

7 *Pulp Mills on the River Uruguay (Argentina v Uruguay)*, [2010] ICJ Reports 14.

8 Geographers might beg to differ and qualify the conception of space underlying this as outdated, ignoring the idea that territory tends to be relational rather than fixed. I think theirs is a plausible position, but if taken seriously, it renders the rest of my discussion moot – it would deny that the concept of the regional international organization can even exist in any meaningful way. I eventually reach a similar conclusion, but via a different route. One statement on the relational nature of space is Doreen Massey, 'Geographies of Space' (2004) 86 *Geografisker Annaler, Series B: Human Geography*, 5–18.

9 The International Law Commission's Draft Conclusions on Customary International Law recognize the possible existence of 'particular' law (including 'regional' customary international law), but does little to further elucidate the notion of the regional.

10 This can be contested, of course, e.g., by pointing out that Cuba is more or less situated in-between.

to continue these in an international organization based on a shared language or some shared cultural institutions. Thus, the Organisation Internationale pour la Francophonie and the Lusophone Organization (the Community of Portuguese Language Countries) are dominated by colonial powers France and Portugal, respectively, and much the same applies to the Netherlands Language Union (Nederlandse Taalunie), comprising Holland, Belgium and Surinam. The former Soviet Union found some continuation in the Commonwealth of Independent States, while the United Kingdom wallows in imperial nostalgia through the Commonwealth and a fondness for cricket. Some of these may remain vehicles for cultural cooperation but not much more, but the Commonwealth is still of some relevance in international law, to the extent that the UK refuses to submit most disputes with other Commonwealth members (present and past) to the jurisdiction of the ICJ – such disputes are better seen, from a UK perspective, as more or less 'internal debates'.[11]

What this suggests is that the notion of 'region' is not so easy to define, and may show considerable overlap. This is further illustrated by the European situation alone. Europe is home to a multitude of international organizations, doing a multitude of things. In random order, uncontroversial European international organizations, comprising only states located in Europe, include the Council of Europe and its offspring (such as the Council of Europe Development Bank), the EU and its offspring (such as the European Investment Bank), the Nordic Council and its offspring (Nordic Investment Bank, etc.), the Benelux (and its offspring, such as the Benelux Office for Intellectual Property), the Council of Baltic Sea States, Black Sea Economic Cooperation, the Helsinki Commission for the Protection of the Baltic Sea, the Visegrad Group, the European University Institute, the European Forest Institute, the Office Franco-Allemand pour la Jeunesse, the Energy Community for South East Europe, the European Bank for Reconstruction and Development, the European Space Agency, the European Centre for Medium-Range Weather Forecasts, the European Free Trade Area, Eurocontrol, the European Patent Office, the Black Sea Trade and Development Bank, the Rhine Commission and other river commissions, the European Molecular Biology Laboratory, the Conseil Européen pour la Recherche Nucleaire, the European Southern Observatory, and the Office of the Secretary-General of the European Schools – the list is unlikely to be exhaustive. And then there are some entities whose formal

11 The UK's declaration, in its most recent (2017) version, accepts the jurisdiction of the ICJ over all disputes arising after 1 January 1987, but with some exceptions. These include, in Article 1(ii), 'any dispute with the government of any other country which is or has been a Member of the Commonwealth'.

status is uncertain, such as the various forms of cooperation under the label Northern Dimension or the above-mentioned Office Franco-Allemand pour la Transition Énergétique (which calls itself a 'platform'). Missing from this list are organizations with European membership and comprising some more or less adjacent states, such as the North Atlantic Treaty Organization and the Organization for Security and Cooperation in Europe (both comprising the USA and Canada), or the Union for the Mediterranean (covering the EU and a number of Mediterranean states) and the European and Mediterranean Plant Protection Organization, while the UN Economic Commission for Europe (UNECE) comprises some states in Asia (Kazakhstan and others), as do the Eurasian Economic Union (Kazakhstan and Kyrgyzstan, in addition to Armenia, Belarus and Russia) and the Collective Security Treaty Organization (the same five plus Tajikistan) which, its name notwithstanding, displays a very relaxed attitude about collective security – having done very little to stop Azeri aggression with respect to Armenia in 2023. Here too there are entities of uncertain status, such as the Hybrid Center of Excellence (full name: European Center of Excellence for Countering Hybrid Threats). Similar lists can no doubt be composed with respect to other continents.

While continents would seem to be an obvious way to delimit the idea of 'regional', some states are located on more than one continent: think only of Russia and Turkey, while the French, English and Dutch still have territorial possessions outside Europe. Others are in-between continents, so to speak: Armenia, Azerbaijan and Georgia are neither clearly in Europe (though they are members of various European international organizations) nor clearly in Asia, and for different reasons, much the same applies to Israel.[12] And that suggests that such states can also meaningfully belong to two regions, as is indeed the case with Russia, which was until its attack on Ukraine a member of the Council of Europe and is still a member of several other European organizations, but also of the Asia-oriented Shanghai Cooperation Organization. Russia and Belarus (partly and wholly in Europe, respectively) are part of the aforementioned Eurasian Economic Union and the Collective Security Treaty Organization.

The point to arrive at is that the notion of 'regional international organization' is rather elusive, something nicely illustrated by the Arctic Council. For, the Arctic Council comprises states from the Arctic region (a distinct region by

12 Israel also participates in European sports competitions and the extravaganza known as the Eurovision song contest; the latter, for reasons unknown, also allows Australia to compete. These competitions are not, it should be added, organized under auspices of intergovernmental organizations.

most standards), but located on different continents – which is why the Arctic Council can be seen as regional in a manner which does not apply to NATO, OECD, or OSCE, of which Canada and the US are also members. More generally, the conclusion presents itself that 'regional international organization' is, at best, an imprecise shorthand academic label, useful for some analytical purposes perhaps but not a distinct legal category: it lacks the required precision.

3 What about the EU?

The convocation of this meeting suggests that the EU is a regional organization from which lessons can be learned – presumably by other regional organizations, or even by international organizations generally, and maybe also by federal and confederal states; Europe's hubris has always been pronounced. This will be discussed in the current section and the next. But before going there, a preliminary question needs to be put on the table: can one even meaningfully think of the EU as an international organization, whether regional or otherwise?

Our political imagination is limited. Since Westphalia, for a long time, the notion of political community referred to the state. This remains visible in the label reserved for all other communities. These are 'non-state actors', a label that is not very precise and is negative in tenor: it can only group things together by specifying what they are not, rather than by any positive characteristics. So, when the first international organizations were created, observers had difficulties finding ways to describe them and to think of them. The great Lassa Oppenheim, e.g., had no idea what to make of the League of Nations.[13] Somehow, in the late nineteenth century, the term international 'unions' was in vogue, a term still reflected in some classic organizations (Universal Postal Union, International Telecommunications Union) but rarely used for newer entities – the International Union for the Protection of New Varieties of Plants, set up in 1961, is an exception.

Arguably, the stage of uncertainty has never quite been overcome, as Orford also suggests when endorsing that international lawyers pay some serious attention to regions. But, as she rightly warns, regional projects, from the nineteenth century Monroe doctrine via Schmitt's *Grossraum* to China's Belt and

13 Lassa Oppenheim, 'Le caractère essentiel de la Société des Nations' (1919) 26 *Revue Générale de Droit International Public*, 234–243; Lassa Oppenheim, *The League of Nations and Its Problems* (London: Longmans, Green and Co., 1919).

Road Initiative, are often hegemonic projects – or, in her more diplomatic terms, often manifest 'asymmetric relations between a central state and formally independent but weaker states'.[14]

The discipline suffers, one might say, from *aphasia*: international lawyers can more or less observe what goes on, but lack the language, the vocabulary, to think about it, discuss it, and comprehend it. This goes back to the early days of international organizations. These mark forms of cooperation between states but, as Jellinek noted in 1882, so do regular processes of state formation: so what then is the difference between the creation of Italy and the creation of the Universal Postal Union? For him, the answer resides in their final objective: the entities creating Italy had as their goal a new state (*Staatszweck*); the entities setting up the UPU were, by contrast, having an administrative goal (*Verwaltungszweck*) in mind, something nowadays often referred to as a function.[15] The linguistic confusion has remained a constant, with people distinguishing 'supranational' from 'international' or 'intergovernmental organizations', or even distinguishing the latter two from each other: an 'intergovernmental' organization, some suggest, has no officials but remains strictly 'between governments', with all the work being done by government representatives. An 'international' organization, on such a view, has more autonomy and some staff of its own.[16]

On such lines of thought, the EU is often seen as supranational, because it has some characteristics that other organizations lack. It has, e.g., some decision-making powers: the EU can set rules that are binding for its entire membership. This, in itself, incidentally, while rare, is not unique and actually has a surprisingly long history. A century ago, the International Sugar Union could do something similar: setting prices which would be considered binding for its entire membership.[17] And logic dictates that the same applies to some of the work of entities such as the Bureau International des Poids et Mesures: it cannot be the case that a metre differs in length in different member states, or that a kilogram is heavier in some than in others.

In addition, the EU is special in that, since its early days, it envisaged there to be a popular component (the Parliamentary Assembly, now referred to as

14 Anne Orford, 'Regional Orders, Geopolitics, and the Future of International Law' (2021) 74 *Current Legal Problems*, 149–194, 191.

15 Georg Jellinek, *Die Lehre von den Staatenverbindungen* (Berlin: Hölder, 1882).

16 Through this logic, Yao can refer to the Rhine Commission as 'intergovernmental', while the Danube Commission is 'international'. See Joanne Yao, *The Ideal River: How Control of Nature Shaped the International Order* (Manchester: University of Manchester Press, 2022).

17 Francis B. Sayre, *Experiments in International Administration* (New York: Harpers, 1919).

the European Parliament). As its Court of Justice recognized early on, this could only mean going beyond classical inter-state cooperation. And that same Court conveniently labelled the EU first as a 'new legal order of international law',[18] and then slowly dropped the reference to international law, and it conveniently suggested that the effect of EU law in its member states depends on EU law which also happens to be superior to member state law. As a result, the EU is often seen as 'supranational'.

The use of such a label is intriguing. It suggests that the EU falls into a different category than other organizations, but that it nonetheless fits into such a category. The legal mind is very adept at doing this, also finding the EU to fit other boxes having other labels. Thus, in addition to being 'supranational', the EU is also deemed a 'regional economic integration organization', and in addition to those two labels, it is often seen as 'sui generis': the label for those that cannot be labelled. The interesting consequence is this. The *sui generis* label suggests that the EU is in a category of its own – this is literally what *sui generis* means: the EU does not fit any existing category.[19] The label 'supranational' is open to the existence of several species of that genus, but on closer scrutiny it is generally accepted that thus far it only describes the EU – no other international organization in existence can meaningfully be described as supranational, and in one of those lovely circularities that the law is so rich in, the supranational organization actually cannot meaningfully described except by reference to the EU and its characteristics. And since no organization is exactly (or even approximately) like the EU, it follows that none is supranational, except the EU.

The same logic eventually applies to the regional economic integration organization (REIO). But it does so with a twist. As with 'supranational', REIO can only be defined by pointing to the EU, but no putative candidate-REIO has characteristics coming close to those of the EU. General bindingness, popular involvement, direct effect, supremacy: these all apply to the EU, but in combination they only apply to the EU. A quick Google search of REIO suggests that there might be almost thirty in existence, but this is hugely deceptive.[20] Not

---

18 Case 26/62, *Van Gend and Loos*, ECLI:EU:C:1963:1.

19 This does not exclude the possibility of others being *sui generis*; when most or all are *sui generis*, as may actually be the case with international organizations, the discussion becomes very complicated indeed.

20 https://www.google.com/search?q=regional+economic+integration+organizations&rlz=1C1GCEA_enFI879FI879&oq=&gs_lcrp=EgZjaHJvbWUqCQgAECMYJxjqAjIJCAAQIxgnGOoCMgkIARAjGCcY6gIyCQgCECMYJxjqAjIJCAMQIxgnGOoCMgkIBBAjGCcY6gIy>CQgFECMYJxjqAjIJCAYQIxgnGOoCMgkIBxAjGCcY6gLSAQkxMjY5ajBqMTWoAgiwAgE&sourceid=chrome&ie=UTF-8 (visited 19 September 2023).

only are the EU and the EEC listed separately, but the list also contains forms of economic cooperation between states that are not at all even geared towards integration (think European Free Trade Area, OECD, African Union, UNECE), and some of the remaining others meet one or two of the EU's characteristics, but not all of them. This then can mean one of two things. It can mean, first, that the EU is the only REIO currently in existence, and other putative REIOs can only properly be considered as such if and when they meet the characteristics the EU possesses. Or it can mean, second, that the criteria for REIO are pretty relaxed: the EU may meet them in abundance, but a number of entities also meet them. The first option has the drawback that it is highly selective (perhaps unreasonably selective), but at least it has analytical rigour. The second is more inclusive (all sorts of entities can be included), but has fairly little analytical traction: it seems that every form of inter-state economic cooperation can qualify as long as it is not completely universal, and if that is the case, the label loses much of its utility.

These musings may come across as an academic conceit, but that is not really what they are. After all, it is one of the core tasks of academics to provide taxonomies, to help understand the world by providing categories and classifications, regardless of whether these have an immediate real-world effect. Taxonomies are the tools of bureaucracy, if nothing else, the tools of 'seeing like a state',[21] but also provide frames on our social existence: there is a difference between being married and cohabitating, or between being married and being single, or being a confirmed bachelor and being divorced. It makes a difference whether one belongs to the Lutheran or the Catholic Church, and for customs purposes the differences between hard cheese and soft cheese may well be of relevance. And it matters much whether one is a woman, a man or self-identifies differently. Indeed, the latter example emphasizes the social importance of taxonomy: it may be experienced as hugely important in which category one is considered to belong.[22]

But taxonomies also create hierarchies, none more so than the constant quibbling over the EU. For whether supranational or not, a regional economic integration organization or not, a proto-state or not, a quasi-federation or not, *sui generis* or not, there can be little doubt that many hold the EU to be the 'most developed' form of international organization, whatever exactly this may mean. The EU is something all other international organizations should strive for, so most of us would agree. But why? Why not strive for a loose

21 James C. Scott, *Seeing Like a State* (New Haven CT: Yale University Press, 1998).

22 See generally also Alex Wright, *Cataloging the World: Paul Otlet and the Birth of the Information Age* (Oxford University Press, 2014).

platform, where participants can freely speak their minds undisturbed by power relations or other restrictions, and where no judicial organ is needed to block overly zealous management? Why not prioritize a quasi-Habermasian ideal speech situation entity over the massively managerial EU? The answer will be fairly obvious: international organizations are expected to do things and achieve results; political leaders are expected to regulate, govern and administer, achieving managerial success and ideally with some democratic input. So the EU is placed on top, as it is both more effective (by the above metrics) and invasive than any (other) international organization.[23]

Either way, as with all social constructions, 'essentialism' should be avoided. The question whether the EU is an international organization (regional or otherwise) can be useful for some purposes, and fruitless for other purposes. For teaching international organizations law, it may be useful to refer to the EU on occasion, to show a possible trajectory. For other purposes, however, it may be considerably less useful, for instance for purposes of devising a general theory of international organizations – for such purposes, the EU is too much of an outlier.[24] And then there is what philosophers refer to as 'conceptual pluralism':[25] the same thing can have different meanings to different people. For public lawyers, the EU may come close to statehood; for international lawyers, it is bound to stay close to being an international organization, and a prominent private law theorist once referred to the EU as a Jack-in-the-Box:[26] open the box and something unexpected and slightly scary jumps out – and that seems appropriate enough.

4 Lessons from the EU

The convocation to this meeting also wonders what sort of questions are raised by regional international organizations such as the EU, and aims to

23 The novelist may add that the 'main function' of politicians 'is to disappoint'. Julian Barnes, *Elizabeth Finch* (London: Penguin, 2022) 40.

24 This is the questionable premise of Liesbeth Hooghe, Tobias Lenz and Gary Marks, *A Theory of International Organization* (Oxford University Press, 2019).

25 Hilary Putnam, *Ethics Without Ontology* (Cambridge MA: Harvard University Press, 2005).

26 Thomas Wilhelmsson, 'Jack-in-the-Box Theory of European Community Law' reproduced in Lars Eriksson and Samuli Hurri (eds.), *Dialectic of Law and Reality: Readings in Finnish Legal Theory* (Helsinki: Forum Iuris, 1999) 437–454.

find answers to some of those questions. While the EU does confront international law with a number of puzzles, few of these actually arise from the EU being a regional organization. The label is useful for conversational purposes, but is not a fixed legal category – indeed, international law lacks such fixed categories altogether. Whereas in domestic law it can be said that a 'foundation' has certain rights and obligations which may differ from those of a 'limited liability company' or an 'association', international law lacks categories to which particular rights and obligations are attached. In other words, being called a regional international organization has little or no particular legal effect in and of itself, and as mentioned earlier, the continent of Europe counts at least some thirty of such entities, of different size, scope and structure.

The general point is that in international law, legal status comes with very few concrete rights and obligations attached. At best, the accepted subjects of international law can be said to enjoy certain capacities. International organizations enjoy few such capacities, regardless of whether they are universal or regional, technical or political. They do not have a general capacity to join other international organizations, except on a high level of abstraction: they may join if they have the competence to do so, and if the organization to be joined is open to embracing other organization – a combination that does not happen all that often. They lack standing before the International Court of Justice and most other international courts and tribunals, with the possible exception of arbitration panels. It is by no means self-evident that they have the capacity to contribute to customary international law as actors in their own right and if so, whether this applies across the board (all international organizations, all policy domains) or comes with limitations. The few general capacities that come to mind are the capacity to conclude treaties (this is codified in the 1986 Vienna Convention) and perhaps the capacity to exercise self-defence in case of an armed attack or resort to counter-measures if and when appropriate. While such situations are unlikely to occur, one can nonetheless imagine attacks on peacekeeping missions, refugee settlements or migration processing centres or the offices of military alliances, or wrongful acts directed against an organization's headquarters.[27] In addition, interna-

27 Additionally, a general capacity to speak up in international affairs can be thought of, but this is such a broadly applicable capacity that its analytical utility remains limited: non-governmental organizations, religious leaders, rock singers and film stars share the same capacity.

tional organizations may enjoy a capacity to be held responsible, at least in theory.[28]

Put differently, there will not be many questions arising for international law from the mere circumstance that the EU happens to be a regional international organization. Such questions as have arisen and will arise, will stem from features, ambitions and policies of the EU itself – as EU. It could hardly be otherwise, for the simple but sufficient reason that in international law, treaties are merely a 'thing between the parties' (*res inter alios acta*). Each treaty regime, and *a fortiori* each international organization, has its own features. None are identical, and few are even similar.[29]

But, that said, the EU as such has generated quite a few legal issues over the years: it has given rise to situations forcing others to adapt or resist – usually adapt. And most of those stem from the one aspect where the EU is truly unique among international organizations: its enjoyment of exclusive powers and the resulting pre-emption of member states. The basic idea is simple: member states delegate competences to the EU (as they do to other international organizations), and do so to such an extent that those member states no longer hold the competence – the members can no longer act in the same way.[30] There is a certain logic to doing this: if one wants a common market, it makes sense to have a common customs tariff, and in order to have a common customs tariff, there is merit in having a common commercial policy. And that only works (or works best) by excluding dissenting voices. Thus, it has been clear from the start of the EU that the EU would be exclusively competent in matters of international trade and commerce, and it rapidly became clear that the same was to apply in fisheries.

This generates internal difficulties. It is, for instance, by no means clear what belongs to the policy domain 'common commercial policy', and what does not, and those categories have proved fluid over time, with 'foreign direct

28 This is the premise underlying the International Law Commission's Articles on the Responsibility of International Organizations (ARIO) – thanks to Ramses Wessel for reminding me.

29 The closest in terms of similarity are the multilateral development banks, which are mostly set up following certain time-honoured ideas and showing similar structures: see, e.g., Susan Park and Jonathan Strand (eds.), *Global Economic Governance and the Development Practices of the Multilateral Development Banks* (Abingdon: Routledge, 2016).

30 Unless those powers are transferred back or 'repatriated', but that is a story for another day.

investment' only being included since the Lisbon Treaty. And likewise, it is not self-evident what belongs to the policy domain of 'fisheries', and what does not. Consequently, often enough, the member states have contested the claim of exclusivity, all the more so if and when at issue is international action spanning several policy domains. The classic example is the 1982 Law of the Sea Convention (UNCLOS), which says one or two things about fisheries, but also quite a few things about other issues, from maritime boundary delimitation to the exercise of jurisdiction by coastal states, from marine environmental research to dispute settlement. On fisheries the EU can claim exclusive competence, but not on most other topics addressed in UNCLOS. Practically speaking, then, both the EU and its individual member states join the incipient regime, a practice referred to as 'mixity'[31] and even heralded as the EU's contribution to the political philosophy of federalism.[32] Consequently, this exclusivity gives rise to an international law question: how are the EU's treaty partners to know when the EU is supposed to do (or refrain from doing) something, or when the member states are supposed to act or not to act? The answer typically has been to ask the EU to declare the division of competences but this, in turn, meets with reluctance on the part of the EU, which is unwilling to carve the division of powers in stone.

Mixity, resulting from exclusivity, presupposes that the treaty partners are willing to work with it. This is sometimes precluded. The ILO, for one, only accepts states as members, and the fact that the EU can claim some exclusive competences on policy domains partly covered by the ILO is to no avail. In such circumstances, the EU has no choice but to insist that its member states defend its interests, and do so in good faith.[33] By contrast, the Food and Agriculture Organization changed its constitution to accommodate EU membership; when the EU joined, things such as voting rights and financial contribution needed to be arranged.[34] This was deemed more plausible than to rely on the earlier adopted succession theory, according to which the EU could succeed to selected rights and obligations of member states in case of an internal

31 Seminal is Joni Heliskoski, *Mixed Agreements as a Technique for Organizing the International Relations of the European Community and Its Member States* (Leiden: Martinus Nijhoff, 2001).

32 J.H.H. Weiler, 'The External Legal Relations of Non-Unitary Actors: Mixity and the Federal Principle' reproduced in J.H.H. Weiler, *The Constitution of Europe* (Cambridge University Press, 1999) 130–187.

33 Opinion 2/91 (*ILO*), ECLI:EU:C:1993:106.

34 Rachel Frid, *The Relations between the EC and International Organizations* (Dordrecht: Martinus Nijhoff, 1995).

transfer of powers.[35] As a general matter, mixity leads to lots of coordination issues for the member states, and some legal issues as well, mostly again affecting the member states. Questions may relate to the jurisdiction of domestic courts, the competence to propose amendments, and much, much more.[36]

A variation on the same theme is where the EU engages in a particular practice which, because of the special nature of the EU, differs from the practice of states, even though the basic facility used is the same. Perhaps the leading recent example relates to the provisional application of treaties. This is generally regulated (or non-regulated, rather) in Article 25 of the Vienna Convention on the Law of Treaties (VCLT), which effectively stipulates that the practice exists and can take several forms, but does not say much more. Consequently, it is no surprise that it was remanded to the International Law Commission, partly in response to a burgeoning EU practice. This amounts to the following: in treaties involving the EU and its member states on the one hand, and a third party on the other, the EU and its members sometimes form one meta-party, with the EU suggesting that the treaty concerned can be applied provisionally throughout the EU, awaiting the ratification by the member states. The novelty here is to treat the EU and its members as a single meta-party, and trust that the EU's promise ('we shall apply provisionally') will be respected by its member states, even if the domestic law of those member states may stipulate conditions to provisional application.[37] While this practice can in principle be copied by other organizations, it presupposes a burgeoning treaty-making practice on the part of the organization.

An earlier EU-based innovation was a variation on the faculty of treaty reservations. The Vienna Convention's regime is complicated and works on a case-by-case basis, so to speak: states conclude a treaty, and prospective parties can submit reservations which then need to be accepted by other prospective parties, customizing bilateral relations between dyads of states. This is cumbersome if all EU member states are to join the incipient regime, and all would have to go through this routine. Hence, in some cases, the EU proposed a different way of doing things. In particular with respect to treaties concluded under auspices of the Council of Europe, the EU proposed a so-called 'discon-

---

35 Joined Cases 21–24/72, *International Fruit Company*, ECLI:EU:C:1972:115.

36 Some of these are discussed in Jan Klabbers, *The European Union in International Law* (Paris: Pédone, 2012).

37 For a useful overview, see Merijn Chamon, 'Provisional Application of Treaties: The EU's Contribution to the Development of International Law' (2020) 31 *European Journal of International Law*, 883–915.

nection clause',[38] giving preference or supremacy to EU law in relations between EU members in cases where the prospective treaty would conflict with EU law. The experiment remained limited to the Council of Europe setting, probably because in that setting the EU member states can muster a healthy majority and thus essentially provide the other states with a *fait accompli*, further aided perhaps by the circumstance that some Council of Europe member states might one day wish to join the EU and thus can be counted on to be submissive. Such persuasive circumstances were lacking in other settings, which might help explain why the practice remained by and large limited to the Council of Europe setting, and now seems to have become a thing of the past.

The EU has also pioneered (well, almost) the practice of replacing a multitude of bilateral instruments by something more 'multilateral', if that is the word to use. The prime examples are how the EU replaced a number of bilateral agreements concluded by its individual member states with the US on the topics of extradition and mutual legal assistance, with two agreements in which the EU replaced those various individual member states, to become the only treaty partner of the US. As a general technique, this had been done before: the 1957 European Extradition Convention, a multilateral treaty, replaced a number of bilateral extradition treaties. And as a general technique, this has also happened later: within the framework of UNCITRAL, the Mauritius Convention on Transparency in Treaty-based Investor-State Arbitration is an example, and a similar technique is also discussed in the framework of UNCITRAL to harmonize investor-state dispute settlement procedures, while the BEPS treaty of the OECD offers a variation.

These three mechanisms (the multilateral treaty to replace bilateral agreements; the disconnection clause, and provisional application) are all examples of techniques that can be learned from the EU, and many more can be identified also outside the sphere of the EU's external relations: think only of the preliminary ruling procedure; the invention of the directive as a legal instrument; the widespread use of codes of conduct, guidelines and the like; the intense recourse to the principle of loyalty, and perhaps even the formal disavowal of implied powers. And that leaves particular policy fields still unmentioned; the EU, it seems fair to say, has been a global pioneer on topics such as environmental protection and data protection. The important thing to note is that these lessons (if that is what they are) can be learned from the EU be-

---

38 Alexandre Kolliopoulos, 'La clause de déconnexion en faveur du droit communautaire: une pratique critiquable' (2006) 110 *Revue Générale du Droit International Public*, 273–302.

cause of the characteristics and policies of the EU – owing very little to the fact that the EU can be seen as a regional organization. Whether this means, e.g., that there really ought to be a separate law of treaties-convention for the EU is questionable, and it may also be doubted whether the 'Brussels Effect' is limited to Brussels.[39]

But inasmuch as lessons can be learned from the EU, so too can lessons be learned from other international organizations, regional or not. The old GATT is perhaps a classic example: set up as a free trade arrangement and only creating organs over the years; moreover, its technique of bilateral tariff negotiations in large multilateral trade rounds was highly instructive, as was its creative use of the classic Most-Favoured-Nation principle. From the WHO, lessons emerge about collaboration with private entities, given hands and feet in the Global Fund, GAVI the Vaccine Alliance, and other public-private partnerships.[40] The Contact Group on Piracy off the Coast of Somalia taught a few lessons about the possibilities (and limits, perhaps) of multi-stakeholder 'governance mechanisms',[41] and lessons from the failure of the League of Nations in the security field (it was far more important in other walks of life) were taken to heart when the United Nations was established. The UNECE has pioneered regulation of the mundane (think road signs, or maximum working hours for lorry drivers), and the above-mentioned technique of multilateralizing a series of bilateral treaties was originally invented by the Council of Europe.[42]

5 At Last

So where does this lead us? It seems clear that the idea of a regional international organization is highly elusive: there is uncertainty even as to the notion of 'region'. More importantly though, convenient as the label may be, it does

39 Delano Verweij, *The European Union, the European Community and the Law of Treaties* (The Hague: Asser Press, 2004); Anu Bradford, *The Brussels Effect: How the European Union Rules the World* (Oxford University Press, 2020). Note, in fairness, that Bradford happily recognizes at least one similar forerunner, in the form of the California Effect.

40 Useful is Liliana Andonova, *Governance Entrepreneurs* (Cambridge University Press, 2017).

41 Douglas Guilfoyle, 'Prosecuting Pirates: The Contact Group on Piracy off the Coast of Somalia, Governance and International Law' (2013) 4 *Global Policy*, 73–79.

42 See generally Jan Klabbers, 'Europe's Interaction with the Rest of the World', in Anne van Aaken et al. (eds.), *The Oxford Handbook of International Law in Europe* (Oxford University Press, 2023).

not come with a specific legal connotation, let alone with specific rights or obligations. To be a regional international organization signifies, at best, that its member states have something in common, in that they are geographically closely located. But beyond that, the category is rather empty and appeared randomly in the professional discourse, as the counterpart to universal. The intellectual dividing lines could have been drawn differently: Big Power international organizations versus Small Power international organizations, e.g.; or regulatory international organizations versus policing international organizations, or standard-setting versus operational, or imperialist versus liberation-minded. Incidentally, such distinctions are also made, but usually in a secondary manner: the OECD may or may not be regional, but it is generally also seen as a rich nations' club, whereas the ILO is seen to be on the side of the oppressed, as was UNCTAD once upon a time.

Geographer John Agnew once astutely observed that international studies suffer from what he referred to as the 'territorial trap': scholars of international affairs (and this would include international lawyers, it may be presumed) think in spatial terms, and have a hard time re-directing their thoughts.[43] So too with international organizations: these are depicted as collections of territorial units, either spanning the globe or part thereof. And this is, of course, accurate enough. But instead of squeezing as much as possible out of ideas such as 'universal' or 'regional', it may perhaps be more fruitful to see if different perspectives can be employed to make sense of international organizations.

43 John Agnew, 'The Territorial Trap: The Geographical Assumptions of International Relations Theory' (1994) 1 *Review of International Political Economy*, 53–80.

CHAPTER 2

The EU Is Not a Role Model! Why Other Regional Organizations around the World Do Not Follow the Path of European Integration

Sebastian Krapohl

Abstract

Already the neofunctionalists of the 1960s were analyzing regional organizations in South America in order to find a second case for their theory. Later, the New Regionalism of the 1990s led to a revival of comparative regionalism studies. But despite a high number of regional organizations around the world, none of these match the European Union (EU) in terms of economic and political integration. The unique development of European integration is due to two conditions that have not been met simultaneously by any other region. First, the level of economic interdependence within Europe has always been high, which created a stable demand for market integration. And second, the EU has never been dominated by a hegemon, but the member states established complex institutions to stabilize cooperation. These preconditions created the background for spill-over processes and the emergence of a new polity. Regional organizations around the world have copied the EU model, but due to a lack of economic interdependence, the diffusion of EU institutions has not produced similar results elsewhere. Only two other regions – North America and East Asia – show levels of economic interdependence similar to Europe, but both regions have not created regional institutions that match the European example.

Keywords

Comparative Regionalism – Integration Theory – Intergovernmentalism – Market Integration – Neofunctionalism – New Regionalism – Regional Organizations – Regional Trade

 | DOI:10.1163/9789004700659_004

1 Introduction

The question of whether European integration is a unique or a replicable process has always been debated since the European Communities were founded in the 1950s. Already the early neofunctionalists under the lead of Ernst B. Haas were looking out for other cases of regional integration, mainly on the South American continent.[1] However, the Latin American Free Trade Association (LAFTA) – on which they put much of their hope – did not take off and neofunctionalist spill-over effects were not found anywhere. This contributed to Haas's frustration, when he finally declared his theory to be obsolete.[2] As a result of the New Regionalism during the 1990s, the field of comparative regionalism gained new upwind. The newly established or re-started regional integration projects around the world were influenced by the famous European example of regional integration, and the European Union (EU) itself became very active in exporting its own development model to other world regions.[3] Until today, scholars of the re-emerging comparative regionalism literature are exploring the resulting patterns of institutional diffusion, and the EU is usually at the centre of such comparisons.[4] Nevertheless, despite

1 See, generally, Ernst B. Haas, 'International Integration: The European and Universal Process' (1961), *International Organization* 15:3, 366–392; Ernst B. Haas and Philippe C. Schmitter, 'Economics and Differential Patterns of Political Integration: Projections about Unity in Latin America' (1964), *International Organization* 18:4, 705–737; Philippe C. Schmitter, 'Central American Integration: Spill-over, Spill-around or Encapsulation?' (1970), *Journal of Common Market Studies* 9:1, 1–48.

2 Ernst B. Haas, 'The Obsolescence of Regional Integration Theory (UCP, 1975). See also Ernst B. Haas, 'Turbulent Fields and the Theory of Regional Integration' (1976), *International Organization* 30:2, 173–212.

3 On the EU's influence on the diffusion of regionalism, see Anja Jetschke and Philomena Murray, 'Diffusing Regional Integration: The EU and Southeast Asia' (2012), *West European Politics* 35:1, 174–191; Anja Jetschke and Tobias Lenz, 'Does Regionalism Diffuse?: A New Research Agenda for the Study of Regional Organizations' (2013) *Journal of European Economic Policy* 20:4, 626–637; Tobias Lenz and Alexandr Burilkov, 'Institutional Pioneers in World Politics: Regional Institution Building and the Influence of the European Union' (2017), *European Journal of International Relations* 23:3, 654–680. On the export of the EU's model, see Tobias Lenz, 'Spurred Emulation: The EU and Regional Integration in MERCOSUR and SADC' (2012), *West European Politics* 35:1, 155–173; Anja Jetschke, 'Regional Integration Support by the EU in Asia: Aims and Prospects' in Thomas Christiansen and others (eds.), *The Palgrave Handbook on EU-Asia Relations* (Palgrave, 2013), 226–243.

4 Anja Jetschke and others, 'Patterns of (Dis)similarity in the Design of Regional Organizations: The Regional Organizations Similarity Index (ROSI)' (2021), *International Studies Perspective* 22:2, 181–200; Diana Panke, 'Regional Cooperation through the Lenses of States: Why Do States Nurture Regional Integration' (2020), *The Review of International Organizations* 15:2, 475–504.

the ever-growing numbers of regional organizations and the corresponding academic attention, this chapter argues that the EU is still a unique case, and that we should not expect any other regional integration project to follow the European path of regional integration anytime soon.

The EU is, in fact, an exceptional case and not a role model of regional integration. The dynamic of European integration is due to the interaction of two very specific preconditions, and in no other region on this globe are these two preconditions met at the same time. First, there exists a high degree of economic interdependence on the European single market, which finds its expression in a share of intraregional trade above 60%. As a result, there exists a high economic need for regional market integration, and business has a constant interest to push for harmonized rules on this market. And second, Europe is not dominated by a single and undisputed regional hegemon which could dominate the integration process with its particular interests. Thus, the European countries needed to find other ways to stabilize their long-lasting and peaceful cooperation after WWII. Instead of relying on a hegemonial power, they created strong supranational institutions, which gained more and more influence over the years. The interaction between these two variables – economic interdependence and supranational institutions – lies at the core of the constitutionalization of European law.[5] It needed intraregional economic interdependence in order to create a steady flow of cases on which the European Court of Justice (ECJ) could decide. But of course, these trade conflicts would not have had the same effect on the EU, if dispute settlement was not delegated to such a strong supranational body.

No other regional organization in the world fulfils the two preconditions of intraregional economic interdependence and the absence of a hegemonical power at the same time. The only other regional organization with a similar degree of intraregional trade to the EU is the United States-Mexico-Canada Agreement (USMCA) that replaced the North American Free Trade Agreement (NAFTA) in 2018. Although this free trade agreement only consists of three member states, these countries nevertheless trade more than 40% of their international trade with each other. However, due to the dominance of the US within that region, supranational institutions were neither included in NAFTA nor in the USMCA. Instead, North American integration

5 Alec Stone Sweet and Thomas L. Brunell, 'Constructing a Supranational Constitution: Dispute Resolution and Governance in the European Community' (1998), *American Political Science Review* 92, 63–81; Alec Stone Sweet, *The Judicial Construction of Europe* (OUP, 2004).

follows more a plutocratic model, where Canada and Mexico adapt to US rules to gain access to their neighbour's market.[6] The only other world region where economic interdependence would be high – and steadily growing due to enormous economic dynamics – is East Asia, which would include China, Japan, and Korea, as well as the member states of the Association of Southeast Asian Nations (ASEAN). However, these countries are not yet members of one regional organization, but they are only loosely connected through the so-called ASEAN+3, in which the three external countries mainly cooperate bilaterally with ASEAN.[7] The potential economic gains of deeper market integration would be high, but ongoing rivalry and hostility between the two regional powers China and Japan make it unlikely that the two countries will subsume their sovereignty under strong regional institutions any time soon.

Some (although by far not all) regional organizations of the Global South are heavily influenced by the example of the EU and have consequently adopted more complex and formal regional institutions.[8] For example, the Andean Community (Spanish: Comunidad Andina, CAN) knows the Andean Court of Justice (ACJ), the Common Market of South America (Spanish: Mercado Común del Sur, MERCOSUR) has a permanent appellate court for its dispute settlement mechanism, and the Southern African Development Community (SADC) has set up the SADC Tribunal. However, regional organizations in the Global South are distinguished by much lower levels of intraregional economic interdependence,[9] and they are more dependent on extra-regional trade with and investments from other world regions like Europe or North America. As a result, the dynamics of regional integration depend much more on the regions' extra-regional economic relations and the regional institutions cannot rely on the same support by domestic economic actors as in the

6 Kathleen J. Hancock, *Regional Integration: Choosing Plutocracy* (Palgrave Macmillan, 2009).

7 Sebastian Krapohl, 'Financial Crises as Catalysts for Regional Cooperation? Chances and Obstacles for Financial Integration in ASEAN+3, MERCOSUR and the Eurozone' (2015), *Contemporary Politics* 21:2, 161–178; Sebastian Krapohl, 'ASEAN' in Sebastian Krapohl (ed.), *Regional Integration in the Global South: External Influence on Economic Cooperation in ASEAN, MERCOSUR and SADC* (Palgrave, 2017) 115–146. See also Douglas Webber, 'Two Funerals and a Wedding? The Ups and Downs of Regionalism in East-Asia and Asia-Pacific after the Asian Crisis' (2001), *The Pacific Review* 14:3, 339–372.

8 Jetschke and Murray (n 3); Jetschke and Lenz (n 3); Lenz and Burilkov (n 3). See also Thomas Risse, 'The Diffusion of Regionalism' in Thomas Risse and Tanja A Börzel (eds.), *The Oxford Handbook of Comparative Regionalism* (OUP, 2016), 87–108.

9 Probably the highest level of intraregional trade within the Global South is reached by ASEAN, where it fluctuates between 20 and 25% (see Figure 1.1 below).

EU.[10] Under these circumstances, regional integration becomes more unstable, and regional institutions develop less strength and influence than within the EU – even if they may appear rather similar on paper. In other words, under different structural economic circumstances the same formal institutions have very different effects on regional integration, and analysing the formal institutions alone does not help much to understand factual integration dynamics.

In the following, this chapter proceeds in three steps. First, it discusses the argument that the dynamics of European integration have largely been dependent on an interaction between the high degree of intraregional economic interdependence, the absence of a hegemonial power, and the existence of strong supranational institutions. Second, the paper lays down that no other regional organization on this globe is based on similar levels of economic interdependence, balance of power and institutional strength at the same time. In some regions one of these preconditions is given, but nowhere can these factors interact with each other as they have done within the EU. As a result, the conclusion argues that the EU cannot be a role model for regional integration in other world regions as long as the necessary preconditions are not met. Consequently, we should not expect that other regional organizations develop similar integration dynamics and institutional strength as the EU after WWII.

2 The Demand and Supply of Regional Integration

As Walter Mattli has argued in 1999, the success of regional integration depends on the presence of demand and supply factors.[11] First, there needs to be sufficient societal demand within the participating countries that makes it worthwhile to give up some of the countries' sovereignty. And second, there needs to be a way to solve collective action problems between the regional countries to produce a constant supply of regional integration. Importantly, both of these conditions need to be steadily fulfilled for a relatively long period

10 Sebastian Krapohl, 'Two Logics of Regional Integration and the Games Regional Actors Play' in Sebastian Krapohl (ed.), *Regional Integration in the Global South: External Influence on Economic Cooperation in ASEAN, MERCOSUR and SADC* (Palgrave, 2017), 33–62; Sebastian Krapohl, 'Games Regional Actors Play: Dependency, Regionalism, and Integration Theory for the Global South' (2020), *Journal of International Relations and Development* 23:4, 840–870.

11 Walter Mattli, *The Logic of Regional Integration: Europe and Beyond* (CUP, 1999).

of time in order that regional integration can unfold and becomes a process rather than a one-shot cooperation project.

2.1 *Different Societal Demands for Regional Integration*

The reasons why countries choose to cooperate regionally are manifold, but we can distinguish at least three different kinds of societal demands for regional integration that are often discussed in the academic literature. First, regional integration may help countries to address regional security problems.[12] The set-up of the European Communities during the 1950s may also be seen as such a reaction to security issues, as it was deemed to be a response to the 'German problem' and to the perceived threat by the Communist bloc in central and eastern Europe. Security problems often have a regional dimension. They either result from conflicts between neighbouring countries, or from external threats that address more than one regional country, or from the negative externalities of social unrest within single countries. Thus, it suggests itself to react to such problems with some form of regional cooperation. However, such regional demands for security cooperation are not dynamic. Once the regional security issues are sufficiently addressed, there is no need to integrate the regional countries any step further. The demand for regional cooperation only continues if the security problems could not be solved, but such situations are hardly prone to successful regional integration. As a result, demands for security cooperation can hardly carry a dynamic regional integration process over longer time periods.

Second, in the discussion about the so-called 'New Regionalism' of the 1990s, it is often argued that regionalism can be an instrument to open developing regions to international trade and to integrate them into global markets.[13] Regional integration bears positive size and stability effects, which may improve the economic competitiveness of developing regions. Regional markets are necessarily larger than each of the participating national markets, and well-integrated regions are politically more stable. When speaking with one voice, such integrated regions can gain more weight in international trade negotiations, and they become more attractive addressees of foreign direct

12 Yoram Z. Haftel, 'Designing for Peace: Regional Integration Arrangements, Institutional Variation, and Militarized Interstate Disputes' (2007), *International Organization* 61:1, 217–237; Ingo Hennenberg, 'Local Hero? Introducing the Regional Organisations Security Activity Dataset for Africa (ROSADA)' (2022), *South African Journal of International Affairs* 29:2, 161–185; Robert E. Kelly, 'Security Theory in the "New Regionalism"' (2007), *International Studies Review* 9:2, 197–229.

13 Stefan A. Schirm, *Globalization and the New Regionalism: Global Markets, Domestic Politics and Regional Cooperation* (CUP, 2002).

investments. This economic attractiveness constitutes an important demand for integration in regions that are largely dependent on trade with and foreign direct investments from other world regions (like Europe, North America, and – increasingly – East Asia). Unfortunately, the member states of developing regions do not only compete with other world regions for their shares of global exports and investments, but they also compete with each other for these common pool resources – and this results in the instability of demands for regional integration.[14] Sometimes, single member states of developing regions can gain a competitive advantage vis-à-vis neighbouring economies if they act unilaterally and against the common regional interest. For example, they may increase their own export shares at the costs of their neighbours by signing bilateral trade agreements with important extra-regional trading partners or by devaluing their domestic currencies unilaterally. Of course, regional integration is likely to stagnate as a result of such unilateral actions. This explains, why regional integration in the Global South often starts rather enthusiastically but stagnates after some first steps.

Finally, the third kind of societal demand for regional integration results from trade and investment between countries within a particular region.[15] Importantly, this kind of demand becomes stronger the more developed and diversified the regional economies are. The neighbouring countries need to be attractive markets for each other's exports in order to utilize comparative cost advantages and economies of scale by intraregional trade and investment. If the regional countries depend very much on the export of few commodities to other world regions, the potential for intraregional economic exchange is low. However, if the regional economies are diversified and constitute large consumer markets, economic actors export to and invest in neighbouring countries as soon as these countries lift the first barriers for intraregional economic exchange. And once economic actors export to neighbouring markets, or if they invest in neighbouring countries, they have a vested interest in regional market integration and will constantly push for the abolishment of ever more trade and investment barriers. Here, the demand for regional integration is dynamic and expansive, and it is unlikely to be satisfied with some initial steps of regional cooperation. The more trade and investment is liberalized,

14 Sebastion Krapohl and others, 'Regional Powers as Leaders or Rambos of Regional Integration? Unilateral Sanctions of Brazil and South Africa and their Negative Effects on MERCOSUR and SADC' (2014), *Journal of Common Market Studies* 52:4, 879–895; Krapohl, 'Two Logics' (n 10); Krapohl, 'Games Regional' (n 10).

15 Mattli (n 11).

the more businesses become active on the regional market, and the stronger become the societal demands for regional integration.

To sum up, the societal demands for regional integration can be very different, and this is very likely to have effects for the dynamics of these demands over time. If regional cooperation takes place to address security problems, it can either be successful and the need for cooperation is satisfied, or it is unsuccessful and the respective region remains in political turmoil. In any case, such security issues alone do not bear the seeds for increasing societal demands for further regional integration. Security problems may be a starting point for regional cooperation, but they cannot carry a dynamic integration process over longer time periods. Things are a bit different, if regions integrate to become more attractive economic partners on the global stage. Here, the demand for regional integration may indeed increase, if these regions are successful, and if more trade and investment lead to economic diversification and intraregional trade. However, the problem is that the regional member states also compete with each other for their shares of extra-regional exports and investments. This always bears the risk that member states look for a competitive advantage by acting unilaterally, which of course hinders the regional integration process.[16] The most dynamic and sustainable demand for regional integration results from intraregional economic interdependence. If economic actors can profit from economic exchange on the regional market, they may still compete for trade and investment shares, but they have no outside option as long as these gains are predominantly generated within the region itself. Thus, the societal demand for regional integration should be more stable. Besides, it is very likely that successful integration creates more economic interdependence, which in turn leads to increasing demands for regional integration.

2.2 *Regional Hegemony or Supranational Institutions*

When cooperating and integrating their markets, the neighbouring countries repeatedly and steadily need to solve collective action problems.[17] First, when deciding about regional rules, the countries usually face coordination prob-

16 Krapohl and others, 'Regional Powers' (n 14); Krapohl, 'Two Logics' (n 10); Krapohl, 'Games Regional' (n 10).

17 Geoffrey Garrett and Barry R. Weingast, 'Ideas, Interests, and Institutions: Constructing the European Community's Internal Market' in Judith Goldstein and Robert O. Keohane (eds.), *Ideas and Foreign Policy: Beliefs, Institutions, and Political Change* (Cornell University Press, 1993), 173–206; Arthur A. Stein, 'Coordination and Collaboration: Regimes in an Anarchic World' (1982), *International Organizations* 36:2, 299–324; Michael Zürn, 'Problematic Social Situations and International Institutions: On the Use of Game The-

lems with distributive consequences. In other words, even if they agree to cooperate in principle, they prefer different regional policies and need to agree on compromises. And second, when implementing regional rules, the countries still need to reinforce compliance with these rules. Here, the collective action problem is a prisoner's dilemma, wherein each country faces incentives to free ride on the cooperation of others. Generally, there exist two different ways to solve such collective action problems: the hegemonic dominance by one particular country, or the establishment of regional institutions that stabilize cooperation.

The necessary existence of benevolent hegemons to achieve stable international cooperation is usually stressed by realist scholars. According to hegemonic stability theory, it needs the resources of an economically and militarily dominant country in order to solve cooperation problems.[18] As long as such a dominant country has an interest in international cooperation itself, it solves coordination problems by setting positive incentives for other countries and by compensating them for possible losses, and it mitigates the enforcement problem by monitoring and punishing non-compliant countries. Realists argue that other countries than the hegemon profit in absolute and relative terms from such a situation, because they can enjoy the gains of international cooperation whereas the costs are largely carried by the hegemon.

Following the realist argument, a benevolent regional hegemon may indeed provide a stable supply of the collective good 'regional integration' on behalf of its neighbours – but the question is, whether this results in regional integration as we know it from the European example.[19] Of course, a regional hegemon is not a neutral arbitrator, but it has economic and political interests of its own, and these interests influence the supply of regional integration. In the case of coordination problems with distributive consequences, the outcomes are likely to be very close to the hegemon's interests. And in the case of prisoner's dilemmas, the compliance with regional norms of the hegemon itself is difficult to monitor and to enforce. The resulting integration process will probably be very asymmetric – in fact, it may very much look like plutocratic integration, i.e., the one-sided adaptation of the other member states to

---

ory in International Politics' in Frank R. Pfetsch (ed.), *International Relations and Pan-Europe: Theoretical Approaches and Empirical Findings* (Münster, 1993), 63–84.

18 See, generally, Robert Gilpin, *War and Change in World Politics* (CUP, 1981); Charles P. Kindelberger, *The World in Depression, 1929–1939* (UCP, 1973); Stephen D. Krasner, 'State Power and the Structure of International Trade' (1976), *World Politics* 28:3, 317–347.

19 Mattli (n 11).

the interests of the regional hegemon.[20] The smaller member states will still profit from regional integration – they may gain military protection from the regional hegemon or market access to the region's largest economy –, but a new regional polity with member states on par with each other will not emerge.

Another school of thought in international relations – namely institutionalism in its various forms – stresses the importance of international regimes (in other words, international institutions) to achieve and stabilize cooperation.[21] Accordingly, it is not one dominant country that carries the burden of stabilizing cooperation, but international institutions reduce the transaction costs of coordination and enforcement. Coordination problems can be eased by delegating agenda-setting power to an agent or by agreeing on some form of majority rule, whereas compliance problems can be mitigated by institutionalized monitoring and by delegating dispute settlement to court-like bodies.[22] Importantly, whenever tasks are delegated to some newly-established agents, new actors with own interests are entering the playing field. Of course, these agents do not have the same material resources as countries, but they need to get some independence and competencies in order to fulfil their tasks – and they may use these institutional resources in their own particular ways.

Whenever the collective good of 'regional integration' is supplied with the help of regional institutions and supranational bodies, new actors emerge that automatically have an interest in more regional integration.[23] We can assume that the personnel of supranational bodies have an interest to advance their own careers and to gain political influence. Generally, they can achieve that by strengthening the influence of the supranational bodies, which implies that regional integration proceeds. Thus, the supranational bodies are more neutral in respect to the interests of particular member states, but they surely have an own interest in pushing regional integration forward. As a result, the supply of 'regional integration' is not only stable, but

20 Hancock (n 6).

21 See, generally, Peter A Hall and Rosemary C. R. Taylor, 'Political Science and the Three New Institutionalisms' (1996), *Political Studies* 44:5, 936–957; Mark A. Pollack, 'The New Institutionalism and EC Governance: The Promise and Limits of Institutional Analysis' (1996), *Governance* 9:4, 429–458.

22 Kenneth W. Abbott and others, 'The Concept of Legalization' (2000), *International Organization* 54:3, 401–419; Mark A. Pollack, 'Delegation, Agency, and Agenda Setting in the European Community' (1997), *International Organization* 51:1, 99–134.

23 Pollack, 'Delegation, Agency' (n 22); Mark A. Pollack, *The Engines of European Integration: Delegation, Agency, and Agenda-Setting in the EU* (OUP, 2003).

in fact even expansive, because the regional bodies actively use their discretion to the advantage of regional integration.[24] Of course, how successful the regional bodies are with their endeavour to push for more regional integration depends very much on the configuration of member states' interests and on the concrete institutions of the respective regional organization. But in any case, it is more likely that a new regional polity emerges than in the case of hegemonic dominance, where one member state alone can direct, control and veto the process of regional integration.

To sum up, both hegemonic dominance and regional institutions can help to generate a supply of 'regional integration', but the consequences for the regional integration process are likely to be very different. In situations of regional hegemony, regional decision-making is dominated by one single country alone. The smaller member states may still profit economically and politically from such a constellation, but they probably need to adapt largely to the rules set up by the regional hegemon and a new regional polity does not emerge. In contrast, the establishment of supranational bodies creates new actors with an inherent interest in regional integration. It depends on the concrete institutional design, how influential these actors really are, but under favourable circumstances, they may become the seeds of a new regional polity.

2.3 *The Interaction of Different Demand and Supply Factors*

The main argument of this paper is that dynamic regional integration similar to the European example can only occur, if the most favourable demand and supply conditions interact with each other over a longer period of time. In other words, dynamic regional integration requires both: the expansive demands resulting from intraregional economic interdependence and the expansive supply resulting from the lack of a regional hegemon and the existence of supranational institutions. This is in fact a neofunctionalist and institutionalist argument (Fligstein and Stone Sweet 2002; Pierson 1996; Stone Sweet and Sandholtz 1997), but it explicitly takes the economic preconditions for regional integration on the demand side into account.[25] Existing

---

24 See, for example, Neil Fligstein and Alec Stone Sweet, 'Constructing Polities and Markets: An Institutionalist Account of European Integration' (2002), *American Journal of Sociology* 107:5, 1206–1243; Paul Pierson, 'The Path to European Political Integration: A Historical Institutionalist Analysis' (1996) *Comparative Political Studies* 29:2, 123–163; Pollack (n 22); Alec Stone Sweet and Wayne Sandholtz, 'European Integration and Supranational Governance' (1997), *Journal of European Economic Policy* 4:3, 297–317.

25 Fligstein and Stone Sweet (n 24); Pierson (n 24); Stone Sweet and Sandholtz (n 24).

theories of regional integration were all developed along the example of European integration, and they rely rather implicitly on the precondition of intraregional economic interdependence.[26] Thus, they face difficulties explaining why neofunctionalist spill-overs or path-dependent institutional dynamics do not take off in other world regions than Europe.

When interacting with each other, intraregional economic actors and supranational institutions can set in motion a virtuous circle of regional market integration and a gradual empowerment of the supranational bodies.[27] Accordingly, the first steps of regional trade liberalization are used by economic actors to utilize comparative cost advantages and economies of scale. Growing intraregional trade and investment inevitably lead to conflicts between market participants and member states' remaining trade regulations (which still constitute trade barriers). These conflicts need to be resolved in some form by the supranational bodies. For example, a regional dispute settlement body may decide whether member states' particular policies are in conflict with existing regional commitments. Alternatively, economic actors can also lobby supranational bodies for a concretization of the regional norms. In the next step, the supranational bodies use their discretion (as big or small as this may be) to push for integration-friendly decisions. The results are new regional norms – either in the form of case law or of new regional agreements – that are likely to allow for more intraregional trade and investment. At this point, intraregional economic interdependence gets reinforced and the virtuous circle starts again. Alec Stone Sweet and his co-authors have shown in several articles how such trade disputes on the European single market and the responding activities of the ECJ led to a constitutionalization of the EU.[28]

The virtuous circle described above can be broken on either the demand or supply side of regional integration. First, if supranational bodies are not backed up by economic interests on the regional market, initial steps of regional integration will not lead to increasing intraregional trade and investment, and there will not be sufficient societal demands for the abolishment of

26 For example, the neofunctionalist concept of spillovers requires intraregional economic interdependence as a kind of transmission-belt that connects different product sectors and policy problems with each other, see Jeppe Tranholm-Mikkelsen, 'Neofunctionalism: Obstinate or Obsolete? A Reappraisal in the Light of the New Dynamism of the EC' (1991), *Millennium* 20(1), 1–22. And also Andrew Moravcsik's liberal intergovernmentalism is built up on asymmetric interdependence between different economic interests, see Andrew Moravcsik, *The Choice for Europe: Social Purpose and State Power from Messina to Maastricht* (Cornell University Press, 1998).

27 Stone Sweet and Brunell (n 5); Stone Sweet (n 5).

28 Stone Sweet and Brunell (n 5); Stone Sweet (n 5).

even more trade and investment barriers. Increasing extra-regional trade and investment cannot make up for that, as the intraregional competition for these resources always bears incentives for single member states to gain a competitive advantage by defecting against their neighbours. Thus, without the potential for intraregional economic interdependence, the risk is always that the virtuous circle gets broken on the demand side, and that the supranational bodies cannot gain strength and influence on the supply side. Formally, the regional institutions may still look strong and independent, but they have much less substantive effects on the ground. In its most extreme form, regional organizations may become 'Potemkin villages' that resemble the usual blueprint of regionalism but without significant factual consequences for the member states and their people.

And second, intraregional economic interdependence alone is also not sufficient for the generation of a dynamic regional integration process, if the respective region is dominated by one single hegemon. In this case, the regional hegemon can always break the virtuous circle of regional integration at the supply side, if this is in its own interest. In this case, independent and strong supranational bodies are very unlikely to exist, because the hegemon mitigates coordination problems and sanctions non-compliance. Here, the economic demands for the abolishment of more and more trade and investment barriers need to be addressed to the hegemonic member state. It is very likely that the reaction to such demands is very asymmetric, and favour the hegemon's own economy. Thus, economic demands from the hegemon's own economy are more likely to be fulfilled than the economic demands coming from other member states. Obviously, such a supply of regional integration is unlikely to be expansive. Due to the different weights of their economies, the smaller member states gain more from access to the hegemon's market than vice versa. Thus, the smaller member states are likely to have more demands for regional integration than the hegemon, but it is the regional hegemon who has control over the supply of regional integration. As a result, the supply of regional integration will be insufficient in respect to the average of economic demands across all member states.

There also exists the possibility that a particular region is not dominated by a regional hegemon, but that the member states nevertheless could not agree on setting up independent and strong supranational bodies. In this case, regional integration would need to be supplied by intergovernmental negotiations alone without the administrative support of a Commission-like body, and without an independent arbitrator in form of a regional court. Here, the supply of regional integration would not be constrained by the particular interests of one single dominant member state, but it would still resemble the lowest common denominator of member states' interests (Moravcsik 1998).[29] However, these interests of the member states would probably be more in favour of regional cooperation than the interests of a regional hegemon would be. If no single member state peaks out in respect to its market size or other material resources, the importance of regional coordination should increase for all member states, and the incentives to act unilaterally should be correspondingly low. A virtuous circle between dynamic economic interdependence and integrationist supranational bodies can still not occur – because these supranational bodies are missing –, but at least there does not exist a single and powerful country that is always tempted to go alone without taking the interests of its neighbours into account.

To sum up, the preconditions for a dynamic regional integration process are quite specific and demanding: there needs to be a huge potential for intraregional trade and investment on the regional market, and there should be no regional hegemon that may restrict the supply of regional integration with its particular interests. Only then do the regional countries face a functional need to establish independent supranational bodies, which reply to growing demands for market integration with a growing supply of regional norms. It has been this interaction between dynamic economic demands and a dynamic political supply which has constantly pushed the European integration process through all its ups-and-downs during the last seventy years – not without periods of frustration and stagnation, but in only one direction: namely the gradual emergence of a new regional polity. However, no other regional organization in the world meets both of the preconditions at the same time

3 Regional Integration around the World

In academic and political debates, the EU is often seen as a role model for regional integration around the world, and the European Commission itself is actively supporting regional integration efforts elsewhere.[30] However, this Eurocentrism is highly problematic, because the dynamics of the European integration process rely on very specific preconditions that cannot easily be copied elsewhere. First, the potential to utilize comparative cost advantages and economies of scale by intraregional trade and investments on the European market has always been high. Already in 1962 – when the first data is

29 Moravcsik (n 26).

30 Jetschke (n 3); Lenz (n 3).

available – the share of intraregional trade among the original six member states of the European Communities (EC) was almost 40%. During the 1970, it increased to more than 50%, and nowadays the 27 member states of the EU trade more than 60% of their international trade with each other (see Figure 2.1).[31] And second, there does not exist a clear and undisputed regional hegemon within the EU. Germany is the largest member state, but its GDP makes up for only about a quarter of the EU's GDP. For a long time, European integration has been pushed by the so-called Paris-Berlin axis,[32] i.e., by cooperation between the two largest member states France and Germany. To stabilize cooperation between France and Germany, as well as an ever increasing number of member states, the EU has the strongest and most independent institutional setup of all international organizations existing nowadays. As a result, scholars have even started to analyse the EU as a political system *sui generis* and not as an international organization anymore.[33]

The interaction of economic interests and strong regional institutions pushed the European integration process through all the various crises on its way. For example, at the times of Eurosclerosis in the 1970s, decision-making in the Council was largely blocked by *de facto* unanimity rule, but the CJEU passed some path-breaking judgements – including the *Cassis-de-Dijon* decision that paved the way for the Single European Act a couple of years later.[34] Of course, the CJEU could only become so active, because economic activities on the common market provided a large number of legal cases to decide on. Thirty years later, during the Euro crisis beginning in 2010, it was mainly the European Central Bank (ECB) that rescued and stabilized the common currency with its monetary policy.[35] However, it is hard to imagine that the member states would have agreed to the far-reaching actions of the ECB, if they were not aware of the economic losses that would certainly have occurred on the European Single Market if the Euro had broken down. To sum up, the supranational bodies of the EU have been very influential throughout its his-

31 Trade numbers obtained from the Regional Integration Knowledge System (RIKS) of UNU-CRIS (https://riks.cris.unu.edu/).

32 Paris-Bonn axis before Berlin became the capital of a reunited Germany in 1990.

33 Simon Hix, *The Political System of the European Union* (Palgrave Macmillan, 1999).

34 Karen Alter and Sophie Meunier-Aitsahalia, 'Judicial Politics in the European Community: European Integration and the Pathbreaking Cassis de Dijon Decision' (1994), *Comparative Political Studies* 26:4, 535–561.

35 Jeffry Frieden and Stefanie Walter, 'Understanding the Political Economy of the Eurozone Crisis' (2017), *Annual Review of Political Science* 20:1, 371–390; Peter A. Hall, 'The Economics and Politics of the Euro Crisis' (2012), *German Politics* 21:4, 355–371.

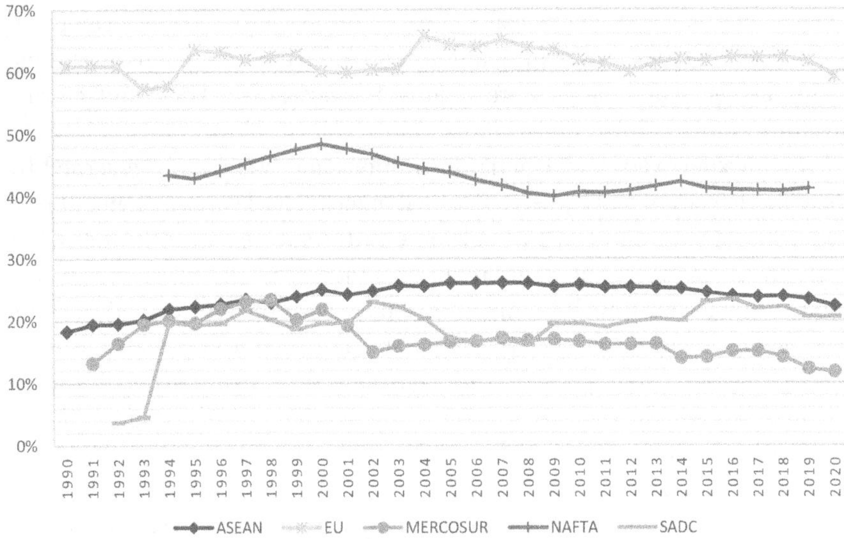

FIGURE 2.1 Intraregional trade shares of selected regional organizations
OWN CALCULATION BASED ON DATA FROM THE REGIONAL INTEGRATION KNOWLEDGE SYSTEM (RIKS) OF UNU-CRIS (https://riks.cris.unu.edu/).

tory, but they could only develop this strength because they answered to demands that resulted from strong economic interdependence on the regional market.

3.1 *Regionalism in North America*

The only regional organization that came close to the intraregional economic interdependence on the early European common market was the North American Free Trade Agreement (NAFTA). Although NAFTA only consisted of three member states (Canada, Mexico and the United States (US)), intraregional trade almost reached 50% at the turn of the millennium, and even if it declined somewhat during the 2000s and 2020s, it always stayed above 40% (see Figure 2.1). This relatively high number of intraregional trade has mainly resulted from trade between Canada and the US, as well as between Mexico and the US, whereas trade between Canada and Mexico has remained rather low.[36] Because labour costs are so much lower in Mexico, production has become outsourced from the US, and then the respective products have been exported from Mexico into the US market. This intraregional trade and

36 David Bartlett, 'The Renegotiation of NAFTA' *The European Financial Review* (14 August 2017) last accessed on 26 November 2023 at https://www.europeanfinancialreview.com/the-renegotiation-of-nafta/.

investment (and a bailout package from the US) stabilized the Mexican economy after the Peso-crisis of 1994, but of course also contributed to the chronic US trade deficit and the pressure on jobs and wages in the US manufacturing sector.[37]

NAFTA knew very few regional institutions and was mainly governed by one intergovernmental agreement signed in 1994. The dispute settlement procedures were basically NAFTA's only noteworthy governance institutions, but they were less independent and influential than even the WTO's dispute settlement mechanism with its Appellate Body. Nevertheless, NAFTA's dispute settlement mechanism was used regularly, and some rudimentary form of legal integration took place.[38] Although the NAFTA treaty explicitly stated that decisions of the dispute settlement mechanism did not constitute precedents for following cases, the different dispute settlement panels nevertheless developed a consistent interpretation of NAFTA norms over time. Within a regional organization that does not know any supranational legislative bodies, and whose constituting treaty was not reformed until 2019, the case law of the dispute settlement mechanism was basically the only way to develop any regional norms. Importantly, some of these interpretations were favouring the smaller member states Canada and Mexico, which are on equal footing with the US in legal terms in front of the dispute settlement mechanism, but not in terms of economic power. Nevertheless, the overall impact of such legal integration in NAFTA was very modest, and the regional organization was extremely static until 2019.

How asymmetrical regionalism in North America really is, and how much it is dominated by the US, became obvious between 2017 and 2019, when NAFTA was renegotiated and became the United States – Mexico – Canada Agreement (USMCA). Under President Donald Trump, the US provoked and accompanied these renegotiations of NAFTA by raising tariffs on aluminium and steel against all its trade partners – including the NAFTA members Canada and Mexico.[39] Additionally, tariffs on car imports were repeatedly discussed, and the US also threatened to leave NAFTA, if a new agreement

---

37 Maxwell A. Cameron and Vinod K. Aggarwal, 'Mexican Meltdown: States, Markets and Post-NAFTA Financial Turmoil' (1996), *Third World Quarterly* 17:5, 975–988; Bradford De Long and others, 'The Case for Mexico's Rescue: The Peso Package Looks Even Better Now' (1996), *Foreign Affairs* 75:3, 8–14.

38 Sebastian Krapohl and others, 'Judicial Integration in the Americas? A Comparison of Dispute Settlement in NAFTA and MERCOSUR' in Finn Laursen (ed.), *Comparative Regional Integration: Europe and Beyond* (Ashgate, 2010), 169–192.

39 Kristen Hopewell, 'Trump & Trade: The Crisis in the Multilateral Trading System' (2021), *New Political Economy* 26:2, 271–282.

could not be reached. Thus, the negotiation for the USMCA was dominated by US interests and in particular by Donald Trump's attempt to reduce the US trade deficit. This is also reflected in the adopted reforms. *Inter alia*, Canada opened up parts of its dairy market for US imports, the rules of origin for the tariff-free trade of cars were tightened, the minimum wage for labour employed in Mexico's automobile industry was increased, and intellectual property rights were extended.[40] All-in-all, it is fair to see the USMCA negotiations as an adaptation of the old NAFTA to the interests of the regional hegemon, i.e., the US.

To sum up, strong economic interdependence within North America has not been sufficient to generate a regional integration process as we know it from Europe. The three countries Canada, Mexico and the US have never set up regional institutions like in the EU, and the regional market is governed in a purely intergovernmental way. The only exception to this is the regional dispute settlement mechanism, which, however, is much weaker than the ECJ and cannot make up for a general lack of regional governance institution. The undisputed regional hegemon, i.e., the US, can dominate regional politics with its economic and political power. This became clearly visible during the presidency of Donald Trump, when NAFTA was renegotiated according to US interests and became the USMCA.

3.2 *Regionalism in South America and Africa*

In the developing world, the levels of intraregional trade are much lower than in Europe and North America. For example, in MERCOSUR and in SADC, intraregional trade has never been more than 23% of all international trade since the 1990s (see Figure 2.1). In other regional organization of Africa and South America, the numbers are even lower: 13% in the Andean Community (CAN), 14% in the East African Community (EAC) and 12% in the Economic Community of West African States (ECOWAS).[41] These low numbers are due to the low level of economic diversification within the respective regions. Many of these regional economies are dependent on exporting few commodities and agricultural products, and the markets for these products are not neighbouring countries, but more developed and diversified economies in East Asia, Europe and North America. However, this does not necessarily mean that intraregional trade is equally unimportant for all regional countries. Due to pure size effects,

---

40 Mary E. Burfisher, 'NAFTA to USMCA: What Is Gained? (2019) *IMF Working Paper WP/19/73*.

41 Trade numbers obtained from the Regional Integration Knowledge System (RIKS) of UNU-CRIS (https://riks.cris.unu.edu/).

the smaller member states may still profit a lot from access to the larger markets of regional hegemons – but in case of such asymmetries, the regional market is less important for the economically and politically more powerful countries.[42]

The two most prominent regional organizations in Africa and South America – namely MERCOSUR and SADC – are distinguished by the hegemony of one regional country, and by relatively weak regional institutions. The Republic of South Africa (RSA) makes up for 51% of SADC's GDP, and Brazil even makes up for 72% of MERCOSUR's GDP. Within both regions, the regional powers have refused to give away far-reaching competencies to regional bodies.[43] MERCOSUR and SADC have a more complex institutional setup than NAFTA, but the dispute settlement mechanisms are the only exceptions to purely intergovernmental decision-making. MERCOSUR has a two-level dispute settlement mechanism, and the second stage takes place in front of the Permanent Review Tribunal in Asuncion.[44] SADC established a relatively powerful tribunal in 2005, but the member states already suspended its operation in 2010 after the Tribunal's second decision judged that the farm evictions in Zimbabwe were an unlawful discrimination of white farmers.[45] Since then, the SADC tribunal has stayed passive. The legal procedures of MERCOSUR are also used very rarely by the member states. The Permanent Review Tribunal has so far decided on six cases, and the Ad Hoc Tribunals of the first legal instance have decided on 12 cases.[46] No disputes have been brought in front of MERCOSUR's dispute settlement mechanism since 2012. Unsurprisingly, under these circumstances, the dispute settlement mechanisms of MERCO-

42 Simon Fink and Daniel Rempe, 'Trade Network Analyses' in Sebastian Krapohl (ed.), *Regional Integration in the Global South: External Influence on Economic Cooperation in ASEAN, MERCOSUR and SADC* (Palgrave, 2017), 91–112; Sebastian Krapohl and Simon Fink, 'Different Paths of Regional Integration: Trade Networks and Regional-Institution-Building in Europe, Southeast Asia and Southern Africa' (2013), *Journal of Common Market Studies* 51:3, 472–488.

43 Mahrukh Doctor, 'Prospects for Deepening MERCOSUR Integration: Economic Asymmetry and Institutional Deficits' (2013), *Review of International Political Economy* 20:3, 515–540; Johannes Muntschick, *The Southern African Development Community (SADC) and the European Union (EU): Regionalism and External Influence* (Palgrave, 2018).

44 Christian Arnold and Berthold Rittberger, 'The Legalization of Dispute Resolution in MERCOSUR' (2013), *Journal of Politics in Latin America* 5:3, 97–132.

45 Laurie Nathan, 'The Disbanding of the SADC Tribunal: A Cautionary Tale' (2013), *Human Rights Quarterly* 35:4, 870–892.

46 https://www.tprmercosur.org/es/sol_contr_laudos.htm (24–11–2023).

SUR and SADC had no real impact on regional integration in South America and Southern Africa.[47]

Because intraregional economic interdependence is low in the Global South, the respective regions integrate their markets not so much in order to benefit from intraregional trade and investment, but they take regionalism as a step to integrate their economies into global markets. Regional integration bears size and stability effects, which make well-integrated regions more attractive as addresses of foreign direct investments and as partners in international trade negotiations.[48] The problem is that intraregional competition for extra-regional trade and investment can also destabilize the demand for regional integration. Sometimes, single member states can gain a competitive advantage vis-à-vis their neighbours, if they defect from regional integration and go for privileged relations with extra-regional economic partners.[49] This also happened in MERCOSUR and SADC, and it had devastating consequences for the respective regional integration processes.

First, when the MERCOSUR economies faced pressure to devaluate their currencies at the turn of the millennium, Brazil floated its currency without even consulting its neighbour Argentina. The result was that the Real devaluated massively, that Brazilian exports became much cheaper on the global market, and that Brazil witnessed an export boom during the 2000s. This turned out to be the death blow for the Argentinean economy, which became uncompetitive, could not stabilize its currency anymore, and entered the well-known Argentinean crisis.[50] In the following years, regional integration stag

47 Krapohl and others (n 39).

48 Tim Büthe and Helen V. Milner, 'The Politics of Foreign Direct Investment into Developing Countries: Increasing FDI through International Trade Agreements?' (2008), *American Journal of Political Science* 52:4, 741–762; Mordechai E. Kreinin and Michael G. Plummer, 'Effects of Regional Integration on FDI: An Empirical Approach' (2008), *Journal of Asian Economics* 19:5–6, 447–454; Edward D. Mansfield and Eric Reinhardt, 'Multilateral Determinants of Regionalism: The Effects of GATT/WTO on the Formation of Preferential Trading Arrangements' (2003), *International Organizations* 57:4, 829–862; Jim Markusen, 'Regional Integration and Third-Country Inward Investment' (2004), *Business and Politics* 6:1, 1–24.

49 Krapohl and others, 'Regional Powers' (n 14); Krapohl, 'Two Logics' (n 10), Krapohl, 'Games Regional' (n 10).

50 Giselle Datz, 'What Life after Default? Time Horizons and the Outcome of the Argentine Debt Restructuring Deal' (2009), *Review of International Political Economy* 16:3, 456–484; Krapohl, 'Financial Crises' (n 7); Katharina L. Meissner, 'MERCOSUR' in Sebastian Krapohl (ed.), *Regional Integration in the Global South: External Influence on Economic Cooperation in ASEAN, MERCOSUR and SADC* (Palgrave, 2017) 147–178.

nated and MERCOSUR has never reached the same dynamics as in the 1990s again.[51]

Second, despite far-reaching plans of market integration in SADC, the RSA signed a bilateral Trade, Development and Cooperation Agreement (TDCA) with the EU in 1999.[52] Thus, the region could not establish a homogeneous negotiation group, when the EU started to renegotiate its trade relations with the so called ACP-countries (former European colonies in Africa, the Caribbean and the Pacific) after the Cotonou Agreement. As a result, the SADC member states negotiated as members of three different groups about Economic Partnership Agreements (EPAS) with the EU.[53] The RSA has finally joined the SADC EPA group in 2004, but the agreement signed in 2016 only includes six of the 16 SADC member states. Obviously, by agreeing to three different trade regimes towards their most important trade partner in Europe, the regional countries forwent the chance of establishing a customs union or a common market that includes all 16 member states.

To sum up, both preconditions for a dynamic regional integration process have not been met by MERCOSUR and SADC. Both regions have low levels of intraregional trade, and both regions are dominated by regional hegemons that put their own parochial interests first at crucial occasions. As a result, whereas the initial steps of integration were taken with huge enthusiasm during the 1990s, the integration processes stagnated after the turn of the millennium. This stagnation is not due to a lack of demand for integration. Especially the small member states would profit a lot from more market integration, and also the large member states could profit from an increased leverage on the global stage, if they could speak on behalf of well-integrated regions. However, the dominance of single countries leads to instability in the supply of regional integration. Both regions depend largely on the cooperation of Brazil and South Africa, respectively, but if the regional powers profit more from unilat-

51 Andrés Malamud, 'Interdependence, Leadership and Institutionalization: The Triple Deficit and Fading Prospects of MERCOSUR' in Søren Dosenrode (ed.), *Limits to Regional Integration* (Farnham, 2015) 163–178.

52 Magdalena Frenhoff Larsén, 'Trade Negotiations between the EU and South Africa: A Three-Level Game' (2007), *Journal of Common Market Studies* 45:4, 857–881.

53 Johannes Muntschick, 'SADC', in Sebastian Krapohl (ed.), *Regional Integration in the Global South: External Influence on Economic Cooperation in ASEAN, MERCOSUR and SADC* (Palgrave, 2017), 179–208; Christopher Stevens, 'Economic Partnership Agreements: What Can We Learn?' (2008), *New Political Economy* 13:3, 211–223; Aurelie Walker, 'The EC-SADC EPA: The Moment of Truth for Regional Integration' (2009), *Trade Negotiations Insights* 8:6, 1–3.

eral action than from regional cooperation, they can damage the respective integration processes considerably and permanently.

3.3 *Regionalism in East and Southeast Asia*

From among all regional organizations in the developing world, ASEAN has the highest share of intraregional trade. As Figure 2.1 shows, the ten ASEAN member states trade up to 26% of their international trade with each other. Aside from that, ASEAN is not dominated by a single hegemonic power. Indonesia is the biggest regional economy, and makes up for 36% of ASEAN's GDP. However, there are also other strong economies in the neighbourhood like Malaysia, Thailand or the small but very prosperous Singapore. Despite the lack of a clear hegemon, the regional organization does not have any supranational institutions and decides purely by intergovernmental negotiations and often outside of formal procedures. Although ASEAN exists since 1967, it took until the ASEAN charter of 2007 that a first formal and legally binding agreement was signed and ratified by all ten member states.[54] The ASEAN charter includes the provisions for a dispute settlement procedure, which, however, has never been used so far. The intergovernmental and mostly informal style of decision making has become widely known as the 'ASEAN-way'. Obviously, the regional integration process in ASEAN cannot rely on a stable supply of integration by strong supranational bodies – but it is not dominated by the interest of one single member state either.

In contrast to MERCOSUR and SADC, the integration process in ASEAN has been more stable since the 1990s. East and Southeast Asia were also hit by a financial crisis during the 1990s, but this crisis had not the same devastating effects on regional integration as the Argentinean crisis had in MERCOSUR.[55] On the contrary, the Asian crisis became the nucleus of further regional integration during the 2000s. After the crisis, the so-called Chiang-Mai-Initiative – a set of bilateral swap agreements that later became a regional

---

54 Katja Freistein, 'A Living Document': Promises of the ASEAN Charter' (2013), *The Pacific Review* 26:4, 407–429; Lee Leviter, 'The ASEAN Charter: ASEAN Failure or Member Failure?' (2010), *NYU Journal of International Law and Politics* 42:159, 159–210.

55 Heribert Dieter and Richard Higgott, 'Exploring Alternative Theories of Economic Regionalism: From Trade to Finance in Asian Co-operation?' (2003), *Review of International Political Economy* 10:3, 430–454; Jürgen Rüland, 'ASEAN and the Asian Crisis: Theoretical Implications and Practical Consequences for Southeast Asian Regionalism' (2000), *The Pacific Review* 13:3, 421–451; Michael Wesley, 'The Asian Crisis and the Adequacy of Regional Institutions' (1999), *Contemporary Southeast Asia* 21:1, 54–73.

liquidity fund –[56] started an intensive cooperation between ASEAN, on the one hand, and the non-member states China, Japan and South Korea, on the other hand. In the following years, each of the three external countries also signed a bilateral trade agreement with ASEAN. The so-called ASEAN+3 group does not constitute a regional organization on its own, but it relies heavily on ASEAN as a focal point of cooperation.[57] The ASEAN member states were able to improve their leverage vis-à-vis the +3-countries considerably, by acting through ASEAN instead of acting unilaterally on their own. Importantly, none of the ASEAN member states is big and powerful enough to achieve similar results on its own. This has provided incentives for more regional integration in ASEAN, and, in 2007, the member states could agree on the ASEAN charter and the establishment of an ASEAN Economic Community (AEC).[58]

Nevertheless, in comparison to the EU, regional integration in Southeast Asia is less dynamic and far less advanced. The regional institutions in ASEAN still do not look in any way similar to those of the EU, and they do not really indicate a commitment of the member states towards advanced regional integration. The member states form the ASEAN Economic Community (AEC), but this is merely a free trade area as it does not harmonize external tariffs. Yet, ASEAN is still an example for how developing countries can profit from regionalism by speaking with one voice to extra-regional partners. Thereby, the absence of a regional hegemon within ASEAN seems to have been an advantage rather than a disadvantage. An economically and politically powerful country could have faced considerable incentives to cooperate bilaterally with China, Japan and South Korea instead of taking the interests of its regional neighbours into account. However, Indonesia – the largest economy of ASEAN – preferred to operate within the ASEAN context, and this unity proved decisive for the success of ASEAN within the ASEAN+3.

The prospects for regional integration in East and Southeast Asia would look rather different, if ASEAN+3 became a regional organization on its own. The economies of China, Japan and South Korea are much more developed and diversified than the ASEAN economies, and they also trade and invest heavily with each other. In addition, the already existing North-South division of labour within East Asia could become much more efficient. Therein, the

56 William W. Grimes, 'East Asian Financial Regionalism: Why Economic Enhancements Undermine Political Sustainability' (2015), *Contemporary Politics* 21:2, 145–160.

57 Richard Stubbs, 'ASEAN's Leadership in East Asian Region-Building: Strength in Weakness' (2014), *The Pacific Review* 27:4, 523–541.

58 John Ravenhill, 'Fighting Irrelevance: An Economic Community with ASEAN Characteristics' (2008), *The Pacific Review* 21:4, 469–488.

ASEAN countries take a similar position than Mexico in NAFTA and become the 'work-bench' of East Asia, whereas the +3-countries – similar to the US in NAFTA – invest heavily in the economies of their Southern neighbours. As a result, intraregional economic interdependence within a possible East Asian Community would be huge, and it would achieve similar level as within NAFTA or even the EU. In fact, an East Asian Single Market could become the nucleus of a regional integration process that could be comparable in its dynamics to that within Europe. However, the hostility and rivalry between the two regional powers China and Japan have so far prevented any form of effective cooperation – not to mention the establishment of a common regional organization.[59] After WWII, East Asia followed a very different historical trajectory than Europe, and – unlike France and Germany – China and Japan never have taken serious efforts of reconciliation. Currently, the chances of an East Asian integration process similar to the one in European is blocked by seemingly unbridgeable political differences between the two largest economies of that region.

4 Conclusion

The EU is often seen as a role model of regional integration, but this is highly problematic, because the European integration process has built up on very specific preconditions. First, there has always been a high potential for intraregional economic interdependence on the European Single Market. And second, regional integration was never restricted by the interests of one single dominant power, but the absence of an undisputed hegemon in Europe allowed for the development of strong regional institutions. Throughout the history of European integration, the economic demand and the institutional supply of regional integration have interacted and reinforced each other. However, there exist no other world regions where these two preconditions are met at the same time (see Figure 2.2). Only a possible East Asian Community including the ASEAN member states, China, Japan and South Korea would satisfy both conditions, but it is blocked by political animosities between China and Japan. NAFTA shows relatively high numbers of intraregional trade and investment, but the dominance of the US and the absence of regional institutions prevent a more dynamic supply of regional

59 Lay Hwee Yeo, 'Japan, ASEAN, and the Construction of an East Asian Community' (2006), *Contemporary Southeast Asia* 28:2, 259–275; Takashi Terada, 'Forming an East Asian Community: A Site for Japan-China Power Struggles' (2006), *Japanese Studies* 26:1, 5–17.

integration. MERCOSUR and SADC are also distinguished by such asymmetries and the existence of regional hegemons, but in addition to that the potential to utilize comparative cost advantages and economies of scale on the regional markets is also low. ASEAN takes a middle position where intraregional economic interdependence is also relatively low, but where the region is at least not dominated by one single hegemon. As a result, regionalism in ASEAN and NAFTA is more stable than in MERCOSUR and SADC, but none of these regions achieves the same dynamic as the EU.

There is often the hope among academics and politicians that regional integration in other world regions takes off as soon as the member states build up similar regional institutions as the EU. As a result of this, the EU model diffused around the globe, and many regional organizations adapted some institutions similar to those existing in Europe. At the macro-level, the setup of MERCOSUR looks similar to the EU, but all its bodies decide through intergovernmental negotiations. SADC once had a tribunal that followed the example of the ECJ, but it was suspended quickly. This demonstrates that the establishment of regional institutions alone does not yet generate the necessary commitment for an ongoing and dynamic integration process. The regional institutions need constant support from actors within the member states in order to develop their influence on the integration process. Such constant support is given if high intraregional trade and investment create dynamic demands for more and more regional integration. Other rationales of regional integration – like security concerns or the strengthening of regional competitiveness on the global market – do not seem to generate the same stability. Unfortunately, it is very difficult to generate the preconditions for intraregional economic interdependence. Even if developing regions are successful in attracting extra-regional investments and negotiating interregional trade agreements, intraregional trade and investments only take off after a long time of economic development and diversification. If single member states face incentives to act unilaterally to improve their competitiveness vis-à-vis their regional neighbours, it proves very difficult to keep regional integration

		Dominance by one regional hegemon	
		Yes	No
High intraregional economic interdependence	Yes	NAFTA	EU [East Asian Community]
	No	MERCOSUR SADC	ASEAN

FIGURE 2.2 Overview about the preconditions of regional integration

stable enough in order that economic development and diversification can take place. In this respect, it seems to be an advantage for ASEAN that it is not dominated by a regional hegemon, which could easily act unilaterally without considering its neighbours' interests. Because such a dominant player does not exist in Southeast Asia, it is easier for the ASEAN member states to keep their unity in relation to extra-regional players like China and Japan.

For developing regions in the Global South, it is not so much the EU but ASEAN that could and should serve as a role model of regional integration. The ASEAN member states have managed to keep their unity when negotiating with China, Japan and South Korea about the Chiang-Mai-Initiative and the ASEAN+1 trade agreements. This has made ASEAN a significant actor in the international economic relations of East and Southeast Asia. It is highly unlikely that the individual ASEAN member states would have been able to negotiate similarly beneficial deals, if they all acted on their own. Thus, ASEAN proves that there exist significant gains of regionalism also in developing regions. In contrast, MERCOSUR and SADC have not been able to keep their unity in their extra-regional affairs. Brazil's unilateral devaluation of the Real, South Africa's TDCA with the EU, and the fragmentation of SADC into different EPA negotiation groups demonstrate how difficult it is for developing countries to stick to regional commitments, if extra-regional economic interests are at stake. Thereby, strong supranational institutions do not seem to be the most decisive factor for regional integration in developing regions, as ASEAN's institutions are as weak or even weaker than those of MERCOSUR of SADC. Instead, the hegemonic dominance of one singular country seems to be the main problem for regional integration in the shadow of extra-regional economic dependency.

CHAPTER 3

Solving European Problems with Regional Solutions? Conceptualizing 'the Region' in EU Higher Education and Climate Change Policies

Andrew Telford[1] *and Anne van Wageningen*[2]

Abstract

Understanding the EU as a Regional International Organization (RIO) raises several questions, including what the term 'regional' means in this designation and how the EU can be understood as a specific type of RIO. Drawing on a theoretical framework from regional geography and a legal analysis of the constitutional aspects of EU regional politics, we argue that the EU employs multiple conceptions of 'region' in its policymaking. In education policy, we explore how the European Higher Education Area has developed into a loose organization of higher education in Europe, drawing on multiple conceptions of 'region' which to an extent transcend nation-state boundaries. In climate policy, we explore how subnational regions play a role in the European Green Deal's 'just transition'. Both cases illustrate key dimensions of the EU as a RIO: first, that the 'regions' constructed in these policies 'exceed' their legal and political foundations (especially the assumption of a territorially-bounded, sovereign nation-state); and second, that the state is (re)constituted as a multi-scalar regional actor in EU politics. We conclude with reflections on the difference regional thinking makes to understanding the EU as a regional organization.

Keywords

Region – Territory – Just transition – Climate mitigation – European Education Area – EHEA – Developing competences – Education policies

---

1 Assistant Professor in European Studies, University of Amsterdam (a.j.telford@uva.nl).
2 Senior Lecturer in European Studies, University of Amsterdam (a.c.vanwageningen@uva.nl).

 | DOI:10.1163/9789004700659_005

1 Introduction

What do we mean when we call a territorial unit a 'region'? This question is paraphrasing Stein Rokkan's question: what do we mean when we call a territorial unit a 'nation'?[3] And a lawyer may want to ask what we mean when we call a territorial unit a 'state'? These questions have animated scholars from a range of disciplines, including politics, history, law and geography. As Wolfgang Reinhard has shown, the state as we know it today is a product of historical development.[4] Floris de Witte provides an in-depth overview of the connections between legal studies and geography.[5] Going a step further Gail Lythgoe[6] proposes 'a fundamental reconceptualization of territory and the spatially mediated concepts of sovereignty and jurisdiction and actorhood, indeed the entire spatial imaginary of international law'. This is to remedy the 'orthodox state-centric concept of territory [viewing] the territorial structure of the global legal space as essentially flat, that is not allowing any "territorial" overlaps'[7] In making these claims, Lythgoe's argument, from a legal perspective, provides a means through which lawyers and other scholars can avoid what geographer John Agnew terms the 'territorial trap' in international relations: the assumption of states as fixed, sovereign units of territorial space with clear borders separating the 'domestic' from the 'foreign'.[8]

In this chapter, we identify how thinking about regional organizations is deeply connected to thinking about the locus of public authorities, especially nation-states or federal states. We analyse two cases, higher education policies and climate policies, to interrogate these loci and show that regional politics in the EU is complex and not organized in a linear manner from either top down or bottom up. In fact, higher education and climate policies offer different examples of regional constitutional arrangements which ques-

3 Stein Rokkan, 'Introduction: Centre-Formation, Nation-Building and Cultural Diversity: Report on a UNESCO Programme' in Shmuel Noah Eisenstadt and Stein Rokkan (eds.), *Building States and Nations* (Sage Publications, 1973).

4 Wolfgang Reinhard, *Geschichte der Staatsgewalt : eine vergleichende Verfassungsgeschichte Europas von den Anfängen bis zur Gegenwart* (Beck, 2000).

5 Floris de Witte, 'Here be Dragons: Legal geography and EU law' (2022) 1 *Eur L Open*, 113–125. https://doi.org/10.1017/elo.2021.2.

6 Gail Lythgoe, *The Rebirth of Territory* (Cambridge University Press, 2024) 255.

7 Ibid., 254.

8 John Agnew, 'The Territorial Trap: The Geographical Assumptions of International Relations Theory' (1994) 1 *Review of International Political Economy* 53.

tion the traditional territory/function dichotomy,[9] including an intermediate level between states and international organizations, but also the interaction between states, supranational international organizations (e.g., the EU) and intranational transborder regional organizations (e.g., Euregions).

Whether it is considered as a RIO, in terms of 'macro-regions' (e.g., the 'Mediterranean') constructed as part of its external relations, or in terms of the role that subnational regions play in Cohesion policies, the EU is a thoroughly *regional* actor. We contend that regions in the EU, whether it is the European Higher Education Area (EHEA) or the subnational regions identified as part of the European Commission's 'just transition', have important political implications. Specifically, we argue that regional thinking in these contexts has two key characteristics. Firstly, there are legal and political ambiguities (especially in the case of Higher Education policy) in which, although there are legal codifications in place, the construction of the region exceeds these frameworks and is grounded in a wider, more ambiguous set of political and legal relationships. Secondly, although the Higher Education region and Just Transition regions disrupt the nation-state-territory relation to an extent, particularly the Westphalian notion of territorial sovereignty, this does not mean that the state, and national governments more specifically, are not central to regional thinking in these cases. Instead, both in terms of the role that national governments play in formulating Higher Education and Just Transition policies and in decision-making about the definition/constitution of these regions, the nation-state is a central actor in these policy areas. As such, the 'state' is constituted not only at the 'national' or 'international' levels, but is instead an effect of policymaking across a range of geographical (including 'regional') scales.

We therefore argue that in order to understand the EU as a Regional International Organization (RIO), it is crucial to examine how the concept of 'region' is utilized in EU policymaking and law: what the word 'regional' connotes in these configurations. To unpack this argument, we first provide a theoretical discussion of the concept of 'region' and its role in EU scholarship, informed in particular by work in critical geography and legal studies. Second, we expand on the first of two case studies, the EU's Just Transition Mechanism (JTM), a regulation designed to respond to the distributional effects of climate mitigation policies. The second case study explores EU higher education policies, and particularly the legal evolution of the EHEA which has 49 adherents, also members of the Council of Europe. European Higher Education is there-

9 Catherine Brölmann, 'Review: Interactions between Regional and Universal Organizations: A Legal Perspective' (2020) AJIL 335.

fore not an exclusive EU policy area, but is certainly influenced by the EU. And the EU will use higher education as a stepping stone toward an EU Education Area (EEA). Finally, the chapter concludes with a comparative discussion of these case studies and reflections on what they suggest about the constitution of the EU as a RIO and its implications for European (dis)integration.

2 Conceptualizing Regional Thinking

As a geographical construct, the concept of 'region' is important for research in many academic disciplines.[10] Regions come in all shapes and sizes, sometimes with a clearly demarcated and long history, other times as an administrative invention with little cultural grounding in the specific geographical area.[11] Nevertheless, regions are usually understood in one of two ways: as a *subnational* spatial unit below the level of the nation-state (entities such as Tuscany), or as a spatial unit which is *supranational* in character (e.g., the Mediterranean).[12] With regard to the first understanding, regions are a delimited space, a territorial container defined on the basis of administrative, cultural, historical or physiographic characteristics.[13] In the second sense, regions are comprised of groups of nation-states with shared regional interests. 'Regions' can be further qualified according to functional characteristics, for example 'mining regions', 'agricultural regions' or 'peri-urban regions'.[14] Paasi argues that geographers have conceptualised regions in three ways. The first is as a type of administrative or statistical category, for example the EU's NUTS regional classification, which can be used for governance and applied research purposes. Second are regions constructed as a consequence of geographical research: bounded spaces produced on the basis of formal or functional classifications of spatially divided phenomena. Finally are regions as political constructs – spaces of contested borders, identities and histories.[15] Taylor also

10 Gordon Macleod and Martin Jones, 'Territorial, Scalar, Networked, Connected: In What Sense a 'Regional World'?' (2007) 41 *Regional Studies* 1177.

11 Jon Anderson, *Understanding cultural geography: people and traces* (Routledge, 2000).

12 Luiza Bialasiewicz, Paolo Giaccaria and Claudio Minca, 'Re-scaling 'EU'rope: EU macro-regional fantasies in the Mediterranean' (2012) 20 *European Journal of Urban and Regional Studies* 59.

13 Ibid. 59–61.

14 Tiffany Morrison, 'The meta-governance of regions and the need for a political geography of planning' (2016) 21 *International Planning Studies* 298.

15 Anssi Paasi, 'Regional geographies of climate change' (2023) 114 *Tijdschrift voor Economische en Sociale Geografie* 71.

identifies another conception of 'region' in geography: regions as a *synthetic* form which bring together social and biophysical phenomena in complex, entangled relationships.[16]

These contested definitions of region are reflected in the history of geography in Western Europe and North America. Regional geography developed in the late 19th century as a means to investigate the particularities of both geographical types (coastal regions) and individual geographical spaces (Cornwall).[17] Inspired by French geographer Paul Vidal de Blache's studies of the relationships between land, cultural history and social practices in particular places (their *genres de vie*), regional geography focused on detailed examination of particular areas of the Earth's surface and the distinctive characteristics of these areas (areal differentiation).[18] More recently, a 'new regionalism' has developed which examines connections between economic globalization and regions, including development of regional political identities and organizations, e.g., the African Union.[19] Studies of new regionalism also focus on subnational entities in the context of economic globalization, neoliberalism and financialization, for example the development of California's 'Silicon Valley'.[20]

More recently human geographers, including Doreen Massey, Nigel Thrift and Ash Amin, have also advocated for a 'new regional geography' which critiques the notion of regions as static territorial units and instead posits a 'relational' understanding of regional constructs.[21] Here, regions are understood as contingent bundles of geographical, political and historical relations: they are not pre-defined spaces, but instead socially constructed and characterized by porous, shifting boundaries.[22] As Amin, Massey and Thrift note, regions are thus 'sites within networks of varying geographical composition ... spaces of movement and circulation (of goods, technologies, knowledge, people, infor-

---

16 Peter Taylor, 'The geographical ontology challenge in attending to anthropogenic climate change: regional geography revisited' (2023) 114 *Tijdschrift voor Economische en Sociale Geografie* 63.

17 Martin Jones, 'For a 'new new regional geography': plastic regions and more-than-relational regionality' (2022) 104 Geografiska Annaler: Series B, Human Geography 43.

18 Richard Hartshorne, *The nature of geography* (American Association of Geographers 1939).

19 Kevin Bloor, 'Regionalism and the European Union' (*E-International Relations*, 21 May 2022) <https://www.e-ir.info/2022/05/21/regionalism-and-the-european-union/#google_vignette> accessed 19 November 2023.

20 Gordon Macleod and Martin Jones, 'Territorial, Scalar, Networked, Connected: In What Sense a 'Regional World'?' (n 10) 1177–1179.

21 Ibid. 1177–1179.

22 Martin Jones, 'For a 'new new regional geography': plastic regions and more-than-relational regionality' (n 17) 43–45.

mation)'.[23] In this paper, we draw on this concept of 'region' to examine the EU as a *regional* international actor.

Building on two case studies – the EU's Just Transition Mechanism, and the European Higher Education Area – we argue that regions (as politically contested, relational constructs) play a fundamental role in EU policymaking. Regions are both fundamental in the drafting and justification of EU regulations and policies (for example, as tools to delimit the distributional effects of decarbonization), and as contingent products of the network of laws, policies, and institutions which underpin EU policies (the EU 'higher education area', for example). In making these claims, we are not trying to make conclusive judgements about whether the EU *is* a region, or indeed a regional organization, but rather to emphasize that different constructions of 'regions' – what we call *regional thinking* – are central to how the EU can be conceptualized as a regional international actor (including as a RIO), including the fundamental role of 'state' actors in these regional constructions.

3 The Just Transition Mechanism and European Higher Education Area as Case Studies

To unpack our argument in more depth, we focus on two cases in this chapter: the EU's JTM (part of its broader 'European Green Deal'), and the EHEA. On one level, these are very different policy areas involving different political actors, decision-making procedures and legal competences. However, we contend that when these cases are examined together, they provide a number of key insights into regional thinking in the EU. The first is that they both highlight, albeit in different ways, the ways in which EU policies are geographically 'scaled' and embedded in particular spatial contexts (the 'supranational' for higher education, and the 'subnational' for the JTM). Secondly, both highlight a key ambiguity in the legal and political formation of regions in the EU: regions are both constructs of particular networks of policies, laws, and decisions by political actors on the one hand, and yet also exceed these processes of construction, exhibiting a 'life of their own' in the further evolution of these policy areas. Thirdly, they also reveal a key insight about the role of Member States in the EU's regional thinking: that 'the state' manifests at multiple, interconnecting geographical scales, including as a 'regional actor' (subnational and supranational) which arguably disrupts the conventional under-

23 Ash Amin, Doreen Massey and Nigel Thrift, *Decentering the nation: a radical approach to regional inequality* (Catalyst 2003) 17.

standing of the state's sovereignty as restricted to a particular territorial jurisdiction. In these respects, we argue that examination of these policies together is fruitful for providing insights into the EU's regional thinking. We start with an examination of the EU's Just Transition Mechanism and its particular regional configurations.

3.1 *The EU's Just Transition Mechanism*

The EU has long presented itself as a leader in international climate policy. Ursula von der Leyen has made climate policy a central commitment of her presidency of the European Commission (EC): speaking on 11 December, 2019, von der Leyen introduced the 'European Green Deal', a package of policy measures which she described as 'Europe's man on the moon moment'.[24] The European Green Deal (EGD) has three priorities: first, a target of no net emissions of greenhouse gases (GHGs) by 2050 (climate neutrality); second, to decouple economic growth from resource use; and third to ensure a 'just transition' in which 'no person' and 'no place' is 'left behind'.[25] The first of these aims, to reach 'climate neutrality' by 2050, was enshrined in the 'European Climate Law' (Regulation 2021/1119) adopted in July 2021.[26] To meet the EGD's third objective, a 'just transition', the European Commission proposed a regulation for a 'Just Transition Mechanism' (JTM) in January 2020 with a focus on the distributional effects of climate mitigation (particularly for regions more heavily reliant on fossil fuels).[27] The Commission's proposal partially springs from a larger international 'just transition' movement, embodied most clearly in the International Labour Organization's (ILO) *Guidelines for a Just Transition* which stress the need for social dialogue, well-paying jobs and high-quality educational opportunities as part of decarbonization.[28] The 2018

24 Lorna Hutchinson, "Europe's man on the moon moment': Von der Leyen unveils EU Green Deal' (*The Parliament*, 11 December 2019) <https://www.theparliamentmagazine.eu/news/article/europes-man-on-the-moon-moment-von-der-leyen-unveils-eu-green-deal> accessed 23 November 2023.

25 Commission, The European Green Deal (2023) <https://commission.europa.eu/strategy-and-policy/priorities-2019-2024/european-green-deal_en> accessed 4 November 2023.

26 Commission, European Climate Law (2023) <https://climate.ec.europa.eu/eu-action/european-climate-law_en> accessed 4 November 2023.

27 European Parliament, 'Legislative train schedule: Just Transition Fund' (2023) <https://www.europarl.europa.eu/legislative-train/theme-regional-development-regi/file-just-transition-fund> accessed 20 November 2023.

28 International Labour Organization, 'Guidelines for a just transition towards environmentally sustainable economies and societies for all' (2019) <https://www.ilo.org/

'Silesia Declaration on Solidarity and Just Transition' was also endorsed by the European Commission at COP24 in Katowice, with the Polish Presidency leading this initiative under pressure from mining unions.[29] The *Gilet Jaunes* demonstrations, partly connected to Emmanuel Macron's decision to increase fuel duties, also inspired the European Commission's turn towards just transition policy.[30] With von der Leyen's Presidency of the EC in December 2019, a political window opened for just transition policy at the EU level.

3.1.1 Funding of the Just Transition Mechanism

The proposal for the JTM introduced in January 2020 has three components: a Just Transition Fund (JTF) worth 7.5 billion euros, a specific just investment scheme under InvestEU, and a public sector loan facility at the European Investment Bank to mobilize additional investment.[31] Reflected in the drive to have green transition recognized in the EU's recovery from COVID-19, the JTF's budget was increased to 40 billion euros in May 2020.[32] However, in the European Council meeting on 17–21 July (2020), the budget of the JTF was reduced to 17.5 billion euros).[33] A provisional agreement was reached in trilogy in December 2020 on a JTF of 17.5 billion euros (with 7.5 billion from the EU's Multiannual Financial Framework (agreed in 2020) and 10 billion from the Next Generation EU COVID-19 recovery package), and the final act was published in the Official Journal on June 18, 2021.[34] Investments in fossil fuels and nuclear energy are excluded from the JTF, with the provisos that up to 1% of European Regional Development Funds can go to fossil fuel projects and

wcmsp5/groups/public/@ed emp/@emp_ent/documents/publication/wcms_432859 .pdf> accessed 31 October 2023.

29 Aparajita Banerjee and Geertje Schuitema, 'How just are just transition plans? Perceptions of decarbonisation and low-carbon energy transitions among peat workers in Ireland' (2022) 88 *Energy Research & Social Science* 1.

30 Georg Zachmann and Simone Tagliapietra, 'What the "gilets jaunes" movement tells us about environment and climate policies' (*Bruegel*, 30 November 2018) <https://www.bruegel.org/comment/what-gilets-jaunes-movement-tells-us-about-environment-and-climate-policies> accessed 10 October 2023.

31 Anna Kyriazi and Joan Miró, 'Towards a socially fair green transition in the EU? An analysis of the Just Transition Fund using the Multiple Streams Framework' (2023) 21 *Comparative European Politics* 112.

32 Ibid. 112–113.

33 European Parliament, 'Briefing: Just Transition Fund' (2021) <https://www.europarl.europa.eu/RegData/etudes/BRIE/2020/646180/EPRS_BRI(2020)646180_EN.pdf> accessed 27 November 2023.

34 Ibid.

that full JTF funding will only be allocated on the basis of a Member State accepting the 2050 climate neutrality target.[35]

The JTM and JTF, in particular, are grounded in a territorial model based on the regional implications of climate mitigation policy.[36] Each Member State is required to draw up a 'Just Territorial Transition Plan' (JTTP) in order to request funding under the JTF.[37] Funding is allocated to regions which are most economically and socially impacted by a move away from fossil fuels and as part of their JTTP Member States need to justify funding on the basis of the regions' dependence on fossil fuels.[38] JTTPs are evaluated by the Commission on the basis of the importance of carbon-intensive industries to regional economies, impacts on employment, reskilling and educational opportunities, the risk of depopulation, and negative environmental impacts associated with transition.[39] JTF funding is jointly managed between Member States and the European Commission.[40] As of January 2023, 93 regions had been accepted for funding under the JTF (on the basis of 67 JTTPs).[41]

3.1.2 Regional Politics of the JTM

We argue that two aspects of the JTM (and in particular the JTF) – the political demarcation of administrative regional boundaries in the JTF, and the politics of 'partnership' in the JTTPs – are pertinent for debates on the EU's regional thinking. In relation to the first of these points, Cohesion (or Regional) Policy forms a major part of EU spending (392 billion euros for 2021–2027).[42] As part of this, the EU prioritizes territorial cohesion (embedded in Article 174 of the Treaty on the Functioning of the EU): promoting 'balanced and harmonious development' across EU territory, with the particular aim of reducing regional

35 Simo Sarkki, Alice Ludwig, Maria Nijnik and Serhiy Kopiy, 'Embracing policy paradoxes: EU's Just Transition Fund and the aim "to leave no one behind"' (2022) 22 *International Environmental Agreements: Politics, Law and Economics* 761.

36 Amandine Crespy and Mario Munta, 'Lost in transition? Social justice and the politics of the EU green transition' (2023) 29 *Transfer* 235.

37 Commission, 'The territorial just transition plans' (Communication) COM 275 final.

38 Ibid.

39 Ibid.

40 Ibid.

41 European Commission, 'Just Transition Fund to ensure a smoother road to carbon-neutral regions' (19 April 2023) <https://ec.europa.eu/regional_policy/whats-new/panorama/2023/04/19-04-2023-just-transition-fund-to-ensure-a-smoother-road-to-carbon-neutral-regions_en> accessed 19 November 2023.

42 Ibid.

disparities.[43] The EU uses the 'Nomenclature of territorial units for statistics' (NUTS) classification of regions as the basis for its cohesion funding. First introduced in the early 1970s and amended via subsequent regulatory iterations, the NUTS classification is divided into NUTS 1 (major socio-economic regions with a minimum population of 3,000,000), NUTS 2 (regions with a minimum population of 800,000, the basic unit for most EU Cohesion policies), and NUTS 3 (small regions for specific priorities, with a minimum population of 150,000) regions.[44] The NUTS classification generally reflects existing administrative geographical divisions in the Member States.[45] Under the JTF, funding is available at the level of NUTS 3 regions.[46] The European Commission initially identified, based on a narrow set of pre-allocation criteria (such as employment rates in coal and lignite, or in carbon-intensive industries), a set of NUTS 3 regions that could be eligible for JTF funding.[47] In its opinion on the JTF proposal (July, 2020), the Committee of the Regions recommended that JTF funding be available at the NUTS 2 instead of NUTS 3 regional level to take account of any spillover of carbon-intensive activities across regional boundaries.[48] In the final regulation, the allocation criteria were changed so that they are not determined on the basis of emissions-based criteria, or on existing NUTS 2 regions used in Cohesion Policy, but instead a bespoke model based on identification of affected actors and regions as part of the negotiated Just Territorial Transition Plans.[49] These changes point to a scalar politics of regional demarcation under the JTF (between the larger NUTS 2 and smaller NUTS 3 regions). Despite the statistical, almost apolitical character of the NUTS classification, these administrative categories are fundamentally political, based on choices about quantifiable (economic, social, environmental,

43 European Parliament, 'Economic, social and territorial cohesion' (2023) <https://www.europarl.europa.eu/factsheets/en/sheet/93/economic-social-and-territorial-cohesion> accessed 24 November 2023.

44 Eurostat, 'NUTS – Nomenclature of Territorial Units for Statistics' (2023) <https://ec.europa.eu/eurostat/web/nuts/background> accessed 3 November 2023.

45 Ibid.

46 European Parliament, (n 33).

47 European Commission, European Semester: Overview of Investment Guidance on the Just Transition Fund 2021–2027 per Member State (Annex D) (27 February 2020) <https://commission.europa.eu/publications/2020-european-semester-overview-investment-guidance-just-transition-fund-2021-2027-member-state_en> accessed 3 November 2023.

48 Committee of the Regions, 'Opinion Factsheet: Just Transition Fund' (2020) <https://cor.europa.eu/en/our-work/Pages/OpinionTimeline.aspx?opId=CDR-418-2020> accessed 19 November 2023.

49 Simo Sarkki, Alice Ludwig, Maria Nijnik and Serhiy Kopiy, (no 35) 761.

etc.) criteria and geographical boundaries which are shifting and embedded in political contestation.[50]

The political construction of JTF regions is clearest in the decision to base funding allocation on regions identified in Just Territorial Transition Plans. The drawing up of these plans is at the behest of Member States, with each granting the responsibility to a relevant national ministry.[51] The JTF regulation states that Member States shall prepare JTTPs 'together with the relevant local and regional authorities of the territories concerned' (Article 11), working in 'partnership' with a range of actors (local and regional authorities, civil society organizations, research bodies) under the remit of Article 8 of the Common Provisions Regulation.[52] However, in practice the involvement of regional and other stakeholders in the creation of JTTPs has been mixed, with concerns about a lack of transparency (for example in selection of stakeholders to consult, or in information gathering), as well as capacity building issues (for example a lack of technical assistance or expertise in regional authorities).[53] There are also concerns about the social inclusiveness of JTTP consultations, for example on the involvement of youth representatives in the process.[54] This is reflected in the prioritization of economic issues in many JTTPs (for example support for businesses) as opposed to social and environmental concerns (e.g., gender equality, childcare or water quality).[55] In many Member States, the consultation process has only taken place after the national ministry already formulated a draft of the JTTP, making it difficult to amend or contribute to the document from a stakeholder perspective.[56]

---

50 Anssi Paasi, (no 13) 71.

51 Lorenzo Manca and Jens Hunsbeth Schreuder, 'The state of youth engagement in the implementation of the EU's Just Transition Mechanism' (2022) <https://gceurope.org/wp-content/uploads/2022/05/REPORT.-The-state-of-youth-engagement-in-the-implementation-of-the-EU-Just-Transition-Mechanism-May-2022.pdf> accessed 19 November 2023.

52 Commission, 'The territorial just transition plans' (Communication) COM 275 final.

53 Inanna Tribukait and Kevin Le Merle, 'Improving territorial justice: Transparency, inclusiveness, capacity-building and strategy in the Territorial Just Transition Plans' (2023) <https://feps-europe.eu/wp-content/uploads/2023/06/Improving-territorial-justice-1.pdf> accessed 14 November 2023.

54 Lorenzo Manca and Jens Hunsbeth Schreuder, (no 51).

55 Michiel Stapper, 'The road to a just transition' (24 April 2023) <https://feps-europe.eu/publication/the-road-to-a-just-transition/> accessed 20 November 2023; World Wildlife Fund, Territorial Just Transition Plan Scorecard Assessment (2023) <https://www.wwf.eu/?9036866/Territorial-Just-Transition-Plan-Scorecard-Assessment> accessed 15 October 2023.

56 Lorenzo Manca and Jens Hunsbeth Schreuder, (no. 51).

Perhaps the starkest example is Bulgaria, which, due to recent political instability and the country's strong dependence on coal, chose not to submit a JTTP in 2022 and lost out on its JTF funding for that year.[57] The public consultation in Bulgaria was carried out by PwC Bulgaria and involved a range of stakeholders (e.g., WWF and Bankwatch), but due to contractual limitations between PwC and the Bulgarian Ministry of Energy, the outcomes of the consultation could not be released publicly.[58] These findings reveal that the interpretation of 'partnership' in the formation of JTTPs leads to mixed results across EU Member States. What is clear is that although regional and non-governmental actors play a role in consultation over the JTTPs (with differing levels of transparency and inclusiveness), the power to draft JTTPs is one which rests at the level of the Member State. Furthermore, in terms of which regions are selected for funding (approved JTTPs), this selection process is a product of negotiation between the European Commission and the Member States, not decision-making by subnational regional actors.

Both of these points – on the choice of administrative NUTS regions, and the role of 'partnership' in consultation over the JTTPs – reveal a scalar politics of regional construction in the EU's JTM (and JTF more specifically). For NUTS regions, there is contestation over the capacity of such regions to capture the GHG intensity of economic activities (the risk of 'spillover' at certain geographical scales). In the drawing up of JTTPs, in which regions for JTF funding are negotiated, there are unequal political dynamics in relation to consultation of regional and non-governmental actors in this process, with these regional constructions ultimately dependent on agreement between the Commission and Member States. Overall, the JTM (JTF) case study highlights that the EU's regional thinking is contingent, with shifting regional boundaries depending on the political dynamics of just transition funding. In this sense, the EU's territorial politics in the context of just transition is not comprised of static regional 'containers' over which states (and other actors) exercise sovereignty.[59] Rather, the EU's regional thinking is 'relational',[60] with regions as contingent bundles of contested political, economic and social relations, the

57 Krassen Nikolov, 'Bulgaria risks €10 billion over coal addiction' (*Euractiv*, 7 April 2023) <https://www.euractiv.com/section/politics/news/bulgaria-risks-e10-billion-over-coal-addiction/> accessed 15 November 2023.

58 Lilo Rösch and Daniele Epifanio, 'Just transition in 7 central and eastern European countries: What works and what does not' (2022) <https://euagenda.eu/upload/publications/2022-04-just-transition-in-7-ceecs.pdf> accessed 17 November 2023.

59 Andreas Faludi, 'Territorial Cohesion, Territorialism, Territoriality, and Soft Planning: A Critical Review' (2013) 45 *Environment and Planning A: Economy and Space* 1302.

60 Gordon Macleod and Martin Jones, (n 8) 1177.

products of unequal power relations in which Member States and the European Commission have a clear political advantage. In this political process, the 'state' is also shown to be not only confined to a fixed territorial unit, but rather is a dynamic actor which manifests at multiple interacting geographical scales. Focusing on a supranational region, the European Higher Education Area, the next section explores these processes in the context of higher education policy.

3.2 *The European Higher Education Area and the European Education Area*

European education policies have been subject to different integration processes. Initially these processes were isolated from each other, but European education polices have developed over time and have become increasingly interconnected.[61] We focus on the nexus between the EU and its Member States. This nexus has been developed indirectly by case law of the Court of Justice of the European Union (CJEU) (Section 3.2.1) and informally on the basis of governmental agreements resulting from the Bologna Process and subsequently within the framework of the European Higher Education Area (EHEA) (Section 3.2.2). The EHEA includes the participation of most European states, including non EU member states. Although the EHEA is not the result of a treaty, we consider it to be a RIO. Our aim is to show that different degrees of commitment to the EHEA can be identified depending on the legal force and scope of agreements of other RIOs, such as the European Economic Area,[62] or RIOs on the basis of Association Agreements with the EU, and the EU as such (Section 3.2.5). In parallel, mainly using the EHEA as a support (Section 3.2.4) and using some Association Agreements to regulate education, the EU has been establishing a legal basis for its education policy (Section 3.2.5).

3.2.1 The Prelude

A concerted European education policy had to wait until the launch of the Bologna Process in 1999.[63] Nevertheless, EU Member States were already

61 Anne van Wageningen, 'The Legal Constitution of Higher Education Policy and Governance of the European Union' in Jeroen Huisman, Harry de Doer, David D Dill and Manuel Souto-Otero (eds.), *The Palgrave International Handbook of Higher Education Policy and Governance* (Palgrave Macmillan, 2015).

62 https://www.efta.int/ accessed 31 October 2024.

63 'The Bologna Declaration of 19 June 1999' (*European Higher Education Area*) <https://ehea.info/media.ehea.info/file/Ministerial_conferences/02/8/1999_Bologna_Declaration_English_553028.pdf> accessed 31 October 2024.

experiencing increased European influence on their education systems. Soon after the establishment of the European Economic Community it became clear that taking internal market freedoms, including the free movement of workers, seriously would also require that education rights would need to be taken seriously. It furthermore implied the necessity of Member States to accept diplomas issued in other Member States. This has led to a string of cases decided by the Court of Justice of the European Union (CJEU) on education.[64] It led to cases on the free movement of students, tuition fees, study grants, tax rulings and selection criteria. This list of examples is not exhaustive. Important to note is that the CJEU, only deciding on individual cases, has not aimed to change national education policies, although its case law has produced this effect.

Whilst this string of cases was a normal outcome of the functioning of the EU, it did nevertheless create policy problems for Member States.[65] Evidently if one EU student, using the freedom of services, was allowed to follow higher education under the same conditions as students from the host Member State then every EU student could,[66] which for the concerned minister created a problem due to a potential influx of students.[67] This might also create problems in other policy domains, which was at least the claim of Belgium in the cases of Blaizot[68] and later Bressol[69] in which Belgium put forward the argument that free access to (para)medical studies impaired the Belgium healthcare system. However, this is only negative integration removing barriers, not creation of new policies.

In principle, the EU's role in the development of education policy is limited. Member States have limited all EU education competences within the treaties to 'actions to support, coordinate or supplement the actions of Member States', moreover 'fully respecting the responsibility of the Member States

64 Anne van Wageningen, 'Free movement, citizenship and the regulation of higher education: A constitutional and institutional stress test' in H. Mercenier, E. Ni Chaoimh, L. Damay, & G. Delledonne (eds.), *La libre circulation sous pression: Régulation et dérégulation des mobilités dans l'Union européenne* (Bruylant, 2018).

65 Peter Kwikkers and Anne van Wageningen, 'A Space for the European Higher Education Area: The Guidance from the EU Court of Justice to Member States', *Higher Education Policy* 25 1.

66 Case 293/85 Gravier v City of Liège, [1985] ECR 593.

67 Case-147/03, Commission of the European Communities v Republic of Austria, [2005] ECR 2005 I-05969.

68 Case 24/86 Blaizot [1988] ECR 379.

69 Case C-73/08, Bressol and Others and Céline Chaverot and Others v Gouvernement de la Communauté française, [2010] ECR *2010 I-02735*. See also Peter Kwikkers and Anne van Wageningen (n. 61).

for the content of teaching and the organisation of education systems and their cultural and linguistic diversity' (Articles 6 & 165 and 166 TFEU).

Although the CJEU has ruled on education drawing on internal market rationales and case law on the freedom of services and the free movement of workers, it didn't aim to rule on educational policies.[70] It only ruled on free access to education without discrimination on the basis of nationality. The firm exclusion of the EU to pursue independent education policies backfired on the Member States in the early 2000s. They then perceived that globalization and the challenges of a new knowledge-driven economy necessitated a concerted European answer.[71] However, that answer was given as a concerted intergovernmental approach to assist in the management of complex national higher education systems. This intergovernmental approach became known as the Bologna Process, leading to the European Higher Education Area (EHEA).

3.2.2 The Genesis of the European Higher Education Area

The European Higher Education Area was launched in Paris in 1998, though formally only since 2010.[72] The Ministers of Education of France, Germany, Italy, and the United Kingdom gathered to celebrate the 800th anniversary of the Sorbonne. They also convened to discuss a more uniform and aligned system of higher education in those four countries. For the occasion, the French Minister of Education had drawn up the Sorbonne Declaration,[73] and invited his colleagues to sign.[74] In that year, these states were all members of the EU and represented the most important and largest education systems in Europe. In addition, these four Member States represented 68% of the inhab-

70 Case 9/74 Casagrande v. Landeshauptstadt München. [1974] ECR p. 773.

71 'Presidency Conclusions' (European Council, 23 and 24 March 2000) www.consilium.europa.eu/media/21038/lisbon-european-council-presidency-conclusions.pdf accessed 31 October 2024.

72 'Budapest-Vienna Declaration (Europea Higher Education Area, 12 March 2010) https://ehea.info/Upload/document/ministerial_declarations/Budapest_Vienna_Declaration_598640.pdf accessed 31 October 2024.

73 'Ministerial Declarations and Communiqués' (European Higher Education Area) https://ehea.info/page-ministerial-declarations-and-communiques, accessed 22 September 2024; 'Sorbonne Joint Declaration' (European Higher Education Area, 25 May 1998) https://www.ehea.info/media.ehea.info/file/1998_Sorbonne/61/2/1998_Sorbonne_Declaration_English_552612.pdf accessed 22 September 2024.

74 Pauline Ravinet, 'Comment le processus de Bologne a-t-il commencé ? La formulation de la vision de l'Espace Européen d'Enseignement Supérieur en 1998' *Éducation et Sociétés*, n° 24, 29.

itants of the then EU Member States.[75] The French Minister of Education hoped to initiate national reforms in higher education in France and sought support from his German and Italian counterparts who needed reforms in their respective countries as well. The three ministers hoped to reform higher education under the aegis of an alleged European necessity to do so.[76] The UK also signed because not signing would entail the danger of being excluded from a joint European development of higher education.[77]

One year later (1999), alongside the celebrations of the 800th anniversary of the founding of the University of Bologna, the Italian Minister of Education hosted a conference on higher education. At that moment, 29 states joined the conference and signed the Bologna Declaration, considered to be the official start of the Bologna process and the unofficial start of the EHEA, although the latter entity had not yet taken on this name.[78]

Oddly, the European Union was left out of this process, but from the onset the European Commission joined as full member.[79] Two institutional aspects of this process are particularly significant. Firstly, it was a governmental process, pushed by the ministers of education, and secondly all of the policies decided upon were implemented on a voluntary basis in the Member States. Contrary to EU directives, even the propositions and agreements on new national higher education laws were and had to be the result of voluntary national legal action.

Moreover, the European Commission's full membership is remarkable for two reasons. Firstly the Bologna process was intended to be intergovernmental without any influence of the EU,[80] and secondly according to the EHEA[81]

75 Eurostat demographic data via: http://appsso.eurostat.ec.europa.eu/nui/show.do?dataset=demo_gind&lang=en accessed 14 May 2018.

76 Pauline Ravinet, 'Comment le processus de Bologne a-t-il commencé ? La formulation de la vision de l'Espace Européen d'Enseignement Supérieur en 1998' *Éducation et Sociétés*, n° 24, 29.

77 Ibid.

78 'The Bologna Declaration of 19 June 1999' (*European Higher Education Area*) <https://ehea.info/media.ehea.info/file/Ministerial_conferences/02/8/1999_Bologna_Declaration_English_553028.pdf> accessed 31 October 2024.

79 'European Commission' (European Higher Education Area) https://ehea.info/page-european-commission, accessed 22 September 2024.

80 Pauline Ravinet, 'From Voluntary Participation to Monitored Coordination: Why European Countries Feel Increasingly Bound by Their Commitment to the Bologna Process' *Eur J of Education,* Vol. 43 p 353.

81 'Members' (European Higher Education Area) https://ehea.info/page-members, accessed 22 September 2024.

becoming a full member is only open to states that have also ratified the European Cultural Convention.[82] The European Commission is not competent to ratify a treaty, nor is it a state.

3.2.3 The Lisbon Declaration of the Council

At approximately the same time as the Bologna process started, the European Council, in their Lisbon meeting, issued its conclusions setting out a strategic goal which was fully outside of the scope of EU competences of that time. The objectives were set out in point 5 in which the European Council stated:[83]

> The Union has today set itself ***a new strategic goal*** for the next decade: *to become the most competitive and dynamic knowledge-based economy in the world capable of sustainable economic growth with more and better jobs and greater social cohesion.* Achieving this goal requires an ***overall strategy*** aimed at:
> - preparing the transition to a knowledge-based economy and society by better policies for the information society and R&D, as well as by stepping up the process of structural reform for competitiveness and innovation and by completing the internal market;
> - (…).

The quote highlights four areas in which the EU had no competence: the knowledge economy is divided into education and research[84] as well as economic policy[85]; better jobs in terms of labour market policy[86]; and social cohesion[87] which may mean that a European welfare state might be created. For the first time this statement also describes the Open Method of Coordination (OMC), an important development which would be used in the Bologna Process as well. In point 37 of its Conclusions, the European Council noted, 'Implementation of the strategic goal will be facilitated by applying a new open method of coordination as the means of spreading best practice and

82 'Details of Treaty No.018' (Council of Europe) https://www.coe.int/en/web/conventions/full-list?module=treaty-detail&treatynum=018, accessed 22 September 2024.

83 European Council Presidency Conclusions (Lisbon, 23 – 24 March 2000) https://www.consilium.europa.eu/ueDocs/cms_Data/docs/pressData/en/ec/00100-r1.en0.htm.

84 Now Articles 165 and 166 TFEU (Title XII Education, vocational training, youth and sport) and title XIX TFEU (Research and technological development and space).

85 Title VIII, chapter 1 (Economic policy) TFEU.

86 Title IX (Employment) TFEU.

87 Title X (Social policy.) TFEU.

achieving greater convergence towards the main EU goals'.[88] This method uses fixed European guidelines and specific timetables; indicators and benchmarks to compare best practices; national and regional policies to implement these European guidelines; and periodic monitoring, evaluation and peer review organised as mutual learning processes.

The OMC would become fundamental in the subsequent development of the Bologna Process and the European Higher Education Area.

3.2.4 Explaining the Bologna Process and the EHEA

When it started in 1999, the Bologna Process involved 29 European states,[89] and since then the number of members has risen to encompass 48 participating states and the European Commission. Initially, the Bologna Process was legally insignificant. The participating states have taken clear measures to ensure this. The Bologna Process was conducted in a comparable way to the OCM. States developed or changed policies, reported on these policies, and then they compared their policies to other states' policies.

Subsequently, the Process has evolved into a politically significant process that succeeds in achieving goals using similar techniques to those employed under the OMC.[90] Ravinet describes how the Bologna Process started to be monitored by the Bologna Follow Up Group (BFUG).[91] This group produces trend reports, from which participating states can see what they and the other states have done. The logical next step in this process was that Member States started to write the reports themselves. Ravinet notes:

> These reports have a powerful effect. Besides their content or reliability, the simple fact of being obliged to produce such a report that will subsequently be made public, and especially the fact that these reports became standardised after several years of collective labour, give them significant impact. Through them, it becomes simpler to find out about national implementations of the Bologna Objectives, and with the standardisation of the reports, it becomes easy to compare the perfor-

88 Lisbon declaration: Conclusions of the European Council of 23/24 March 2000.

89 'History' (European Higher Education Area) http://www.ehea.info/pid34248/history.html accessed 22 September 2024.

90 Isabelle Bruno, Sophie Jacquot and Lou Mandin, 'Europeanization through its instrumentation: benchmarking, mainstreaming and the open method of co-ordination…toolbox or Pandora's box' *Journal of European Public Policy* Vol. 13 519.

91 Pauline Ravinet, 'From Voluntary Participation to Monitored Coordination: Why European Countries Feel Increasingly Bound by Their Commitment to the Bologna Process' *Eur J of Education,* Vol. 43 p 353.

mance of different countries. This allows for a naming shaming mechanism to develop.[92]

Initially, the EHEA was intended to be fully intergovernmental.[93] Nevertheless, the OMC helps the European Commission to gain influence in the Bologna Process, which is not an EU-only process. EU Member States and non-EU states continue to participate in the Bologna Process due to the fact that the European Commission, as an EU Representative using the Lisbon Strategy to determine the Bologna agenda, sells the Bologna Process as an opportunity to put Europe back on the map as a knowledge continent in the world.[94] There is no legal coercion deriving from the Bologna Process. Moreover, for the non-EU states non-coercion and the knowledge continent argument will positively influence their involvement.

For the Member States of the Union the interaction with the single market and the four freedoms partly change the voluntary nature of the Process. The Commission may use its administrative powers to take legal actions against Member States before the Court of Justice of the European Union (CJEU) if it considers that the Member State has been in breach of the Treaties. Garben describes the Belgian-Austrian saga in which these Member States were convicted of breaches of the Treaties because they indirectly discriminated against non-national students trying to enrol at their universities.[95] Under the guise of European citizenship and the violation of the four freedoms, the Commission has had a direct impact on the higher education law of the Member States.[96] The right to go to court is a prime instrument for the Commission to put pressure on the Member States. What matters here is the direct influence on higher education policy and its funding. Moreover, the Commission's case against Austria revealed that the Court directly influences admission

92 Ibid., 362.

93 Ibid.

94 Ruth Keeling, 'The Bologna Process and the Lisbon Research Agenda: The European Commission's Expanding Role in Higher Education Discourse' *Eur J of Education* Vol. 41 p 203.

95 Sacha Garben, *EU higher education law: the Bologna process and harmonization by stealth* (Kluwer Law International 2011); Case-147/03 *Commission of the European Communities v Republic of Austria* [2005] ECR 2005 I-05969; Case-65/03 *Commission of the European Communities v Kingdom of Belgium* [2004] ECR 2004 I-06427.

96 Anne van Wageningen, 'Free movement, citizenship and the regulation of higher education: A constitutional and institutional stress test' in H. Mercenier, E. Ni Chaoimh, L. Damay, & G. Delledonne (eds.), *La libre circulation sous pression: Régulation et dérégulation des mobilités dans l'Union européenne* (Bruylant, 2018) 185–204.

requirements for higher education programs with a *numerus fixus*.[97] The latter requirement belongs to the elements that are 'regulated' through the Bologna Process.

The Bologna Process influences higher education in Europe. To be able to participate in the process as a full member, two formal requirements need to be met. First of all, the state must be affiliated with the Council of Europe's European Cultural Convention.[98] Secondly, the Member State must endorse and implement the objectives of the Bologna Process in its own higher education system. The affiliated states and organizations are committed to bring this process into one single area for European Higher Education. This space called the European Higher Education Area was established 12 March 2010 by the declaration of Budapest-Vienna.[99] The purpose of this space is to create a European higher education space in which it does not matter where someone has studied. Previously, all Member States agreed that a similar minimum level had to be achieved within courses.[100] Furthermore, this space must be a knowledge buffer in a globalizing world.[101] This space would also contribute to a better job market. Therefore, the Bologna Process is also supported by the European Union as a reinforcement for and in interaction with the Lisbon objectives of 2000.[102] It has also played an important role in helping the EU to create an EU education Area.

3.2.5 The Last Legal Keystone for an Independent EU Education Policy: The Adoption of Treaties with Georgia, Moldova and Ukraine

Since the Maastricht Treaty, and the subsequent Treaty changes (Amsterdam 1997; Nice 2000; Lisbon 2009; and several accession treaties), EU higher education law has developed significantly.[103] Member States could have decided to stop the development of an EU education policy by changing the Treaty

97 Case-147/03 *Commission of the European Communities v Republic of Austria*, ECR 2005 I-05969.

98 'Members' (European Higher Education Area) https://ehea.info/page-members, accessed 16 September 2024.

99 https://media.ehea.info/file/2010_Budapest_Vienna/64/0/Budapest-Vienna_Declaration_598640.pdf, accessed 14 May 2018.

100 https://media.ehea.info/file/2009_Leuven_Louvain-la-Neuve/06/1/Leuven_Louvain-la-Neuve_Communique_April_2009_595061.pdf, pt 19-pt 22 accessed 14 May 2018.

101 https://media.ehea.info/file/2007_London/69/7/2007_London_Communique_English_588697.pdf, pt 1.3, accessed 14 May 2018.

102 Cristina Sin, Amélia Veiga and Alberto Amaral, *European Policy Implementation and Higher Education: Analysing the Bologna Process* (Palgrave Macmillan, 2016).

103 Anne van Wageningen, 'Gelijke academici, gelijke baretten?' in Victoria Daskalova and Michiel. A. Heldeweg, eds. *Constitutionele Mogelijkheden En Beperkingen Voor Experi-*

provisions, but they chose not to do so. On the contrary, as with most treaty changes or enlargement treaties, they have added possibilities. Furthermore, the Member States have used these possibilities to add or change secondary rules, like directive 2004/38 which absorbed different directives including student directive 93/96. Its goal was to regulate access and residence rights for individuals in Member States other than their state of origin.

Three additions to the legal framework are Association Agreements with Georgia, Moldova, and Ukraine. These Association Treaties have given legal bases to develop higher education policies, albeit in three different modes. No agreement has the same text. Nevertheless, the Member States and the Union are bound to each of these three treaties. The first basis concerns the Association Agreement with Moldova and is stated in Articles 122 and 123.[104] The second basis is stated in Articles 358 and 359 of the Association Agreement with Georgia, which has a different wording from the Association Agreement with Moldova.[105] The third basis concerns the Association Agreement

---

menteel Handelen En Experimentele Wetgeving : Staatsrechtconferentie 2016 (Wolf Legal Publishers WLP, 2017).

104 Association Agreement between the European Union and the European Atomic Energy Community and their Member States, of the one part, and the Republic of Moldova, of the other part, [2014] OJ L 260, 4–738.
Article 122
The Parties shall cooperate to promote lifelong learning and encourage cooperation and transparency at all levels of education and training, with a special focus on higher education.
Article 123
That cooperation shall focus, inter alia, on the following areas:
(a) | [...]
(b) | [...]
(c) | promoting convergence in higher education, deriving from the Bologna process and the EU higher education modernisation agenda;
(d) | reinforcing international academic cooperation and participation in EU cooperation programmes, increasing student and teacher mobility;
(e) | [...]
(f) | [...].

105 Association Agreement between the European Union and the European Atomic Energy Community and their Member States, of the one part, and Georgia, of the other part [2014] OJ L 261, 4–743.
Article 358
The Parties shall cooperate in the field of education and training to intensify cooperation and dialogue, including dialogue on policy issues, seeking approximation to relevant EU policies and practices. The Parties shall cooperate to promote lifelong learning, encourage cooperation and transparency at all levels of education and training, with a special focus on higher education.

with Ukraine, worded in Articles 430 and 431, and has a totally different tone to the previous agreements.[106]

Such treaties bind every signatory, especially since the treaty is agreed on in every (member) state according to their own constitutional procedures. The Association Agreement with Georgia provides the most comprehensive legal basis. Efforts are being made to adapt to EU policies and practices that are relevant alongside a dialogue on policy issues. Quality in higher education is promoted through the Bologna Process and the EU Agenda for Modernization of Higher Education. In addition, this Association Agreement includes more areas for further cooperation.

This far-reaching form of cooperation is lacking in the association agreement with Moldova. However, it is in relation to the agreement with Ukraine that a significant difference becomes apparent. That agreement uses a wording similar to that of Article 165 TFEU. In Article 430 of the Association Agreement, which reiterates full respect for 'the content of each other's curriculum, the organization of each other's education system and their cultural and linguistic diversity', the tone and scope of Article 165 TFEU can be read. That reluctance cannot be found in the agreement with Georgia. Furthermore, Article 359 of the Georgia Agreement includes the obligation of consistency with the EU Modernisation Agenda for Higher Education, an obligation which is not mentioned in the Ukraine Agreement.

The Association Agreements create different kinds of spaces and particular effects. There is one Bologna Process, but each EU Member State now has

---

Article 359

This cooperation in the field of education and training shall focus, inter alia, on the following areas:

106 Association Agreement between the European Union and its Member States, of the one part, and Ukraine, of the other part, OJ L 161, 29.5.2014, p. 3–2137.

Article 430

Fully respecting the responsibility of the Parties for the content of teaching and the organisation of education systems and their cultural and linguistic diversity, the Parties shall promote cooperation in the field of education, training and youth in order to enhance mutual understanding, promote intercultural dialogue and increase the knowledge of their respective cultures.

Article 431

The Parties shall undertake to intensify cooperation in the field of higher education, aiming, in particular at:

(a) [...];

(b) promoting convergence in the field of higher education deriving from the Bologna process;

(c) [...]

(f) [...].

three legal regimes to consider. For EU Member States the highest bar to meet is with Georgia and among themselves. Thus, for the EU Member States the commitments in the Association Agreement with Georgia are the most extensive commitments between the EU, Member States and a third country and those commitments also regulate Member State's education policies.

The three Association Treaties refer to the Bologna Process, which makes part of the content of those treaties no longer dependent on the wishes of the contracting parties, but on the wishes of a third organization that manages the European Higher Education Area. In addition, an institutionally interesting experiment on guarding the content of treaties between the EU, Member States and third States has also been established by a rotating secretariat, which is not necessarily held by an EU Member State. Although the content of the three Association Treaties may differ, these differences will vanish if these states eventually join the EU. What might be still open, is the connection with the Bologna Process as an independent legal entity.

3.2.6 Mapping the State-EU-EHEA Nexus

By mapping the different relationships between states in the EHEA, some differences become apparent. The first relationship is between all 49 members. For instance the relation between the UK and Serbia is fully regulated within the EHEA. It is a voluntary relationship committed to the different objectives set in multiple documents published on the EHEA website. A little more complex is the relationship between Ukraine and the UK. Ukraine has committed to the Association Agreement with the EU and although not a Member State yet, EU regulations on the internal market cast their effect already. This is even more so between Ukraine and the Netherlands. This relationship is not only regulated by the EHEA, but also by the provisions of the Association Agreement. Because of the wording of the agreement, the relationship between Georgia and the Netherlands is substantively deeper than between Ukraine and the Netherlands. The most profound relationship is between the Netherlands and Belgium. These EU Member States are not only bound by the TFEU, but also by the Association Agreements, especially with Georgia, and the EHEA. Adding complexity to this relationship there is no relevant Belgian entity in higher education, but Flanders and Wallonia are adding another layer to the map. The Venn diagram beneath (Figure 3.1) visualizes the intensity of the actual legal connections between different EU Member States or other states. It is clear that these legal connections can create different relevant legal spaces, which are wider than the EU legal space. The EU thus is part of a Regional International Organization, the EHEA, as well as itself being a one.

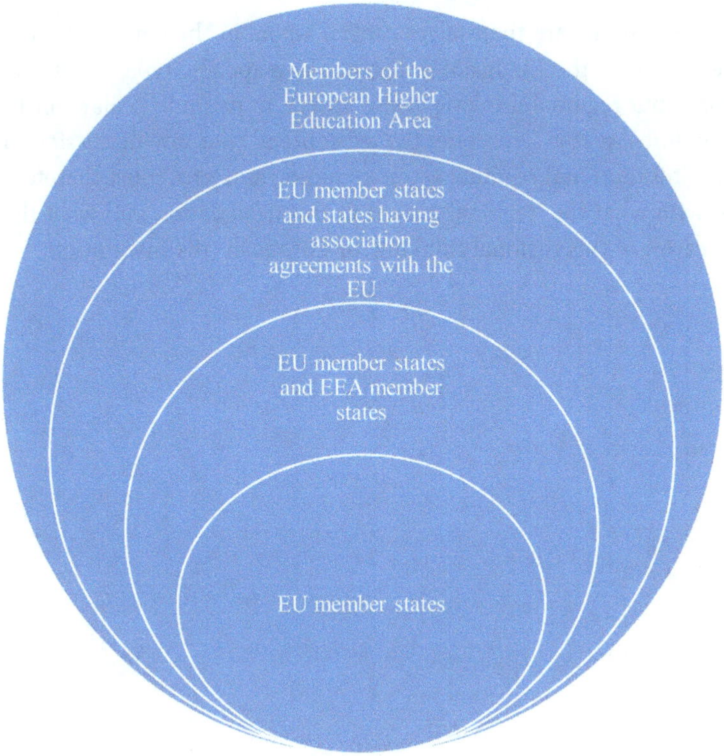

FIGURE 3.1 A mapping of the relationships in European higher education policy

4 Conclusion

In this paper we have explored the regional thinking which underpins how the EU can be understood as *regional* international organization. We have argued that for both the Just Transition Mechanism and the European Higher Education Area, regions are constructed at different geographical scales and these regions exhibit particular political dynamics with two key characteristics. Firstly, although both the Just Transition regions and the European Higher Education Area are grounded in particular legal and political codifications, both regional constructs also 'exceed' these basic codifications and are enrolled into a complex politics which questions the notion of EU (and especially Member State) territorialities as embedded in fixed, clearly bounded spatial units. Secondly, these examples also highlight the role of the EU and Member States as 'regional' actors in policymaking: whilst 'regions' are often constructed as either subnational or supranational entities, different from the national or EU scales of governance, the Member States and the EU institutions are themselves central actors in the construction of these spaces. As such, the EU is not only a RIO as a specific type of political and legal form, but regional thinking is also crucial to its multi-scalar constitution as a political actor. Consequently, we contend that any discussion of the EU as an international regional actor, including as a RIO, must therefore first reckon with what the 'regional' means in this designation and what the consequences are of this regional thinking for European (dis)integration.

PART 2

EU Regionalism in Practice

CHAPTER 4

Enhancing Global Health and Human Rights Law through Regionality?: The Case of EU International Cooperation for Pharmaceuticals

Katrina Perehudoff[1]

Abstract

Regional international organisations (RIOs) (e.g. the EU) can have significant impacts on international lawmaking and external legal orders. The EU's impact on global health law, an emerging field of international law, is one salient example. Recent global crises (e.g. Covid-19 pandemic) underscore how the EU's international cooperation can protect and promote human rights within and beyond the Union's borders. However, the normative standards for the EU's international cooperation are scarcely defined with regards to social and health rights. The International Covenant on Economic, Social and Cultural Rights (ICESCR), and the principle of international cooperation therein, offers guidance to fill this gap. Although the EU is not a contracting party to the ICESCR, the EU Treaties reference to the UN Charter illustrates the potential for RIOs to be a vehicle for regional law and practice consistent with international human rights law (IHRL). This chapter explores the EU's practice of international cooperation regarding pharmaceuticals, questioning how it aligns with the IHRL principle of international cooperation, and how regionality affects the coherent application of this principle through three EU laws: the Joint Procurement Agreements; Trade Diversion Regulation; Regulation on Clinical Trials Partnership. While the EU generally adheres to IHRL in its legal conception of international cooperation, the EU's practice could be more coherent with this principle. For example, the EU's decision to leverage its market power and prioritize Covid-19 vaccine access for its own market over the global market highlights the need for better alignment between EU law and the ICESCR standards.

1 Katrina Perehudoff is affiliated to the Law Centre for Health and Life, University of Amsterdam, Postbus 15859, 1001 NJ Amsterdam, the Netherlands.

 | DOI:10.1163/9789004700659_006

Keywords

European Union – international human rights law – pharmaceuticals – access to medicines – external relations

1 Introduction

Regional international organizations (RIOs), such as the EU with its autonomous legal order, can have significant impacts on international lawmaking and (both directly and indirectly) on external legal orders.[2] The formulation and practice of global health law, an emerging field of international law, is one example of the EU's influence in this regard. Global health law is composed of the legal frameworks, processes and institutions necessary to enable people worldwide to achieve the highest standards of physical and mental health.[3] Relevant legal frameworks for the present chapter are, for example, the WTO Agreement on Trade Related Aspects of Intellectual Property and the International Covenant on Economic, Social and Cultural Rights (ICESCR). Global health law seeks to foster health-promoting actions among key stakeholders – such as governments, businesses and international organizations – by advancing research, mobilizing resources, setting priorities, coordinating initiatives and enforcing standards.[4] Central to the regime of global health law is the principle of social justice, and as such, the regime seeks to prioritize equitable access to health services, particularly for the most impoverished populations globally.[5]

The EU has the potential to mitigate and/or alleviate the repercussions of global health crises (such as the 2009 avian flu, the COVID-19 pandemic or antimicrobial resistance) at least in part through international cooperation with third countries and international organizations in the field of health, a competence which the EU derives from to Article 168(3) Treaty on the Functioning of the European Union (TFEU).[6] For example, the COVID-19 pandemic underscored this potential, notably through the 'Team Europe' initiative – a

2 Samantha Besson and Eva Kassoti, 'The International Law of Regional Organizations – Mapping the Issues' (2024) 21 *International Organisations Law Review* 4–5.

3 Lawrence O. Gostin and Allyn L. Taylor, 'Global Health Law: A Definition and Grand Challenges' (2008) 1 *Public Health Ethics* 53, 55.

4 Ibid.

5 Ibid.

6 Consolidated version of the Treaty on the Functioning of the European Union [2016] OJ C202/47-388 (TFEU).

collaborative framework that brings together the European Union, its member states, financial institutions, and other partners to enhance and coordinate their global development efforts.[7] This initiative played a pivotal role in global fundraising for vaccine research, COVID-19 response efforts, and the provision of financial support and vaccine donations to benefit developing countries.

However, the permissible scope and/or requirements of the EU's international cooperation (i.e., cooperation with entities outside of the EU) are scarcely defined with regards to social rights and (public) health.[8] Meanwhile, international human rights law (IHRL) offers normative guidance on the scope and content of the principle of international cooperation, which is enshrined in the Charter of the United Nations (hereinafter UN Charter) that the EU has committed to respect in 'its relations with the wider world'.[9] In the field of social rights, the principle of international cooperation is a legal obligation of the 171 state parties to the ICESCR.[10] The EU is not a party to the ICESCR and therefore does not have a direct legal obligation to implement the commitments in the Covenant through its institutions. Nevertheless, the reference to the UN Charter in the EU Treaties illustrates the potential for RIOs such as the EU to be a vehicle for driving law, policy and actions that are consistent with international law.

Therefore, this chapter asks the questions: What is the EU's practice of international cooperation in the field of pharmaceuticals? How does the EU's practice align with the principle of international cooperation under IHRL? Why is the regional element relevant to the coherent application of the principle of international cooperation? To what extent is the EU's practice threatening or enhancing IHRL? These are timely questions as the EU has increasingly expanded its actions in the field of (global) health and pharmaceuticals (e.g., 2022 EU Global Health Strategy, 2020 Pharmaceutical Strategy for Europe) which include international cooperation despite having little in-

7 Council of the European Union, 'Council conclusions on Team Europe' 7894/21, 23 April 2021.

8 Marco Liverani and Richard Coker, 'Protecting Europe from Diseases: From the International Sanitary Conferences to the ECDC' (2012) 37 *Journal of Health Politics, Policy and Law* 915; Azzopardi-Muscat N., Schroder-Bäck P. and Brand H., 'The European Union Joint Procurement Agreement for Cross-Border Health Threats: What Is the Potential for This New Mechanism of Health System Collaboration?' (2017) 12(1) *Health Economics, Policy, and Law* 43.

9 See art 3(5), Consolidated version of the Treaty on European Union [2016] OJ C202/1-45 (TEU); Arts 55 and 56; Charter of the United Nations (signed 26 June 1945, entered into force 24 October 1945) 1 UNTS XVI.

10 Art 2(1) International Covenant on Economic, Social and Cultural Rights (adopted 16 December 1966, entered into force 3 January 1976) 993 UNTS 3 (ICESCR).

ternal normative guidance for Union action on this matter.[11] As this chapter will show, this potential of RIOs is realized by the EU when it leverages its capacity to regulate the single market to shape companies' extraterritorial trade activity in such a way to protect human dignity and the human rights of people outside Union borders and in accordance with the UN Charter and the EU's own principles and objectives of external action.

This chapter examines selected examples of the EU's practice of international cooperation in relation to pharmaceuticals. Part two explores the EU as a RIO and its relationship with the ICESCR. Part three elucidates the relevant provisions of Article 2(1) ICESCR and its subsequent authoritative interpretations by the UN Committee on Economic, Social and Cultural Rights (hereinafter Committee), for the EU's practice of international cooperation. The analytical framework applied in this chapter draws on the normative development of Covenant rights by the Committee to delineate the nature, scope and content of 'developed' states' obligations with regard to international cooperation, where the receiving states are usually low- and middle-income countries (LMICs). Part four examines to what extent selected examples of EU law satisfy the duties to respect, to protect and to fulfil ICESCR rights through international cooperation. The analysis considers whether and how the EU's practice of international cooperation aligns with the substantive aspects of this duty under the ICESCR. Finally, in part five this chapter draws some conclusions about whether the EU's practice threatens or enriches the principle of international cooperation with regards to pharmaceuticals under the ICESCR – a pillar of global health law.

This chapter advances the state of knowledge about the EU as a RIO in several respects, highlighting how the regional dimension is crucial in the interplay between the EU's (global) regulatory power and the Union's potential to catalyse state and regional practices consistent with IHRL. First, this chapter investigates international cooperation provisions in EU laws the primary objective of which is regulating the internal market (in contrast to most literature on the EU's international cooperation which focuses on the EU's explicit external actions). This approach builds the knowledge base of the EU's under-addressed global regulatory influence over pharmaceuticals through its internal market actions.[12] Second, this chapter contributes to un-

11 European Commission, 'Pharmaceutical Strategy for Europe' COM(2020) 761, 25 November 2020; European Commission, 'EU Global Health Strategy' COM(2022) 675, 30 November 2022.

12 Examples of internal market actions are, e.g., coordination of internal and external research funding; provision of expertise to external regulators; 'capacity building' and

derstanding the potential contributions of the practice of RIOs, such as the EU, to emerging fields of international law, namely global health law. This chapter's contribution stands alongside more established strands of scholarship regarding the EU's contribution to international economic, environmental and criminal law.[13]

2 The EU as a RIO

The EU is understood as both an autonomous legal order and an international organization under international law. This chapter focuses on the EU as an international organization whereby the EU is founded and empowered by the Member States of the EU to discharge certain functions outlined in its Treaties.[14] The implications of the EU's status as a RIO are illustrated by the words of UN Special Rapporteur Michael Wood: '...international organisations do act on the behalf of their members States; but in doing so they are actors in their own right'.[15] International law also gives the EU legal personality that imposes on it certain 'rights' and obligations.[16] As such, when the EU is acting within its conferred (full, shared or parallel) competences that are 'functionally equivalent' to the public powers exercised by states, the International Law Commission finds that the practice of international organizations is comparable to the practice of States.[17]

This chapter concerns the EU's international cooperation and humanitarian aid competences, which are parallel competences held by both the Union and its Member States, such that measures by both entities should not be

technical assistance to third countries. See, generally, Katrina Perehudoff et al., 'Impact of the European Union on access to medicines in low- and middle-income countries: A scoping review' (2021) 9 *Lancet* – Regional Health Europe 100219, 1–9.

13 Frank Hoffmeister, 'Chapter 3. The contribution of EU Practice to International law' in Marise Cremona (ed.), *Developments in EU External Relations Law* (Oxford University Press, 2008) 112–124.

14 Robert Schütze, *An Introduction to European Law* (3rd edn, Oxford University Press, 2020) 75.

15 Michael Wood, *Fifth report on identification of customary international law.* (International Law Commission, 14 March 2018) Paragraph 44.

16 International Law Commission (ILC), 'Draft conclusions on identification of customary international law, with commentaries 2018' (adopted by ILC in 2018 at 17th session, submitted to GA as part of Commission's report on work of that session) A/73/10, Conclusion 4, Paragraph 2.

17 Art 4(2)(k) TFEU; Ibid., Paragraph 4.

identical but rather 'complement and reinforce each other'.[18] Pharmaceuticals are the empirical subject of this chapter, and in this regard the EU has a complementary competence to protect and improve public health except in a limited set of circumstances (e.g., for the safety of the pharmaceutical supply) whereby the EU may harmonise national laws.[19] Due to its limited competences in the field of public health, the EU has adopted internal market regulation governing health matters (that could include pharmaceuticals) on the legal basis of safeguarding the functioning of the internal market (in Article 114 TFEU). However, since the Lisbon Treaty, the protection of human health has become legally recognized in Article 9 TFEU as an overarching objective of the Union that should be considered in all EU policies and actions, and without territorial limitation.[20]

All EU Member States are party to the ICESCR, one of the main UN human rights treaties enshrining social, economic and cultural rights relevant to the provision of pharmaceuticals for the protection and promotion of human dignity. Notably, according to the ICESCR only states may become contracting parties to the instrument, which therefore excludes RIOs from being directly bound by this UN human rights treaty.[21] The legal obligations enshrined in the ICESCR impose a duty on states to act 'individually and through international assistance and cooperation, especially economic and technical, to the maximum of their available resources' to progressively realise ICESCR rights 'through all appropriate means'.[22] ICESCR rights include the right to the highest attainable standard of mental and physical health, which includes the provision of essential medicines, and the right to enjoy the benefits of scientific progress which is crucial for ensuring the availability of innovative pharmaceuticals.[23]

There are several justifications for the EU to have indirect obligations flowing from the ICESCR. First, from an EU law perspective, while ICESCR obligations are not directly legally binding on the Union, it is required by virtue of its own constitutional treaties to respect the principles of the UN

18 Art 4(4) TFEU and Article 208(1) TFEU, as explained by Klamert, Marcus, 'Article 4 TFEU', in Manuel Kellerbauer, Marcus Klamert, and Jonathan Tomkin (eds.), *The EU Treaties and the Charter of Fundamental Rights: A Commentary* (online edn, Oxford Academic 2019) 370–371, https://doi.org/10.1093/oso/9780198759393.003.75, accessed 21 Sept. 2024.

19 Art 168 TFEU.

20 De Ruijter, Anniek. *EU health law & policy: the expansion of EU power in public health and health care.* (Oxford University Press, 2019) at 77–78.

21 Article 26 ICESCR.

22 Article 2(1) ICESCR.

23 Articles 12 and 15 ICESCR.

Charter and international law.[24] Moreover, from an international law perspective, the UN Charter establishes the primacy of the obligations arising from the Charter in cases where they conflict with other international agreements.[25] According to Ahmed and de Jesús Butler, obligations that arise from the UN Charter 'include the obligation to guarantee human rights as they are elaborated in subsequent UN-sponsored instruments such as… the International Convention on Economic, Social and Cultural Rights'.[26] Another justification for the EU's indirect obligations imposed by the ICESCR is found in the monitoring mechanism for this UN treaty. EU Member States, as contracting parties to the ICESCR, receive instructions from the ICESCR's monitoring body, the Committee, about how to act with regards to ICESCR duties as independent states *and* as member states of the EU, which is an international organization also bound by the UN Charter. This accountability pathway lends weight to the argument that the EU, albeit through its Member States, has some indirect obligations flowing form the ICESCR. Therefore, it can be argued that the ICESCR obligations are indirectly incumbent on the EU as a RIO.

3 The Principle of International Cooperation under the ICESCR

The Committee has further developed a common understanding of the norm of international cooperation through its statements, general comments and concluding observations.[27] In the context of the right to science, for instance, the Committee reminds state parties that those 'participating in decisions as members of international organizations cannot ignore their human rights obligations'.[28] Further to this observation, state parties 'should direct their ef-

24 Article 21(1) TEU.

25 Article 103 UN Charter. See Tawhida Ahmeda and Israel de Jesús Butler, 'The European Union and human rights: An international law perspective.' (2006) 17(4) *European Journal of International Law*, 771–801.

26 Ibid., 772.

27 International cooperation is a key tenant of international human rights and global health law. Initially established in the UN Charter (Articles 55 and 56), international cooperation among states and other entities are also crucial for protecting and promoting the realization of health rights. This is acknowledged in Article 44 of the World Health Organization (WHO) International Health Regulations (for the prevention and control of infectious disease outbreaks), which are applicable to all Member States of the WHO.

28 UN CESCR, 'Public debt, austerity measures and the International Covenant on Economic, Social and Cultural Rights' (22 July 2016) E/C.12/2016/1.

forts and exercise their voting powers in these organizations' for the realization of ICESCR rights.[29] Moreover, the Committee calls upon international organizations concerned with ICESCR rights, and specifically with trade, to 'cooperate effectively with States parties, building on their respective expertise' for the implementation of ICESCR rights.[30] Additionally, the Committee calls for the 'incorporation of human rights law and principles in the programmes and policies of international organizations' in order to 'greatly facilitate the implementation' of ICESCR rights.[31] Moreover, several of the Committee's Concluding Observations on the treaty monitoring reports submitted by EU Member States criticised their inaction and/or called for their future action within the RIOs and international organizations they are members of 'in advocating for universal, equitable and affordable access to COVID-19 vaccines and drugs' based on Articles 2(1), 12 and 15 ICESCR.[32] This is evidence that the Committee's guidance with implications for international organizations extends into its accountability mechanisms for the realization of ICESCR rights.

The Committee has noted that the duty expressed in the UN Charter to respect the human rights of all is 'without any territorial limitation, and should be taken into account when addressing the scope of States' obligations under human rights treaties'.[33] Although international cooperation is enshrined in other UN human rights treaties, the ICESCR is the focus of this chapter given its broad applicability to all population groups (i.e., not limited to women, children, migrants, people with disabilities, etc.) and the global recognition of ICESCR rights shown by having secured 171 state parties.

---

29 UN CESCR, 'General comment No. 25 (2020) on science and economic, social and cultural rights (Article 15 (1) (b), (2), (3) and (4) of the International Covenant on Economic, Social and Cultural Rights)' (30 April 2020) E/C.12/GC/25, para 83.

30 Namely the right to social security. See UN CESCR, 'General Comment No. 19: The right to social security (Art. 9 of the Covenant)' (4 February 2008) E/C.12/GC/19, para 82.

31 This statement was made in relation to the right to social security. Ibid, para 84.

32 UN CESCR, 'Concluding observations on the second periodic report of Latvia' (15 February – 5 March 2021) UN Doc E/C.12/LVA/CO/2, para 40 and 41(e); UN CESCR, 'Concluding observations on the seventh periodic report of Finland' (30 March 2021) UN Doc E/C.12/FIN/CO/7, para 8–9. Cited in Katrina Perehudoff and Jennifer Sellin, 'The Right to Science as a Guidepost for Fair Access to COVID-19 Vaccines: Investigating the Interpretive Role of the United Nations Committee on Economic, Social and Cultural Rights' (2022) 24 Health and Human Rights 191–204, at 199–201.

33 UN CESCR, General Comment No. 24 (2017) on State obligations under the International Covenant on Economic, Social and Cultural Rights in the context of business activities (adopted 10 August 2017) E/C.12/GC/24, para 27 (hereinafter: General Comment No. 24).

With regards to the private sector, the Committee recognises the private business sector's responsibilities in relation to human rights, and specifically the right to health, by stating that

> while only States are parties to the Covenant and thus ultimately accountable for compliance with it, all members of society [...] [including] the private business sector – have responsibilities regarding the realisation of the right to health.[34]

The Committee's authoritative interpretations of state obligations in the ICESCR constitute a duty to respect, protect and fulfil ICESCR rights with regards to international cooperation.[35] The duty to respect requires developed states to act with restraint by not interfering with or preventing meaningful/beneficial international cooperation in the realization of ICESCR rights 'in particular the rights of vulnerable groups within the recipient society'.[36] In general, the duty to protect in relation to international cooperation implies that developed states prevent deleterious acts by non-state entities under their jurisdiction, even if (and particularly when) those non-state entities are acting extraterritorially or their actions have extraterritorial effects.[37] The second aspect is to ensure ICESCR rights are protected when negotiating, ratifying and implementing international agreements and to avoid the violation of ICESCR rights as a result of the programmes or policies of international organizations of which states are a member.[38] The obligation to fulfil Covenent rights within the framework of international cooperation can be considered a composite of three positive obligations, namely, the duty to facilitate, to

34 UN CESCR, 'General Comment No. 14: The Right to the Highest Attainable Standard of Health (Art. 12)' (11 August 2000) E/C.12/2000/4, para 42.

35 See generally Magdalena Sepúlveda Carmona, 'Obligations of 'International Assistance and Cooperation' in an optional protocol to the international covenant on economic, social and cultural rights' (2006) 24(2) *Netherlands Quarterly of Human Rights* 271–303.

36 Ibid., 280. citing, among others, General Comment No. 14 (n 34) para. 39. Non-interference includes refraining from imposing embargoes and burdensome conditionalities on international assistance. Bid., 281 citing, among others, UN CESCR, 'General Comment No. 8: Poverty and the International Covenant on Economic, Social And Cultural Rights' (4 May 2001) E/C.12/2001/10.

37 Ibid., p. 282 citing, among others, General Comment No. 14 (n 28) para 39.

38 Ibid., p. 282 citing, among others, General Comment No. 14 (n 28) para. 39. Also Carmona (n 35) 283, citing SIM, The Maastricht Guidelines on Violations of Economic, Social and Cultural Rights, SIM Special No. 20 (Utrecht, 1998) guideline No. 19.

provide and to promote.[39] The duty to promote is most relevant for the present chapter because it requires aiding a state receiving overseas development assistance regarding the fulfilment of the ICESCR's obligations,[40] and raising attention to the Convent's rights through international cooperation and assistance while simultaneously empowering individuals to defend their rights in a participatory environment.[41]

Beyond the ICESCR, the UN Guiding Principles on Business and Human Rights are increasingly relevant to the perennial challenge of regulating transnational health-related industries (e.g., pharmaceutical, tobacco, food) such that their policies and activities support, or at least do not deter, the attainment of health rights. The Guiding Principles were formulated by the Special Representative of the Secretary-General Mr. Ruggie, and endorsed by the Human Rights Council in 2011.[42] The Guiding Principles offer authoritative (albeit non-binding) normative guidance regarding the contours of corporate conduct consistent with human rights standards.[43] These principles establish a framework for the private business sector to discharge their human rights responsibilities, emphasizing the responsibilities to 'protect, respect and remedy'. International cooperation is an important component of commercial actors' responsibilities to undertake due diligence activities to identify and mitigate potential adverse impacts of their activities on the enjoyment of human rights.[44]

39 General Comment No. 19 (n 30) para 55. Carmona (n 35) 286, 288–289, citing, among others, UN CESCR, 'General Comment No. 18: The right to work (art. 6)' (6 February 2006) E/C.12/GC/186 para 29; General Comment No. 14 at para. 40 (see note 27); UN CESCR, 'General Comment No. 15: The right to water (arts. 11 and 12)' (20 January 2003) E/C.12/2002/11 para 34.

40 Carmona (n 35) 289.

41 ibid.

42 Human Rights Council, 'Resolution 17/4 on Human rights and transnational corporations and other business enterprises' (July 2011) Seventeenth session. A/HRC/RES/17/4.

43 In an effort to establish binding obligations that 'mutually reinforce' and complement the UN Guiding Principles, an intergovernmental working group was established in 2014 to elaborate a binding instrument to regulate business enterprises with respect to human rights. The discussions about a binding instrument are ongoing. See OHCHR, Guiding Principles on Business and Human Rights: Implementing the United Nations 'Protect, Respect and Remedy' Framework https://www.ohchr.org/sites/default/files/documents/publications/guidingprinciplesbusinesshr_en.pdf., para. 24 and principle 17.

44 ibid.

4 Legal Basis and Context of the EU's International Cooperation

'International cooperation' is discussed within the EU treaties in relation to cooperation with third countries and other international organizations for development, economic, financial, technical measures, humanitarian aid and the protection of human health.[45] The respect and promotion of human rights standards is a cross-cutting EU value that the Union must uphold in the external aspects of all of its policies, including international cooperation and its internal policies with external effects.[46] References to the EU's values, principles and objectives in the context of its external relations are scattered throughout the TEU. The EU's values are enshrined in Article 2 TEU, which states that (emphasis added) 'the Union is founded on the values of respect for human dignity, freedom, democracy, equality, the rule of law and respect for human rights (…)'.[47] These values must be upheld and promoted through the EU's 'relations with the wider world', which indicates to some scholars the 'legally binding nature' of these values on EU external action.[48]

Furthermore, the EU's international action 'shall be guided by the principles which have inspired its own creation, development and enlargement, and which it seeks to advance in the wider world' including through its relations with third countries and international organisztions.[49] These principles include:

> the universality and indivisibility of human rights and fundamental freedoms, respect for human dignity, the principles of equality and solidarity, and respect for the principles of the United Nations Charter and international law.[50]

Article 21(2) TEU enumerates some of the substantive objectives of the EU's policies, actions and cooperation in international relations, including to 'safeguard its values', and 'consolidate and support (…) human rights and the prin-

45 Title III TFEU and Article 168(3) TFEU.

46 Article 21 TEU.

47 Aricle 2 TEU.

48 Article 3(5) TEU. See also, Ramses A. Wessel and Yuliya Kaspiarovich, 'The Role of Values in EU External Relations: A Legal Assessment of the EU as a "Good" Global Actor' in Elaine Fahey and Isabella Mancini (eds.), *Understanding the EU as a Good Global Actor* (Edward Elgar Publishing, 2022) 93 and 96.

49 Article 21(1) TEU.

50 Article 21(1) TEU.

ciples of international law'.[51] Moreover, Article 21(3) TEU requires that the EU's external action and the 'external aspects of its other policies' 'respect the principles and pursue the [Union's] objectives'.[52]

To help achieve these objectives, the EU is empowered to engage in international development cooperation, economic, financial and technical cooperation with third countries, and humanitarian aid.[53] EU actions considered to be part of international cooperation consist of implementing multiannual cooperation programmes with developing countries, concluding agreements and/or cooperating with third countries or international organizations to help achieve the objectives of the EU treaties, coordinating policies or actions and/or undertaking joint actions between the EU and the Member States, and where relevant other international organizations, providing economic, financial and technical cooperation and assistance to third countries other than developing countries, and 'provide ad hoc assistance, relief and protection for people in third countries who are victims of natural or man-made disasters'.[54] In the fields of development cooperation and humanitarian aid, the EU has the competence to 'conduct a common policy', which does not preclude Member States from pursuing their own policies.[55]

With regards to the protection of human health, the EU is empowered to 'foster cooperation with third countries and the competent international organizations' in the field of public health.[56] Moreover, the EU may adopt 'measures setting high standards of quality and safety for medicinal products and devices for medical use', and adopt 'incentive measures designed to protect and improve human health and in particular to combat the major cross-border health scourges'.[57] In this respect, the EU has two mainstreaming obligations relevant for international cooperation. The first is to consider its objectives in the field of development cooperation (namely, poverty reduction and eradication) in the development and discharge of its other policies 'which are likely to affect developing countries'.[58] The second is to ensure a high level of human health protection 'in the definition and implementation of all Union policies and activities', thereby also requiring the EU

51 Article 21(2) TEU.
52 enshrined in Article 21(1–2) TEU.
53 Articles 208–211, 212–213, and 214 TFEU, respectively.
54 Articles 209(1), 210, 211, 212(1,3), 214(1,4,6–7) TFEU.
55 Article 4(4) TFEU.
56 Article 168(3) TFEU.
57 Articles 168(4)(c) and 168(5) TFEU.
58 Article 208(1) TFEU.

to take steps to protect human health in its cooperation with third countries.[59]

Against the backdrop of the legal basis and context of the EU's international cooperation policy and activities, the following section describes the rationale for selecting three cases – the Health Threats Regulation and Joint Procurement Agreement (JPA, Section 5.1), the EU Trade Diversion Regulation (Section 5.2), and the European and Developing Countries Clinical Trials Partnership (Section 5.3) – to investigate the EU's practice in this regard.

5 The EU's Practice of International Cooperation

This chapter examines selected, non-exhaustive examples of EU legislative and administrative acts as evidence of the EU's practice of international cooperation in relation to pharmaceuticals. The EU laws selected for analysis represent examples of the EU practicing each type of state obligations (i.e., respect, protect, fulfill) towards the realization of ICESCR rights as indicated in Table 4.1 below. First, the EU's joint purchase of vaccines (enshrined in the Health Threats Regulation and JPA) offers a case to examine the EU's practice of non-interference and respecting access to pharmaceuticals through international cooperation.[60] The second example of the EU Trade Diversion Regulation to avoid the re-importation into the EU of medicine shipments destined for developing countries integrates the protection of ICESCR rights.[61] Third, the European and Developing Countries Clinical Trials Partnership is an example of the EU's practice of the duty to fulfil ICESCR rights through international cooperation.[62]

59 Article 168(1) TFEU.

60 European Commission, 'Commission Implementing Decision on the Joint Procurement Agreement to Procure Medical Countermeasures' [2014] OJ L117/4; Regulation (EU) 2022/2371 of the European Parliament and of the Council of 23 November 2022 on serious cross-border threats to health and repealing Decision No 1082/2013/EU (Text with EEA relevance) [2022] OJ L314/26.

61 Regulation (EU) 2016/793 of the European Parliament and of the Council of 11 May 2016 to avoid trade diversion into the European Union of certain key medicines (codification) [2016] OJ L135/39.

62 Decision 556/2014/EU of the European Parliament and of the Council of 15 May 2014 on the participation of the Union in a second European and Developing Countries Clinical Trials Partnership Programme (EDCTP2) jointly undertaken by several Member States [2014] OJ L169/38.

TABLE 4.1 Overview of cases of EU legal instruments analysed in this chapter

Cases of EU law	Predominant type of state duty under ICESCR		
	Respect	Protect	Fulfil
Joint vaccine purchases (section 5.1)	X		
Trade Diversion (section 5.2)		X	
Clinical Trials Partnership (section 5.3)			X

5.1 *Respecting Human Rights When Jointly Purchasing Vaccines*

The COVID-19 pandemic illustrated that the EU's coordination of the joint procurement of vaccines primarily destined for the internal market, can have implications for the supply of vaccines externally, and consequently for the respect of ICESCR rights abroad. For example, the European Commission's vaccine contracts had the perverse effect of detracting from the scarce global supply of vaccine doses available for the rest of the world, including LMICs.

The EU's joint procurements are facilitated by the Health Threats Decision on serious cross-border health threats (later repealed by 'Health Threats' Regulation of 2022) and by the JPA with EU Member States.[63] The Health Threats Decision (and subsequent Regulation) established the aims and methods of EU support for Member States in response to such threats, including through the joint procurement of medical supplies (e.g., vaccines).[64] The Decision provides for the administrative infrastructure allowing the European Commission to manage and support Member States to engage at a European level in voluntary and complementary actions to their own national measures.[65] The

63 European Commission, 'Commission Implementing Decision on the Joint Procurement Agreement to Procure Medical Countermeasures' [2014] OJ L117/4. Regulation (EU) 2022/2371 of the European Parliament and of the Council of 23 November 2022 on serious cross-border threats to health and repealing Decision No 1082/2013/EU [2022] OJ L314/26.

64 Article 5, Decision No 1082/2013/EU of the European Parliament and of the Council of 22 October 2013 on serious cross-border threats to health and repealing Decision No 2119/98/EC. OJ L 293, 5.11.2013, 1–15.

65 See, generally, E. McEvoy and D. Ferri, 'The Role of the Joint Procurement Agreement during the COVID-19 Pandemic: Assessing Its Usefulness and Discussing Its Potential to Support a European Health Union' (2020) 11(4) European Journal of Risk Regulation 851–863.

FIGURE 4.1
EU's joint procurement of COVID-19 vaccines through Advanced Procurement Agreements (APAs) with transnational pharmaceutical companies

Decision is based on Article 168(5) TFEU, which empowers the Council and the European Parliament to adopt measures to combat cross-border health threats, and serves an internal market objective.[66]

The JPA lays down the rules and practical arrangements for participating states and the EU institutions to jointly purchase medical supplies in the event of a serious cross-border health threat.[67] The JPA provides the operational infrastructure for the Commission to facilitate Member States' decisions to participate and support and manage the joint purchases. By April 2020, 37 countries had signed the JPA including EU Member States and non-EU states including EEA countries, the UK, and countries in the Western Balkans. In this way, the EU leverages its market power and capacity to mobilise state resources to construct from this group of countries a collective 'buyer' of vaccines. Some developing countries (i.e., candidate countries for EU membership, including Bosnia and Herzegovina, Montenegro, North Macedonia, Serbia, Albania and Moldova) have signed the JPA to procure medical countermeasures coordinated by the European Commission, which corresponds to the duty on developed states to aid foreign states in fulfilling ICESCR rights through international organizations of which they are parties.[68]

66 Ibid.

67 Recitals 18–19, Regulation (EU) 2022/2371 of the European Parliament and of the Council of 23 November 2022 on serious cross-border threats to health and repealing Decision No 1082/2013/EU, PE/40/2022/REV/1 OJ L 314, 6.12.2022, p. 26–63.

68 European Commission, 'Signing Ceremonies for Joint Procurement Agreements' https://health.ec.europa.eu/health-security-and-infectious-diseases/preparedness-and-response-planning/signing-ceremonies-joint-procurement-agreement_en, accessed 22 September 2024.

On the basis of this Decision, the EU entered into several advanced purchase agreements with manufacturers for COVID-19 vaccine doses to be distributed amongst members of the JPA. Advanced purchase agreements (APAs) intend to encourage and de-risk the development of products (i.e., pandemic vaccines) that society needs, and often that are not lucrative for companies to develop.[69] APAs can accelerate the development of new products and their availability on the market. However, the terms and conditions in APAs will impact how quickly, widely and affordably these products will be made available. This is a practical example of the EU's role in shaping the global business environment to facilitate the private pharmaceutical industry to discharge its human rights responsibilities.[70]

During the COVID-19 pandemic, European politicians, German Chancellor Angela Merkel and French President Emmanuel Macron, both endorsed the notion that a COVID-19 vaccine ought to be a 'global public good' despite the absence of a clear definition of this term in European affairs. Among other international organizations, such as the International Monetary Fund, the term 'global public good' generally refers to goods that are available to all people of the world and where the enjoyment of these goods by one person does not diminish the benefits that can be enjoyed by other people.[71] Notably, this terminology is found in the European Commission's 2020 agreement with Member States on procuring COVID-19 vaccines, which includes in an Annex to its Decision approving the APA the following commitment:

> In the negotiations with the pharmaceutical industry under the present Agreement, the Commission will promote a COVID-19 vaccine as a global public good. This promotion will include access for low and middle income countries to these vaccines in sufficient quantity and at low prices.
>
> The Commission will seek to promote related questions with the pharmaceutical industry regarding intellectual property sharing, espe-

69 P. Boulet et al., *Advanced Purchase Agreements for Covid-19 Vaccines. Analysis and Comments* (The Left in the European Parliament, July 2021) https://left.eu/issues/publications/eu-vaccine-deals-with-big-pharma-failed-to-protect-the-public-interest-study/. Last accessed: 8 January 2025.

70 General Comment No. 14 (n 28).

71 Global public goods are considered non-excludable and non-rival. See Moya Chin, 'What are global public goods' (International Monetary Fund, December 2021) https://www.imf.org/en/Publications/fandd/issues/2021/12/Global-Public-Goods-Chin-basics, accessed 22 September 2024. Comparable definitions are used by the UN Department of Economic and Social Affairs, and the WHO.

cially when such IP has been developed with public support, in order to these objectives.[72]

The Commission's commitments to promote access to COVID-19 vaccines in developing countries are consistent with the duties of developed states under the right to science to promote access to research results for developing countries and their citizens in an 'affordable manner'.[73] Moreover, the Commission's promotion of IP sharing, in the context of global COVID-19 vaccine access, echoes the UN CESCR's framing of the social function of intellectual property and the responsibility of developed states to share the benefits and applications of science with LMICs.[74] Notably, although the Commission's language is generally supportive of intellectual property (IP) sharing particularly for vaccines developed with public financing, it does not require Member States to regulate private actors (e.g., pharmaceutical companies) to create a supportive business environment for the realization of human rights, which is also a duty under the right to health.[75]

Whether the EU has delivered on these agreements with Member States can be in part determined in an analysis of the terms and conditions of the APA contracts. For example, the contracts between the EC and Astra-Zeneca, Moderna and CureVac (where not redacted) bear no commitment to making vaccines a 'global public good'.[76] Moreover, the contracts allow the companies to retain IP ownership including over the know-how and data.[77]

Beyond the EU's JPA for vaccines, the EU contributed to the global COVAX initiative that supplied vaccine doses as donations or at discounted prices to LMICS; however, these doses usually arrived later and in smaller quantities than those purchased by more affluent buyers such as through the EU's joint

72 European Commission, Annex to 'Commission Decision C (2020) 4192 final of 18 June 2020 on approving the agreement with Member States on procuring COVID-19 vaccines on behalf of the Member States and related procedures' [2020].

73 UN CESCR, General Comment No. 25: Science and economic, social and cultural rights (art. 15(1)(b), (2), (3), and (4))' (30 April 2020) E/C.12/GC/25 para 79.

74 UN CESCR, 'Statement on the coronavirus disease (COVID-19) pandemic and economic, social and cultural rights' (17 April 2020) E/C.12/2020/1. General Comment No. 25, para. 79 (see note 79). See also Human Rights Council, Report of the UN Special Rapporteur in the Field of Cultural Rights, Farida Shaheed, UN Doc. A/HRC/20/26 (2012), para. 68.

75 General Comment No. 14 (n 28).

76 Boulet et al. (see note 59). Although there is no legal definition of the term 'global public good', it was understood by Boulet et al. to mean 'to ensure the public benefits from public funding' into the development of COVID-19 vaccines.

77 Ibid.

procurement.[78] On the one hand, it is questionable whether through its cooperation with non-EU countries on joint procurement, the EU has acted with restraint and observed the principle of non-interference of the enjoyment of ICESCR rights, in particular for vulnerable groups in developing countries who stand to benefit the most from the first COVID-19 vaccine doses. On the other hand, the EU's contribution to the COVAX initiative, and the resulting low-priced or donated vaccine doses to developing countries, can be understood as a step towards the duty to provide disaster relief.[79]

Notably, in parallel with the EU's commitment to vaccines as 'global public goods' in annex to some of its APAs and the Union's contributions to COVAX, the EU has also taken steps at the WTO to frustrate the scale-up of COVID-19 vaccine production worldwide. At the WTO, EU representatives opposed interpretations of the TRIPS Agreement that would support the sharing of the IP, knowledge and know-how needed to increase the global production of COVID-19 vaccines.[80] This course of action seems to ignore the fact that the WTO TRIPS Agreement also includes in Article 7 a clause recognizing the imperative that IP promotes social welfare and that the protection and enforcement of IP 'should… contribute to the transfer and dissemination of technology'.[81]

In the case of the EU's COVID-19 vaccine procurement, the Commission agreement with EU Member States appears to respect and promote health rights when pursuing its joint vaccine purchases. However, the likely unintended, although perhaps not entirely unforeseen, consequence of a large-

78 Usher A. D., 'Uncertainties over EU COVID-19 vaccine sharing scheme.' (2021) 397 *The Lancet* 1171.

79 General Comment No. 14 (n 28) para 40.

80 One of the major practical hurdles to increasing the global supply of COVID-19 vaccines during the pandemic was pharmaceutical manufacturers reticence to license or otherwise share their vaccine know-how (i.e., undisclosed commercial information) with other producers. India and South Africa proposed a 'TRIPS waiver' to address the intellectual property-related barriers to global access to COVID-19 health products and technologies. However, the EU delegation to the WTO opposed this interpretation and maintained that minor changes in the interpretation of compulsory licensing permitted under Articles 31 and 31bis of the TRIPS Agreement could provide the solution. See Kohler, Jillian, Anna Wong, and Lauren Tailor. 'Improving access to COVID-19 vaccines: An analysis of TRIPS waiver discourse among WTO members, civil society organizations, and pharmaceutical industry stakeholders.' (2022) 24(2) *Health and Human Rights*: 165–166.

81 See, generally, E. 't Hoen. 'Protecting public health through technology transfer: the unfulfilled promise of the TRIPS agreement' (2022) 24(2) *Health and Human Rights* 211–214.

scale vaccine purchase by the EU is a reduction in global vaccine doses for the rest of the world, which suggests that there are limits to the EU's respect for the extraterritorial right to health in its internal health policy. The impact of this consequence of the Union's internal procurement decision is exacerbated by the EU's opposition at the WTO of an interpretation of the TRIPS Agreement aiming to facilitate global licensing and/or sharing of the intellectual property, knowledge and know-how necessary for producing more vaccines to alleviate the (then) global shortage. Committing to respect human rights to health and science in one domain (i.e., through EU joint vaccine procurement) does not absolve the Union from respecting these human rights in other domains related to the supply of pandemic vaccines (i.e., through international declarations interpreting global trade law in a manner supportive of enhanced vaccine production). At the macro level, this case illustrates the broader implications of EU legal instruments and actions for the development of global health law. The case of JPA of COVID-19 vaccines during a pandemic highlights the potential of RIOs to leverage their market power in in a manner contrary to the rights to health and science, as enshrined in the ICESCR, which has inevitable implications for the realization of individual rights worldwide and for (re)actions by other states and regions.

Turning now to the duty to protect, the following case in Section 5.2 illustrates the scope of EU law and practice with regards to the protection of human rights through measures promoting global trade in lower priced medicines.

5.2 *Protecting Human Rights by Avoiding the Re-importation of Essential Medicines*

The Trade Diversion case illustrates one way in which the EU leverages its own internal market to attempt to influence company conduct regarding the trade in medicines destined for developing countries that can result in the protection of human rights externally. This Regulation attempts to incentivise transnational pharmaceutical companies active in the EU to export certain medicines to 'the poorest developing countries' at a lower price (compared to the Union).[82] Based on Article 207(2) TFEU, this instrument's primary aim is to promote the Common Commercial Policy in line with 'the principles and

82 Regulation (EU) 2016/793 of the European Parliament and of the Council of 11 May 2016 to avoid trade diversion into the European Union of certain key medicines (codification) [2016] OJ L 135/39

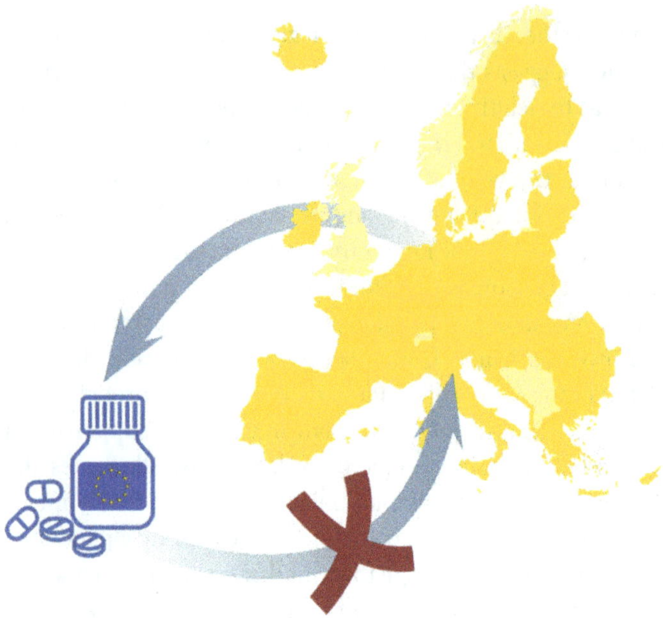

FIGURE 4.2 EU Regulation 2016/793 to avoid the re-importation of lower-priced medicines destined for 'the poorest developing countries'

objectives of the Union's external action'.[83] By adopting rules for the registration and identification of medicines shipments destined for developing countries in the Regulation, EU lawmakers attempt to mitigate the risk that company drug donations or heavily price-reduced products would re-enter EU borders and be sold at lower prices, thereby eroding these manufacturers' pricing policies in the EU. This is one example of how the EU, as a RIO, leverages its regulatory capacity to shape or incentivise companies' extraterritorial behaviours that are consistent with the protection of human dignity, human rights and the UN Charter.

In this respect, EU law is therefore indirectly supporting the Committee's interpretation of ICESCR obligations, namely where: 'States parties also have an extraterritorial obligation to regulate and monitor the conduct of multinational companies over which they can exercise control…'.[84] Moreover, the EU

83 These principles include namely 'democracy, the rule of law, the universality and indivisibility of human rights and fundamental freedoms, respect for human dignity, the principles of equality and solidarity, and respect for the principles of the United Nations Charter and international law'. in Article 21(1)TEU.

84 General Comment No. 25 (n 29) para 84.

is contributing to what the Committee considers an international environment that supports the realization of ICESCR rights, including by encouraging 'business actors whose conduct they are in a position to influence to ensure that they do not undermine the efforts of the States in which they operate to fully realize the Covenant rights'.[85]

5.3 *Fulfilling Human Rights through Clinical Trials Partnerships*

Finally, the European and Developing Countries Clinical Trials Partnership (EDCTP, hereafter Partnership) is an example of how developed states can facilitate international cooperation for the development and testing of new pharmaceuticals against infectious diseases. The Partnership was initially established through Decision 1209/2003/EC of the European Parliament and the Council.[86] This legal framework establishes a Partnership for coordinating Member States' research and development funding for clinical interventions that are effective against HIV/AIDS, malaria and tuberculosis, mainly in Sub-Saharan African countries.[87] This is in line with the legal basis of these instruments (Article 185 TFEU) that allows for joint participation of the EU and its Member States in research and development (R&D) programmes.[88] The EDCTP focuses on enhancing cooperation and networking in two formations: one, a 'coherent approach' among European national R&D programs, and two, a 'long term partnership' between European and developing countries.[89] The latter formation is the focus of this section.

The EU's role in the Partnership is to financially contribute through its research framework programme budget and to play a coordinating role. These roles are consistent with the right to science and the duty of states to provide adequate financial support to research in the public interest.[90] According to the Executive Director of EDCTP, Dr. Charles Mgone, the 'ultimate goal' of European states acting through the EDCTP:

85 General Comment No. 24 (n 33) para 37.

86 Decision No 1209/2003/EC of the European Parliament and of the Council of 16 June 2003 on Community participation in a research and development programme aimed at developing new clinical interventions to combat HIV/AIDS, malaria and tuberculosis through a long-term partnership between Europe and developing countries, undertaken by several Member States [2003] OJ L169/1.

87 Ibid., recitals 5 and 11.

88 Formerly Article 169 TEC.

89 Decision No 1209/2003/EC, (n 76) recitals 5 and 11.

90 General Comment No. 25 (n 29) para 62.

FIGURE 4.3 The European and Developing Countries Clinical Trials Partnership for the development and testing of new pharmaceuticals against infectious diseases

> is to achieve a joint programme whereby the participating member states will have an integrated research programme on poverty-related diseases with a common administration, peer-review and funding mechanism.[91]

In this way, the EU contributes to promoting an enabling environment for the advancement of science.[92]

The Partnership's research agenda attempts to address areas where there is a dearth of research in the public interest, particularly for interventions necessary for realizing the rights of vulnerable groups. This approach is consistent with the 'special responsibility' of developed states to assist developing counterparts with access to the benefits of science, particularly for 'communities living in the poorest groups with special needs and vulnerabilities'.[93] EDCTP funding has supported the research and testing of various therapeutic products, and has notably contributed to the development of a malaria vaccine, which was approved for use in two African countries in 2023.[94]

91 C. S. Mgone and W. Salami, 'EDCTP: a genuine north–south partnership' (2009) 14(11) *Tropical Medicine & International Health* 1327–1328, 1327.

92 General Comment No. 25 (n 29) para 77.

93 Ibid., para 80.

94 EDCTP funded a phase II trial of vaccine R21/Matrix-M. Following clinical tests demonstrating its efficacy, two countries (Ghana and Nigeria) have approved its use in 2023. See

The European Union's financial contributions to the EDCTP are conditional upon several criteria. One criterion is that there is a 'high level of involvement of developing countries'.[95] To that end, Mgone and Salami also state that all partners are involved at all levels of the programme including through agenda and priority setting, 'determination of the capacity needs; and ownership and delivery of the programme'.[96] Another criterion is the establishment by participating states of a structure with legal personality for the implementation of the Partnership, as well as assuring a high level of scientific excellence and the observance of ethical principles.[97] In practice, Mgone and Salami explain that the Partnership supports the development of local institutional infrastructure in the form of a regulatory framework for ethics review and trials registration.[98] This is consistent with the requirement of international assistance programmes by developed countries to provide institutional frameworks for the enjoyment of ICESCR rights.[99] A third criterion is the formulation of IP rights arising through the work of the Partnership in a manner that:

> also aim[s] at ensuring that the people of developing countries have easy and affordable access to the research results produced by activities under the EDCTP Programme and to the products directly deriving from its results.[100]

In this way, the affordability and accessibility of the products resulting from this research Partnership remains a priority, in line with the Committee's conception of the 'social function' of IP.

EDCTP also encourages the participation of the private sector in different capacities, including as donors.[101] To illustrate the scale of financial support

EDCTP. Annual Report 2022. Section 9.1. https://publications.edctp.org/edctp-annual-report-2022/malaria-vaccine.

95 See Article 2(e) of Decision 1209/2003/EC (n 86).

96 Mgone and Salami, (n 91) 1327, citing F. Binka, 'Editorial: North-South research collaboration: a move towards a true partnership?' (2005) 10 *Tropical Medicine and International Health* 207–209.

97 Article 2(c & f) of Decision 1209/2003/EC (n 86).

98 These measures are considered good practices and are consistent with the EU's own internal regulation on these matters. See Mgone & Salami (n 91).

99 Magdalena Sepúlveda Carmona. 'The obligations of 'international assistance and cooperation' under the International Covenant on Economic, Social and Cultural Rights. A possible entry point to a human rights based approach to Millennium Development Goal 8' (2009) 13(1) *The International Journal of Human Rights* 86–109, 92.

100 Article 2(g) of Decision 1209/2003/EC (n 86).

101 Ibid., recitals.

that the EDCTP has garnered, for each euro that the EU has invested in EDCTP, it has secured an additional €1.50 from other public and private funders between 2003 and 2011.[102] Although the present chapter makes no assessment of what level of financial support for biomedical research would be considered 'adequate', the foregoing evidence illustrates how the EU takes steps to provide financial support through individual national/state efforts and through international and technical cooperation for research that is 'important' for the realization of ICESCR rights.[103]

6 Conclusion: Is the EU's Practice Threatening or Enhancing IHRL?

This chapter set out to determine whether the EU – a prominent RIO – exercises its regulatory power in the field of pharmaceuticals in a manner that impacts on the development of global health law. Specifically, this chapter sought to assess the conformity of the EU's legal instruments and practice in this field with the principle of international cooperation flowing from the ICESCR. The three cases explored in this chapter illustrate that, through its international cooperation activities for pharmaceuticals, the EU appears to adhere to many of the human rights standards of the ICESCR. In this way, international law serves as a normative framework to determine whether the actions and omissions of the EU with regards to international cooperation conform with IHRL.

Is EU law influencing the formulation, interpretation or implementation of international law? Each of the three cases of EU practice analysed in this chapter demonstrate that EU law prescribes actions that are aligned with much of the Committee's conception of developed countries' obligations with regards to international cooperation. However, EU law also stops short of explicitly recognizing these duties as flowing from the ICESCR. In this way, secondary sources of EU law can be characterized as 'quietly' adhering to international human rights standards (with regards to international cooperation on social rights) rather than being a 'full bodied' acknowledgement of international law as a source for such specific standards. Therefore, the (internal) laws of RIOs that have external impacts may be an avenue through which such organizations can indirectly promote adherence to human rights stand-

102 PolicyCures, DSW. Saving lives and creating impact: EU investment in poverty-related neglected diseases. October 2012. http://policycures.org/downloads/DSWreport.pdf.

103 General Comment No. 25, (n 29) para 62.

ards (enshrined in the ICESCR) by the international organization itself, its member (states) and the non-state actors it engages with.

Through its internal market laws explored in this chapter, the EU may directly or indirectly shape the actions of the private business (pharmaceutical) sector in third countries. When those laws promote human rights standards, the EU may be an important conduit for socializing and externalising such standards among private for-profit actors on the global market place because they are active on the EU internal market and therefore, particular activities of theirs are regulated by EU law. In this way, the EU may be enhancing the implementation of human rights responsibilities (related to the ICESCR) of the private business sector, which offers a unique perspective to the thorny issue of the role of non-state actors in human rights realization. Interestingly, although the EU's international cooperation practices examined in this chapter take steps to engage with and/or regulate the private business sector, these practices do not foresee penalizing 'harmful behaviour[s]' by 'prosecut[ing] perpetrators at the domestic level'; nor do these practices provide remedies for victims of rights violations.[104] These are important aspects of the duty to protect ICESCR rights through international cooperation.

The analysis of EU law in this chapter also demonstrates the various roles (i.e., coordinator, financier/donor, regulator, procurement agent...) the EU as a RIO may take on to advance ICESCR rights realization. Through its coordinating role (i.e., between EU Member States, and between European-developing countries), the EU leverages its capacity to manage administrative processes and to mobilise financial resources from European and non-EU governments and the private sector around a singular, coherent procurement order and/or research agenda.

Acknowledgements

The author wishes to acknowledge the research assistance of Kaja Ippel and Estela Pires, the figures provided by Crescendo Consulting, and the helpful suggestions from the editors on an earlier version of this book chapter. This manuscript is part of the 'Global access to medicines through EU law and policy' project of the Veni talent research programme which is financed by the Dutch Research Council (NWO).

104 General Comment No. 25 (n 29) para 84. Carmona (n 35) 282.

CHAPTER 5

Can the EU Not Promote Free Movement of Persons in the External Action on Migration? Neglecting Regional Mobility in EU–Africa Cooperation

Eleonora Frasca[1]

Abstract

This chapter investigates to what extent free movement of persons, as a regional integration objective, is promoted in the EU external action when the EU cooperates with non-EU States belonging to other regional international organisations (RIOs) on migration in Africa. The tenets of the EU free movement regime and the importance of free movement of persons for Africa's integration are scrutinised. Focusing on the EU's external migration policies and the external funding financing these policies, EU-Africa migration cooperation illustrates that free movement initiatives in the African region are not taken into account in the EU external migration policies. These external policies are not based on a common understanding of migration, but on the EU's interest in preventing irregular migration from Africa to the EU. This chapter problematises how the objective of preventing irregular migration in EU – Africa cooperation can undermine free movement initiatives in Africa and, in particular, in RIOs.

Keywords

Free movement of persons – Regional migration – Regional integration – EU-Africa cooperation on migration – EU external action – EU external funding – Irregular migration

1 Dr. Eleonora Frasca, Faculty of Law, Université catholique de Louvain (UCLouvain), Place Montesquieu 2, 1348, Louvain-la-Neuve, Belgium.
E-mail: eleonora.frasca@uclouvain.be.

 | DOI:10.1163/9789004700659_007

1 Introduction

The term 'region' has several meanings in both European and African contexts.[2] Similarly, the term 'migration' is a multifaceted concept.[3] A working definition of regional international organizations (RIOs) has been developed by the International Law Association.[4] However, the legal relevance of the concept remained debated.[5] Besides conceptual disputes, it is undoubted that different RIOs provide for different forms of inter-State cooperation on migration.[6] They can do that *internally*, developing more or less advanced forms of integration (including through international law-making), and they can also engage in *external* forms of cooperation on migration.

The European Union (EU), one of the many RIOs in Europe, developed supra-national legislation on migration, including on free movement of persons. In this field of law, the EU has achieved a high degree of integration, building a border-free area of circulation and gradually developing a set of rights related to free movement, as well as regional citizenship which 'is destined to be the fundamental status of nationals of the Member States'.[7] Thanks to specific bilateral agreements, some countries that are not members of the

2 As argued in the International Law Association (ILA) report 'The International Law of Regional Organizations', 2024, 'RIOs can be 'regional' in a strict geographical sense, but also that the term 'regional' is applied in a wider context beyond the location of its members', p. 8.

3 On this topic, Samson Maekele Tsegay, 'International Migration: Definition, Causes and Effects' (2023) 3 Genealogy 7, 61.

4 International Law Association (2024) 'The International Law of Regional Organizations' Final Report, 2024. The adopted definition is the following: A Regional International Organization (RIO) is an international organization whose membership consists of States (and international organizations) that share similar geographical, linguistic, cultural, economic, political, legal or other characteristics', p. 13.

5 See the contribution to this edited volume by Jan Klabbers, 'The Soft Phenomenology of the Regional International Organisation'.

6 The approach undertaken in this paper is one that focuses on migration as primarily regional phenomenon and on experiences of inter-States of cooperation on migration at the regional level.

7 Article 21 of the Treaty on the Functioning of the European Union (TFEU) establishes that every citizen of the Union has the right to move and reside freely within the territory of the Member States, subject to the limitations and conditions laid down in the Treaties and to the measures adopted to give effect to that right, O.J., C 202, 7 June 2016. Article 45 of the Charter of Fundamental Rights of the European Union (CFR) also guarantees the right of every EU citizen to move and reside freely within the territory of the Member States, O.J., C 326, 26 October 2012, 391. See also Case C-184/99 *Grzelczyk* [2001] ECR I-06193 para 31.

EU/RIO can also participate in the EU free movement regime, thus enlarging the personal and geographical scope of free movement rights beyond the EU citizens and territory. The sophisticated free movement regime not only involves EU citizens' movement across the territories of the Member States, but also includes certain categories of non-EU citizens while contextually excluding others.[8] Moreover, through differentiated integration, EU Member States and non-EU States participate in the border-free Schengen area to different extents. This means that integration in the free movement regime goes beyond the EU Member States, enabling regular migration within the broader European region and different forms of participation in the EU legal order by non-EU States.

In Africa, there are many different RIOs. It is estimated that an average African State is a member of no less than eight different regional bodies.[9] The African Union (AU), which succeeded the Organization of African Unity (OAU), is an inter-governmental regional organization comprising 55 African Member States.[10] Regional Economic Communities (RECs) are also RIOs, as they consist of groups of neighbouring or nearby African States of a sub-region, and they are considered the building blocks of the African Economic Community.[11] The African Union coordinates and harmonises the RECs policies 'for the gradual attainment of the objectives of the Union'.[12] Free movement of persons is one of the objectives of African integration, and several RECs have provisions on free movement within the sub-regional spaces.[13]

---

8 Third-country nationals who are applicants and beneficiaries of international protection do not enjoy free movement rights across Member States. On this topic, see: Iris Goldner Lang, 'Freedom of movement of EU citizens and mobility rights of third-country nationals: where EU free movement and migration policies intersect or disconnect?' in E. Tsourdi and P. De Bruycker (eds.), *Research Handbook on EU Migration and Asylum Law* (Edward Elgar, 2023) 98.

9 Bruce Byiers, 'Regional organisations in Africa – Mapping multiple memberships' (ECDPM, 15 September 2017), check also the interactive map.

10 Constitutive act of the African Union, done in Lome, Togo, 11 July 2000, and Protocol on amendments to the constitutive act of the African Union, done in Addis Ababa, 3 February 2003.

11 There are eight Regional Economic Communities (RECs) in Africa: the Arab Maghreb Union (AMU), the Community of Sahel–Saharan States (CEN–SAD), the Common Market for Eastern and Southern Africa (COMESA), the East African Community (EAC), the Economic Community of Central African States (ECCAS), the Economic Community of West African States (ECOWAS), the Intergovernmental Authority on Development (IGAD), and the Southern African Development Community (SADC).

12 Article 3 (l) of the Constitutive act of the African Union.

13 Articles 2, 27(1), 27(2) of the Treaty establishing the ECOWAS. Article 2 of the Protocol on the Free Movement of Persons, the Right of Residence and Establishment of the ECO-

One might wonder if (regional) free movement law and integration techniques – and the undoubted expertise that the EU has developed in abolishing obstacles to the free movement of persons in and beyond the regional organization – could be promoted among other regional organizations worldwide, and how. Such promotion, on the one hand, could derive from Article 21(1) TEU and, on the other hand, from recent global developments in collaborative solutions to migration governance.[14]

Article 21(1) TEU not only provides that the EU values must be safeguarded in the EU's international relations, but also links these values to a more extensive set of principles that should guide the Union's action on the international scene.[15] These are 'democracy, the rule of law, the universality and indivisibility of human rights and fundamental freedoms, respect for human dignity, the principles of equality and solidarity, and respect for the principles of the United Nations Charter and international law'.[16] While the reference to the notion of 'fundamental freedoms' in this specific part of the Treaty does not concern 'freedom of movement of persons', one could argue that the fundamental freedom of movement of persons is, more broadly, one of the principles that have inspired the Union's 'own creation, development and enlargement'. The second subparagraph of Article 21(1) TEU requires the Union to 'develop relations and build partnership with third countries, and international, *regional* or global organizations which share the principles referred to in the first subparagraph'.[17] Free movement at the regional level could be considered a 'principle' that the EU shares with many other regional organizations.

WAS. Article 40 of the Treaty Establishing the ECCAS. Article 3 and 10 of the SADC Protocol on Facilitation of Movement of Persons under. Articles 2 (4(b), (c), (d), and (e)) of the Protocol on the Establishment of EAC. Articles 3, 9, 11, and 12 of the COMESA Protocol on the Free Movement of Persons, Labour, Services, the Right of Establishment and Residence. Article 3 of the Protocol on Free Movement of Persons in the IGAD. Article 2 of the Treaty Establishing the AMU. Article 3(f) of the Treaty Establishing the CEN–SAD. On this topic, Sonja Nita, 'Regional free movement of people: The case of African Regional Economic Communities' (2013) 3 Regions and Cohesion 8.

14 On this topic, see Vincent Chetail, 'The politics of soft law: Progress and pitfall of the Global compact for safe, orderly, and regular migration' [2023] Frontiers in Human Dynamics.

15 Treaty on European Union (consolidated version 2016), O.J., C 202, 7 June 2016. For a commentary on Article 21 TEU, see Thomas Ramopoulos, 'Article 21 TEU', in M. Kellerbauer, M. Klamert, and J. Tomkin (eds.), *The EU Treaties and the Charter of Fundamental Rights: A Commentary* (Oxford Academic 2019).

16 Article 21(1) TEU.

17 *Ibid.*, emphasis added.

On the other hand, promoting free movement of persons in other regional contexts might result from recent global developments in international migration law. One of the principles established in the Global Compact for Safe, Orderly and Regular Migration (GCM) is that of 'advancing a common understanding of migration' in which the production of knowledge and the understanding of migration should be a joint effort.[18] How States come together to build regional free movement regimes is an important factor contributing to a shared understanding of migration.

This chapter explores if and to what extent free movement, as a regional integration objective, is taken into account and potentially promoted in EU–Africa cooperation on migration. The interest of this research question lies in the fact that migration, as a global phenomenon, requires policies that respect the rights of migrants and provide opportunities to migrate legally and safely. For now, regional free movement initiatives are where these policies take effect and develop in a way that contributes to regional development. The regional dimension is quintessential to migration and migration policies.

To the contrary, by over-focusing on preventing Africa-to-Europe migration, EU external migration policies pose a disruptive challenge to regional migration and existing free movement initiatives in the African continent. These policies are based on the EU's interest of controlling irregular migration rather than on a 'common understanding of migration, shared responsibilities and unity of purpose regarding migration', as the Global Compact on Migration requires.[19] To demonstrate how the objective of preventing irregular migration in EU–Africa cooperation can undermine free movement initiatives in Africa and, in particular, in RIOs with provisions on free movement of persons, the chapter is structured as follows.

In the next section on the regionalization of migration, the tenets of the EU free movement regime and the importance of free movement of persons for Africa's integration are briefly presented. The terminology 'mobility' vs 'migration' is discussed (Section 2). The following section shows that the EU's understanding of how free movement regimes contribute to regional development is currently absent from region-to-region cooperation, both in discourse and practice (Section 3). Building a 'common understanding of migration' is one of the guiding principles of the GCM. It calls for 'international efforts' in strengthening the 'knowledge and analysis of migration' as 'shared understandings will

18 United Nations General Assembly, Global Compact for Safe, Orderly and Regular Migration (A/RES/73/195), 19 December 2018.

19 *Ibid.*, point 9.

improve policies that unlock the potential of sustainable development for all'.[20]

This chapter will argue that the expertise that the Union has built up in developing its free movement regime is not or seldomly included in the understanding of migration promoted in the EU external action, even where conditions are there to reinforce shared knowledge on the issue. The EU external migration policies implemented in the African continent mainly aim to prevent irregular migration from Africa to Europe. This objective is pursued through policies of so-called externalization, securitization and informalization of migration law, which impact *all* migration from Africa, including intra-African regional migration.[21]

2 The Regionalization of Migration: Free Movement Regimes

In migration studies, the regional dimension is key to understanding the migratory phenomena, as international migration occurs primarily within regions.[22] As explained in the World Migration Report, '[n]otwithstanding increasing globalization, geography is one of the most significant factors shaping patterns of migration and displacement. Many people who migrate across borders do so within their immediate regions, to countries that are close by'.[23] However, regional integration comes with the cost of 'an intensification of border control at the region's external frontiers and a tightening of its asylum and immigration policy'.[24]

High degrees of inequalities characterise migrants' access to the so-called Global Mobility Infrastructure.[25] As a matter of fact, migration is far from

20 *Ibid.*, point 10.

21 Africa-to-Europe migration only represents a small part of African migration worldwide, the majority being intra-Africa migration. See UN DESA, 'Global Migration Database'. Similarly, irregular migration to the EU only represents a small part of all migration to the EU. See Eurostat, 'Migration and migrant population statistics'. See also IOM and the African Union, 'Connecting the Threads: Linking policy, practice and the welfare of the African migrant', 2nd Africa migration report, 2024: 'Migrants from West, Central, Southern, and East Africa predominantly reside in neighbouring African nations'.

22 On this topic, see Andrew Geddes, Marcia Vera Espinoza, Leila Hadj Abdou and Leiza Brumat, *The dynamics of regional migration governance* (Edward Elgar, 2019).

23 McAuliffe, M. and L.A. Oucho (eds.), 2024. *World Migration Report* (IOM, 2024) 55.

24 Jean-Yves Carlier, 'General Report: Regional Integration', in M.-C. Foblets, J.-Y. Carlier (eds.), *Law and Migration in a changing world* (Springer, 2022), 8.

25 Thomas Spijkerboer, 'The Global Mobility Infrastructure: Reconceptualising the Externalisation of Migration Control' (2018) 20 European Journal of Migration and Law 452.

being liberalised at the global level. If the idea of a borderless *world* is utopian, that of borderless *regions* already shows its feasibility.[26] Through regionalization, partial liberalization of migration has happened in many parts of the world.[27] In this context, regionalization can be broadly understood as a set of legal measures taken at the regional level – through international agreements or more legally complex transfer of competence to a RIO – to address regional migration, with a view to facilitating free movement of nationals of the States members of the RIO.

Regional answers to migration can profoundly impact regional development, bringing economic prosperity and fostering regional identities.[28] Through time, groups of States have come together in regional fora to discuss and potentially adopt *rules* – often gradually – that aim to facilitate cross-border movement at the regional level. Such rules range from lighter measures in terms of international cooperation, such as the facilitation of inter-regional short-term travel to visa liberalization, to progressively deeper measures, such as the establishment of fully-fledged free movement rights and regional citizenship.[29]

Due to the importance of the regional dimension in the regulation of migration, it is not surprising that Regional Consultative Processes (RCPs) have emerged as important fora in developing inter-States dialogues on migration, which can eventually stimulate and lead to the adoption of formal binding rules. RCPs are informal cooperation structures where States come together at the inter-governmental level. They are informal and non-binding, but nonetheless crucial to building a shared understanding of migration.[30] In the New York Declaration for Refugees and Migrants of 2016, RCPs were identified

---

26 On this topic, Sonja Nita *et al.* (eds.), *Migration, free movement and regional integration* (UNESCO Publishing and UNU Institute on Comparative Regional Integration Studies 2017).

27 Sonja Nita, 'Free movement of people within regional integration processes: A comparative view', in S. Nita et al., *Migration, free movement and regional integration* (UNESCO Publishing and UNU Institute on Comparative Regional Integration Studies, 2017) 3.

28 Organisation for Economic Cooperation and Development (OECD), *The Contribution of Migration to Regional Development, OECD Regional Development Studies* (OECD Publishing 2022).

29 Sandra Lavenex, Flavia Jurje, Terri E Givens and Ross Buchanan, 'Regional Migration Governance' in T. A. Börzel and T. Risse (eds.), *The Oxford Handbook of Comparative Regionalism* (Oxford University Press, 2016) 457.

30 It should be noted that this dynamic was followed by the EU Member States for the creation of the Schengen area. The Schengen Convention was initially conceived in informal structures of cooperation, governed by unanimity rules and decided upon in inter-governmental settings, and later brought into EU law. On this topic, Elspeth Guild

as having a significant role in the preparation and negotiations of the Global Compact for Safe, Orderly and Regular Migration (GCM).[31] Moreover, the GCM is subject to rounds of *regional* reviews where States commit to reviewing the progress made in the GCM's implementation within their respective regions. Both the EU and the AU have developed or are developing free movement regimes, as mobility is seen as a factor contributing to regional integration.

2.1 *The EU Free Movement Regime and the Broader European Region*

The EU is the most prominent example of an intra-regional free movement regime. This complex field of EU law results from two entangled developments: freedom of movement in the EU internal market and the abolition of internal border controls in the Area of Freedom, Security and Justice.[32] On the one hand, the freedom of movement of persons, recognised as one of the four fundamental freedoms of the EU internal market, has evolved progressively and is now one of the most cherished rights of EU citizens.[33] On the other hand, establishing an Area of Freedom, Security and Justice where internal border controls have been abolished, required the creation of an EU (common) migration policy to enforce border controls at the EU's external borders. These parallel developments created crucial differences in relation to migration, exemplified by the dichotomous legal categories in which EU law qualifies international migration (i.e., EU citizens/third-country nationals, free movement/migration, irregular migration/legal mobility, etc.).[34]

---

and Paul Minderhoud (eds.) *The First Decade of EU Migration and Asylum Law* (Martinus Nijhoff, 2012).

31 See para 54 of the New York Declaration for Refugees and Migrants, 19 September 2016: 'We will build on existing bilateral, *regional* and global cooperation and partnership mechanisms [...]. We will strengthen cooperation to this end [...], including through *regional consultative processes*' (emphasis added). See also para 14 of the Annex II to the New York Declaration: 'Regional consultations in support of the negotiations would be desirable, including through existing consultative processes and mechanisms, where appropriate'.

32 Philippe De Bruycker, 'The European Union: from freedom of movement in the internal market to the abolition of internal borders in the area of freedom, security and justice' in S. Nita et al. (eds.), *Migration, free movement and regional integration* (UNESCO Publishing and UNU Institute on Comparative Regional Integration Studies, 2017) 287.

33 According to the Eurobarometer, 'a large majority of respondents cherish the free movement of people within the EU, with 89% agreeing that it benefits them personally and 83% that it benefits the economy'. See Commission, Eurobarometer on citizenship and democracy, December 2023 (2971/FL528).

34 On this topic, Elspeth Guild, *The Legal Elements of European Identity: EU Citizenship and Migration Law* (Wolters Kluwer, 2004).

Freedom of movement within the EU/RIO is defined differently depending on whether the person circulating is an EU citizen or a third-country national. In addition, depending on the third country of origin, different rules apply with regard to freedom of movement – so that some countries bordering the EU are linked to the EU free movement regime by rules that extend, in whole or in part, mobility rights to these non-EU countries' citizens. In other words, the current EU free movement regime results, on the one hand, from the progressive and broad interpretation of the notion of 'freedom of movement', as an EU law principle and as a right which belongs primarily to the EU citizens (nationals of an EU Member States) – and, on the other hand, from a patchwork of international agreements, including trade agreements, with non-EU States and internal legislation which allows several but not all categories of non-EU citizens (third-country nationals) to enjoy a set of mobility rights to and within the EU.[35]

As for EU citizens, while, initially, free movement was conceived to protect, essentially, *workers* – economically active EU citizens circulating within the regional organization, the then European Economic Community, for economic reasons –, it progressively expanded its personal scope to become a regime related to free movement of *persons*. As early as 1986, the Court of Justice of the European Union identified the freedom of movement not merely as an 'instrument of economic integration' but as 'one of the fundamental principles of the Community'.[36]

In parallel, being a major regional integration achievement, the EU promotes free movement of persons in its external relations to third countries geographically located in Europe, which have been integrated or could potentially integrate into the EU free movement regime. Mobility is a core aspect of the EU cooperation with third countries that are not (or not yet) part of the EU/RIO. This promotion has both a symbolic and economic value for countries cooperating with the EU, especially in the context of the EU Neighbourhood Policy and enlargement negotiations. Among these groups of countries, a distinction is drawn between countries of the European Economic Area and Switzerland (a), countries which achieved visa liberalization for their citizens who enjoy visa-free travel to the Schengen area, such as neighbouring States of the Western Balkans and the Eastern Partnership (b) and countries to which visa liberalization has been promised but not fulfilled because of protracted

---

35 On this topic, Jean-Yves Carlier and Marie-Claire Foblets, 'General Report: Regional Integration', in M.-C. Foblets, J.-Y. Carlier (eds.), *Law and Migration in a changing world* (Springer, 2022), 7–9.

36 Case C 66/85 *Lawrie Blum* [1986] ECR 02121 paras 11 and 16.

negotiations on other aspects of migration cooperation, such as neighbouring States of the Euro-Mediterranean Partnership (c).[37] It is no coincidence that the latter group of countries, although physically close to the European Union, does not belong to the geographical region 'Europe'.

2.1.1 Free Movement and Schengen-Associated Countries

The EU has integrated certain non-EU countries into the area without internal border controls. Several countries participate in the EU single market thanks to international agreements on free movement and Schengen membership, their participation resulting in a form of de *jure* integration into the EU free movement regime.[38] Iceland, Liechtenstein and Norway concluded the European Economic Area agreement, which includes provisions on free movement of persons.[39] Similarly, Switzerland concluded a set of bilateral treaties with the EU, which also cover free movement of persons.[40] The four countries – Iceland, Liechtenstein, Norway and Switzerland – have signed association agreements with the EU to be members of the Schengen area. They apply EU rules relating to the crossing of borders and have harmonised the conditions of entry and short stay visas and visa types.

2.1.2 Visa Liberalization and States Candidate to the EU Membership

With countries of the Western Balkans and with countries of the Eastern Partnership, the EU has resorted to methods of legal 'co-option'.[41] The fulfilment of the promise of visa liberalization of nationals of these countries depends on their progress in implementing domestic reforms in fields related to respect for the rule of law, the fight against organised crime, and migration governance.[42] In this context, their EU membership is at stake. This normative

37 Daniel Thym, *European Migration Law* (Oxford University Press, 2023), 555.

38 On this topic, see Bruno de Witte, Andrea Ott and Ellen Vos (eds.) *Between flexibility and disintegration: the trajectory of differentiation in EU law* (Edward Elgar, 2017).

39 Agreement on the European Economic Area, O.J. L 1, 3 January 1994, 3–522.

40 Agreement between the European Community and its Member States, of the one part, and the Swiss Confederation, of the other, on the free movement of persons in the sectors free movement of persons, air and land transport, public procurement, scientific and technological cooperation, mutual recognition in relation to conformity assessment, and trade in agricultural products, O.J. L 353, 31 December 2009, 71–90.

41 On the basis of visa liberalization dialogues, the EU granted visa-free travel to nationals of Montenegro, Serbia and North Macedonia in December 2009, Albania and Bosnia and Herzegovina in 2010, Moldova in 2014, Georgia in 2017 and Ukraine in 2017, Kosovo in 2024.

42 For the kind of normative alignment required, see European Commission, 'EU Action Plan on the Western Balkans', press release of 8 December 2022.

alignment foresees their full adoption of EU law if and when these countries will be granted accession. The European Commission claims that visa-free travel for their nationals

> provides a strong incentive for Western Balkan partners to intensify their fundamental reform efforts. As such, it greatly helps to advance the accession process. It is a powerful tool in facilitating people-to-people contacts and in strengthening ties between the EU and citizens of visa-free countries.[43]

The 'strategic use' of visa-free travel allows the EU to 'persuade third States to support migration management by means of domestic reforms'.[44] Non-EU countries' compliance with the Schengen rules is attained in exchange for access to short-stay Schengen visas for their nationals, *de facto* integrating those third-country nationals in the EU free movement regime. The EU has formally cooperated with these countries by combining readmission agreements (EURAs) with visa facilitation agreements.[45] The negotiations of an EU visa facilitation agreement followed the entry into force of an EURA. However, to obtain visa facilitation agreements granting their citizens (limited) mobility rights to the European Union, non-EU countries must align their visa rules to the Schengen *acquis*.[46] Marise Cremona and Jorrit Rijpma refer to this phenomenon as 'the promotion, by the EU, of its own *acquis* towards third countries, and their adoption of that *acquis* into their own domestic legal orders'.[47] As such, several non-EU countries of the broader European region are partially incorporated into the EU free movement regime. They have indirectly adopted EU rules into their domestic legal orders as a result of this external promotion by the Union.

---

43 European Commission, 'Visa liberalisation: Commission reports on the continued fulfilment of requirements by the Western Balkans and Eastern Partnership countries', press release of 10 July 2020.

44 Daniel Thym, *European Migration Law* (Oxford University Press, 2023), 283.

45 On the topic of readmission agreements, see Eleonora Frasca and Emanuela Roman, 'The Informalisation of EU Readmission Policy: Eclipsing Human Rights Protection under the Shadow of Informality and Conditionality' (2023) 8 European Papers 2, 931–957.

46 Lena Laube, 'The Relational Dimension of Externalizing Border Control: Selective Visa Policies in Migration and Border Diplomacy' (2019) 7 Comparative Migration Studies 1.

47 Marise Cremona and Jorrit Rijpma, 'The Extra-Territorialisation of EU Migration Policies and the Rule of Law' (EUI Working Papers, 2007), 1, 15.

2.1.3 Standoff with Associated Countries of the Euro-Mediterranean Partnership

Differently, with associated countries of the Southern European Neighbourhood, such as Morocco, Tunisia and Algeria, integration on mobility is not achieved, resulting in unresolved tension.[48] The European Commission obtained its first negotiating mandate for securing an EURA with Morocco in 2000, and a mandate for the signature of a visa facilitation agreement in 2013, after the adoption of the EU–Morocco Mobility Partnership.[49] Despite several rounds of negotiations held in more than two decades, no agreement has been adopted so far.[50] In 2016, parallel negotiations for a visa facilitation and a readmission agreement started with Tunisia, but soon stagnated.[51]

The case of Morocco and Tunisia is interesting. Until the creation of the Schengen area and the Europeanization of visa policy, citizens of both countries could travel freely to neighbouring Mediterranean EU countries. Visa obligations were introduced for citizens of these countries at the time when the EU visa policy was established. Therefore, free movement in the Mediterranean, which was once possible, came to a standstill.[52] There is no prospect of integrating the citizens of these countries into the EU free movement regime. This circumstance makes these countries reluctant to cooperate with the Union in other aspects of migration policies – at least through formal means – as it is the case for readmission cooperation.

2.2 *Free Movement Initiatives in Africa*

On a continental level, initiatives related to the free movement of persons accompany the history of Africa's regional integration, even if the full implementation of a continental free movement regime is far from being accomplished.[53] As a regional integration objective, free movement has historically

48 See Tasnim Abderrahim, 'A Tale of Two Agreements: EU Migration Cooperation with Morocco and Tunisia' (2019) PapersIEMed 7.

49 Migration and mobility partnership signed between the EU and Morocco, 7 June 2013.

50 For the example of Morocco see: Sergio Carrera and others, 'EU-Morocco Cooperation on Readmission, Borders and Protection: A Model to Follow?' (2016) CEPS 87; Nora el Qadim, *Le gouvernement asymétrique des migrations Maroc/Union européenne* (Dalloz, 2015).

51 European Commission, 'Brussels the EU and Tunisia start negotiations on visa facilitation and readmission', press release of 12 October 2016.

52 On this topic, see Simone Paoli, 'The Schengen Agreements and their Impact on Euro-Mediterranean Relations. The Case of Italy and the Maghreb' (2015) Journal of European Integration History, 125.

53 See Ikechukwu P Chime et al., 'The AU Free Movement Protocol: Challenges in Its Implementation' (2023) *Journal of African Law*, 1; Alan Hirsch, 'The African Union's

been linked to the intellectual and political movement of Pan-Africanism and nationalist movements across the continent, as a contestation of the African States' borders, a legacy of colonialism.[54] Through time, both hard and soft legal initiatives have supported this endeavour.[55] In the context of the realization of African Union 'Agenda 2063', the leading continental political framework, it is acknowledged that

> free movement of people is a pillar of African integration and accelerated growth of intra-African trade. This programme aims at transforming Africa's laws, which remain generally restrictive on movement of people despite political commitments to bring down borders with the view to promoting the issuance of visas by Member States and enhance free movement of all African citizens in all African countries by 2018.[56]

On the hard law spectrum, the Africa Union adopted a Protocol relating to the free movement of persons in 2018, advancing regional integration on mobility, notwithstanding current practical challenges.[57] Other initiatives concern the African States' facilitation of inter-regional travel through liberalization or relaxation of visa requirements.[58] On the soft law spectrum, the African Union

Free Movement of Persons Protocol: Why has it faltered and how can its objectives be achieved?' (2021) 28 *South African Journal of International Affairs* 497; Samuel Kehinde Okunade and Olusola Ogunnubi, 'The African Union Protocol on Free Movement' (2019) 8 *Journal of African Union Studies*, 73.

54 Alan Hirsch, 'A strategic consideration of the African Union Free Movement of Persons Protocol and other initiatives towards the freer movement of people in Africa' (South African Institute of International Affairs, 2021).

55 African Union, 50th Anniversary – Solemn Declaration, 26 May 2013.

56 African Union, 'A shared strategic framework for inclusive growth and sustainable development and a global strategy to optimize the use of Africa's resources for the benefit of all Africans', also known as 'Agenda 2063. The African we want by 2063', September 2015, 1, 107.

57 Treaty Establishing the African Economic Community Relating to the Free Movement of Persons, Right of Residence and Right of Establishment (AU Free Movement Protocol), signed in Addis Ababa, 29 January 2018. The Protocol codified the binding commitment expressed in 1991 in the Treaty establishing the African Economic Community. Major challenges concern signature and ratification. Fifteen ratifications are required for the Protocol to come into force, but this threshold has not yet been reached.

58 On this topic, see the Africa Visa Openness Index (AVOI), which measures the extent to which each country in Africa is open to visitors from other African countries, available at www.visaopenness.org. African Development Bank and African Union Commission, Africa Visa Openness Report, 12 December 2023. The report of 2023 established that

Passport was launched 2016 to facilitate mobility within the continent.[59] A specific African Union's Migration Policy Framework shows that regional mobility sits high in the priorities of the African Union, and the Pan African Forum on Migration (PAFOM) – the continental inter-state dialogue – testifies to the importance of regional cooperation structures in fostering a common understanding of migration.[60] These 'pre-law' efforts have great potential, as they can lay the foundation for further strengthening regional free movement initiatives in Africa.

The African Regional Economic Communities (RECs) developed more advanced forms of free movement regimes at the sub-regional level. The African Union recognises RECs as essential vehicles for African integration, although their level of integration, institutional structures and centre of interest might differ.[61] Free movement is one aspect of integration in the RECs, through the recognition of fully-fledged free movement rights as well as community citizenship.[62] For instance, already in 1979, the Economic Community of West African States (ECOWAS) made free movement of persons a reality for the citizens of its Member States, and regional cross-border movements within the sub-region are part of the identity of West Africans.[63] The ECOWAS Protocol on free movement of persons and the right of residence and establishment allows for a right to entry and a 90 days visa-free stay.[64] One might wonder if

the majority of the African countries 'currently offer visa-free entry privileges to the citizens of at least one other country'. Four countries 'offer a visa on arrival to the citizens of *all* other African countries'. Roughly 60% of the African countries 'offer visa-free travel to at least 10 other countries' and other four countries 'now offer visa-free entry to the citizens of the rest of the continent'.

59 African Union Assembly, Decision on free movement of persons and the African passport, AU/Dec.607 (XXVII), 1.

60 Migration Policy Framework for Africa and Plan of Action (2018–2030), which recommends 'the harmonization and strengthened implementation of AU and REC free movement provisions related to residence and establishment, as well as enhanced cooperation among Member States in regard to the facilitation of free movement', 5.

61 On this topic, see Inocent Moyo, Jussi P Laine, Christopher Changwe Nshimbi (eds.) *Intra-Africa Migrations Reimaging Borders and Migration Management* (Routledge 2021)

62 The majority of the Treaties establishing the RECs have provisions on free movement of persons and labour, the rights of establishment, and residence, and they provide for the gradual realization of these rights. See footnote 7.

63 Achille Mbembe, 'The idea of a borderless world', Chimurenga's Chronic, on circulations and the African imagination of a borderless world, October 2018.

64 ECOWAS, Protocol Relating to Free Movement of Persons, Residence and Establishment, 29 May 1979, A/P 1/5/79. On this topic, see Aderanti Adepoju, Alistair Boulton and Mariah Levin, 'Promoting integration through mobility: free movement under ECOWAS' (2010) 29 Refugee Survey Quarterly 120.

the importance of free movement regimes in both the EU and the AU is currently reflected in region-to-region cooperation.

2.3 *A Common Understanding of Regional Migration?*

One of the principles of the Global Compact for Migration is that of 'advancing a common understanding of migration' in which the production of knowledge about migration should be a joint effort.[65] Andrew Geddes and others observed that

> there are important instances of regional cooperation to promote mobility or free movement between participating states, which introduces a legal and political distinction between those who move between states within the regional grouping (labelled *mobility*) and those who move from outside this regional setting (labelled *international migration*).[66]

This means that the regional 'element' in migration law is so vital that it gives the same phenomenon a particular semantic. This distinction in terminology is particularly significant in the EU context, and it is mirrored in EU law. The free movement of EU citizens *and* migration are carefully distinct from a legal perspective. This dichotomous view of migration can be found in legal categories such as EU citizens as opposed to third-country nationals or the risk of irregular migration as opposed to the promotion of legal mobility opportunities and visa-free travel. While in law, the categories are more complex than

65 Global Compact for Migration, point 10: 'We shared our realities and heard diverse voices, enriching and shaping our common understanding of this complex phenomenon. We learned that migration is a defining feature of our globalized world, connecting societies within and across all regions, making us all countries of origin, transit and destination. We recognize that there is a continuous need for international efforts to strengthen our knowledge and analysis of migration, as shared understandings will improve policies that unlock the potential of sustainable development for all. We must collect and disseminate quality data. We must ensure that current and potential migrants are fully informed about their rights, obligations and options for safe, orderly and regular migration, and are aware of the risks of irregular migration. We also must provide all our citizens with access to objective, evidence-based, clear information about the benefits and challenges of migration, with a view to dispelling misleading narratives that generate negative perceptions of migrants'. See, for instance, International Organization for Migration (IOM), 'Advancing a common understanding of migration governance across regions', Assessment Report (IOM, 2019).

66 Andrew Geddes, Marcia Vera Espinoza, Leila Hadj Abdou and Leiza Brumat, *The dynamics of regional migration governance* (Edgar Elgar Publishing, 2019) 2, emphasis added.

dichotomies, they broadly reflect the regional or non-regional nature of migration.[67] Citizens of the countries who are geographically located in Europe might aspire to gradual access to mobility rights – from partial integration of citizens of States candidates for the EU membership to full integration of citizens of non-EU countries who are simultaneously Schengen members. A value judgment is attached to the concepts of 'migration' and 'mobility', where mobility is often presented as good and positive and migration as bad and risky.[68] Iris Goldner Lang observes that

> [w]hereas one refers to 'free movement rights' in relation to EU citizens, third-country nationals are associated with the term 'migration'. The words 'rights' and 'free' are consciously omitted in reference to 'migration'. The term 'mobility', on the other hand, can be used in relation to both EU citizens and third-country nationals, but it seems to refer exclusively to 'desirable' migrants (e.g., tourists, students, researchers, business people, and short-term visitors) and is of a circular and temporary character.[69]

This is not *per se* a problem, but the distinction can be criticised when EU external migration policies undermine mobility within non-EU regional spaces, as is the case in EU–Africa cooperation, where regional mobility dynamics are often neglected. Moreover, at the global level, the GCM calls for 'facilitating mobility', making migration policies more coherent.[70]

3 EU–Africa Cooperation on Migration

In the context of EU–Africa cooperation, for a long time, migration featured as one of the main cooperation objectives, as evidenced in the Cotonou

---

67 On this topic, see Godfried Engbersen, Arjen Leerkes, Peter Scholten, Erik Snel, 'The intra-EU mobility regime: Differentiation, stratification and contradictions' (2017) 5 *Migration Studies* 3, 337–355.

68 Sergio Carrera, Raluca Radescu and Natasja Reslow, 'EU external migration policies. A preliminary mapping of the instruments, the actors and their priorities' (2015) Report for the EURA-net project, 12.

69 Iris Goldner Lang, 'The European Union and migration: An interplay of national, regional, and international law' (2017) 111 AJIL Unbound 509, 512.

70 François Crépeau, 'Towards a mobile and diverse world: "facilitating mobility" as a central objective of the global compact on migration' (2018) 30 *International Journal of Refugee Law*, 650.

international agreement,[71] now substituted by the Samoa agreement,[72] as well as in policy frameworks such as the EU–Africa Strategy (2007)[73] and the new EU–Africa Strategy (2020).[74] The African States were the primary targets of the external dimension of EU migration law, as testified in the subsequent policy frameworks: the 2005 Global Approach on Migration (GAM),[75] substituted in 2012 by the Global Approach on Migration and Mobility (GAMM) in 2012.[76] The renaming of the GAM in GAMM had also a symbolic significance. It officially dissociated the concept of 'migration' from the concept of 'mobility' in the EU external policy discourse towards African migration:

> [m]igration is hence related to border controls, expulsions and readmission, while mobility is [...] a much broader concept aimed at facilitating visas for certain categories of third-country nationals, which may be of strategic importance for the Union such as tourists, business communities or scientists.[77]

71 Article 13 (1) of the Cotonou agreement established that '1. The issue of migration shall be the subject of in-depth dialogue in the framework of the ACP-EU Partnership'. Partnership agreement between the members of the African, Caribbean and Pacific Group of States of the one part, and the European Community and its Member States, of the other part, signed in Cotonou on 23 June 2000, O.J., L 317, 15 December 2000, 3–353.

72 The Samoa agreement was signed on 15 November 2023, but it has not yet been ratified. It contains several provisions on migration. See Council Decision (EU) 2023/2861 of 20 July 2023 on the signing, on behalf of the European Union, and provisional application of the Partnership Agreement between the European Union and its Member States, of the one part, and the Members of the Organization of African, Caribbean and Pacific States, of the other part ST/8371/2023/DCL/1, O.J. L, 2023/2861, 28 December 2023.

73 Commission, Communication 'EU Strategy for Africa: Towards a Euro-African pact to accelerate Africa's development', SEC(2005)1255 and Communication 'From Cairo to Lisbon – The EU–Africa Strategic Partnership', SEC(2007) 855.

74 Commission and the High Representative of the Union for Foreign Affairs and Security Policy, Joint communication 'Towards a comprehensive Strategy with Africa', JOIN/2020/4 final, 9 March 2020.

75 European Council, Presidency Conclusions, Brussels, 15–16 December 2005, point 4 and Annex I, 'Global Approach to Migration: Priority actions focusing on Africa and the Mediterranean'.

76 Commission, 'The Global Approach to Migration and Mobility', COM (2011) 743, 18 November 2011.

77 Sergio Carrera, Raluca Radescu and Natasja Reslow, 'EU external migration policies. A preliminary mapping of the instruments, the actors and their priorities' (2015) Report for the EURA-net project, 1, 12.

These policy frameworks were complemented by the New Migration Partnership Framework in 2016[78] and the EU Pact on Migration and Asylum of 2020, making migration cooperation with third countries even more central to the EU migration policies.[79] Numerous studies on EU–Africa relations discuss the broader legal and policy implications of such frameworks, critically engaging with the unequal structures of cooperation and power imbalance.[80] The EU approaches Africa-to-Europe migration mainly as a single issue, that of irregular migration, which must be prevented. Free movement within and from the African continent, rather than an exercise of (regional) freedom, is treated with suspicion and perceived as a potential threat to the Union's security.[81] According to EU law, virtually all African citizens embed a potential migratory risk.[82] This particular understanding of African migration, grounded in the idea of containment, is reflected in the Union's external action.[83] For instance, the EU agency Frontex runs different projects to support the African States in

78 Commission, 'Communication on establishing a new Partnership Framework with third countries under the European Agenda on Migration', COM (2016) 385.

79 Commission, 'Communication on a New Pact on Migration and Asylum', COM (2020) 609.

80 Toni Haastrup, Luis Mah and Niall Duggan (eds.), *The Routledge Handbook of EU–Africa Relations* (Routledge, 2021); Valeria Fargion and Mamoudou Gazibo (eds.), *Revisiting EU–Africa Relations in a Changing World* (Edward Elgar Publishing, 2021); Adekeye Adebajo and Kaye Whiteman, *The EU and Africa. From Eurafrique to Afro-Europa* (Hurst, 2012); Maurizio Carbone, *The European Union in Africa. Incoherent policies, asymmetrical partnership, declining relevance?* (Manchester University Press, 2016).

81 Ferruccio Pastore and Emanuela Roman, 'Migration Policies and Threat-based Extraversion. Analysing the Impact of European Externalisation Policies on African Polities' (2020) 36 Revue européenne des migrations internationals 133.

82 While all EU citizens can visit the majority of the African States without arranging a visa prior to travel, all African States figure on the EU common list of countries whose citizens must secure a visa to travel to an EU Member State for a short stay, the so-called Schengen visa. See Council Regulation (EU) 2018/1806 of the European Parliament and of the Council of 14 November 2018 listing the third countries whose nationals must be in possession of visas when crossing the external borders and those whose nationals are exempt from that requirement (codification) PE/50/2018/REV/1, O.J., L 303, 28 November 2018, 39–58. According to Schengen visa statistics, the refusal rate of visa applications is the highest for African countries than in any other region of the world. See www.statistics.schengenvisainfo.com. On the broader topic, see Esra Demir-Gürsel and Jens Theilen, 'Framing Europe in Human Rights, Framing Human Rights in Europe: Authoritarianism, Migration, and Climate Change in the Council of Europe' (2023) 12 ESIL reflections 1.

83 Iriann Freemantle and Loren B Landau, 'Migration and the African Timespace Trap: More Europe for the World, Less World for Europe' (2022) 27 Geopolitics 791.

collecting data and sharing information about border security threats affecting the African countries and the EU.[84]

3.1 *Normative Misalignment in EU–Africa Cooperation on Migration*

Most EU migration cooperation is directed towards preventing irregular migration, epitomised by the EU's request that the African States reaffirm their sovereign control over borders.[85] This objective is pursued through policies of so-called 'externalization', 'securitization' and 'informalization' of migration law. While none of these terms has a single definition, externalization is the process whereby the EU and its Member States perform their border control functions extra-territorially or through delegation to a third party,[86] securitization is the process whereby migration emerged as a security issue,[87] and informalization of law-making is the process whereby the EU concludes international agreements on migration with third countries bypassing substantive and/or procedural rules.[88] Many studies have the merit of demystifying Europe-to-Africa migration as well as irregular migration.[89] The richness and importance of mobility within the African continent are accurately docu-

84 Africa-Frontex Intelligence Community (AFIC). – Can you refer to the official document establishing this?

85 For a critical analysis: Elaine Fahey, 'Unravelling the subjects and objects of EU external migration law' in D. Bigo et al. (eds.) *The Routledge Handbook of Critical European Studies* (Routledge 2020) 441.

86 Among many, Violeta Moreno-Lax and Martin Lemberg-Pedersen, 'Border-induced displacement: The ethical and legal implications of distance-creation through externalisation' (2019) 56 Questions of International Law 5.

87 Among many, Didier Bigo, 'The (in)securitization practices of the three universes of EU border control: Military/Navy – border guards/police – database analysts' (2014) 45 Security Dialogue 209; Vicki Squire, 'The Securitisation of Migration: An Absent Presence?' in G. Lazaridis and K. Wadia (ed.) *The Securitisation of Migration in the EU. The European Union in International Affairs* (Palgrave Macmillan, 2015) 19.

88 Among many: Eva Kassoti and Narin Idriz (eds.), *The Informalization of the EU's External Action in the Field of Migration and Asylum* (T.M.C. Asser Press 2022); Paul James Cardwell, 'Rethinking Law and New Governance in the European Union: the Case of Migration Management'(2016) 41 European Law Review, 362; Paula García Andrade, 'The external dimension of the EU migration policy: the legal framing of building partnerships with third countries' in E. Tsourdi and P. De Bruycker (eds.) *Research Handbook on EU Migration and Asylum Law* (Edward Elgar 2023), 365; Andrea Ott 'Informalization of EU bilateral instruments: Categorization, contestation, and challenges' (2020) 39 Yearbook of European Law, 569; Ramses A Wessel, 'Normative transformations in EU external relations: the phenomenon of soft international agreement' (2021) 44 West European Politics 72.

89 Marie-Laurence Flahaux, 'Demystifying African Migration: Trends, Destinations and Returns' in G. Carbone (ed.) Out of Africa. Why People Migrate (Ledizioni, 2017) 31;

mented and put the spotlight on the general lack of common understanding of migration between the two continents from a normative perspective.[90] While regional free movement is key to the EU development in the wider region, making the EU a leading example of integration in this field, capable of integrating into its free movement regions neighbouring States through a complex system of incentives, the EU does not support nor promote free movement in regional contexts in its external action.[91]

Despite the EU policies targeting mainly Africa-to-Europe migration, they impact all migration from Africa, including intra-African regional and sub-regional migration. For this reason, factually wrong visions of African migration, reflected in the substantive aspects of EU migration cooperation, clash with legal efforts on free movement in the African sub-regions.[92] In other words, the current EU migration cooperation with States members of RIOs, such as the ECOWAS, might threaten the coherence of their regional free movement regimes.[93] The predominance of security-dominated cooperation without, at the same time, fostering efforts to integrate and facilitate cross-border movements in regional space is detrimental to African integration efforts.

3.2 *Scaling-Up EU–Africa Cooperation on Migration*

Since the Valletta Joint Political Declaration and Action Plan of 2015, the scale of EU–Africa cooperation on migration changed significantly. Political, financial and legal actions on migration are increasingly taking precedence over other objectives of EU–Africa cooperation. As a matter of fact, the African countries are increasingly targeted by the Union's external migration

Anna Triandafyllidou (ed.), Irregular Migration in Europe. Myths and Realities (Routledge, 2016).

90 Olivier Bakewell and Loren B Landau (eds.), *Forging African Communities. Mobility, Integration and Belonging* (Palgrave MacMillan, 2022); Asfa-Wossen Asserate, *African Exodus: Migration and the Future of Europe* (Haus Publishing, 2018); Cris Beauchemin (ed.), *Migration between Africa and Europe* (Springer, 2018); Mehari Taddele Maru, 'Migration Policy-making in Africa: Determinants and Implications for Cooperation with Europe' (2021) Robert Schuman Centre for Advanced Studies Research Paper no 54.

91 Amanda Bisong, 'Trans-regional institutional cooperation as multilevel governance: ECOWAS migration policy and the EU' (2019) 45 *Journal of Ethnic and Migration Studies*, 1294.

92 On this topic, see Kwaku Arhin-Sam, Amanda Bisong, Leonie Jegen, H. Mounkaila, Franzisca Zanker, 'The (in) formality of mobility in the ECOWAS region: The paradoxes of free movement' (2022) 29 *South African Journal of International Affairs*, 187.

93 On this topic, Christina Oelgemöller, 'How freedom of movement infringes on the right to leave' (2023) 5 *Front. Hum. Dyn.* 1.

policies, in particular through informal agreements accompanied by external funding.[94]

Informal agreements are widespread in the EU contemporary practice of international law-making on migration.[95] Mobility Partnerships,[96] Migration Compacts,[97] Common Agendas on Migration and Mobility,[98] informal readmission agreements,[99] Memorandum of Understanding[100] as well as Joint Declarations[101] are prevalent in the EU external action. These informal agreements often constitute the basis for technical cooperation on migration. They are accompanied by funding for cooperation on migration control to fulfil the commitments they spell out.[102] External funds are used to persuade third

---

94 Eva Dick and Benjamin Schraven, 'Regional cooperation on migration and mobility: experiences from two African regions' in A Geddes *et al.* (eds.) *The dynamics of regional migration governance* (Edward Elgar Publishing, 2019) 109; Micheal Imran Kanu, 'Towards purposeful economic integration in Africa: Free movement of persons instead of illegal migration' (2020) *Journal of the African Union Commission of International Law* 165.

95 On this topic, Eleonora Frasca, 'Informal agreements and quasi-legal mechanisms in EU–Africa cooperation on migration: how the EU takes advantage of the GCM commitments' (2023) 5 Frontiers in Human Dynamics, 1. Informal agreements on migration are not concluded exclusively with the African States, but in prevalence.

96 Mobility Partnerships were signed with Cape Verde (5 June 2008); Morocco (7 June 2013) and Tunisia (3 March 2014).

97 Commission, 'Communication on Establishing a New Partnership Framework with third countries under the European Agenda on Migration', COM (2016) 385, 3, footnote 7.

98 Joint Declaration on a Common Agenda on Migration and Mobility between the Federal Democratic Republic of Ethiopia and the European Union and its Member States (11 November 2015) and Joint Declaration on a Common Agenda on Migration and Mobility between the Federal Republic of Nigeria and the European Union and its Member States (12 March 2015).

99 EU-Guinea good practices for the efficient operation of the return procedure (16 July 2017); EU–Ethiopia admission procedures for the return of Ethiopians from European Union Member States (1 November 2017); EU–Ivory Coast Joint document on the procedures for identification and readmission of migrants presumed to be Ivorian nationals staying irregularly in the European Union (2018) and EU–The Gambia good practices for the efficient operation of the identification and return procedures of persons without authorization to stay (2018).

100 Memorandum of Understanding on a strategic and global partnership between the European Union and Tunisia (16 July 2023).

101 Joint Declaration establishing a migration partnership between the Islamic Republic of Mauritania and the European Union (8 March 2024) and EU–Egypt Joint Declaration (17 March 2024).

102 Migration control funding comes from the EU Trust Fund for Africa, see Constitutive agreement establishing the European Union Emergency Trust Fund for stability and addressing root causes of irregular migration and displaced persons in Africa, and its

countries to change their domestic legislation or enforce it in a manner instrumental to the EU's interest in migration control, losing sight of the objectives of international cooperation and development.[103] Negative conditionality also plays a role in EU–Africa cooperation on migration. The main financial instrument for external funding on migration in Africa was created *ad hoc* and constituted at the Valletta Summit. It is called the EU Emergency Trust Fund for 'stability and addressing root causes of irregular migration and displaced persons in Africa' and it was created 'to address the root causes of instability, forced displacement and irregular migration and to contribute to better migration management'. Its creation shows how the EU approaches African migration, namely negatively, more as a problem 'to be solved' or 'managed' than positively, as part of continental integration, a challenge primarily for Africa rather than the EU.

In the implementation of the Trust Fund, which has been the main driver of migration cooperation in Africa, the Union approaches migration individually with each third country, focusing on border control, preferring bilateral cooperation on migration (EU-to-third–country) instead of region-to-region cooperation. Although, at the implementation level, it would be more difficult to interact with the RECs, due to lack of capacity of the REC itself, such a task is not impossible. Under the EUFTA, only one project out of 251 projects aims to support free movement within the African RECs.[104] Moreover, the 'regional' distribution of projects financed by the Trust Fund is artificial. In fact, three regions are identified: the Sahel, North Africa and the Horn of Africa. These three regions do not correspond to African RIOS /RECs. Some projects are implemented at a regional level, but do not take into account the specificities that characterise the countries' membership to a RIO nor their citizens' free movement rights within that region. The implementation of the EU Trust fund for Africa shows that a securitarian approach prevails in the projects

internal rules, done at La Valletta, on 12 November 2015, and from the Global Europe Regulation (EU) 2021/947 of the European Parliament and of the Council of 9 June 2021 establishing the Neighbourhood, Development and International Cooperation Instrument – Global Europe, PE/41/2021/INIT OJ L 209, 14 June 2021, 1.

103 Eleonora Frasca, 'The EU's legal influence on migration in the African States: The normative content of development cooperation projects' in M. Neuman, R. A. Wessel, and T. de Zee, *A Geopolitical EU in the Making? The EU's Actorness in a (De-)Globalizing World* (T.M.C. Asser Press, 2025).

104 One is the project 'Towards Free Movement of Persons and Transhumance in the IGAD region' (project identification number EUTF05-HoA-REG-19. Another project, called 'FMM West Africa: Support to Free Movement of Persons and Migration in West Africa' is also funded by the European Union, but not under the EU Trust for Africa.

funded under this instrument, with migration control objectives being at the forefront of cooperation.

3.3 *Undermining Free Movement in Africa*

By advising, equipping and persuading the African States to comply with or better enforce migration law in line with the EU's interests, the EU exercises a legal influence in their domestic legal orders. Much of the EU funding reinforces non-EU countries' border control capacities, and is aimed at preventing irregular migration to the EU. In doing so, EU–Africa cooperation on migration neglects the importance of migration for the regional identity of the RECs, in particular in the ECOWAS, and for African integration. When cooperating with States belonging to RIOs that developed or are developing free movement regimes, the EU defends its own migration regional interests – containment and securitization – thus undermining the facilitation of migration as a driver and objective of regional integration in those regions. Claire Castillejo notes that

> the EU should adopt a broader and longer-term perspective on migration that could rebalance the current narrow, short-term focus on irregular migration. This would begin with a recognition that the vast majority of people migrate within Africa, that harnessing the potential of such intraregional and intracontinental movement is the priority for African actors, and that this requires long-term sustained support.[105]

In addition, the EU external migration policies are based on factually wrong assumptions about African migration, such as an over-emphasis on irregular migration to the European Union, which remains a marginal phenomenon in comparison with the overall scale and types of regular migration to the Union, and the unidirectional migration from Africa to the European Union without sufficiently taking into account that the majority of international migration of African citizens is regional and continental.[106] This one-sided and counter-productive narrative heavily influences the EU decision-making and policy choices regarding EU–Africa cooperation. The EU should refrain from adopting external migration policies that are counter-productive and short-sighted

105 Clare Castillejo, 'The influence of EU migration policy on regional free movement in the IGAD and ECOWAS regions' (2019) DIE Discussion Paper no. 11, 1, 44.

106 On this topic, the work of geographers is of great interest: Henk van Houtum and Rodrigo Bueno Lacy, 'The migration map trap. On the invasion arrows in the cartography of migration' (2020) 15 Mobilities 196.

and live up to the commitments of the GCM to facilitate mobility, even if only limited to regional spaces. The EU external migration policies are in stark contrast not only with regional free movement of persons, but they also run counter the efforts of 'facilitating mobility' globally.

4 Conclusion

This chapter focused on the failure of the European Union to foster a common understanding of migration in its external action. Regional free movement of persons, an area where the EU has developed invaluable expertise, is rarely prioritised when cooperating with the African States. The underlying concern in external cooperation with third countries is the control of irregular migration. However, the EU's own external action framework pleads in favour of promoting free movement in regional spaces. Article 21(1) TEU provides that the Union's action on the international scene shall be guided by the principles that have inspired its own creation. There is room for arguing that these include freedom of movement of persons. Global developments in migration law also plead in favour of paying special attention to regional mobility. The GCM calls for 'advancing a common understanding of migration' which should be based on a careful and detailed study of international migration dynamics, also focusing on regional migration and the benefits it can bring to regional integration. The Union should refrain from promoting external migration policies that hinder migration regionalization dynamics already underway in Africa. The prevailing approach of the EU is one that promotes EU's own regional interests (the prevention of irregular migration from Africa) to the detriment of regional free movement initiatives in Africa. The role of the European Union as an international legal actor in migration can be questioned. Indeed, free movement of persons is an essential objective of African integration and a reality in sub-regional organizations such as the ECOWAS, which the EU should respect and support.

CHAPTER 6

The Notion of Regionalism in the Context of Sanctions Adopted by Regional International Organizations in the Defence of the General Interest

Maruša T. Veber[1]

Abstract

The notion of regionalism has traditionally been understood in geographical terms, as a concept confined to the governance of a group of members of a particular region, who share distinctive interests and values. Such understanding is based on the binary universal–regional dimension, whereby one prevails over the other. This chapter argues that the traditional understanding of regionalism fails to properly capture practice related to sanctions adopted by regional international organizations (RIOs) in their external relations (against non-member states) for the protection of the general interest. Deriving from the practice of the adoption of sanctions by the EU this chapter therefore proposes a novel understanding of regionalism, whereby universal and regional engage in mutual (rather than hierarchical or exclusionary) relationships. Framing the practice of the adoption of sanctions by RIOs in their external relations under the realm of regionalism (as opposed to universalism), helps us understand how regional interests are on such occasions exported externally and may influence the universally general posited interest (*erga omnes* obligations). This has important ramifications as it discloses the possible hegemonic influences of RIOs when engaging in their sanctioning practices and at the same time, allows RIOs to contest the universally posited interests.

Keywords

regionalism – regional international organizations – Chapter VIII of the UN Charter – European Union – sanctions – erga omnes obligations – general interest

---

1 Maruša T. Veber, Assistant Professor, Director of the Institute for International Law and International Relations, Faculty of Law, University of Ljubljana.

 | DOI:10.1163/9789004700659_008

1 Introduction

There does not exist a shared understanding of regionalism in international law, however, this notion has traditionally been understood in geographical terms, as a concept limited to the governance of a group of members of a particular region, which share distinctive interests and values.[2] This understanding seems to be embedded in the scholarly discussions on regional international law[3] and has also been the basis for drafting Chapter VIII of the United Nations (UN) Charter, governing the role of regional international organizations (RIOs) in matters relating to international peace and security.[4] These traditional understandings of regionalism are based on the binary universal – regional dimension, whereby typically one prevails over the other: regional legal rules as an exception to the universal international rules,[5] and regional organizations vs. universal organizations.[6]

This chapter argues that the traditional understanding of regionalism fails to apprehend an important segment of the practice of RIOs relating to their external relations and proposes a novel understanding of regionalism, whereby universal and regional engage in mutual (rather than hierarchical or exclusionary) relationships. It develops such a novel concept of regionalism focusing on practice related to sanctions adopted by RIOs in the defence of the general interest in their external relations (adopted against non-member states), focusing in particular on the practice of the European Union (EU).

2 Mathias Forteau, 'Regional International Law', *MPEPIL* (2006) para. 1; Laurence Boisson de Chazournes, *Interactions between Regional and Universal Organizations* (Brill Nijhoff, 2017) 8–14; Catherine Brolmann, 'Interactions between Regional and Universal Organizations' by Laurence Boisson de Chazournes [2020] 114(2) AJIL 335.

3 ILC, 'Draft Conclusions on the identification of customary international law', YILC 2018, vol. II, Part Two, conclusion 16; *Asylum case (Colombia v Peru)* (Merits) [1950] ICJ Rep 266.

4 Charter of the United Nations (Opened for signature 24 June 1945, entered into force 24 October 1945) 1 UNTS XVI, chapter VIII.

5 ILC, Fragmentation of international law: difficulties arising from the diversification and expansion of international law, 'Report of the Study Group of the International Law Commission', Finalized by Martti Koskenniemi (13 April 2006) UN Doc. A/CN.4/L.682 45 ff. See also, Draft Conclusion 16, ILC, 'Draft Conclusions on the identification of customary international law' (2018).

6 Christoph Schreuer, 'Regionalism v. Universalism' [1995] 6(3) EJIL 477, 483. See, e.g., in relation to Article 53 of the UN Charter Ademola Abass, *Regional Organisations and the Development of Collective Security: Beyond Chapter VIII of the UN Charter* (Hart Publishing, 2004).

It will be explained in this chapter that regionalism should be conceptualized in an inter-relational, rather than exclusionary sense, thereby bringing regional and universal into a relationship(s) allowing for the mutual understanding and construction of the otherwise disputed general interest in international law. In the context of the adoption of sanctions, such an inter-relational approach to regionalism allows us to understand that regionalism encompasses, not only sanctions adopted by RIOs within their respective regions, but also sanctions adopted by RIOs in their external relations, i.e., against non-member states. On such occasions, their internally defined interests are projected externally on the international level. Thereby the particular (regional, e.g., European) understanding of RIOs interests is claimed as being international, universal, and thus also applicable to the targeted third state. This is possible because RIOs, as autonomous actors in international law and based on their capacity to enforce their internal rules[7] and capacity to react to breaches of international law,[8] are entitled to adopt internal, institutional sanctions, as well as external sanctions in the form of countermeasures in defence of the general interest, that is, in response to violations of obligations *erga omnes*.[9] The proposed claims will be exemplified by the analysis of the sanctioning practice of the EU, mentioning, however, also the practice of other RIOs such as the African Union (AU) and the Arab League (AL).

This novel understanding of regionalism is important because framing such practice under the realm of regionalism (as opposed to practice pertaining to universalism), helps us understand how regional interests may be exported externally thereby influencing and contributing to the understanding and construction of the universally posited general interest. It helps us understand that sanctioning practice of RIOs projects regional interests to the universal level thereby disclosing their possible hegemonic nature, but may, at the same time provide for legitimation and contestation as to the understanding and interpretation of the controversial universally posited general interest (i.e., *erga omnes* obligations). This broader understanding, therefore, transposes

7 Maruša T. Veber, 'Sanctions adopted by international organizations in the defence of the general interest', Ph.D. Thesis, Faculty of Law, University of Ljubljana (2022) 160–164; Henry G. Schermers and Niels M. Blokker, *International Institutional Law: Unity Within Diversity* (5th edition Martinus Nijhoff 2011) 873, para. 1390; Kirsten Schmalenbch, 'International Organizations or Institutions, Supervision and Sanctions' [2020] MPEPIL.

8 *Reparation for injuries suffered in the service of the United Nations* (Advisory Opinion) [1949] ICJ Rep 174 184–185.

9 See ILC, Articles on Responsibility of International Organizations (ARIO), YILC 2011, vol. II, Part Two, Articles 49 and 57; ILC, Articles on Responsibility of States for Internationally Wrongful Acts (ARSIWA), YILC, 2001, vol. II (Part Two) Articles 48 and 54.

the above-mentioned traditional binary approach (in the sense where either universal or regional prevails) and acknowledges the intersections and mutual influences between the two, while simultaneously also transcending traditional scepticism and fear about the fragmentation,[10] particularization or regionalization of universal international law.[11]

Three preliminary caveats must be formulated before further developing the main claim of this chapter. First, this chapter does not specifically address the question of the entitlement of RIOs under general international law to adopt sanctions in the general interest under the law of countermeasures, nor answer the entangled question of identification of the general interest (*erga omnes* obligations) in international law.[12] Rather, it attempts to propose a novel understanding of regionalism by explaining that through the adoption of sanctions, RIOs can contribute to the understanding and construction of the universally posited general interest. Second, this chapter leaves aside the conduct of RIOs relating to their internal sanctioning practices, in relation to their member states in the form of, e.g., suspension from the privileges of membership.[13] More important for this research are sanctions adopted by RIOs in their external relations. Third, this chapter does not address the *Kadi*-like questions concerning the entangled relationship between the UN and the EU when implementing the United Nations Security Council (UNSC) resolutions adopting sanctions,[14] as it focuses on the autonomous sanctions of the EU, adopted outside the realm of the UNSC resolutions.

---

10 For analysis of different arguments concerning the fragmentation of international law see: Anne-Charlotte Martineau, 'The Rhetoric of Fragmentation: Fear and Faith in International Law' [2009] 22 *LJIL* 1.

11 See, e.g., Michael Wood, 'A European vision of international law: for what purpose?' in Helene Ruiz Fabri, Emmanuelle Jouannet, Vincent Tomkiewicz (eds.) [2008] 1 *Select Proceedings of the European Society of International Law*, 151; Alexander Orakhelshvili, 'The Idea of European International Law' [2006] 17(2) *EJIL* 315–347. See also, Inis L. Claude, *Swords Into Plowshares: The Problems and Progress of International Organization* (Random House 1971) 102–113; Anastassia, Obydenkova, Alexander Libman, *Authoritarian Regionalism in the World of International Organizations: Global Perspective and the Eurasian Enigma* (First edition OUP, 2019).

12 For further analysis see: Christian J. Tams, *Enforcing Obligations Erga Omnes in International Law* (CUP, 2005); Frédéric Dopagne, *Les contre-mesures des organisations internationales* (Anthemis, 2010).

13 See also, Schermers and Blokker (n 7) 919, para. 1455; Jerzy Makarczyk, 'Legal Basis for Suspension and Expulsion of a State from an International Organization' [1982] 25 *German Yearbook of International Law* 476, 480.

14 T-315/01 *Yassin Abdullah Kadi v. Council of the European Union and Commission of the European Communities* [2005] ECLI:EU:T:2005:3322005; C-402/05 and C-415/05 *Yassin Abdullah Kadi and Al Barakaat International Foundation v. Council of the European Union*

Following this introduction, the chapter first outlines the traditional understanding of regionalism as a geographical and binary concept by analysing the role of RIOs within Chapter VIII of the United Nations (UN) Charter (section 2). It then proceeds to introduce a new understanding of regionalism by focusing on practice and legal thought related to sanctions adopted by RIOs in the defence of the general interest in their external relations (adopted against non-member states). After presenting the controversial notion of the general interest in international law, as a constructed concept necessitating re-examination (section 3.1.), it outlines that RIOs may be perceived as an embodiment of regional interests under the traditional understanding of regionalism (section 3.2.). Turning to the sanctioning practice of RIOs for the protection of the general interests in their external relations, it then presents a novel understanding of regionalism, which has important ramifications, as it helps us appreciate and disclose RIOs twofold role in the understanding and construction of the general interest in international law (section 3.3.). Finally, the chapter offers some concluding remarks.

2 Traditional Understanding of Regionalism: RIOs and Chapter VIII of the United Nations Charter

Regionalism has traditionally been understood in geographical terms, as a notion limited to the governance of a group of members of a particular geographic region, which share distinctive interests and values.[15] It was first introduced in international law through the idea of regional international law which was formed as a 'reaction' to the rules of traditional international law.[16] The essence of such regional law was exceptional, as it 'called upon with the idea of escaping the 'old' international law'.[17] This binary

and the Commission of the European Communities [2008] ECLI:EU:C2008:461; T-85/09 *Yassin Abdullah Kadi v. European Commission* [2010] ECLI:EU:T:2010:418; C-584/10 P, C-593/10 P and C-595/10 P *European Commission and Others v. Yassin Abdullah Kadi* [2013] ECLI:EU:C2013:518; Jean d'Aspremont, and Frédéric Dopagne, 'Two Constitutionalisms in Europe: Pursuing an Articulation of the European and International Legal Orders' [2008] 68 ZaÖRV 939–977.

15 Forteau (n 2) para. 1; Boisson de Chazournes (n 2) 8–14; Dietrich Schindler, 'Regional International Law' in Rudolf Bernhardt, *Encyclopedia of public international law* (1984) 161. Generally on regionalism, see: Joseph Nye, *International Regionalism* (Little Brown & Company, 1968).

16 Judge Ammoun sep. op. *Barcelona Traction, Light and Power Company, Limited* (*Belgium v. Spain*) (Merits) [1970] ICJ Rep 3, 290, para. 5.

17 Forteau (n 2), para. 5; ILC (n 5) 45 ff.

approach continued through the acknowledgement of the possible existence of particular customary international law, which is specific to a limited number of states (often also linked in geographical senses),[18] governing their relations *inter se*,[19] and is contrasted with the universally posited customary international law.[20]

More important for our discussion, regionalism in international law gained prominence through institutionalization and the emergence of RIOs, such as the AU, AL and EU, in the 20th century, most prominently in the aftermath of the Second World War.[21] Thereby, institutional regionalism emerged in the form of RIOs, as a notion limited to geographically confined institutional structures governing relations of their member states *inter se*.[22] Moreover, with the emergence of the universal international organization, the UN, the central part of which was the limitation and centralization of the use of force in international relations and the simultaneous establishment of the collective security system, the need arose for acknowledging and clarifying the role of the existing and possible future RIOs in these areas. This paved the way towards a binary approach to the universal-regional relationship.

Within the UN Charter, largely as a result of input from Latin American and Arab countries, a specific reference to regionalism was included (albeit with limited scope).[23] These references to regionalism are, however, confined to the role of RIOs in peaceful settlement of disputes[24] and their role in the international peace and security.[25] Activities of RIOs in other fields are not

18 Draft Conclusions on the identification of customary international law, Commentary to Draft Conclusion 16, para. 4–5. This was confirmed by the ICJ, in the, e.g., *Case concerning rights of nationals of the United States of America in Morocco* (*France v United States of America*) (Counter-claims) [1952] ICJ Rep 176 200; *Case concerning Right of Passage over Indian Territory* (Portugal v India) (Merits) [1960], ICJ Rep 6 39; *Dispute regarding Navigational and Related Rights* (*Costa Rica v Nicaragua*) (Merits) [2009] ICJ Rep 213 233, para. 34.

19 ILC, Draft Conclusions on the identification of customary international law, Commentary to Draft Conclusion 16, para. 6.

20 Ibid., para. 3.

21 For the history of RIOs, see Boisson de Chazournes (n 2) 28–54.

22 See, e.g., working definition of RIO adopted in the final report of ILA study group on 'The International Law of Regional Organizations' [2024] available at: https://www.ila-hq.org/en_GB/documents/ila-study-group-regional-organisations-final-report-may-24 13.

23 Schreuer (n 6) 477.

24 Article 33(1), UN Charter.

25 Chapter VIII, UN Charter. Similar provisions were already included in the League of Nations covenant, which in Article 21 acknowledged the possible existence of regional agreements, provided they are compatible with the objectives of the League of Nations. Boisson de Chazournes (n 2) 45–54.

explicitly addressed in the UN Charter, however, they are implicitly governed by the general conflict rule as embedded in Article 103 of the UN Charter.[26] It is acknowledged, that regionalist elements later came to be recognised in the UN through practice, especially in the form of group systems within different organs and in the election and distribution of positions within different organs.[27] For the purposes of this chapter, I will, however, mainly confine the analysis to Chapter VIII of the UN Charter. The latter encapsulates the traditional notion of regionalism and is the departure point for discussion on regionalism in international law.[28]

In terms of terminology, Article 52(1) does not define RIOs and moreover, refers not to RIOs as such but to 'regional arrangements' and 'regional agencies'. However, it does seem to confer a geographical and member-states oriented understanding, as it refers to 'regional action'[29] and 'local disputes'.[30] The absence of a clear definition spurred terminological debates among scholars,[31] which are, however, not particularly relevant to the analysis of the sanctioning practice of RIOs. It is considered here that 'regional arrangements' and 'regional agencies', as understood for the purposes of Chapter VIII of the UN Charter, are inclusive of RIOs, which are commonly considered a specific type of closed international organizations.[32] In practice some international organ-

---

26 Schreuer (n 6) 479, 489;

27 Schreuer (n 6) 477 479–481.

28 See, e.g., Laurence Boisson de Chazournes, *Les relations entre organisations régionales et organisations universelles*, RdC (Martinus Nijhoff 2011); Boisson de Chazournes (n 2); Abass (n 6); Ana Peyró Llopis, *Force, ONU et organisations régionales: répartition des responsabilités en matière coercitive* (Bruylant, 2012); Alena F. Douhan, *Regional Mechanisms of Collective Security: the New Face of Chapter VIII of the UN charter?* (Editions L'Harmattan, 2013).

29 Article 52(1) UN Charter.

30 Article 52(2) and (3) UN Charter.

31 Christian Walter, 'Chapter VIII Regional Arrangements Commentary to Article 52' in Simma et al. *The Charter of the United Nations, A Commentary* (3rd edition, Vol. I OUP 2012) 1451; Report of the Secretary-General Boutros Boutros-Ghali, An Agenda for Peace, Preventive Diplomacy, Peacemaking and Peace-keeping (31 January 1992), para. 61; Abass (n 6) 37.

32 Henry G. Schermers and Niels M. Blokker, *International Institutional Law: Unity Within Diversity* (Martinus Nijhoff, 2018), para. 53ff; Boisson de Chazournes (n 2) 5–28; Chittharanjan Felix Amerasinghe, *Principles of the Institutional Law of International Organizations* (2nd revised edition CUP, 2005) 11. For a definition of an international organization in international law see: José E. Alvarez, *International Organizations as Law-makers* (OUP, 2005) 6; Schermers, Blokker (n 7), paras. 32–45; Jan Klabbers, *An Introduction to International Institutional Law* (2nd edition CUP 2009) 6–12.

izations were explicitly recognized as 'regional' or 'sub-regional'[33] by the UN,[34] or made declarations themselves, confirming that they consider themselves to be a RIO.[35] It is undisputed that the EU falls under the category of RIOs.[36]

In essence, the UN Charter in Article 52 recognizes the freedom of UN member states to create RIOs mandated with matters relating to international peace and security,[37] as long as their activities are compatible with the purposes and principles of the UN Charter.[38] This requirement seems to prevent members of RIOs from avoiding their obligations arising from the UN Charter by relying on the constitutive instrument of an RIO, thus reinforcing Article 103 obligations for UN member states. It would be erroneous, however, to assume that the provisions of Articles 52 and 103 oblige RIOs as autonomous legal subjects, to this hierarchical relationship, as is sometimes implied.[39]

In terms of the substantive activities of RIOs, the UN Charter acknowledges the important, primary, role of RIOs in solving regional disputes (peaceful settlement of local disputes).[40] However, on the other hand, Article 53 establishes the primacy of the universal (UN) over the regional in relation to the adoption of enforcement action relating to international peace and security.[41] The scope and meaning of the notion of 'enforcement action' have been subject to different interpretations: is UNSC authorization needed solely for the adoption of forcible action, or does it also apply to non-forcible actions, i.e., sanctions?[42] The UN Charter itself does not provide any clarity in this regard,

---

33 Report of the Secretary-General, A regional-global security partnership: challenges and opportunities (28 July 2006), UN Doc. A /61/204– S /2006/590, paras. 77–84.

34 An Agenda for Peace: Preventive Diplomacy, Peacemaking and Peace-keeping (1992).

35 Conference for Security and Co operation in Europe, Helsinki Document 1992, The Challenges of Change, Helsinki Summit (9–10 July 1992), para. 25. See also, Article 1, Charter of the Organization of American States (30 April 1948, entered into force 13 December 1951), UNTS vol. 119, 3.

36 See, e.g., statement made by the EU, UNSC 4739th meeting (11 April) 2003 S/PV.4739, 29; Sola Natavidad Fernandez, 'The European Union as a regional organization within the meaning of the UN Charter' 32 [2012] *Polish Yearbook of international law*, 259.

37 Walter, 'Chapter VIII Regional Arrangements Commentary to Article 52' in Simma *et al.* (n 31) 1446.

38 Article 52(1) UN Charter.

39 Walter (n 31) 1457.

40 Article 33(1) and 52(2) UN Charter.

41 Article 53(1) UN Charter. See also, Report of the Secretary-General's High-Level Panel on Threats, Challenges and Change from 2004, 'A more secure world: Our Shared Responsibility', United Nations, 2004 85; Boisson de Chazournes (n 2) 163.

42 See, e.g., Walter (n 31) 1481; Christian Dominicé, 'Co-ordination Between Universal and Regional Organizations' in Niels M. Blokker, Henry G. Schermers (eds.), *Proliferation of*

since it employs different terms, such as 'action',[43] 'measures'[44] and 'enforcement action',[45] in other relevant provisions.

In the *Certain Expenses* case, the International Court of Justice (ICJ) seems to have understood the notion of 'enforcement action' as including all obligatory measures adopted by the UNSC.[46] However, the systemic and teleological interpretations of the UN Charter, as well as the practice of RIOs, speak in favour of understanding the term 'enforcement action' in Article 53 as not covering the adoption of non-forcible unilateral measures, e.g., economic sanctions.[47] This can be inferred from the fact that members of the UN themselves, are also not precluded from adopting unilateral sanctions, outside the UN system, based on other international legal regimes.[48] The notion of enforcement action under Article 53 should thus be associated with the adoption of forcible measures, which are, as is well known, limited under international law to self-defence and Article 42 UNSC measures.[49]

There were some discussions on the need for UNSC authorization under Article 53 in the context of the adoption of sanctions by the Organization of American States Organization of American States (OAS) against the Dominican Republic and Cuba[50] in the 1960s. However, subsequent practice in this

International Organizations (Martinus Nijhoff, 2001) 75–82; Boisson de Chazournes (n 2) 164–166.

43 Article 42 UN Charter.

44 Article 41 UN Charter.

45 Article 2(5) UN Charter.

46 *Certain Expenses of the United Nations (Article 17, paragraph 2, of the Charter)* (Advisory Opinion) [1962] ICJ Rep 151, 164–165.

47 Walter (n 31) 1482–1484; Boisson de Chazournes (n 2) 164–166. See, however, Dominicé who seems to argue that the only unilateral action outside the UNSC authorization can relate to responses to serious violations of obligations *erga omnes* obligations or *jus cogens* norms. Dominicé (n 42) 82. See also, Abass (n 6) 51–52 stating that 'where a group of states imposes collective non-military sanctions on another state for the purpose of coercing or pressuring it, in order to compel it to desist from, or conform to certain behaviours, such an action constitutes an enforcement action.' He concludes, however, that the chapter VIII of the UN Charter has become obsolete after the end of the Cold War, as enforcement measures are commonly adopted by regional organizations outside provisions of the chapter VIII of the UN Charter. *Ibid* 64.

48 Nico Krisch, 'Commentary to Article 41' in Bruno Simma, et al. (eds.), *The Charter of the United Nations: A Commentary*, Vol. I (3rd edition OUP, 2012) 1305.

49 Chapter VII and Article 51, UN Charter. Generally on the use of force, see Christine Gray, *International Law and the Use of Force* (3 ed OUP, 2008).

50 See, e.g., Statement made by the Soviet delegation, UNSC Official Records (8 September 1960), UN Doc. S/PV.893 5; UNSC Provisional Agenda (27 February 1962) UN Doc. S/PV.991. See also, Elena Kastelli Proukaki, *The Problem of Enforcement in International*

regard confirmed that no such authorization is needed when RIOs adopt sanctions,[51] including the judicial practice of the Court of Justice of the European Union (CJEU).[52] In fact, RIOs regularly adopt sanctions relating to matters of international peace and security in the absence of UNSC sanctions and authorizations.[53]

Finally, Article 54 of the UN Charter provides that the UNSC is to be kept fully informed of activities undertaken by RIOs for the maintenance of international peace and security.[54] The practice in this respect is, however, far from being uniform and possible non-reporting does not seem to attract criticism by the UNSC.[55]

The above analysis confirms that the notion of regionalism under Chapter VIII of the UN Charter is framed around the traditional geographical sense and continues to perpetuate the universal-regional binary. Disputes are either solved at a regional (as a primary means[56]) or universal level and the universal enjoys primacy over the regional when it comes to enforcement actions. However, and importantly for the purposes of the present chapter, the adoption of sanctions of RIOs departs from this traditional understanding in two ways.

First, chapter VIII of the UN Charter seems to endorse the traditional understanding of regionalism in cases were RIOs adopted sanctions within their regions, against their member states (in their internal relations). Such sanctions are geographically confined to the concerned RIO. However, the UN Charter neither precludes nor gives a special entitlement to RIOs for the adoption of autonomous sanctions either against their members or against third states. In other words, the classification of a particular international organization as an RIO[57] has no bearing on the analysis of its sanctioning practice. Rather, this is a matter of internal, institutional law, of a concerned RIO. If

Law: Countermeasures, the Non Injured State and the Idea of International Community (Routledge, 2010) 115.

51 See also, Christine Gray, *International Law and the Use of Force*, 3 ed (OUP, 2008) 403ff; Walter (n 31) 1484–1487.

52 See, e.g., C-348/12P *Council v Manufacturing Support & Procurement Kala-Naft* [2013] ECLI:EU:C2013:776 para. 109; T-65/18 *République bolivarienne du Venezuela v Council of the European Union* [2023] ECLI:EU:T:2023:529, para. 95–98. See also, Marco Gestri, 'Sanctions, Collective Countermeasures and the EU' [2023] 32(1) *The Italian Yearbook of International Law* 67, 80–81.

53 For a detailed account of practice, see T. Veber (n 7).

54 Article 54 UN Charter. Emphasis added.

55 Walter (n 31) 1531–1534.

56 Boisson de Chazournes (n 2) 158.

57 Report of the Secretary-General, A regional-global security partnership: challenges and opportunities (2006), paras. 77–84.

the adoption of such sanctions is prescribed in the RIO's constitutive act, it will be entitled to adopt them. This has important legal ramifications as it confirms the coexistence of both, universal and regional sanctions regimes. Even though Chapter VIII seems to perpetuate a traditional, binary, understanding of regionality, in practice it came to be acknowledged that certain competencies of the UN and RIOs in matters relating to international peace and security are concurrent and complementary, in the sense that neither the UN nor RIOs are precluded from adopting sanctions about a particular situation.[58] Therefore, they coexist, rather than forming a hierarchical relationship.

Second, Chapter VIII of the UN Charter seems to be confined to the activities of RIOs within their respective regions, while external activities of RIOs fall outside its scope. In other words, sanctions adopted by RIOs in their internal relations (against their member states) fall squarely within the traditional understanding of regionalism, however, this is not the case for sanctions that RIOs adopt in their external relations (against non-member states).[59] Such external activities, in relation to non-member states, do not disqualify the concerned RIO of its status of 'regional organization' for the purposes of Chapter VIII of the UN Charter.[60] However, such activities fall outside the scope of 'traditional' regionalism under the UN Charter.[61] Traditional conceptions of regionalism thus fail to apprehend an important segment of practice, by implying the universal nature of RIOs' sanctioning practices in their external relations. As will be explained below, from the point of view of international law, such sanctions adopted in the external relations of an RIO are to be governed by international law, the law of countermeasures in particular, but should nevertheless pertain to regionalism (as opposed to universalism).

3 A Novel Understanding of Regionalism

The previous sections have outlined the limited relevance of the traditional understanding of regionalism. The criteria of regionalism being geographical

58 Walter (n 31) 1482–1484

59 Further on distinction between internal and external relations of international organizations, see T. Veber (n 7) 173–183.

60 In relation to the EU it is considered that it possess all important features of a regional organization as specified under the chapter VIII (Article 3(5) TEU expressly stipulates respect of the EU for the principle of the UN Charter and encompasses membership of states in a particular region.) See, e.g., Nigel White, 'The ties that bind: the EU, the UN and international law' [2006] 37 *Netherlands Yearbook of International Law* 57, 91.

61 Article 52(2) of the UN Charter refers to 'local disputes'.

and membership-oriented, seem to be at odds with the practices of some RIOs. The traditional understanding does not acknowledge that universal and regional sanctions mechanisms coexist and fails to apprehend the sanctioning practices of RIOs in their external relations. These controversies have contributed to the lessening of the role of Chapter VIII in practice[62] and have led some scholars to doubt the appropriateness and utility of the notion of regionalism as such.[63]

However, it is argued here, that the above-mentioned controversies do not imply that the concept of regionalism must be discarded. Rather, regionalism is essential for the understanding of the universal–regional dynamics. To fully apprehend this, regionalism should be approached in an inter-relational sense, going beyond the traditional understanding thereby also encompassing external activities of RIOs and acknowledging the coexistence of the regional with the universal. To grasp the relevance of the novel understanding of regionalism in the context of the adoption of sanctions by RIOs in the defence of the general interest, we first have to spell out certain characteristics of the concept of 'general interest' in international law.

3.1 *The General Interest in International Law: A Constructed Notion in Need of Re-examination*

The existence of interests, transcending bilateral nature, and giving the entitlement for their protection to subjects irrespective of their individually sustained injury,[64] have been present in international law since the emergence of States as independent international actors.[65] However, the notion of the general in-

62 In this respect the UNSC, for example, authorized EU forces in Bosnia (2004) and DR Congo – Artemis (2003) under chapter VII (article 42) of the UN Charter, rather than Chapter VIII. UNSC Resolution, 1525 (30 January 2004), UN Doc. S /RES/1525 and UNSC Resolution 1484 (30 May 2003), UN Doc. S /RES/1484.

63 Schermers, Blokker (n 7), para. 54.

64 Other authors have also adopted a broad definition of general or community interests, see, e.g., Christian Tams, 'Individual States and Guardians of Community Interests' in Fastenrath, Ulrich, Geiger, Rudolf, Khan, Daniel-Erasmus, Paulus, Andreas, von Schorlemer, Sabine and Vedder, Christoph, *From bilateralism to community interest in international law, Essays in Honour of Judge Bruno Simma* (OUP, 2011) 380; Isabel Feichtner, 'Community Interest' [2007] *MPEPIL*, para. 4.

65 Santiago Villalpando, 'The Legal Dimension of the International Community: How Community Interests are Protected in International Law' [2010] 21(2) *EJIL* 387, 390; Georges Abi-Saab, 'Whither the International Community?' [1998] 9(2) *EJIL* 248, 254; Laura Picchio Forlati, 'The Legal Core of International Economic Sanctions' in Laura Picchio Forlati, Linos-Alexandre Sicilianos (eds.), *Les sanctions économiques en droit international/Economic sanctions in International Law* (Martinus Nijhoff, 2004) 144. See also:

terest is often perceived as carrying an essentially imperialist, civilizing, colonial connotation.[66] In particular, the general interest in international law came to be explicitly recognized in the case law of the ICJ through the notion of *erga omnes* obligations, as obligations owed towards the international community as a whole, giving all states a legal interest in their protection.[67] Controversially, the Court did not, however, further explain in its case law how such obligations come into existence and what the consequences of their violation are. The latter were clarified in the work of the International Law Commission (ILC) on the responsibility of states and international organizations[68] as the entitlement of subjects other than the injured subject to invoke responsibility and adopt countermeasures in response to the violations of *erga omnes* obligations.[69]

It is beyond the scope of this chapter to elaborate further on the notion of the general interest in international law, suffice only to focus on two characteristics of this notion, that are important for our discussion: (1) the general interest in international law is ill-defined and often perceived as notoriously controversial and (2) the ever-evolving, inter-relational character of the general interest, which means that its content is constructed from relations formed by international subjects.

Joaquín Alcaide Fernández, '*Hostes Humani Generis*: Pirates, Slavers, and Other Criminals' in Bado Fassbender and Anne Peters (eds.) *The Oxford Handbook of the History of International Law* (OUP, 2012) 120–143; Georg Nolte, 'The International Law Commission and Community Interests' in Eyal Benvenisti, Georg Nolte, and Keren Yalin-Mor (eds.), *Community interests across international law* (OUP, 2018) 101–120.

66 B.S. Chimni, 'Third World Approaches to International Law: A Manifesto' [2006] 8 *International Community Law Review* 3; George Abi-Saab, 'The Third world and the future of the international legal order' [1973] 79 *Revue Egyptienne de Droit International* 27, 31–32; Ruth Buchanan, 'Writing Resistance into International Law' [2008] 10(4) *International Community Law Review* 445–454; Zouapet, 'Regional Approaches to International Law (RAIL): Rise or Decline of International Law?' [2021] 11–17. See also, Nico Krisch, 'International Law in Times of Hegemony: Unequal Power and the Shaping of International Legal Order' [2005] 16(3) *EJIL* 369. In relation to human rights, see: Liliana Obregon, 'The civilized and the uncivilized', in Bado Fassbender and Anne Peters (eds.) *The Oxford Handbook of the History of International Law* (OUP, 2012) 928.

67 *Barcelona Traction* (n 16), para. 33–34.

68 See also, IDI, Resolution on Obligations *erga omnes* in international law, Krakow 2005.

69 Articles 48 and 54 ARSIWA, Articles 49 and 57 ARIO. For other effects of *erga omnes* obligations, see Tams (2005) 106–116; Commentary to Article 48 ARSIWA 126–127.

(1) There exists no prescribed method of the identification of *erga omnes* obligations[70] and the question of how various norms have entered into the 'magic' *erga omnes* circle is still largely unanswered.[71] Concrete *erga omnes* obligations have been admitted to international law through ICJ case law,[72] which amounts to rather arbitrary examples of such obligations, without stipulating the means of their identification.[73] The existence of the universally-posited general interest in international law, in the form of *erga omnes* obligations, has therefore been constantly questioned and criticised by scholars on the account of merely reflecting the interests of dominant, powerful, western,[74] states and thereby having essentially imperialist, civilizing, colonial connotation.[75] *Erga omnes* obligations have even been framed as

70 Identification of *erga omnes* obligations is to be differentiated from identification of *erga omnes partes* obligations. The identification of the latter is namely largely a question of the wording of a concerned treaty and treaty interpretation. Therefore, the question of identification of such norms cannot be answered in the abstract but rather depends on the examination of each specific treaty regime entailing such obligations. See Tams (2005) 125–127.

71 Michael W. Reisman, 'Comment' in Jost Delbrück, and Ursula E. Heinz (eds.), *The Future of International Law Enforcement: New Scenarios, New Law?: Proceedings of an International Symposium of the Kiel Institute of International Law*, March 25 to 27, 1992. Vol. 115 (Duncker & Humblot, 1993) 170.

72 See, e.g., *Barcelona Traction* (n 16), para. 33–34; *Nuclear Tests* (*Australia v. France*) (Merits) [1974] ICJ Rep 253; *Case Concerning East Timor* (*Portugal v. Australia*) (Merits) [1995] ICJ Rep 90, para. 29; *Application of the Convention on the Prevention and Punishment of the Crime of Genocide* (*Bosnia and Herzegovina v. Serbia and Montenegro*) (Preliminary Objections) [1996] ICJ Rep 595 616, para. 31; *Questions relating to the Obligation to Prosecute or Extradite* (*Belgium v. Senegal*) (Merits) [2012] ICJ Rep 422, paras. 68–69; *Legal Consequences of the Separation of the Chagos Archipelago from Mauritius in 1965* (Advisory Opinion) [2019] ICJ Rep 95, para. 182.

73 See, e.g., *Barcelona Traction* (n 16), para. 33–34.

74 Anathea Roberts, *Is International Law International?* (OUP, 2012) 9; Zouapet (n 66); Makau Mutua, 'Savages, victims and saviors: the metaphor of human rights' [2001] 42(1) *Harvard International Law Journal* 202; Martii Koskenniemi, 'International Law in Europe: Between Tradition and Renewal' [2005] 16 *EJIL* 113.

75 B.S. Chimni, 'Third World Approaches to International Law: A Manifesto' [2006] 8 *International Community Law Review* 3; George Abi-Saab, 'The Third world and the future of the international legal order' [1973] 79 *Revue Egyptienne de Droit International* 27, 31–32; Ruth Buchanan, 'Writing Resistance into International Law' [2008] 10(4) *International Community Law Review* 445; Zouapet (n 66) 11–17. See also, Nico Krisch, 'International Law in Times of Hegemony: Unequal Power and the Shaping of International Legal Order' [2005] 16(3) *EJIL* 369. In relation to human rights, see: Liliana Obregon, 'The civilized and the uncivilized', in Bado Fassbender and Anne Peters (eds.) *The Oxford Handbook of the History of International Law* (OUP, 2012) 928.

'kitsch' and false universalism.[76] Against this background, to break away from the imperialist view, the need for contestation and participation of regional approaches to the understanding of the general interest is increasingly put forward.[77] The importance of acknowledging the role of regionalism in this respect is twofold: it helps to disclose instances whereby hegemonic regional actors make claims concerning the general interest under the guise of universality and more importantly, to counter the perpetuated perception that the West continues to be the centre of 'proposal and formulation of universal norms while other regions of the world are reduced to a role of validating or consenting proposals without being able to formulate proposals themselves'.[78]

(2) Interests in international law are increasingly understood in a relative, context-dependent and ever-evolving sense as being constructed from relations formed between international subjects. It is especially in the realm of the general interest that one has to acknowledge the inter-subjective 'forces, that drive' their making and their understanding.[79] As argued by Jorgensen, 'the process of perpetually interposing alternative legal ideas against one another remains the most effective force for uncovering hegemonic interests embedded in the rule of law.'[80] Such contextual understanding of the general interest confirms, that 'universality is not and could not mean an unalterable truth',[81] but has to be constructed from the relations formed between various international actors.

This does not mean, that universality should be discarded. According to d'Aspremont 'ever-growing discussion about what constitutes a common interest offers (greater) leverage to promote universality of international law'.[82] Universality does not mean uniformity, but rather richness in variety and di-

76 Koskenniemi (n 74) 113, 122.

77 Robert Jennings, 'Universal international law in a multicultural world' in Maarten Bos, Ian Brownlie (eds.) *Liber Amicorum for the Rt. Hon. Lord Wilberforce* (Clarendon Press, 1987) 41–42. Martti Koskenniemi stresses that if we acknowledge that *erga omnes* are mere instruments of hegemonic struggles, they may turn into something else. Koskenniemi (n 74) 123.

78 Zouapet (n 66) 22.

79 d'Aspremont, Jean, 'The Foundations of the International Legal Order' [2009] 18 *Finnish Yearbook of International Law* 219 224. This understanding shares some similarities with the international relations theory of constructivism.

80 Malcolm Jorgensen, 'Equilibrium & Fragmentation in the International Rule of Law: The Rising Chinese Geolegal Order' [2018] 21 KFG Working Paper Series 37.

81 Zouapet (n 66) 15.

82 d'Aspremont (n 79) 224.

versity.[83] Contestation and differences in the understanding of the general interest may bring about discord over what the content of the universally posited general interest is,[84] however, this should not be seen as an obstacle but rather as 'part of the process of building truly universal international law' thorough the recognition of differences.[85] In the words of Koskenniemi, 'the universal has no voice, no authentic representative of its own. It can only appear through something particular; only a particular can make the universal known.'[86] The general interest in international law is therefore the result of a process, the relationship between different international actors. It is constantly susceptible to subjective appropriations,[87] whereby contestation may balance these subjective approaches. Participation in the understanding of the universally posited *erga omnes* obligations makes it 'possible to order the multiple without reducing it to the hegemonic extensions of single system' and thus contributes to the 'process of universalization'.[88] Universality as a process acknowledges that one's point of view is only partial and the collisions in interpretation and understanding of the general interest have a function of mutualizing the general interest.

It has to be acknowledged that the idea of regional influences going beyond their geographically-limited character and contributing to the development of universal law was already put forward in the past,[89] but has never been explicitly acknowledged in the context of the adoption of sanctions by RIOs.

This section has shown that the general interest in international law is ill-defined and often perceived as controversial. Moreover, it explained the ever-

83 Jennings (n 77) 42.

84 Zouapet (n 66) 31; René-Jean Dupuy, 'Introduction of the subject' in René-Jean Dupuy (ed.), *The future of international law in a multicultural world* (Martinus Nijhoff Publishers, 1983) 29.

85 Zouapet (n 66) 12; See also, Mario Prost, *The Concept of Unity in Public International Law* (Hart, 2012) 211.

86 Koskenniemi (n 74) 115.

87 Helene Ruiz Fabri, 'Reflections on the Necessity of Regional Approaches to International Law through the Prism of the European Example: Neither Yes nor No, neither Black nor White' [2010] 1(1) *Asian Journal of International Law* 83, 95.

88 Zouapet (n 66) 31; Mireille Delmas-Marty, *Les Forces Imaginantes du droit, Le Relatif et l'Universel* (Editions du Seuil, 2004) 54, 412.

89 Judge Alvarez diss. op. *Asylum case* (*Colombia v Peru*) (Merits) [1950] ICJ Rep 266, 293–294; ILC, Fragmentation of international law: difficulties arising from the diversification and expansion of international law (2006), para. 201; Apollin Koagne Zouapet, 'Not a Threat, an Opportunity: Regional Approaches and the Future of International Law' [2023] 48 *South African Yearbook of International Law*; Forteau, 'Regional International Law' [2006], para. 6. See also, *Reservations to the Convention on the Prevention and Punishment of the Crime of Genocide* (Advisory Opinion) [1951] ICJ Rep 15.

evolving, inter-relational character of the general interest, which means that its content is constructed from relations formed by international subjects. In the following section, it will be shown that the inter-relational conception of regionalism in the realm of sanctions helps to disclose such hegemonic influences and at the same time may mitigate the imperialist and civilizing connotation of the general interest by allowing regional actors to contribute to its understanding. By bringing universal and regional in interaction it namely opens the possibility of different world regions to participate in the shaping of the general interest, a concept that has predominantly been shaped by the Global North regions.

3.2 *Regional International Organizations as the Embodiment of Regional Interests*

Interests, transposing bilateral nature in international law are not limited solely to the notion of *erga omnes* obligations. It is nowadays widely recognized that treaties[90] may transcend traditional reciprocal and bilateral relations and may project general interests of a sort.[91] Constitutive acts of RIOs are one example of embodiment of interests transcending individual nature. Indeed, the very *raison d'etre* of the establishment of RIOs is the protection of interests, common to their member states, thereby transcending individual interests of member states.[92] RIOs are established to 'manage common problems' and to enable the pursuance of objectives that cannot be sufficiently addressed by states individually.[93] The constitutive acts of RIOs commonly

90 See, e.g., Jan Klabbers, 'The Community Interest in the Law of Treaties: Ambivalent Conceptions', in Fastenrath *et al.* (eds.), *From Bilateralism to Community Interest: Essays in Honour of Judge Bruno Simma* (OUP, 2011) 768–780.

91 Dörr, Schmalenbach (2012), 1022, para. 1. See also, *South West Africa Cases* (*Ethiopia v South Africa, Liberia v South Africa*) (Merits) [1966] ICJ Rep 6, para. 44 ('In this connection, the provisions of certain treaties and other international instruments of a humanitarian character, and the terms of various arbitral and judicial decisions, are cited as indicating that, for instance, States may be entitled to uphold some general principle even though the particular contravention of it alleged has not affected their material interests;-that again, States may have a legal interest in vindicating a principle of international law, even though they have, in the given case, suffered no material prejudice, or ask only for token damages. The Court simply holds that such rights or interests, in order to exist, must be clearly vested in those who claim them, by some text or instrument, or rule of law.'). It, however, adopted a restrictive approach concerning the interpretation of Article 7(2) of the South West Africa mandate agreement. *Ibid*, 38, para. 63.

92 Apollin Koagne Zouapet, 'States and Regional International Organizations' [2024] 21 IOLR 147, 150.

93 Jan Klabbers, 'Two Concepts on International Organization,' [2005] 2 IOLR 277, 278; Schermers, Blokker (2018), paras. 1–2.

embed specific regional interests and provide for the explicit or implied institutionally-based entitlements for the adoption of sanctions[94] for their protection. This enables RIOs to properly perform the functions for which they were established in the first place.[95] As autonomous actors in international law and based on their capacity to enforce their internal rules, RIOs are entitled to adopt such sanctions in internal relations to enforce their institutionally defined regional interest.[96]

According to Article 2 of the Treaty of the European Union (TEU), the EU for example, is committed to protecting its fundamental values, which include respect for human dignity, freedom, democracy, equality, the rule of law and respect for human rights.[97] EU treaties also presuppose a corresponding internal sanctioning mechanism in Article 7 TEU,[98] to enforce these values in relation to its member states. Similar provisions, whereby RIOs identify their regional interests applicable to all member states and presuppose sanctions for their enforcement are included in the constitutive acts of other RIOs.[99]

---

94 See also, Schermers, Blokker (n 7) 919–958.

95 Gaja argues in his general course that IOs 'may play an important role of protecting the general interests in their respective area of competence.' Giorgio Gaja *The Protection of General Interests in the International Community*, RdC 364 (Martinus Nijhoff Publishers 2011) 30. See also, Eckart Klein, 'Sanctions by International Organizations and Economic Communities' [1992] 30(1) *AVR* 101, for further citations, see p. 102, ft. 3.

96 T. Veber (n 7) 160 ff.

97 Article 2 TEU, Consolidated version of the Treaty on European Union (adopted 26 October 2012) OJ C 326.

98 Stelio Mangiameli and Gabrialla Saputelli, 'Commentary to Article 7 TEU', in Hermann-Josef Blanke and Stelio Mangiameli (eds.), *The Treaty on European Union (TEU), A commentary* (Springer, 2013) 351. See also, European Commission, 'Communication from the Commission to the Council and the European Parliament on Article 7 of the Treaty on European Union: Respect for and promotion of the values on which the Union is based' (15 October 2003), COM (2003) 606 final, point 1.1. More on this Maruša T. Veber, 'Safeguarding Fundamental Values of the EU Through the Adoption of Sanctions' [2020] 4 *University of Vienna Law Review* 37–78.

99 See, e.g., Article 8 of the Statute of the Council of Europe (5 May 1949), 87 UNTS 103; Article 4 and Article 30 of the Constitutive Act of the African Union (AU) (11 July 2000, entered into force 26 May 2001) OAU Doc CAB/LEG/23.15; AU, Decision on the Prevention of Unconstitutional Changes of Government and Strengthening the Capacity of the African Union to Manage Such Situations, Doc. Assembly/AU/Dec. 269(XIV) Rev.1 (2 February 2010); Article 9, Charter of the Organization of American States (30 April 1948, entered into force 13 December 1951), UNTS vol. 119, p. 3; Articles 19 and 21, Inter-American Democratic Charter, adopted by the General Assembly, 28th special session (11 September 2001); ECOWAS, Supplementary Act on Sanctions against Member States that fail to Honour the Obligations to ECOWAS (19 July 2011), Doc. A/SP.2/08/11.

This is an important aspect of regionalism allowing for the development of specific, regional interests whereby RIOs are perceived as an institutional embodiment of regional interests in a traditional sense. However, as will be shown in the next section, through the adoption of sanctions, such regional interests are not solely protected by RIOs within their own regions, among their member states, but are increasingly also transposed externally, to their relations with third states. This has important ramifications and necessitates a novel, inter-relational understanding of regionalism.

3.3 *Sanctions of Regional International Organizations and the Protection of the General Interest: Lessons from the European Union*

In the absence of a general centralized enforcement mechanism in international law that would systematically address illegal behaviour, the notion of sanctions, as unilateral enforcement mechanisms, has had a prominent role throughout the history of international law.[100] It will be explained in the following section that an important part of practice in this respect derives from RIOs, the EU in particular, which commonly adopts sanctions for the protection of general interests.

Arguably the most relevant examples of the adoption of sanctions in the general interest are EU's are restrictive measures, as these sanctions are referred to under EU law.[101] These are one of the EU's tools to uphold respect for human rights, democracy, the rule of law, good governance, international law, as well as the preservation of peace, prevention of conflicts and strengthening of international security in the wider world.[102] EU sanctions are typically

---

100 Omer Yousif Elagab, *The Legality of Non-forcible Counter-measures in International Law* (OUP, 1988) 6; Stephen C. Neff, *War and the Law of Nations: A General History* (CUP, 2005) 76; Olivier Barsalou, 'The History of Reprisals Up to 1945: Some Lessons Learned and Unlearned for Contemporary International Law' [2010] 49 *Military Law and the Law of War Review* 335, 341.

101 Article 29 TEU and Article 215 TFEU. It is acknowledged that the EU regularly adopts sanctions under other regimes, e.g., treaty-based sanctions, however, these are not further analysed here. See, e.g., Article 98(1) of the Partnership agreement between the members of the African, Caribbean and Pacific Group of states of the one part, and the European Community and its Member states, of the other part, signed in Cotonou on 23 June 2000 *OJ L 317, 15.12.2000* (in force) (Cotonou Agreement). T. Veber (2022) 367–376; Clara Portela, 'Aid Suspensions as Coercive Tools? The European Union's Experience in the African-Caribbean-Pacific (ACP) Context' [2007] 3(2) *Review of European and Russian Affairs* 38.

102 Basic Principles on the Use of Restrictive Measures (Sanctions) (7 June 2004) 10198/1/04 rev 1, p. 2; EU, Sanctions: how and when the EU adopts restrictive measures', available at https://www.consilium.europa.eu/en/policies/sanctions/.

adopted in the form of the complete or partial interruption of economic relations, import and export restrictions (embargoes), freezing of foreign assets, bans on the provision of financial services and investment bans.[103] Over 40 different EU sanctions regimes are currently in place against 34 different countries.[104]

It has been explained already that the traditional understanding of regionalism fails to apprehend that RIOs engage, not only in relations with their member states (within their regions) but increasingly also externally, with non-member states. In such situations, RIOs will have to justify the adoption of their sanctions under international law.[105] While some sanctions of RIOs may amount to mere retorsions (*unfriendly act*),[106] and thus do not necessitate specific legal justification, others amount to a violation of an obligation owed by the concerned RIO under international law.[107] While indeed, 'in the absence of specific legal obligations to engage in trade with another State, a general trade embargo of the EU may be a lawful measure'[108] in practice, the EU has various bilateral[109] and multilateral trea-

---

103 See, e.g.,, CEU, 'Guidelines on the implementation and evaluation of restrictive measures' 5664/18 (4 May 2018) 8, para. 14; EU restrictive measures, Factsheet (2014), available at http://www.consilium.europa.eu/uedocs/cms_data/docs/pressdata/EN/foraff/135804.pdf.

104 For an overview of current sanctions in force, see EU Sanctions map, https://www.sanctionsmap.eu/#/main and EU, Restrictive measures (sanctions) in force, available at https://eeas.europa.eu/archives/docs/cfsp/sanctions/docs/measures_en.pdf.

105 About the EU, see Bert Van Vooren and Ramses A. Wessel, *EU External Relations Law, Text Cases and Materials* (CUP, 2014) 5, 208.

106 On retorsion, in general, see also Partsch, Karl Josef, 'Retorsion' in Rudolf Bernhard, *Encyclopedia of Public International Law* (published under the auspices of the Max Planck institute for comparative public law and international law under the direction or Rudolf Bernhardt) (vol. four Elsevier, 2000) 232–233.

107 Article 4 ARIO. T. Veber (n 7) 318 ff; Gestri (n 52) 70–71.

108 Vaughan Lowe and Antonios Tzanakopoulos, 'Economic Warfare,' [2013] *MPEPIL* para. 37; *Case Concerning Military and Paramilitary Activities in and Against Nicaragua* (*Nicaragua v. United States of America*) (Merits) [1986] ICJ Rep 14, para. 276.

109 In relation to EU sanctions against Argentina, Russia and Burundi see, respectively, the Agreement between the European Economic Community and the Argentine Republic on trade in textile products (26 November 1979. No longer in force) OJ L 298, art 16.3; Council Regulation (EEC) No 2557/79 of 30 October 1979 concerning the conclusion of the Agreement between the European Economic Community and the Argentine Republic on trade in textile products' (26 November 1979. No longer in force) OJ L 298, 1; Arrangement in the form of an exchange of letters between the European Economic Community and the Argentine Republic on trade in mutton and lamb' (18 October 1980) OJ L 275, 14–19; Agreement on Partnership and Cooperation establishing a partnership between the European Communities and their Member States, of one part, and the

ties[110] in place governing its economic and trade relations with third states and therefore necessitate international legal justification.[111]

The legal justification for the adoption of such sanctions are typically countermeasures, which are governed by Articles on Responsibility of States for Internationally Wrongful Acts (ARSIWA),[112] Articles on Responsibility of International Organizations (ARIO),[113] and customary international law[114] and are one of the circumstances precluding wrongfulness, giving a state or an international organization injured by a wrongful act of the responsible state a right to take measures that would otherwise be contrary to international law. Apart from these 'classical' countermeasures, the law of responsibility also allows for countermeasures by not-directly affected states or international organizations[115] in cases of breaches of *erga omnes* obligations,[116] which are relevant for the present chapter. Even though the ILC left the legality of the adoption of such measures to be determined through the further development of interna-

Russian Federation, of the other part' (28 November 1997) OJ L 327; Partnership agreement between the members of the African, Caribbean and Pacific Group of states of the one part, and the European Community and its Member states, of the other part, signed in Cotonou on 23 June 2000 *OJ L 317, 15.12.2000* (in force) (Cotonou Agreement). See also, C-72/15 *PJSC Rosneft Oil Company v Her Majesty's Treasury andOthers* [2017] ECLI:EU:C:2017:236.

110 EU restrictions on the trade of goods and services may, for example, be in breach of the EU's WTO obligations, in particular the most-favoured-nation (MNF) status obligations and the general elimination of quantitative restrictions in the GATT, as well as the most-favoured-nation obligation and market access obligations in GATS. Articles I:1 and XI:1 GATT; Articles II:1 and XVI:1 GATS. See, e.g.,, General Agreement on Tariffs and Trade (GATT) 'Trade Restrictions Affecting Argentina Applied for Non-Economic Reasons – Revision' (18 May 1982) L/5319/Rev.1 and 'Minutes of the Meeting Held in the Centre William Rappard on 7 May 1982' (22 June 1982) C/M/157, p. 10 (concerning sanctions adopted against Argentina).

111 Autonomous sanctions of the EU are to be distinguished from the non-autonomous sanctions whereby the EU implements the United National Security Council sanctions, the legal justification for which derives from the underlying UNSC resolution. T. Veber (2022) 245 ff.

112 ARSIWA (2001) YILC, 2001, vol. II Part Two.

113 ARIO (2011) YILC vol. II, Part Two.

114 *Naulilaa Incident Arbitration (Portugal v. Germany)* 2 R.I.A.A. (1928) 1012; *Gabčíkovo-Nagymaros Project (Hungary v. Slovakia)* (Merits) [1997] ICJ Rep 7; *Air Services Agreement of 27 March 1946 between the United States of America and France*, R.I.A.A. (1978) Vol. XVIII.

115 Article 54 ARSIWA.

116 *Barcelona Traction* (1970), para. 33. See also, *The case of East Timor (Portugal v Australia)* (Jurisdiction) [1995] ICJ Rep 90, 102; Report of the International Law Commission (2001) UN Doc. A/56/10, 208.

tional law,[117] the view that they can be lawfully taken has gained traction in modern international law. This is due to increased practice in this regard which is supported by the literature[118] and other important international institutions, such as the *Institut de droit international*.[119] It is assumed here then, that in their capacity to react to breaches of international law[120] RIOs are entitled to adopt sanctions in the form of countermeasures against third states in defence of the general interest, that is, in response to violations of obligations *erga omnes*.[121]

In relation to the sanctioning practice of the EU, the Court of Justice of the European Union (CJEU) in the *Rosneft* case confirmed, that sanctions adopted by the EU in its external relations have to be grounded in international law.[122] Quite controversially the EU General Court, however, in the *Venezuela v Council* case, when confronted with the legality of EU's sanctions against Venezuela under international law, seemed to denounce the application of the 'countermeasures' rationale to its restrictive measures.[123] Rather, the Court perceived

---

117 ARSIWA Commentary to chapter II 139.

118 Martin Dawidowicz, *Third-Party Countermeasures in International Law* (CUP, 2017); Martin Dawidowicz, 'Third-party countermeasures: A progressive development of international law?' [2016] QIL available at <http://www.qil-qdi.org/third-party-counter measures-progressive-development-international-law/> accessed 11 July 2024; Tams (2005); Frédéric Dopagne, *Les contre-mesures des organisations internationals* (Parution, 2010); Frédéric Dopagne, 'Sanctions and Countermeasures by international organisations' in Richard Collins and Nigel D. White (eds.), *International Organizations and the Idea of Autonomy: Institutional Independence in the International Legal Order* (Routledge, 2011); Jean d'Aspremont, 'The Multifaceted Concept of the Autonomy of International Organizations and International Legal Discourse' in Richard Collins and Nigel D. White (eds.), *International Organizations and the Idea of Autonomy: Institutional Independence in the International Legal Order* (Routledge, 2011) 63–86; Elena Kastelli Proukaki (2010). For the contrary view, see James Crawford, *State Responsibility: The General Part* (CUP, 2013) 706, 709.

119 Institut de droit international, Krakow resolution 2005.

120 *Reparation for injuries suffered in the service of the United Nations* (Advisory Opinion) [1949] ICJ Rep 174, 184–185.

121 See Articles 49 and 57 ARIO and Articles 48 and 54 ARSIWA.

122 Case C-72/15, PJSC *Rosneft Oil Company v Her Majesty's Treasury andOthers* [2017] ECLI: EU:C2017:236 in this case the Court confirmed that sanctions of the EU against Russian entities were justified on the basis of Article 99(1)(d) of the EU-Russia Partnership and Cooperation Agreement. More on this, see Maruša T. Veber, Anže Mediževec, 'R. (on the application of PJSC Rosneft Oil Company (formerly OJSC Rosneft Oil Company)) v Her Majesty's Treasury and ors, Judgment, reference for a preliminary ruling' headnote no. 784 (2024), OXIO database.

123 Quite controversially, it stipulated that conditions for the adoption of countermeasures were not met. Case T-65/18 [2023] *République bolivarienne du Venezuela v Council of the*

restrictive measures adopted against Venezuela[124] as 'independent' from international law and based on Articles 3(5) and 21 TEU. It thereby proclaimed EU's 'autonomous external sanctioning power'[125] and dismissed the action of annulment brought by Venezuela which argued that EU's sanctions against this country amounted to unlawful countermeasures. However, upon a careful reading of the judgement, one may notice that the Court at the same time nevertheless implicitly confirmed the embeddedness of restrictive measures in international law by stating that these measures are intended to ensure the fulfilment of *erga omnes* (*partes*) obligations.[126] Indeed, according to the General Court (citing relevant case law of the ICJ) these obligations are in the common legal interest of the international community.[127] Moreover, the Court's proclamation that the entitlement of the EU for the enforcement of the *erga omnes* obligations derives from its internal mandate to observe international law and internal values (democracy, rules of law and human rights)[128] is at odds with fundamental international legal rules on the law of treaties and responsibility. More generally, the Court's pronouncement in the Venezuela case is also in contradiction with the countermeasures rationale that the EU is increasingly engaging in its sanctioning policies.[129]

As explained above, the notion of *erga omnes* obligations under international law is central to the secondary international rules on countermeasures. Even though the EU enjoys well-established internal competence for the

---

European Union, ECLI:EU:T:2023:529, para. 83–92. For a critical analysis, see Eva Kassoti, 'Beyond Collective Countermeasures and Towards an Autonomous External Sanctioning Power? The General Court's Judgment in Case T-65/18 RENV, Venezuela v Council' (2024) 9(1) European Papers 247, 253–259.

124 Council Regulation (EU) 2017/2063 of 13 November 2017 concerning restrictive measures in view of the situation in Venezuela, arts 2, 3, 6 and 7; Council Implementing Regulation (EU) 2018/1653 of 6 November 2018 implementing the contested regulation in so far as that implementing regulation concerns it; Council Decision (CFSP) 2018/1656 of 6 November 2018 amending Decision (CFSP) 2017/2074 concerning restrictive measures in view of the situation in Venezuela, in so far as that decision concerns it.

125 Kassoti (n 123) 247–259.

126 Case T-65/18 [2023] *République bolivarienne du Venezuela v Council of the European Union*, ECLI:EU:T:2023:529, para. 113.

127 Case T-65/18 [2023] *République bolivarienne du Venezuela v Council of the European Union*, ECLI:EU:T:2023:529, para 113.

128 See also, Kassoti (n 123) 249.

129 European Parliament resolution of 20 May 2021 on Chinese countersanctions on EU entities and MEPs and MPs (2021/2644(RSP)), P9_TA(2021)0255, para. H; Case C-72/15, PJSC Rosneft Oil Company v Her Majesty's Treasury andOthers (2017), ECLI:EU:C2017:236, para. 150.

adoption of restrictive measures (sanctions),[130] on the basis of the principle of *pacta tertiis nec nocent nec prosunt*, whereby 'a treaty does not create either obligations or rights for a third State without its consent',[131] non-member states are not internationally bound by the internal rules of the organization. In contractual terms, the rules of the organization are therefore *res inter alios acta*. While the relevant provisions of EU primary law in this case provide the legal basis for the justification of the adoption of sanctions under internal EU law, this does not mean that the EU can justify such measures in the international sphere on its internal (primary) law. Rather, such sanctions will have to be justified internationally.[132] Against this background, it is argued here, that as an autonomous subject of international law, the EU, like other international organizations, may incur responsibility when adopting sanctions against third states, and in turn it may justify the adoption of sanctions on the secondary rules on countermeasures.[133]

When adopting sanctions against third states based on the law of countermeasures, RIOs engage in the construction of the understanding of the generally posited interest in international law, that is, *erga omnes* obligations.[134] On the occasions when a RIO is reacting to a breach of international law which does not directly affect the organization as such, thereby breaching its international obligations, it arguably engages the regime of countermeasures. On such occasions, RIOs project their internally posited interest externally and contribute to the understanding and the construction of the universally posited general interest. This was, in fact, confirmed by the General Court of the EU in the above-mentioned case concerning Venezuela, whereby the Court endorsed the idea of the EU as an 'enforcer of (international) *erga omnes* obligations in accordance with the values and objectives that govern the

130 Article 29 TEU and Article 215 TFEU.

131 Article 34, Vienna Convention on the Law of Treaties (VCLT (1969)) (23 May 1969, entered into force 27 January 1980) UNTS vol. 1155, p. 331.

132 Maruša T. Veber, Anže Mediževec, see supra note 122.

133 T. Veber (n 7). See, however, Gestri (n 52) 92, expressing doubt as to the legal basis of 'collective countermeasures' to justify the adoption of sanctions by the EU against third states.

134 See also, Maruša T. Veber, 'The Making of Custom Through Sanctions of International Organizations' in Sufyan Droubi and Jean d'Aspremont (eds.), *International Organizations, Non-State Actors, and The Formation of Customary International Law* (Manchester University Press, 2020) 284–305; Maruša T. Veber, 'The protection of community interests through countermeasures adopted by international organizations', in Gentian Zyberi, (ed.), *Protecting Community Interests Through International Law* (Intersentia, 2021) 127–162.

EU's external action'.[135] A similar approach was adopted in the *T France v Council* case, whereby the Court clarified that with the adoption of sanctions against Russia, the EU was responding to 'a violation of obligations imposed *erga omnes* by international law in order to counter, using all the measures at its disposal that did not involve the use of force, the military aggression against Ukraine by the Russian Federation'.[136] The EU thereby perceives itself as a global actor, promoting the fundamental values in the international arena.[137] However, it is argued there that this practice of the EU is not to be seen as global or universal, but rather as pertaining to regionalism. This is important, for the following reasons.

Such understanding helps to mitigate the imperialist and civilizing connotation of the general interest by allowing regional actors to contribute to its understanding. By bringing universal and regional in interaction it opens the possibility of mutualizing the understanding of the general interest. Perceiving such practice as 'regional' allows us to transcend the above-mentioned traditional binary approach, in the sense where either universal or regional prevails, and acknowledge the intersections and influences between the two. Such an understanding of regionalism is inter-relational and helps us understand how regional actors influence the understanding of the 'universally' posited general interest. In this respect, RIOs themselves can be seen as actors that either perpetuate hegemonic ideas and influences or as actors aimed at counteracting and balancing such hegemonic domination.[138]

While the practice of the EU is predominant when it comes to such external relations, and discloses its (hegemonic) regional perception of the general interest, it is important that other RIOs are also engaging in the adoption of such sanctions, thereby contributing to the understanding of the 'universal' general interest and subsequently fostering its legitimation. Examples include situations where RIOs adopted sanctions against their members thereby affecting their membership rights, without having the entitlement to do so under their constitutive acts. On such occasions, they arguably engage the international legal regime of countermeasures to justify the adoption of such

135 Kassoti (n 123) 249. *Case T-65/18, République bolivarienne du Venezuela v Council of the European Union*, ECLI:EU:T:2023:529, para. 113.

136 Case T-125/22 [2022] *RT France v Council* ECLI:EU:T:2022:483 para. 86.

137 Kassoti (n 123) 250.

138 Fiti Sinclair, 'Between Functionalism and hegemony: regional International Organizations in the History of International Law' [2024] 65, 77–78; Georges Abi-Saab, 'The Newly Independent States and the Rules of International Law: An Outline' [1962] 8(2) *Howard Law Journal* 97, 105.

sanctions.[139] One example includes the AL measures against Syria in the form of suspension of membership and economic sanctions, including travel bans, freezing of assets belonging to the Syrian government and senior regime officials, suspension of dealings with the central bank of Syria, and a ban on civil aviation.[140] These measures were adopted in response to violence and human rights violations in Syria,[141] although protecting human rights and respecting humanitarian law is not among the AL's functions. The AL pact only includes a provision on the exclusion of members in cases of failure to fulfil the obligations resulting from the pact,[142] and there exists no provision for suspension of members. These sanctions were adopted in the absence of the UNSC response to the outbreak of violence and it has been argued that they can be termed countermeasures in response to *erga omnes* violations, namely to the continuous suppression of civilians and violations of human rights by the Syrian regime.[143] Similar examples could include AL's sanctions (boycott) against Israel[144] and sanctions currently contemplated by the AU against this same country, which already deprived Israel of its observer status and is considering the possible adoption of trade and economic sanctions.[145] Framing this practice under the realm of regionalism, helps us understand how AL and AU in this case are projecting their interest to the universal, international level, thereby contributing to its mutual understanding. While these interests and their understanding to some degree overlap, there is also a possibility of collisions and conflicts between them, thereby working as a sort of checks and balances.

4 Concluding Remarks

This chapter has proposed a novel understanding of regionalism, which is not geographical and membership-oriented, but rather brings regional and universal into a relationship(s). This novel concept of regionalism was derived from the practice related to sanctions adopted by RIOs against non-member

139 Generally on this, see T. Veber (n 7).
140 Arab League Resolution 7442 (27 November 2011).
141 Arab League Resolution 7438 (12 November 2011).
142 Article 18 Charter of the League of Arab States (22 March 1945).
143 See also, Dawidowicz (2017) 224–225; T. Veber (2022) 356–357.
144 Martin A. Weiss, 'Arab League Boycott of Israel' [2017] Congressional Research Service.
145 Africa, Namibia's Call for Sanctions against Israel Draws Mixed Responses (2 March 2024), available at: https://www.voanews.com/a/namibia-s-call-for-sanctions-against-israel-draws-mixed-responses/7511207.html.

states and in the defence of the general interest. The two most prominent characteristics of the general interest in international law, being ill-defined and controversial and its ever-evolving, inter-relational character, justify the proposed inter-relational approach. Once we acknowledge the analysed sanctioning practice of RIOs as pertaining to regionalism we can understand that with such activities, RIOs define their regionally posited general interests, which may be at variance with the universally posited general interest. Transcending traditional scepticism and fear in relation to the fragmentation,[146] particularization or regionalization of universal international law,[147] the inter-relational understanding of regionalism should be perceived as a means enabling the participation of RIOs in the construction and the understanding of the general interest, thereby fostering its legitimacy.[148] Framing such practice under the realm of regionalism (as opposed to practice pertaining to universalism), helps us understand how regional interests and values are on such occasions exported externally and may influence the universally posited interest. This is important, for two reasons: it discloses the possible hegemonic influences of RIOs and at the same time, allows RIOs to contest the universally posited interests and functions as a sort of checks and balances as to the understanding and interpretation of the universally posited interests (i.e., *erga omnes* obligations). In this respect, such understanding of regionalism discloses the perception of RIOs as actors that either perpetuate hegemonic ideas and influences or as actors aimed at counteracting and balancing such hegemonic domination.[149] The above analysis has shown that such an understanding of regionalism currently mainly discloses European influences on the understanding of the general interest. However, as the sanctioning practice of other RIOs evolves, it brings opportunities for contestation and possible con-

---

146 For analysis of different arguments concerning the fragmentation of international law see: Anne-Charlotte Martineau, 'The Rhetoric of Fragmentation: Fear and Faith in International Law' [2009] 22 *LJIL* 1–28.

147 See, e.g., Michael Wood, 'A European vision of international law: for what purpose?' in Helené Ruiz Fabri, Emmanuelle Jouannet, Vincent Tomkiewicz (eds.) [2008] *Select Proceedings of the European Society of International Law, Volume 1 2006* 151; Orakhelashvili, 'The idea of European international law' 315–347.

148 On the legitimacy of international law see: Jutta Bruneé and Stephen J. Toope, *Legitimacy and Legality in International Law: An Interactional Account* (CUP, 2010) 7; Thilo Marauhn, 'The International Rule of Law in Light of Legitimacy Claims' in Heike Krieger, Georg Nolte and Andreas Zimmermenn (eds.), *The International Rule of Law: Rise or Decline?* (OUP, 2019) 282.

149 Fiti Sinclair (n 138) 77–78; Georges Abi-Saab, 'The Newly Independent States and the Rules of International Law: An Outline' [1962] 8(2) *Howard Law Journal* 97, 105.

flicts in the understanding of the universally posited general interest and balancing the hegemonic nature of the general interest in international law.

Acknowledgements

This chapter was written in the course of author's post-doctoral research project 'Seizure of State-owned and private Property under International Law: Mapping the Applicable Legal Rules and Identifying Conditions that Frame and Limit Seizure of Frozen Assets in the Context of the Situation in Ukraine' (Z5-50167) funded by the Slovenian Research Agency (ARIS).

CHAPTER 7

The EU Anti-coercion Mechanism: A Tool for Development or Fragmentation of International Law?

Petr Stejskal[1]

Abstract

In a changing geopolitical environment where trade is weaponized as a method of coercion, the EU adopted an anti-coercion instrument (ACI). This chapter perceives the ACI as another avenue through which the EU as a regional international organization contributes to the interpretation or development of international law. ACI was developed as part of the EU's common commercial policy and enables adopting response measures in reaction to coercion against Member States or the EU. The spectrum of possible measures includes measures otherwise qualified as countermeasures under international law. The instrument brings its own definition of economic coercion. However, it is not settled in international law what forms of economic coercion qualify as prohibited intervention. Moreover, it seems that the EU can adopt anti-coercion measures also when only one or a few Members States are facing coercion. This raises the question of third-party countermeasures. Potential conflict with the WTO dispute settlement raises another legal challenge. The primary goal of this chapter is therefore to contribute to the legal debate on this challenging and multidimensional topic by explaining the main features of the mechanism and pointing to several legal challenges, namely from the perspective of the rules on state responsibility and WTO law.

Keywords

anti-coercion instrument – EU strategic autonomy – economic coercion – countermeasures – WTO dispute settlement

1 Petr Stejskal, Palacký University Olomouc, Faculty of Law, Centre for International Humanitarian and Operational Law (petr.stejskal@upol.cz).

 | DOI:10.1163/9789004700659_009

1 Introduction

The European Union (EU) gradually developed into a regional international organization (RIO) that is a key actor in international relations and trade. The rule of law, a functioning internal market and large global market share are among the essential foundations for its global position. But the EU and its Member States have also become the target of deliberate economic coercion in recent years, as a response to their political or economic actions. One of the most well-known examples concerns China's strong reaction to the decision of Lithuania to allow Taiwan to open Taiwan's Representative Office in Vilnius (using the word 'Taiwan' instead of 'Taipei'). To exert pressure on Lithuania to change its decision, China stopped imports from the country. But China took also further steps to exert economic pressure on Lithuania and pressured international companies (for example, the German company *Continental*) trading with China by rejecting products containing components produced by Lithuanian companies. These measures allegedly affected public opinion in Lithuania and also led to indirect political pressure from within the EU Member States.[2] The threat of economic coercion however also came from the West, with the Trump Administration imposing duties on imports of aluminium and steel and threatening further tariffs on the EU car imports into the US in 2018.[3] Even though Chinese pressure on Lithuania is often mentioned as a cause for adopting the Anti-Coercion Instrument (ACI),[4] the threat of coercion from the US under the Trump administration is in fact considered to be the actual reason for the development of a deterrence tool on the part of the

2 Matthew Reynolds and Matthew P. Goodman, 'China's Economic Coercion: Lessons from Lithuania' (*CSIS*, 6 May 2022) <https://www.csis.org/analysis/chinas-economic-coercion-lessons-lithuania> Accessed 1 October 2023. For a case-study of China's use of economic coercion, see Peter Harrell, Elizabeth Rosenberg and Edoardo Saravalle, 'China's Use of Coercive Economic Measures' (*Centre for a New American Security*, 11 June 2018) <https://www.cnas.org/publications/reports/chinas-use-of-coercive-economic-measures> accessed 31 October 2023.

3 See inter alia, David Savage, 'The fall and partial rise of US-EU trading relations' (*BDO Global*, January 2022) <https://www.bdo.global/en-gb/microsites/tax-newsletters/indirect-tax-news/issue-1-2022/international-the-fall-and-partial-rise-of-us-eu-trading-relations> accessed 24 March 2024.

4 Anh Nguyen, 'Questioning the EU Anti-coercion Instrument – Conflating the Curtailment of 'Strategic Autonomy' with the Erosion of Sovereignty?' (*EJIL:Talk!*, 10 October 2023) <https://www.ejiltalk.org/questioning-the-eu-anti-coercion-instrument-conflating-the-curtailment-of-strategic-autonomy-with-the-erosion-of-sovereignty/> accessed 11 October 2023.

EU, Chinese pressure against Lithuania simply adding further justification.[5] In fact, today's interconnected global economy increases the risk of economic coercion, as it provides countries with enhanced means for such coercion.[6]

The above-mentioned examples of coercive measures[7] should be viewed in the wider context of something that can be described as geoeconomic fragmentation, polarization of international relations and increasing inability of multilateral mechanisms to prevent negative global spillovers from unilateral actions.[8] In response to this, in December 2021, the European Commission introduced its proposal for an anti-coercion instrument to deter and counter the use of economic coercion against the EU or its Member States. In June 2023, after intensive discussions (and after reaching a provisional political agreement on key principles already in March 2023),[9] the European Parliament and the Council reached a final political agreement on the proposed instrument. Throughout the process, the main outstanding issues have been resolved, relating to the role of the Council in determining whether the EU or a Member State is a target of economic coercion, resulting in several changes

5 For more precise details on motivations for developing and negotiating the ACI, see Christian Freudlsperger and Sophie Meunier, 'When Foreign Policy Becomes Trade Policy: The EU's Anti-coercion Instrument' (2024) 62(1) Journal of Common Market Studies 1–17, 13. Among other things, interesting is the fact that the Chinese pressure on Lithuania was not the trigger for the idea of having ACI, but rather another justification to the process that had already started. In their empirical analysis, the authors point to the fact that idea to develop such a mechanism was rather a reaction to political pressure from the US government under the Trump administration. They refer to the sanctions adopted by the US Congress against companies involved in the Nord Stream 2 construction, extraterritorial sanctions against companies conducting business with Iran after the withdrawal of the US from the Joint Comprehensive Plan of Action (known as the Iran nuclear deal) or threats to introduce tariffs on French goods on the basis of the Section 301 of the 1974 US Trade Act.

6 Regulation (EU) 2023/2675 of the European Parliament and of the Council of 22 November 2023 on the protection of the Union and its Member States from economic coercion by third countries [2023] OJ L *2023/2675* recital 6.

7 For other examples of economic coercion, see 'The EU Anti Economic Coercion Regulation: A New Addition to the EU's Toolbox' (*Herbert Smith Freehills*, 14 July 2023) <https://www.herbertsmithfreehills.com/insights/2023-07/the-eu-anti-economic-coercion-regulation-a-new-addition-to-the-eus-toolbox> accessed 12 August 2023.

8 'Geoeconomic Fragmentation and the Future of Multilateralism (Staff Discussion Note, SDN/ 2023/001)' (*International Monetary Fund*, January 2023) <https://www.imf.org/-/media/Files/Publications/sdn/2023/English/sdnEA2023001.ashx> accessed 1 October 2023.

9 'Trade: political agreement on the anti-coercion instrument' (*European Commission*, 28 March 2023) <https://www.consilium.europa.eu/en/press/press-releases/2023/03/28/trade-political-agreement-on-the-anti-coercion-instrument/> accessed 11 January 2024.

to the text[10] from the original ACI proposal.[11] The final act was signed on 22 November 2023 as Regulation (EU) 2023/2675 of the European Parliament and of the Council of 22 November 2023 on the protection of the Union and its Member States from economic coercion by third countries (Regulation).[12] What should be pointed out already at this place is that the EU explicitly formulated the desire to 'contribute to the creation, development and clarification of international frameworks for the prevention and elimination of situations of economic coercion'.[13] This chapter will study how exactly the ACI can contribute to this goal.

The ACI is viewed by some authors as a doctrinal and policy shift in the EU trade and investment policy[14] or as controversial geoeconomic instrument.[15] But this new instrument should also be viewed in the context of the wider issue of *securitization* of the EU commercial policy, as one of several examples of the framework for measures affecting trade and investment. The ACI is part of the Economic Security Strategy of the EU that was introduced in June 2023.[16] The wider toolbox (if we may conceptualize the following mechanisms in such a way) consists of several instruments which vary in terms of their legal basis, purpose and design, institutional setting or implementation. Foreign investment screening regulation should be mentioned as part of that toolbox, as it

10 The changes are visible in the compromise text of the Proposal for a Regulation of the European Parliament and of the Council on the protection of the Union and its Member States from economic coercion by third countries, 2021/0406 (COD) from June 2023, available at <https://www.europarl.europa.eu/RegData/commissions/inta/lcag/2023/06-19/INTA_LA(2023)003909_EN.pdf>.

11 'Press Release: Political agreement on new Anti-Coercion Instrument to better defend EU interests on global stage' (*European Commission*, 6 June 2023) <https://ec.europa.eu/commission/presscorner/detail/%20en/ip_23_3046> accessed 1 July 2023.

12 Regulation (EU) 2023/2675 of the European Parliament and of the Council of 22 November 2023 on the protection of the Union and its Member States from economic coercion by third countries [2023] OJ L, 2023/2675.

13 Ibid., recital 6.

14 See, for example, Thomas Verellen and Alexandra Hofer, 'The Unilateral Turn in EU Trade and Investment Policy' (2023) 28 European Foreign Affairs Review 1.

15 Freudlsperger, Meunier (n 5) 1–2.

16 The proposed strategy sets out a common framework for achieving economic security by promoting the EU's economic base and competitiveness and protecting against risks, among other things. The idea is to develop an approach to minimise risks arising from certain economic flows in the context of increased geopolitical tensions and accelerated technological shifts, while preserving maximum levels of economic openness and dynamism interests. See 'Press Release: An EU approach to enhance economic security' (*European Commission*, 20 June 2023) <https://ec.europa.eu/commission/presscorner/detail/en/IP_23_3358> accessed 12 January 2024.

represents an important tool that the EU Member States can utilise to protect their national, as well as European internal market.[17] In February 2024, the Commission proposed ideas to further strengthen the foreign investment screening mechanism.[18] Interestingly, together with strengthening the existing foreign investment screening regulation, the EU is now also considering a mechanism for screening of outward investments which could apply to dual-use items or sensitive and emerging technologies (such as quantum, advanced semiconductors or AI).[19] Also the Foreign Subsidies Regulation from 2022 or the International Procurement Instrument from 2022 are examples of the newer tools of the EU.[20] Another tool that the EU has in its toolbox is the EU blocking Statute for protection of the EU operators against extraterritorial application of third-country measures.[21] In the wider context of the EU security and autonomy toolbox, sanctions (restrictive measures) could also be mentioned as an important tool as they are used to protect the interests of the EU and its (or international) security. The EU utilises this tool extensively, which

17 Even though this tool is not entirely in the hands of the EU as it is up to the Member States to adopt and adjust their national investment screening mechanism. See Regulation (EU) 2019/452 of the European Parliament and of the Council of 19 March 2019 establishing a framework for the screening of foreign direct investments into the Union [2019] OJ L 79 I/1.

18 See, for example, Jana K. Dammann de Chapto, Philipp Studt and Nicolas Andreas Jung, 'Proposal to Revise EU FDI Screening Regulation – Revolution or Gradual Evolution?' (*Lexology*, 5 March 2024) <https://www.lexology.com/library/detail.aspx?g=aaac861c-c3d0-410c-ae6d-a0218ceb5f93> accessed 28 March 2024.

19 In January 2024, the European Commission released a White Paper on 'Outbound Investments', mapping the policy initiatives that the Commission takes in the field of outbound investments. See Commission, 'White Paper on Outbound Investments' [2024] COM (2024) 24 final. See also, 'EU seeks new controls on outbound investment as security fears mount' (*Herbert Smith Freehills*, 3 August 2023) <https://www.herbertsmithfreehills.com/insights/2023-08/eu-seeks-new-controls-on-outbound-investment-as-security-fears-mount> accessed 28 March 2024.

20 Regulation (EU) 2022/2560 of the European Parliament and of the Council of 14 December 2022 on foreign subsidies distorting the internal market [2022] OJ L 330; Regulation (EU) 2022/1031 of the European Parliament and of the Council of 23 June 2022 on the access of third-country economic operators, goods and services to the Union's public procurement and concession markets and procedures supporting negotiations on access of Union economic operators, goods and services to the public procurement and concession markets of third countries (International Procurement Instrument – IPI) [2022] OJ L 17.

21 Council Regulation (EC) No 2271/96 of 22 November 1996 protecting against the effects of the extra-territorial application of legislation adopted by a third country, and actions based thereon or resulting therefrom [1996] OJ L 309.

is now visible especially in light of the Russian aggression against Ukraine.[22] Apart from these and other legal tools that the EU has at its disposal, we have recently witnessed the birth of a completely new agenda – the so-called Anti-Coercion Instrument.

On the basis of explication of its main features and related legal challenges, this chapter will explain how the practice of the application of the ACI may eventually serve as another avenue through which the EU as a RIO can contribute to the interpretation or development of rules of international law. The ways in which RIOs can contribute to the development of public international law have been ascertained by several experts and demonstrated in various fields. For example, in its report from 2024, the International Law Association's Study Group *The International Law of Regional Organizations* discussed various ways in which RIOs help to identify international law or be the source of the practice impacting the development of customary international law.[23] The ACI is still a new mechanism and it remains to be seen how frequently it will be used. However, given its distinct features which can be even characterised as legal challenges, the utilization of the ACI in practice can in fact provide the opportunity for the EU to either clarify or develop some key concepts of international law. It is probably safe to claim already now that intensity of such contribution will not reach the level which can be seen in RIOs' contribution to the development of international human rights standards, to mention a striking example. But still, the ACI's potential not only to defend the EU against coercion but also to elucidate or develop concepts of public international law is relevant because this eventual secondary effect pertains to some long-lasting issues of international law.

In particular, the ACI enables the EU to adopt various measures as a reaction to identified coercion interfering in the legitimate sovereign choices of the EU or of its Member States. The instrument is primarily designed to deter coercive actions and provides for dialogue and negotiation before having recourse to, as the last resort, response measures. The list of possible response measures prescribes various restrictions related to trade and investments (such as import tariffs, restrictions in trade or public procurement measures,

---

22 'EU adopts 14th package of sanctions against Russia for its continued illegal war against Ukraine, strengthening enforcement and anti-circumvention measures' (*European Commission*, 24 June 2024) <https://ec.europa.eu/commission/presscorner/detail/en/ip_24_3423> accessed 2 August 2024.

23 The International Law Association 'ATHENS CONFERENCE (2024). The International Law of Regional Organizations. Final Report' (*ILA*, 2024) <https://www.ila-hq.org/en_GB/documents/ila-study-group-regional-organisations-final-report-may-24> accessed 21 September 2024, at 40–44.

to name but a few). Response measures can also be adopted as measures which apply to certain natural or legal persons which engage or might engage in activities falling under Article 207 of the Treaty of the Functioning of the EU (TFEU) and which are connected to the government of a third country.[24] As response measures can take the form of non-performance of international obligations in various aspects of trade and investment relations, specific features of the mechanism raise some legal questions. Firstly, the ACI brings about a wide definition of economic coercion and also refers to customary international law and the non-intervention rule (as it will be explained in Section 2). In cases of economic coercion that can be qualified as an international wrongful act, the EU can adopt response measures in the form of non-performance of international obligations. However, in international law, it is not settled under which conditions economic coercion can amount to a breach of customary international law. Secondly, as the mechanism is currently drafted, it seems that response measures in the form of non-performance of international obligations could be adopted by the EU in situations where only one or a few Member States face coercion. When the EU affects *its* international obligations towards a coercing State that exerted coercion affecting international obligations owed *only* to a *Member State*, this raises the question of conformity with the rules on responsibility and the issue of the so-called third-party countermeasures.[25] The issue is even more interesting due to the fact that the ACI envisages qualified majority in the decision making of the Council, in contrast to the restrictive measures adopted in the scheme of the common foreign and security policy which are based on unanimity. Finally, WTO rules, especially the WTO Dispute Settlement Mechanism (WTO DSM), raise another legal challenge should the ACI be used to combat economic coercion in the area of international trade. This is especially the case when the coercion induced against the EU or its Member State would run contrary to WTO-based rules and the EU adopted response measures without utilising the WTO DSM.

Therefore, the primary goal of this chapter is to contribute, by legal analysis conducted from an international law perspective, to the nascent debate on the challenging and multidimensional topic which covers aspects of international law, European law and political science. The chapter starts by explaining the functioning and institutional setting of the ACI, highlighting pertinent legal issues. The first issue addressed is the definition of economic coercion and its

24 Article 8 (3) letter b) of the Regulation.

25 Countermeasures adopted by a State or international organization that is not directly injured by the internationally wrongful act they respond to.

qualification as an internationally wrongful act. Then, this chapter addresses the availability of the EU response measures in the form of countermeasures in situations where only one or a few Members States face coercion constituting an internationally wrongful act. Finally, the chapter provides an overview of the debate concerning consistency of the ACI with the WTO DSM. Notably, in relation to the issue of what forms of economic coercion run contrary to public international law, this chapter also claims that the application of the ACI may eventually serve as another avenue through which the EU as RIO contributes to the interpretation or development of the rules of international law by producing relevant practice.

2 Design and Institutional Setting of the Anti-coercion Instrument

The Regulation laying down rules and procedures concerning the ACI is part of the EU common commercial policy (CCP), pursuant to Article 207 (2) TFEU. It consists of a recital (preamble), 20 articles and two annexes. The ACI aims to ensure effective protection of interests of the EU and its Member States in situations where a third country (or another subject of international law other than the EU or a Member State, 'third country') seeks to coerce the EU or a Member State into adopting or refraining from adopting a particular act. It also builds on the fact that Member States, acting on their own, cannot counteract economic coercion by third countries through measures falling within the area of CCP as this area falls into the exclusive competence of the EU (para 10 of the recital). At the same time, it is repeatedly stipulated in the text of the Regulation that any action shall be consistent with international law. This includes not only customary international law, but also the Agreement establishing the WTO as a cornerstone of the rules-based multilateral trading system.[26]

Interestingly, the ACI brings its own definition of economic coercion, a term which is the cornerstone of the whole mechanism as it determines its scope of application. In Article 2, economic coercion is defined as an interference in the legitimate sovereign choices of the EU or a Member State by seeking to prevent or obtain the cessation, modification or adoption of a particular act by the EU or a Member State. Notably, the ACI applies to such coercion that is made through applying or threatening to apply measures affecting trade or investment. Article 2 (2) of the Regulation provides factors that

26 See Article 1 (2) and Recital 4 (referring to Article 21 (1) of the Treaty on European Union) and Recital 12 of the Regulation.

should be taken into account (by the Commission and the Council, as it will be described later) when determining the existence of such coercion. These factors include, among others, the intensity, severity, frequency, duration, breadth and magnitude of the coercion, actual impact on trade or investment relations, extent to which the coercive measure infringes upon the EU or Member States' sovereignty. What also needs to be considered is whether the third country is acting on the basis of a legitimate concern that is internationally recognised,[27] or whether and in what manner it, before the imposition or application of the coercive measures, made serious attempts, in good faith, to settle the matter through international coordination or adjudication. As it will be explained in the third part of this contribution, a major challenge is not necessarily to establish what conduct qualifies as coercion, but when economic coercion can be considered contrary to international law.

As regards the institutional setting, the ACI confers a strong position on the Commission. The Commission examines any third country measures and determines whether it meets the definition of coercion (both on its own initiative or upon substantiated request). If the Commission determines that third-country measures meet the threshold of coercion in accordance with Article 2, it submits a proposal to the Council for an implementing act determining the existence of economic coercion.[28] The Council may then adopt (also with the possibility to amend) the implementing act determining coercion by a qualified majority (Article 5). If the Council adopts the implementing act, the Commission then informs the third country and requests it to cease the economic coercion. The Commission also requests the third country to repair the injury incurred if that was previously determined by the Council in the implementing act (see Article 5 (2) and (10)). The Commission engages with the third country via direct negotiations, mediation, conciliation or good offices, or international adjudication, provided that the third country enters into consultations with the EU in good faith (Article 6).

The Commission shall adopt the so-called response measures where: (a) the engagement with the third country has not resulted in the cessation of the economic coercion (and in the reparation of the injury where requested), pro-

27 Such as, among other things, the maintenance of international peace and security, the protection of human rights, the protection of the environment, or the fight against climate change. Recital para 15 of the Regulation.

28 In the original proposal of the ACI, it was up to the Commission to determine whether a third-party action qualifies as coercion as defined in the Regulation. The final version, which includes the Council into the determination phase, reflects the will of Member States to keep some degree of control in application of the ACI.

vided that adoption of response measures is also (b) necessary to protect the interests and rights of the EU or Member States and (c) such measures are in the interest of the EU (Article 8). In contrast to the previous step (determination of coercion), the Commission adopts response measures without the Council vote. In this phase (after coercion has been determined), Member States can influence the adoption of response measures only through the (slightly modified) comitology process as response measures are adopted by means of implementing acts.[29] This means that it is much more difficult to bypass the act of the Commission. However, Article 18(2) of the Regulation slightly strengthens the position of Member States by modifying the committee procedure.[30] The European Parliament is *only* informed through the process. The ACI also envisages the process of amendment, suspension and termination of the EU response measures, obliging the Commission to keep under review the economic coercion that have triggered response measures, their effectiveness and their effects on the interests of the EU (Article 12).

With respect to the *teeth* of the ACI – the response measures that may be adopted to combat economic coercion – these can be adopted as (a) measures of general application (thus targeting the coercing country as a whole),[31] or (b) as measures which apply to certain natural or legal persons which are connected or linked to the government of the coercing country and which engage or might engage in activities covered by the EU CCP. Possible forms of response measures are listed in Annex I to the Regulation. These measures include imposition of new or increased customs duties, introduction of any additional charge on the importation or exportation of goods, introduction or increase

29 Article 8 (1) of the Regulation. See also Article 18 of the Regulation (referring to Regulation (EU) No 182/2011 of the European Parliament and of the Council of 16 February 2011 laying down the rules and general principles concerning mechanisms for control by Member States of the Commission's exercise of implementing powers [2011] OJ L 55). For a brief description of implementing acts, see, for example, 'Implementing and delegated acts European Commission.' (*European Commission*) <https://commission.europa.eu/law/law-making-process/adopting-eu-law/implementing-and-delegated-acts_en> accessed 28 February 2024. For more detailed analysis of implementing acts, see, for example, Gijs Jan Brandsma, 'Chapter 17: Delegated and implementing acts: rule-making by the Commission' in Gijs Jan Brandsma (ed.), *Handbook on European Union Public Administration* (Edward Elgar, 2024).

30 Where the Committee delivers no opinion, the Commission shall not adopt the draft implementing act. Where an implementing act is deemed to be necessary, the chair may either submit an amended version of that act to the same committee within 2 months of the vote or submit the draft implementing act within 1 month of the vote to the appeal committee for further deliberation. Article 18(2) of the Regulation.

31 Herbert Smith Freehills (n 7).

of restrictions on the importation or exportation of goods, restrictions on trade in goods made effective through measures applying to transiting goods, measures affecting the right to participate in public procurement, and measures affecting trade in services. Response measures can also include measures that affect the access of foreign direct investment to the Union, restrictions on the protection of intellectual property rights in relation to right-holders that are nationals of the third country concerned or imposition of restrictions for banking, insurance, access to Union capital markets and other financial service activities (for the remaining measures, see Annex I). Importantly, as the formulations in Annex I clearly state, these measures may amount, when necessary, to the non-performance of applicable international obligations.

Article 11 of the Regulation stipulates objective criteria for selecting and designing the EU response measures. They shall be proportionate and shall not exceed the level of injury to the EU, taking into account the gravity of the economic coercion, its economic impact on the EU or a Member State and the rights of the EU and its Member States. Notably, injury to the EU is defined by Article 3 (3) as a negative impact, including economic damage, on the Union or a Member State, including on Union economic operators. When selecting and designing an appropriate response measure, the Commission shall also take into account the effectiveness of the measure in inducing the cessation of economic coercion (and where requested, also the reparation of injury to the EU), avoidance or minimization of negative impacts on the EU actors, on the investment environment in the EU, including on employment and regional development policy, on economic growth or on other EU policies and objectives, among others. Limits of international law are mentioned again as Article 11 (2) letter h) includes in the list 'any other relevant criteria established in international law'. For response measures consisting of measures that affect the access of foreign direct investment to the EU or trade in services, Article 11 (4) prescribes some additional criteria.

3 Legal Issues

One of the distinct features of the ACI is the possibility for the EU to respond to economic coercion with measures in the form of non-performance of international obligations. The text of the Regulation itself qualifies these measures as 'countermeasures' within the meaning of customary international law.[32]

32 See para 7 recital of the Regulation. Understanding of response measures in a form of non-performance of international obligations as countermeasures is shared also by

These are allowed only when the economic coercion against the EU or Member States amounts to an internationally wrongful act (Article 8 (4)). This is indeed a reflection of one of the requirements of the law of international responsibility prescribed for resorting to countermeasures. The ACI stipulates several other substantive and procedural standards for adoption of the EU response measures that are very similar to the requirements for countermeasures as prescribed by the relevant rules on international responsibility.[33] However, some legal questions remain. They relate namely to the definition of economic coercion, conformity of response measures with the rules on international responsibility and also to the possible inconsistency with the WTO dispute settlement.

3.1 *Definition of Economic Coercion and Its Relationship to the Non-intervention Rule*

As described in the previous section, the ACI comes with its own definition of economic coercion in Article 2. The ACI evidently defines coercion without reference to the fact of whether or not the coercive act is unlawful.[34] But all the categories of response measures defined in Annex I may amount, when necessary, to the non-performance of applicable international obligations as regards any tariff concessions. This would, however, be possible only in situations of economic coercion that constitutes an internationally wrongful act, as recognized by Article 8 (4) of the Regulation. This may be the case if a third State breaches an international agreement concluded with the coerced Member State or the EU (such as a trade or investment agreement), or if it acts contrary to customary international law rules. Among the customary rules that can be violated by economic coercion belongs typically the prohibition of intervention in the internal affairs of States. But especially in the context of economic measures, it is a thorny issue of international law to determine what constitutes prohibited intervention. While it is not within the limited scope of this contribution to go into depth of the meaning of the non-intervention principle and the legality of economic coercion, it is necessary to at least provide some observations.

---

commentators. See, for example, Deepak Raju, 'Proposed EU Regulation to Address Third Country Coercion – What is Coercion?' (*EJIL:Talk!*, 6 January 2022) <https://www.ejiltalk.org/proposed-eu-regulation-to-address-third-country-coercion-what-is-coercion/> accessed 12 July 2023.

33 See Articles 7–10 of the Regulation.

34 Raju (n 32).

First, in international law, it has always been difficult to define the notion of economic coercion.[35] There have been some attempts to define *economic coercion* in regional treaties developed mainly by Latin American countries.[36] Thus, already the Charter of the Organization of American States in 1948 stipulated in its Article 19 that 'No State may use or encourage the use of coercive measures of an economic or political character in order to force the sovereign will of another State and obtain from it advantages of any kind.' However, this definition does not really help to better understand what measures of an economic character would reach the threshold of prohibited intervention. Quite notably, however, the recital to the Regulation provides its own definition as to what kind of coercion constitutes a wrongful act under international law. At para 15 it states that:

> [W]hen a country deploys measures such as trade or investment restrictions in order to obtain from another country an action or inaction which that country is not obliged to perform under international law and which falls within its sovereignty, and when the coercion reaches a certain qualitative or quantitative threshold, depending both on the objectives pursued and the means used.

This definition of *illegal economic coercion* seems to be rather vague and not very helpful in determining what actions constitute illegal economic coercion. Not every instance of economic coercion can be qualified as a breach of the non-intervention principle, as pointed out by several commentators.[37] To the contrary, some forms of coercion have always been a feature of international

---

35 UNGA, 'Economic Measures as a Means of Political and Economic Coercion against Developing Countries: Note by the Secretary-General' (15 October 1993) UN Doc. A/48/535, Agenda Item 91(a), at 1.

36 Barry E. Carter, 'Economic Coercion', *Max Planck Encyclopedias of International Law* (September 2009) <https://opil.ouplaw.com/display/10.1093/law:epil/9780199231690/law-9780199231690-e1518?prd=EPIL> accessed 1 September 2023, para 1. For an overview of the UN declarations and resolutions related to the attempts of States to condemn economic interference, see paras 6–8.

37 Omri Sender, 'Economic Coercion', *Max Planck Encyclopedias of International Law* (November 2021) <https://opil.ouplaw.com/display/10.1093/law:epil/9780199231690/law-9780199231690-e1749?rskey=fpJKgW&result=1&prd=EPIL> accessed 1 September 2023, para 18; Raju (n 32); Freya Baetens and Marco Bronckers, 'The EU's Anti-Coercion Instrument: A Big Stick for Big targets' (*EJIL:Talk!*, 19 January 2022) <https://www.ejiltalk.org/the-eus-anti-coercion-instrument-a-big-stick-for-big-targets/> accessed 12 July 2023; Nguyen (n 4); Maziar Jamnejad and Michael Wood, 'The Principle of Non-intervention' (2009) 22 Leiden *Journal of International Law* 2, at 369–372.

relations, even between friendly States.[38] Quite notably, the International Court of Justice in its 1986 Judgement in the *Nicaragua Case* did not find the actions of the United States relating to reduction of sugar quotas and comprehensive trade embargo as a breach of the customary law principle of non-intervention.[39] There has also been an ongoing debate in the doctrine on which economic measures can amount to coercion.[40] Therefore, the Commission and the Council have to be careful in qualifying economic coercion (in order to be able to adopt response measures in the form of non-performance of international obligations) as contrary to customary international law.[41] For example, it can be argued in particular situation that a total economic embargo which in the scenario analysed by the ICJ in the *Nicaragua Case* was not considered a breach of the non-intervention principle can amount to its breach in different scenarios, for example, due to a higher degree of interconnectedness of the concerned economics. As it has been aptly pointed out by Jamnejad and Wood, 'What the ICJ appears to be saying in Nicaragua is that the particular acts at issue in the case did not amount to intervention, which is not to say that they could not in another scenario.' What needs to be analysed in a particular case is whether the sovereign will of the target State could be overcome by the coercive measures at hand.[42]

However, it is claimed here that in this very specific aspect, that is the qualification of economic coercion as legal or illegal, the ACI can serve as an avenue through which the EU as RIO can contribute to the interpretation or development of the rules of international law. As mentioned, there is some degree of unclarity as to when economic coercion can amount to the breach of the non-intervention rule. The practice of the EU in examining coercive measures of third countries and determining whether they constitute a breach of customary international law (allowing the EU to adopt response measures in the form of non-performance of international obligations) can

38 Ibid.

39 Case Concerning Military and Paramilitary Activities in and against Nicaragua (Nicaragua v USA) (Merits) [1986] ICJ Rep 14, para 245.

40 See footnotes 36 and 37 or also some older literature, such as Joyner C. Christopher, 'The Transnational Boycott as Economic Coercion in International Law: Policy, Place and Practice' (1984) 17 *Vanderbilt Journal of International Law* 205.

41 The situation may, in terms of legal clarity, be easier where the actions of economic coercion are contrary to the treaty obligations owed by the coercing State towards the EU or a Member State. But other issues may arise with certain agreements, especially those containing dispute settlement clauses/mechanisms, most notably the WTO agreements, as will be commented on below.

42 Jamnejad and Michael Wood (n 37) 370–371.

constitute practice relevant to understanding or even developing the customary notion of the non-intervention principle. There is indeed growing support for the view that the practice of RIOs may be relevant to the identification or development of customary international law. In this regard, reference could be made to the Draft conclusions on identification of customary international law, adopted by the International Law Commission in 2018. In Conclusion 4(2), it stipulates that 'In certain cases, the practice of international organizations also contributes to the formation, or expression, of rules of customary international law.'[43] In the Commentary to this Conclusion, the Special Rapporteur specifies that this concerns an external practice, involving the relationship of an organization with third States or organizations. The ACI is by its nature exactly this. The Commentary to Conclusion 4 further specifies that relevant practice of international organizations arises mostly where Member States transferred exclusive competences to it. Notably, the Commentary mentions the EU as an example.[44] Especially relevant is the practice of international organizations where they act as independent actors in international law and not merely vehicles of Member States (platforms where organizations only facilitate action of its Member States). And this is the practice to which Conclusion 4(2) applies.[45] In other words, RIOs can provide relevant practice and thus impact on the identification or development of customary international law in two ways: as platform for practice of States or through their own practice, by conduct that is attributable to the organization as such.[46] When one looks again into the institutional setting of the ACI, it could be argued that the EU actually works in both ways here as the Commission (representing the will of the EU as a separate entity) and the Council (representing namely the interests of Member States) are involved in the process of determination of economic coercion. Moreover, after coercion was determined, it is the Commission that then adopts response measures, without the Council vote. Therefore, it is arguable that should there be practice of application of the ACI in future, this practice could be considered relevant for the ascertainment of the contours of the non-intervention principle in the context of economic coercion. However, it

43 Draft conclusions on identification of customary international law, with commentaries (2018) YBILC 2018, vol II, pt 2.

44 Ibid., Commentary to Conclusions 4, para 6.

45 Ibid., para 4. For detailed discussion, see also Jed Odermatt, 'The Development of Customary International Law by International Organizations' (2017) 66 ICLQ 498, 499–503.

46 Fernando Lusa Bordin and Jed Odermatt, 'International Law of Regional Organizations: A Comparative Perspective' (2024) 21 *International Organizations Law Review* 19, 36–38.

remains to be seen whether there will be sufficient practice and experience with the application of the ACI.[47]

Finally, in addition to the legal question of what forms of economic coercion qualify as internationally wrongful acts, there is another related yet different legal issue. Is it at all possible to claim that the prohibition of intervention into internal affairs of States applies also to international organizations, or even to regional ones, such as the EU? The sources addressing the concept of the non-intervention principle often refer to the *domaine reservé*,[48] sovereignty of States,[49] sovereign rights or domestic jurisdiction of States.[50] If non-intervention is mentioned in the context of international organizations, it is usually done in the opposite context – to limit the powers of international organizations to interfere in the internal affairs of Member States.[51] However, doctrinal sources and case-law seem to be silent on the question whether an international organization can be also the target of a violation of the non-intervention rule.[52] However, in the very specific context of the EU, a considerable portion of sovereign powers of its Member States has been delegated to the EU. One could argue that where States delegated sovereign powers to the EU, interference with these powers (albeit while they are exercised by the EU) could be viewed as interference with sovereign choices of Member States. This could be some form of regional shift in the understanding of the rule as applying also to RIOs in certain circumstances. What could also play a role in determining whether international organizations can benefit from the non-intervention rule is the distinction between the subjective and objective personality of international organizations.[53] But the eventual *mere* subjective

47 For more detailed analysis and examples of how RIOs can contribute to the process of interpretation and development of customary international law, see section 4.2 at Teresa Cabrita, 'The integration paradox: an ILC view on the EU contribution to the codification and development of rules of general international law' (2021) 5(1) Europe and the World: A Law Review; or Bordin and Odermatt (n 46).

48 Helal S Mohamed, 'On Coercion in International Law' (2019) 52 *NYU Journal of International Law and Politics* 1.

49 Case Concerning Military and Paramilitary Activities in and against Nicaragua (Nicaragua v USA) (Merits) [1986] ICJ Rep 14, para 205.

50 UNGA Res 2625 (XXV) (24 October 1970).

51 See Charter of the United Nations (adopted 26 June 1945, entered into force 24 October 1945) XV UNCIO 335 (UN Charter), Article 2(7); Articles of Agreement of the International Bank for Reconstruction and Development (adopted 22 July 1944, entered into force 27 December 1945, as amended 16 February 1989), Article IV, sec 10.

52 As far as the author of this contribution is aware at this stage of research.

53 *Reparations for Injuries Suffered in the Service of the United Nations* (Advisory Opinion) [1949] ICJ Rep 174, 15. This distinction concerns the determination whether a particular

personality of the EU does not seem to be an issue in situations where there exist international commitments between the EU and a third State (otherwise there are no obligations in the sense of Annex 1 which are about to be impaired by the ACI response measures). Adoption of the ACI in its current form and mainly its eventual application to situations where coercion interferes *only* with the powers of the EU could be understood as the proof or the *opinion juris* of the EU Member States on accepting the applicability of non-intervention principle also to RIOs.

3.2 *Law of International Responsibility: Permissibility of Countermeasures*

As already mentioned, the ACI also envisages measures that could by qualified as countermeasures under international law as they are in substance contrary to international obligations ('non-performance of applicable international obligations' references in Annex I to the Regulation). However, as the wording of the Regulation is drafted, it seems that response measures could be adopted by the EU as a whole in situations where only one or a few Members States are the target of coercion. This raises the question of the so-called third-party countermeasures. The principal question to analyse is which obligations would be affected by response measures. In accordance with the principle of delegation of powers, the EU would most probably be allowed to adopt response measures that affect only its own obligations (as a distinct legal person acting in its name) towards the coercing State.[54] But a key legal problem may arise when the EU utilises response measures in the form of non-performance of *its* international obligations towards a coercing State in a situation where the latter induced coercion *only* against one or more Member States, or better said, where the coercion impaired international obligations owed to one or more Member States and not the EU. At the same time, if the EU adopts response measures in the form of countermeasures against a third State, also directly non-injured (in terms of rules on international responsibility) EU Member States would have to abide by the adopted EU response measures against the coercing State (depending on the exact formulation of the implementing act). The issue is even more delicate as the ACI envisages qualified majority in the decision making of the Council.

international organization possesses personality only towards its Member States and those third States that recognized it, or whether personality is objective and extends towards the whole international community.

54 The reading of Annex 1 to the Regulation also supports this view as obligations not to be performed as part of a response measure relate to areas where the EU has a competence.

Prima facie, such a situation does not seem to be completely unlikely as Article 3 (3) of the Regulation stipulates that economic damage caused to a Member State by coercion qualifies as injury to the EU. Relevant is also Article 2 (1) of the Regulation that includes in the definition of economic coercion triggering the application of the ACI also interferences into sovereign choices of Member States and not only of the EU. At the same time, the language of the Regulation seems to indicate that where it refers to non-performance of international obligations towards the coercing State, it refers to the obligations of the EU itself and not to obligations owed to the third country by Members States.[55]

It is claimed here that the EU would not be entitled to adopt response measures in the form of non-performance of its international obligations towards the coercing State where there is no obligation owed to the EU itself that was breached by the coercing State (a treaty or non-intervention rule should the latter apply also to RIOs). Illegality of response measures of this nature could not be precluded under the rules on international responsibility as it is only the injured party (a party to whom the breached obligations were owed) that is entitled to invoke countermeasures against the wrongdoer. As indicated by the International Law Commission, the effect of countermeasures in precluding wrongfulness is relative. It concerns the legal relations between the injured State and the responsible State.[56] That a directly non-injured party (in terms of international obligations that are breached) is allowed to engage in countermeasures against a wrongdoer is claimed in context of breaches of obligations of *erga omnes* character, such as the prohibition of aggression (a pertinent example are countermeasures invoked by the EU and several States against Russia in the context of the war in Ukraine). But even in these instances, the views on the legality of the third-party countermeasures are not uniform.[57] At the same time, it is hard to imagine in which

55 See inter alia, recital 13 of the Regulation: 'Union response measures could consist, as necessary, not only in measures consistent with the Union's international obligations, but also in the non-performance of international obligations towards the third country concerned.' See also the wording of Article 8(4) Regulation, making no reference to obligations owed to the third country by Member States.

56 Draft Articles on Responsibility of States for Internationally Wrongful Acts, with commentaries (2001) YBILC 2001, vol II, pt 2, commentary to Article 49, para 4.

57 The issue is complexly addressed in Martin Davidowicz, *Third-Party Countermeasures in International Law* (Cambridge University Press, 2017); one may refer to the Draft articles on the responsibility of international organizations from 2011, but to the author view, these do not offer any specific guidance in relation to permissibility of third-party countermeasures. See inter alia the 'no prejudice' character of Article 57.

scenario economic coercion would amount to a breach of peremptory norms. To the contrary, it may not be clear in a particular case whether economic coercion is illegal at all. For these reasons, if economic coercion is qualified as an internationally wrongful act *only* against a Member State and the EU responds with measures in the form of non-performance of obligations the EU or other (non-injured) Member States owe to the coercing State, it is difficult to qualify these measures as permissible countermeasures under international law. This is a legal limitation the Commission should be aware of in the phase of adoption of response measures.

The distinction between the wrongdoer, the injured party and the legal relationship that can be targeted by response measures is not clear from the text of the Regulation. To the contrary, equalling injury to the Member State or to EU economic operators with the injury to the EU in Article 3 (3) of the Regulation makes the distinction perhaps even more blurred. This poses a risk that response measures adopted by the EU may qualify as impermissible third-country countermeasures under international law. But it is the practice that will show how (and if at all) response measures of the ACI will be applied. One way could be that response measures will be adopted only in situations of economic coercion that affect obligations owed to the EU (trade or investment agreements). It may be difficult for Member States acting on their own to respond to third countries' economic coercion through measures falling under the area of CCP, as the recital to the Regulation acknowledges (para 8). And this is where the ACI could fill the gap and help the EU to better balance the institutional (and to certain extent regional) disadvantage of 'uneven competence base and the lack of an institutionalised interplay between the independent (rather than interdependent) domains of common commercial policy and common foreign and security policy' which its competitors in the geopolitical field acting as individual States do not suffer from.[58] But the consistency of the EU response measures will require careful navigation through and distinction of duty bearers and injured parties in each particular case.

One could argue that the contribution of the EU as a RIO to the development of international law through the ACI could also be identified here, in the field of the law of international responsibility. In particular, it could inform the analysis of relevant practice concerning the legality of third-party counter-

58 Freudlsperger and Meunier (n 5) 4–5.

measures.[59] However, this does not seem to be likely in the case of the ACI. The (contested) permissibility of third-party countermeasures is discussed in the context of breaches of rules of *erga omnes* character (and seems to be out of the discussion in relation to the breaches of dispositive rules).[60] Therefore, to represent relevant practice, response measures in the form of countermeasures would probably have to respond to such economic coercion that would amount to a breach of rules of *erga omnes* character. Should that be the case, the ACI would again represent a source of development of international law through the practice of the EU as a RIO. But this specific situation seems to be rather unlikely in the domain of measures affecting trade and investment, to which the ACI applies. Therefore, it seems that the ACI will not contribute as relevant practice here. To the contrary, if applied wrongly, ACI can rather contribute to the fragmentation of international law. Moreover, when it comes to countermeasures adopted by the EU in the domain of the common foreign and security policy, the EU is already providing quite extensive practice when one looks at the sanction regimes it has adopted in previous years.[61]

To summarize, the text of the Regulation, at least as the author of this contribution reads it, does not offer a sufficient degree of guidance or clarification on the compatibility of the EU response measures in the form of non-performance of international obligations with the rules on responsibility of States and international organization. What the text of the Regulation (and the EU primary law) does provide is a general reference to consistency with international law.[62] However, this general reference might be sufficient if adhered to strictly in the process of application of the ACI. This would mean that the above-mentioned considerations as to the nature of economic coercion and as to the bearers of the international obligations (that are to be disrupted

59 See, for example, Johannes Schäffer, 'The EU Anti-Coercion Instrument: Anti-What, Exactly?' (*CELIS*, 19 February 2024) <https://www.celis.institute/celis-blog/the-eu-anti-coercion-instrument-anti-what-exactly/> accessed 11 September 2024.

60 Based primarily on the argument that by breaching such norm, the wrongdoer legally injures the whole international community. For detailed analysis on the topic of third-party countermeasures, see Davidowicz (n 57) who at p. 283 concludes that 'there is considerable support for the conclusion that third-party countermeasures are permissible under international law' and confirms on p. 284 that 'third-party countermeasures have developed as a *sui generis* form of invocation of State responsibility limited to serious breaches of obligations *erga omnes* (*partes*).'

61 This applies not only to the issue of third-party countermeasures, but newly also to the issue of extraterritorial/secondary sanctions. See Nina M. Hart, 'European sovereignty and development of the international legal order: The EU's economic security and Anti-Coercion Instrument' (2024) 13(1) *Cambridge International Law Journal* 83–102, 100.

62 Recital, paras 2, 4, 5 and Article 1 (3) of the Regulation.

by response measures) must be carefully considered in each case. The Commission should be aware that the EU cannot simply disrupt its own obligations owed to the coercing State in cases where an internationally wrongful act is committed only against one or several Member States. Response measures in the form of non-performance of international obligations of the EU can be adopted only when economic coercion in a particular case is contrary to international obligations owed to the EU itself (be it treaty obligations or customary international law if we agree that the EU as an international organization can also benefit from the non-intervention principle). These measures will not be available in scenarios where economic coercion constitutes violation of international obligations owed *only* to the injured Member State and not to the EU itself.

3.3 *Possible Inconsistency with the WTO Law*

Concerns have also been raised that the ACI could contravene rules of the WTO regime, in particular the WTO DSM (the fact that ACI-based countermeasures are adopted in response to economic coercion contravening WTO substantive standards) but also substantive rules of the individual WTO agreements (which could be impaired by the very own ACI response measures).[63] The issue of the possible contradiction of the ACI and the WTO rules has already been thoroughly analysed elsewhere.[64] However, only a few remarks will be made, namely in relation to the WTO DSM. The question of consistency of the ACI response measures with the WTO law is quite relevant. The WTO agreements seem to be the area of international law to be typically concerned with cases of economic coercion, as demonstrated by practice of States in recent years and also due to the high threshold for meeting (and thus breaching) a customary-based definition of non-intervention rule.[65]

63 See, for example, Cornelia Furculita, 'The Anti-Coercion Instrument. Is the EU Renouncing its 'Multilateralist' DNA?' (2024) Brexit Institute Working Paper Series No 04/2024 <https://papers.ssrn.com/sol3/papers.cfm?abstract_id=4699366> accessed 21 March 2024, referring at p. 4 to GATT 1994 Art. I, XI and XIII.

64 See, for example, Kornel Olsthoorn, 'The EU's Anti-coercion Instrument: A Return of Unlawful Unilateral Trade Countermeasures in Disguise?' (2024) 51 Legal Issues of Economic Integration 47, 67–83 and Furculita (n 63), both addressing the ACI from the point of view of the WTO DSU as well as the WTO substantive rules and the WTO-based defences. More generally, for an overview of scholarly views on applicability of countermeasures in the context of the WTO disputes, see Chien-Huei Wu, 'The EU's Proposed Anti-coercion Instrument: Legality and Effectiveness' (2023) 57 Journal of World Trade 297. See also Nina M. Hart (n 61) 90–97.

65 Investment agreements theoretically represent another area of treaty-based obligations that can be impaired by economic coercion.

Article 23.1 of the WTO Dispute Settlement Understanding (DSU)[66] obliges members to have recourse to and abide by the rules and procedures of the DSU when they seek to redress a violation of obligations or other nullifications or impairment of benefits under the covered agreements, or an impediment to the attainment of any objective of the covered agreements. In these situations, the WTO DSM should be used in exclusion to the customary rules on countermeasures.[67] However, when it comes to the trigger for the ACI, economic coercion by a third State would typically be exemplified through trade restrictions governed by the WTO agreements.[68] The ACI indeed defines coercion quite broadly; Article 2 (1) of the Regulation even prescribes an effect on trade or investment as a compulsory element of the definition of coercion.[69] Is it then possible to fully utilise the ACI in situations where economic coercion affects the WTO-based substantive rules? Does the ACI enable the EU to unilaterally suspend concessions without a decision of the WTO Dispute Settlement Body?

The problem is that the text of the Regulation does not clarify the relationship between the WTO rules and the application of response measures that may take the form of countermeasures.[70] It only stipulates that:

> [T]he Agreement establishing the World Trade Organization (WTO) is the cornerstone of the rules-based multilateral trading system. Therefore, it is important that the Union continue to support that system, with the WTO at its core, and to use its dispute settlement system where appropriate.[71]

The Impact Assessment Report on the ACI prepared by the Commission seeks to address this issue to a certain extent.[72] It points to the fact that there can be

66 Understanding on Rules and Procedures Governing the Settlement of Disputes, Annex 2 to the Agreement Establishing the World Trade Organization (1994).

67 Furculita (n 63) 4.

68 Wu (n 64).

69 Olsthoorn (n 64) 67–68.

70 Furculita (n 63) 4.

71 Recital, para 12 of the Regulation.

72 Commission Staff Working Document. 'Impact Assessment Report Accompanying the document Proposal For a Regulation of the European Parliament and of the Council on the protection of the Union and its Member States from economic coercion by third parties' [2021] SWD (2021) 371 final, at 23: 'cases, where only the WTO breach forms the basis (and claim) for the legal assessment, do not tackle the question of coercion and its illegality under customary international law.' See also p. 43 stating that 'The WTO however is not an effective and suitable forum for debates about the disrespect of non-WTO

instances where the third country's coercive measure is both coercive and represents a breach of substantial commitments under relevant WTO agreement. Arbitrary or selective anti-dumping investigation against certain EU exports not based on any evidence of dumping is provided as an example of action that could be qualified both as coercion and at the same time also as a substantive breach of the WTO Anti-Dumping Agreement. Excessive and discriminatory border checks for sanitary or phytosanitary purposes, or selective import bans or higher-than-bound import duties on products from a particular Member State are listed as another examples of coercive measures that could also be challenged successfully in the WTO DSM (and that were actually brought up by Canada and Australia).[73] However, the Impact Assessment Report points out that the WTO DSM is no substitute for the ACI as the WTO DSM covers only breaches of the WTO substantive obligations and not the very act of coercion contravening obligations under customary international law (e.g., the prohibition of intervention rule). Put differently, the EU needed to adopt ACI as coercion in breach of customary international law does not feature among the possible claims that can be submitted to treaty-made dispute settlement systems such as the WTO DSM.[74] One could arguably interpret this explanation as a statement that in some cases, coercive measures can be simultaneously in breach of customary international law and the WTO obligations, and that the EU would be able to trigger the ACI (including response measures in the form of non-performance of international obligations) also in situations where the coercion violated the WTO law.[75]

Whether or not such interpretation of the Impact Assessment Report is correct, the text of the Regulation seems to be ambiguous enough to allow the EU to proceed in this way. Whether and how the EU will use the ACI (including non-performance of international obligations) in cases of economic coercion that contravenes the WTO rules is yet to be seen. However,

---

rules of international customary law, such as the prohibition of intervention or interference in the internal or external affairs of another country. This however is precisely what the anti-coercion instrument aims to tackle.'

73 'Case WT/DS602 – China – Anti-Dumping and Countervailing Duty Measures on Wine from Australia' (*World Trade Organization*) <https://www.wto.org/english/tratop_e/dispu_e/cases_e/ds602_e.htm> accessed 28 July 2024; 'Case WT/DS598: China – Anti Dumping and Countervailing Duty Measures on Barley from Australia' (*World Trade Organization*) <https://www.wto.org/english/tratop_e/dispu_e/cases_e/ds598_e.htm> accessed 28 July 2024; 'Case WT/DS589: China – Measures Concerning the Importation of Canola Seed from Canada' (*World Trade Organization*) <https://www.wto.org/english/tratop_e/dispu_e/cases_e/ds589_e.htm> accessed 28 July 2024.

74 Impact Assessment Report (n 72) 23.

75 Furculita (n 63) 6–7.

such a scenario does not seem to be completely unlikely when one looks at the practice of the EU (prior to the adoption of the ACI) of triggering the WTO DSM in situations labelled as economic coercion. In particular, commentators refer, for example, to the US – Section 301–310 Trade Act case, as an example of economic coercion where it was actually the EU that made a complaint in front of the WTO panel.[76] References are also made to the fact that the EU filed a dispute settlement case against China at the WTO for 'discriminatory and coercive measures against exports from Lithuania and against exports of EU products containing Lithuanian content'.[77] But this brings again the problem of the definition of economic coercion – it seems that in a typical scenario, the WTO-based substantive rules will be impaired by economic coercion, but it will not at the same time reach the threshold for breaching the customary non-intervention rule. At the same time, if the EU challenges an act of economic coercion at the WTO DSM, it could be difficult to defend a position that response measures that have been adopted in parallel to the WTO proceedings are not taken as a response to the violation of the WTO rules.[78] It is a question then in which scenarios the EU will actually be able to adopt the ACI response measures in the form of non-performance of international obligations when the WTO substantive rules are concerned.

Nevertheless, the ACI leaves the EU the possibility for a careful approach by *simply* not proceeding to response measures in the form of non-performance of international obligations.[79] It should not be forgotten that the ACI would serve well already by providing an institutional framework for identification of coercion, engagement with the third country or resorting to international dispute settlement, including also the WTO DSM itself.[80] Should response measures nevertheless be adopted, they could, for example, consist only of those that are short of non-performance of international obligations.[81] In this context, it is quite interesting to have a look back at the history of the ACI's preparation. According to an empirical analysis, the Commission was reluctant to accept modifications to the ACI that would extend the scope of re-

---

76 *Herbert Smith Freehills* (n 7); Olsthoorn (n 64), 68.

77 'Case WT/DS610: China – Measures concerning trade in goods and services' (*World Trade Organization*) <https://www.wto.org/english/tratop_e/dispu_e/cases_e/ds610_e.htm> accessed 28 July 2024, referred to by Olsthoorn (n 64), 68.

78 Furculita (n 63), 4.

79 Herbert Smith Freehills (n 7).

80 Olsthoorn (n 64), 67.

81 For a discussion how the ACI may be understood as an adjustment to the practice related to the WTO in the environment of growing economic security concerns, see Nina M. Hart (n 61) 93–97.

sponse measures (in the form of countermeasures) to allow the EU to react to breaches of the WTO, an idea proposed by the members of the European Parliament Committee on International Trade.[82] This reluctance was caused by doubts on the legality and risk of further politically undermining the relevance of the WTO platforms. Rather, the Commission began to develop a tool to deter *economic coercion*.[83] This may be the evidence of the true intention of the drafters to create a mechanism that exists in parallel to the WTO DSM (and not to its exclusion). It is true, however, that it does not necessarily prevent the practice of using the ACI contrary to the WTO rules and, again, the ACI could have been more precise as to the relationship with the WTO DSM. This could have helped to better navigate through the regime of Article 23.1 of the DSU, but also to prevent response measures being in contradiction to the WTO substantive rules.

4 Conclusion

This chapter provided an overview of the ACI and on the basis of explanation of possible issues concerning international legal framework it analysed how the practice of utilising the ACI can contribute to the clarification or even development of international law rules. The ACI is an important tool at the hands of the EU as a RIO for defending its internal market and Member States from economic coercion and loss of a certain degree of autonomy. The unique set-up of the EU as a supranational organization with different categories of conferred powers leads to a very specific design of instruments that are adopted on the level of the EU in a need to counter current challenges, which is particularly evident in the case of the ACI. By adopting the ACI, the EU created an institutionalised mechanism on how to respond to cases of economic coercion by stipulating processes, timeframes and institutional set-up. This mechanism is also equipped with tools that should serve as a deterrent towards third countries. Quite notably, the adoption of the ACI brought about an incorporation of countermeasures, a traditional instrument of the common foreign and security policy, into the domain of CCP governed by majority voting in the Council.[84] The ACI may help the EU to better balance the institutional disadvantage rooted in the fact that it is not

82 Freudlsperger, Meunier (n 5), referring at 9 to an interview conducted as part of empirical analysis.

83 Freudlsperger, Meunier (n 5), 9.

84 Ibid., 14.

a State and as an international organization, it operates on the basis of conferral of powers, in contrast to most of its competitors in the geopolitical field. However, and leaving aside policy and legitimacy considerations, the ACI triggers several challenging international law questions, namely from the point of view of customary international law (definition of coercion and requirements for countermeasures) and the WTO law. In light of these legal issues, this chapter analysed how the ACI can provide the EU with the opportunity to further influence identification or development of (customary) international law.

First of all, in light of the non-intervention rule, the ACI brings its own definition of *economic coercion* that could be qualified as an internationally wrongful act and thus allows the EU to adopt response measures in the form of countermeasures. However economic coercion that does not breach treaty obligations of the coercing State would probably have to reach quite a high threshold to constitute a wrongful act. The Commission and the Council must be cautious in qualifying economic coercion (in order to be able to adopt response measures in the form of non-performance of international obligations) as contrary to customary international law. The situation may, in terms of legal clarity, be easier (with some reservation pertaining to the WTO rules) where the actions of economic coercion are contrary to the treaty obligations owed by the coercing State towards the EU or a Member State. In any case, given the lack of clarity of international law as to what forms of economic coercion run counter to the non-intervention principle, the application of the ACI by the EU may serve as a platform through which the EU as a RIO contributes to the interpretation or development of this important concept of international law.

Second, response measures in the form of non-performance of international obligations of the EU can be adopted only when economic coercion is contrary to international obligations owed to the EU itself (be it treaty obligations or customary international law, e.g., prohibition of intervention). These measures will not be available in scenarios where economic coercion constitutes a violation of international obligations owed *only* to the injured Member State and not the EU itself. Equalling the injury to the Member State or to the EU economic operators with the injury to the EU in Article 3 (3) of the Regulation may arguably pose a risk that response measures adopted by the EU may qualify as impermissible third-country countermeasures under international law. Consistency of the EU response measures with international law will therefore require careful navigation through and distinction of duty bearers and injured parties in each particular case. Space for the EU as the RIO to contribute to the practice of third-party countermeasures is rather narrow here. Their permissibility is discussed in the context of breaches of rules of *erga omnes* character and the ACI response measures apply to coercive measures affecting trade and investment which are unlikely to breach *erga omnes* rules. Finally, there are some concerns also in relation to possible contradiction of response measures adopted on the basis of the ACI with the WTO rules, namely the dispute settlement mechanism. Some of the past events of economic coercion against the EU or its Member States that have been referred to in justifications for the development of the ACI have nonetheless been pursued through the WTO DSM. Therefore, several authors warn that response measures adopted on the basis of the ACI could violate Article 23.1 of the DSU as economic coercion is very likely to touch upon WTO-based substantive rules owed to the EU.

This chapter demonstrated that there is a potential to apply the ACI in contradiction to the rules of international law should the interpretation of these rules by the Commission or the Council be wrong in a particular case. However, *strictly speaking*, even though the text of the Regulation may seem ambiguous in some of its parts, adopting response measures contrary to the rules of international law (for wrong qualification of economic coercion, for failing to meet requirements for countermeasures or for violating the WTO rules) would nevertheless infringe the Regulation itself, as well as the EU primary law, as both sources of law repeatedly refer to the consistency with the rules of international law. From the perspective of intra-EU institutional setting, one may argue that there is some risk that the Commission will adopt response measures in the form of non-performance of international obligations against the will of Member States as the Council is not involved at this (second) phase. However, Member States can (and should) influence the determination of economic coercion in the first phase as there the Council is directly involved. For example, if the Council adopts an implementing act determining the actions of a third State as economic coercion, however qualifying it as not being contrary to international law, this should arguably prevent the Commission from adopting response measures contrary to international law (while not preventing it from engaging with the third country in negotiations, consultations and other forms of dispute settlement envisaged by Article 6, and from adopting response measures short of non-performance of international obligations). One may also argue that some degree of ambiguity of the ACI on the issues raised in this chapter is probably nothing new or dramatic as risks of wrongful application are associated also with other mechanisms or policies in the toolbox of the EU. What matters in terms of legality is adherence to international law not only in the formulation of the text that sets up the parameters of a particular tool or policy, but also in its daily application.[85] And in fact the case-by-case operation of the ACI provides an opportunity for the EU as a RIO to produce a practice that is relevant for the identification or interpretation of customary international law, namely when it comes to the definition of illegal economic coercion. In this regard, and as pointed out elsewhere, the reception by the international community of the way the EU utilises the ACI will also be relevant.[86]

Acknowledgements

The research was conducted with the support of the Palacký University Young Research Grant (Grant No. JG-2023-43). The author would like to thank his colleague from the Ministry of Industry and Trade, Natálie Havlíková, for a great inspiration to analyse the anti-coercion draft proposal and for very insightful discussions. All the views and opinions expressed in this chapter as well as any errors belong solely to the author.

85 See Schäffer (n 59) noting that ACI is just the framework for case-by-case practice.
86 Nina M. Hart (n 61) 102.

PART 3

Identity and Outlook

CHAPTER 8

Questioning the Regional Character of EU Citizenship

Victoria Hooton[1]

Abstract

This chapter examines whether the legal construct of European Union (EU) citizenship aligns with the concept of regionalism, reflecting the EU's nature as a regional organisation (RIO). It explores the internal and external dimensions of EU citizenship, identifying significant inconsistencies that challenge its characterisation as a truly regional status. Internally, EU citizenship's derivative nature and ties to free movement rights limit its inclusivity and relevance for large parts of European societies: immobile citizens, third-country nationals, and economically inactive individuals. Externally, its territorial boundaries blur, as evidenced by the potential lack of common values in how EU citizenship can be gained through naturalisation, and by the inclusion of overseas territories in certain applications of EU citizenship law, which stretch the concept beyond a cohesive regional identity. This chapter assesses these dynamics through the lenses of mutual recognition, free movement, and shared values that might otherwise give a regional flavour to EU citizenship, questioning whether it has achieved regional coherence.

Keywords

EU citizenship – free movement of persons – overseas territories – third country national rights – investor citizenship

1 Introduction

This contribution offers some insights into the regional (or not so regional) nature of EU citizenship. Union citizenship was established in Article 8 of the

1 Senior Researcher, Max Planck Institute for Legal History and Legal Theory (Frankfurt am Main).

 | DOI:10.1163/9789004700659_010

Maastricht Treaty in 1992.[2] It is a derivative form of citizenship, meaning it is granted solely on the basis of the individual holding the nationality of one of the 27 Member States, and is neither intended to replace nor significantly add to Member State citizenship. Instead, a rather limited package of rights is offered to the 'Europeans' included in its remit, most notably the right to free movement, and political rights to participate in local and European Parliament elections in the Member State of residence. In its infancy, citizenship of the Union was considered to be either too symbolic to be meaningful or something to be developed in the future.[3] Through the development of secondary legislation, and even more so the jurisprudence of the Court of Justice, the meaning of EU citizenship has slowly been fleshed out. But to what extent has it become a *regional* membership, shaped by the EU's position as an RIO? This chapter challenges the impact of EU regionalism on EU citizenship from both an internal and external perspective.

Internally, the EU fails to have a truly comprehensive *regional* citizenship that applies to the European *people* as opposed to European individuals. The challenges raised in this chapter address the territorial and conceptual limitations of EU citizenship and its meaningfulness to the peoples of Europe. Firstly, EU citizenship does not actually offer meaningful experiences to all the people *in* Europe. This is due to the derivative nature of EU citizenship and the fact that mobility rights have been the most concrete expression of EU citizenship in action. Thus, for immobile or immigrant populations in the Member States, EU citizenship has little to no bearing on their everyday experiences.

Externally, the territorial, regional boundaries of EU citizenship are blurred. Although the status is tied to the nationality of individual Member States, there are several ways in which EU citizenship and attached rights extend beyond European nationals and borders. In particular, Member States with histories of colonialism have overseas territories encompassed in their nationality laws. Thus, EU citizenship is, in certain instances, stretched beyond the regional territory of Europe and into the former colonies of Member States. The debate around *citizenship by investment*, which has been practiced by some Member States, opens a discussion about whether the granting of Member State nationality includes obligations on the granting Member

2 Treaty on European Union [1992] OJ C 191.

3 For example, see Everling, U. 'Reflections on the Structure of the European Union' (1992) 29 Common Market Law Review 1053; O'Leary, S. 'The Relationship Between Community Citizenship and the Protection of Fundamental Rights in Community Law' (1995) 32 Common Market Law Review 519.

State to ensure that foreign investors have some link with their territories (and thus some link with the EU) before they can become a Member State / EU citizen. These debates again highlight not only the territorial challenges to the regionalism of the concept, but also the existence, strength, or lack thereof, of regional attitudes and values towards the meaning of EU citizenship. The fewer common standards there are in the granting of Member State / EU citizenship, the more likely it is that the regional nature of the concept can be challenged.

Before embarking on this analysis, it is important to establish the difficulty that comes with defining what a citizenship shaped by regionalism could look like. While the territorial scope may be the easiest way to define a citizenship as 'regional', this would ignore other factors that might contribute to the regional nature of an international organization and any form of communal membership resulting from it, such as shared objectives, values, histories, culture or language.[4] Forms of citizenship shaped by regionalism play a difficult role in creating a community of belonging whilst respecting inherent differences in the constituent elements making up that community.[5] Any new form of identity has to straddle these paths and highlight commonalities whilst showing deference to inherent differences. In the case of the European Union as an RIO, it is – in any event – difficult to view the citizenship constructed by the Maastricht Treaty as truly regional because it is there to *create* rather than *recognise* a shared identity among the peoples of Europe subject to the EU legal order.[6] Any shared culture and identity that could be found among the Member States, for instance relating to their shared histories and geographical closeness, is relatively weak when compared to the more robustly defined, historically-entrenched identities of the individual Member States.[7] Although a shared objectives prism could be applied, suggesting that EU citizenship is conceptually whole in its reflection of the region, being

4 According to the concept of regionalism unpacked by International Law Association, *'The International Law of Regional Organizations: Final Report'* (2024) <https://www.ila-hq.org/en/documents/ila-study-group-regional-organisations-final-report-may-24-1> accessed on 06.12.24, 8–12.

5 Neuvonen, P. 'Transforming Membership? Citizenship, Identity and the Problem of Belonging in Regional Integration Organizations' (2019) 30 *The European Journal of International Law* 229.

6 Barnard, C. and Leinarte, E. 'The Creation of European Citizenship: Constitutional Miracle or Myopia?' (2022) 24 *Cambridge Yearbook of European Legal Studies* 24, 25–26; Maas, W. 'The Origins, Evolution, and Political Objectives of EU Citizenship' (2014) 15 *German Law Journal* 797, 800–801.

7 Bauböck, R. 'Why European Citizenship? Normative Approaches to Supranational Union' (2007) 8 *Theoretical Inquiries in Law* 453, 465; Becker, MA. 'Managing Diversity in the

based on a clear acceptance of shared objectives in the Treaties, it is once again trounced by the lack of European demos. The *Member States* have clearly shared objectives that they wish to achieve through legal regulation and harmonization. Whether this translates to the European individual is questionable, and the fact that citizenship was created at least in part to create the link between the Union and its peoples suggests otherwise.[8] Thus, the citizenship experienced in the EU may only be nominally shaped by the factors that would otherwise be associated with the regionalism of the Union.

As the EU has a limited scope to suggest the cultural, historical, linguistic or values-based 'glue' between its peoples, it entrenches its citizenship in one of the few benefits it has to create a commonality, and simultaneously draw those people closer to the Union institutions: rights. By offering explicit citizens' rights, and fundamental human rights,[9] the Union creates some commonality between its peoples and some link between that group of membership and its own institutions. In particular, this includes the rights contained in the Treaty provisions on citizenship, many of which are fleshed out more fully in the 2004 Citizens' Rights Directive,[10] which (among other things) lays out the rights to and conditions of residing in another Member State. These rights create some form of commonality between EU citizens. Strumia suggests that a search for greater autonomy, decision making and better living conditions may be the collective good that turns EU citizens exercising individual free movement rights into European peoples expressing some kind of joint political citizenship.[11] This leads to the need for mutual recognition of belonging in other Member States, placing an obligation on Member States,

---

European Union: Inclusive European Citizenship and Third Country Nationals' (2004) 7 *Yale Human Rights and Development Law Journal* 132, 143.

8 Barnard and Leinarte (n 6).

9 Although the interrelation between citizenship and fundamental rights is somewhat debated in the literature on EU citizenship: O'Leary (n 3); van den Brink, M. 'EU citizenship and (fundamental) rights: Empirical, normative, and conceptual problems' (2019) 25 *European Law Journal*, it is nonetheless possible to say that EU citizenship discourse (in the legal language of the Court and the scholarship) is steeped in the language of rights, particularly fundamental rights. It also does not subtract from the fact that one of the few commonalities between EU citizens at large is their enjoyment of both single market and fundamental rights offered by the Union's legal framework.

10 Directive 2004/38/EC of the European Parliament and of the Council on the right of citizens of the Union and their family members to move and reside freely within the territory of the Member States [2004] OJ L 158 (CRD).

11 Strumia, F. 'European Citizenship and EU Immigration: A Demoi-cratic Bridge between the Third Country Nationals' Right to Belong and the Member States' Power to Exclude' (2016) 22 *European Law Journal* 417, 441.

and EU citizens themselves, to recognise other EU citizens' rights in their territories.[12] In some sense, there is an indication of solidarity between Member States, their nationals and other EU citizens. Not in the sense of a concrete, shared identity,[13] but rather in a shared sense of trust, belonging and obligation.[14] The mutual trust flowing from free movement law may be the strongest and most concrete expression of a shared value that one can find in relation to EU citizenship. Nonetheless, it is still arguable whether common rights make a region, or can impart a regional gloss onto the concept of citizenship. In fact, a focus on individual rights may even challenge the truly regional nature of EU citizenship, by limiting the scope of those within the region who are able to actively relate to and experience that form of citizenship. Yet in the absence of any indication of the real *why* behind EU citizenship, the idea of respect for free movement, fundamental rights and mutual recognition of belonging is perhaps the strongest indicator of its regional identity, other than its territorial limits. Thus, this chapter considers whether EU citizenship lives up to having this clear regional identity and territorial reach.

The rest of this chapter is dedicated to highlighting any discrepancies with the characterization of EU citizenship as a regional citizenship. The arguments are split into two key sections. Section 2 of this chapter considers the internal consistency of EU citizenship by addressing how the concept interacts with different parts of the community of people within the EU's borders and larger free movement area. The limited membership of individuals experiencing EU citizenship law in action is highlighted, alongside the stretching of key EU citizenship rights to those outside the scope of its membership (EEA nationals). Thus, the consistency and coherence of the concept is challenged in relation to its regional identity, as there is no clear vision of regional membership in terms of who is an EU citizen and who EU citizenship rights apply to. Section 3 of this chapter looks at EU citizenship from a more external perspective and considers its geographical and social coherence. This section considers the position of overseas territories and the (perhaps now limited) potential for foreign investors to gain EU citizenship by investing in the Member States offering 'golden passports'. Both of these scenarios challenge the regional nature of EU citizenship

12 Strumia, F. 'Supranational Citizenship' in Shachar, A., Bauböck, R., Bloemraad, I. and Vink, M. '*The Oxford Handbook of Citizenship*' (OUP, 2017) 676.

13 Strumia Ibid. 676–679; Kassoti, E. 'The European Union and Other Regional International Organizations: Tales of Solidarity' (2024) 21 *International Organizations Law Review* 190, 200–205.

14 Ibid.

from both a geographical and conceptual perspective, by blurring the ideas about who is European and what it means to be European, as well as posing questions about the nature of the mutual recognition that seems to underpin the free movement rights that are essentially the essence of EU citizenship. Section 4 of this Chapter offers concluding remarks.

2 The Internal Consistency of EU Citizenship: A Truly Regional Affair?

One may expect that a truly regional form of citizenship would be internally comprehensive and coherent, meaning it is relevant for all belonging to the specific region, in so far as they either possess some territorially-defined membership status, or shared objectives and values, or cultural, historical or political ties. Yet EU citizenship has not (yet) been put at the service of recognising the historical, cultural, linguistic and other ties between European nationals, but has rather been a tool by which to cement the specific (and mostly mobility-based) rights of individuals.[15] It is arguable that a truly regional, representative citizenship would require more intentional shaping. EU citizenship has, for the most part, been shaped by the Court of Justice of the European Union, which of course can only react to the scenarios placed in front of it during disputes between Member States and individuals or the Commission and Member States. Therefore, it is little wonder that the results have been individualistic.[16] One could argue that even highly individual rights could suggest some shared commonality or values between those within the group of membership holding those rights.[17] However, as will be discussed below, the experiencing of rights in the Union does not seem to present a coherent vision

15 Menendez, A. 'Which Citizenship? Whose Europe?–The Many Paradoxes of European Citizenship' (2014) 15 *German Law Journal* 907.

16 Ibid. That is not to say that one should ignore the overall impact of the Court's citizenship jurisprudence, I have argued elsewhere that even individual citizenship cases must be viewed in the light of the sum of their parts in terms of the impact for EU-wide migration and the free movement goals of citizenship. However, in terms of setting the agenda for what citizenship can and should impact, individual cases provide a shallow pool from which to draw from, and more engagement from the EU legislature would be welcomed.

17 For instance, the argument noted above by Strumia (n 11) on the common 'European good' being based on shared ideas of autonomy and choice that are denoted by free movement rights, 441.

of what it means to be an EU citizen, and certainly does not seem to reflect the regional nature of EU citizenship.

2.1 *Limited Relevance of EU Citizenship for Non-mobile Citizens*

Article 20 TFEU ties EU citizenship to the nationality of the Member States, stating 'Every person holding the nationality of a Member State shall be a citizen of the Union. Citizenship of the Union shall be additional to and not replace national citizenship.' Thus, the scope of EU citizenship is ultimately determined by the nationality and naturalisation laws of the individual states.[18] This derivative nature of EU citizenship, alongside the choices that have been made as to what EU citizenship means in practice, create a citizenship that is simultaneously too exclusive and too porous to be truly 'regional'. Although citizenship is granted to all nationals of all 27 Member States, and imparts a sense of a territorially-defined 'European' society, the group of individuals actually experiencing EU citizenship is limited by the fact that the rights and protections offered by the status revolve mainly around free movement. EU citizens who do not make use of their free movement receive limited benefits and rights from their status as EU citizens.[19] They retain, for instance, the right to vote in EU parliamentary elections and the right to enforce duties of the EU institutions towards them.[20] Nevertheless, most of the case law interpreting the meaning of EU citizenship revolves around free movement, as do the majority of provisions in the Citizens' Rights Directive. The CJEU, in one of the seminal citizenship judgments, even highlights how the non-discrimination principle afforded by free movement is inherently tied to the substance of EU citizenship. In *Grzelczyk*,[21] when deciding whether EU citizen students should have access to the same social benefits as nationals of a Member State, the Court held that 'Union citizenship is destined to be the fundamental status of nationals of the Member States, enabling those who find themselves in the same situation to enjoy the same treatment in law irrespective of their nationality.'[22] The focus on the prohibition of nationality discrimination inherently centralises mobility (and the ability to be treated comparably with host Member State nationals) within the scheme of EU citi-

18 Closa, C. 'Citizenship of the Union and Nationality of the Member States' (1995) 32 *Common Market Law Review* 487.

19 Kochenov, D. 'EU Citizenship: Some Systemic Constitutional Implications' (2018) European Papers 3 1061, 1065.

20 Bauböck (n 7) 469.

21 C-184/99 *Grzelczyk* [2001] EU:C:2001:458.

22 Ibid. para 31.

zenship rights. As noted by Bauböck, the preamble of the Directive even borrows from the wording of the CJEU judgments on EU citizenship being a 'fundamental status' for those who have opted to move to another Member State, perhaps highlighting that EU citizenship has no such fundamental status for non-mobile EU citizens, who may even be seen as being at a disadvantage in terms of rights allocation in the Union.[23] It may well then be arguable, that the regionalism of EU citizenship is challenged by the fact that the majority of those included in the membership and resident within the region do not actually enjoy the core rights provided by it.

2.2 *The Exclusion of Third Country Nationals from EU Citizenship's Scope*

Another large group within the territory of the Union is also mostly excluded from the enjoyment of EU citizenship as a status: third country (non-Member State) nationals (TCNs). Whether recently migrated or long-term resident, these individuals can only gain EU citizenship via the process of naturalisation in one of the 27 Member States. These processes can be taxing and arbitrary, leaving the possibility of enjoyment of EU citizenship to the individual Member State practice, and often to administrative discretion of national authorities.[24] However, the Union is generally aware of the fact that Member States are made up of diverse populations, and that TCNs make up a significant proportion of the resident population in its jurisdiction. After some debate in the late 90s and early 2000s, the Union made moves to put TCNs who are long-term resident in a host Member State in a 'comparable' situation to EU citizens.[25] This resulted in the Directive 2003/109/EC,[26] the long-term residents directive. After 5 years continuous residence[27] in a host Member State, certain[28] TCNs are granted a long-term residence status that provides some

23 Bauböck (n 7) 469.

24 Strumia (n 11) 431.

25 Becker (n 7) 149; Kostakopoulou, D. '"Integrating" non-EU migrants in the European Union: ambivalent legacies and mutating paradigms' (2002) 8 *Columbia Journal of European Law* 181, 192; European Council, *Tampere Presidency Conclusions* (1999) SN 200/99.

26 Council Directive 2003/109/EC concerning the status of third-country nationals who are long-term residents [2003] OJ L 16.

27 Article 4(1) Directive 2003/109/EC.

28 As per Article 3, the Directive does not apply to those who are only temporarily resident, or who are resident for the purposes of study, for example. As per Article 5 there are conditions for attainment of the status, such as stable financial resources and sickness insurance.

intra-Union mobility rights, such as mobility for the purposes of work or study.[29] This status allows TCNs to be treated akin to nationals in matters of access to employment, tax advantages, and social welfare.[30] Yet there are still significant differences between TCNs with this status and EU citizens. The original or new host Member State can require a TCN applying for long-term residence or using their mobility rights to comply with integration requirements, something that does not apply to EU citizens.[31] Negotiations were ongoing to recast and update the Directive,[32] to strengthen mobility rights and soften the residence conditions to attract TCNs into using the EU legal framework to establish their long-term residence. However, these negotiations have been without success due to the concerns of a number of Member States.[33]

Yet, EU citizenship also has a role to play for TCNs. Those who are family members[34] of EU citizens have rights connected to EU citizenship, found in the 2004 Citizens' Rights Directive. These include the right to enter into[35] and reside[36] in a Member State with the Union citizen family member, and the right to equal treatment and labour market access, which prevail even after death[37] or divorce.[38] These are intended to ensure that EU citizens may undertake their right to free movement without encountering obstacles in the form of immigration laws that prohibit their family members moving with them. As noted by Strumia, the Court of Justice has further developed the

29 Article 14 Directive 2003/109/EC.

30 Article 11 Directive 2003/109/EC.

31 Article 15(3) Directive 2003/109/EC.

32 Council of the European Union, 'Proposal for a Directive of the European Parliament and of the Council concerning the status of third-country nationals who are long-term residents (recast)' (2023) 16000/23 <https://data.consilium.europa.eu/doc/document/ST-16000-2023-INIT/en/pdf> accessed on 09.12.24.

33 Fragomen, Insights: 'European Union: Revised EU Long-Term Residence Directive Negotiations Cease' March 7 2024 <https://www.fragomen.com/insights/european-union-revised-eu-long-term-residence-directive-negotiations-cease.html> accessed on 09.12.24.

34 As defined in Article 2 Directive 2004/38/EC.

35 Article 5(1) Directive 2004/38/EC.

36 Article 6, Article 7(2), Article 16(2) Directive 2004/38/EC.

37 Article 12(2) Directive 2004/38/EC, although (unlike EU citizens) TCNs must have been resident in the Member State for a year before the death in order for their right to residence to be retained.

38 Article 13(2) Directive 2004/38/EC, as above there are also administrative differences for TCNs, they have to have been married for at least three years and in the host Member State with their spouse for at least a year before their retention of residence applies. Otherwise, they must have custody or access rights to minor children, or be in a particular difficult circumstance (i.e., domestic violence).

rights of TCNs in its citizenship / free movement case law.[39] For instance, by imparting a right to residence for TCN parents where the free movement rights of their children would be ineffective if their caretaker were not permitted residence,[40] or permitting Union citizens to bring their TCN family back to their Member State of origin and rely on EU free movement provisions to establish a right of residence, after having resided in another Member State for a period of time.[41] Thus, certain TCNs are privileged by their relation to EU citizens or workers.[42]

Nevertheless, whilst they may acquire some mobility and residence rights, either through those relations or their long-term residence, they are not equals with EU citizens.[43] The biggest indicator of differentiation relates to voting rights. Whereas EU citizens may vote in the municipal and European Parliament elections of their host Member State, the suggestion to extend this to long-term resident TCNs was dropped during the drafting of the Directive.[44] Although steps have been taken towards a more inclusionary approach to rights-granting for these members of EU societies, much is still left to national immigration and naturalisation rules of the individual Member States.[45] This means that a generally exclusionary approach is taken to the granting of residence and related rights, and that there will always be a manner of differentiation between EU citizens and TCNs, and also between different TCNs depending on whether they can prove their connection to an EU citizen.[46] This interferes in the potential regionalism of EU citizenship on two fronts. First, by lowering its relevance for many residents of the territory, and second, by challenging the commitment to fundamental rights protection (and particularly non-discrimination) that seems to otherwise be a core value of the Union and therefore makes up part of its regional identity.[47] Member States populations are not homogenous, and making EU citizenship derivative from national citizenship decreases the territorial relevance of the membership by excluding this significant portion of the EU population from the scope of the rights and duties that it brings.[48] Decoupling EU citizenship from national

39 Strumia (n 11) 421–423.
40 C-200/02 *Zhu and Chen* [2004] ECLI:EU:C:2004:639.
41 C-456/12 *O and B* [2014] EU:C:2014:135.
42 Strumia (n 11) 422.
43 Bauböck (n 7).
44 Ibid. 472.
45 Strumia (n 11); Bauböck (n 7).
46 Strumia (n 11) 434.
47 Becker (n 7) 138; Strumia (n 11) 418.
48 Becker Ibid. 159.

citizenship would better reflect the reality of the region, that is full of diverse Member States with long histories of immigration,[49] and would more accurately reflect the status of EU citizenship as a post-state form of membership[50] built upon different common values and goals than that experienced at the national level.[51] The discriminatory effect of the current EU citizenship model,[52] such as the disparity in voting rights and the chance to politically participate and engage with the Union and its future,[53] throws into question even the most fundamental values highlighted and reflected by the creation of EU citizenship, again throwing into question the regionalism of the concept, if the commitment to regional values and goals crumbles in the face of more nation-centric interests.

2.3 *EU Citizenship and EEA Nationals*

The regionalism of EU citizenship is also challenged by the application of citizenship rights and principles to EEA nationals.[54] The EEA Agreement seems to recognise the regional ties between the EU and EFTA States, noting the 'special relationship' between the two blocs and the territorial proximity as well as a 'common values and European identity'.[55] Despite this, EEA citizens are not EU citizens and there is an explicit agreement that there is no equivalent of the citizenship provisions in the EEA agreement, and that EEA nationals do not have the same political rights as EU citizens.[56] Nevertheless, EEA nationals are apparently in 'objectively comparable' situations to EU citizens according to the Court of Justice.[57] The general overlap occurs mainly in regard to the free movement rights of individuals, which are a central facet of EU citizenship and which much of the citizenship provisions and case law have expanded. Not only has EEA law incorporated the provi-

49 Becker Ibid. 161.

50 Ibid.

51 Strumia (n 11) 442.

52 Kostakopoulou (n 25) 182.

53 Becker (n 7) 159–160.

54 Franklin, C. and Fredriksen, H. H., 'Differentiated citizenship in the European Economic Area' in Thym, D. and Kostakopoulou D., Research *Handbook on European Union Citizenship Law and Policy* (Edward Elgar, 2022).

55 Case C-897/19 *PPU* [2020] ECLI:EU:C:2020:262 para 52.

56 Franklin and Fredriksen (n 54) 299; Joint Declaration by the Contracting Parties to Decision No 158/2007 incorporating Directive 2004/38/EC of the European Parliament and of the Council into the Agreement.

57 *PPU* (n 55) para 58.

sions of the Citizens' Rights Directive,[58] but as noted by Franklin and Frederikson, the parts of EU free movement law that have been built directly or partially on the basis of the citizenship treaty provisions by the CJEU (rather than the secondary legislation, for instance) have also been incorporated into EEA law through the innovative interpretations undertaken by the EFTA Court.[59] For instance, the case law mentioned above[60] regarding the right to residence permitted for EU citizens returning to their home Member State with their TCN family members after a period of time living in another Member State, on the basis that otherwise the home Member State could effectively prohibit or dissuade the application of an EU citizens' free movement rights.[61] This has been incorporated into the EEA legal framework by the EFTA Court recognising a general principle of free movement, albeit whilst recognising that the concept of EU citizenship does not apply to EEA nationals.[62]

Clearly, the incorporation of the citizenship rights framework, without the extension of EU citizenship, has led to – and will continue to lead to – difficult questions for the EFTA court.[63] Decisions of the EFTA Court must ensure homogeneity between the free movement rules as applied in the EEA and in the EU, whilst acknowledging that CJEU free movement jurisprudence derived purely from EU citizenship does not apply to EEA nationals. On the one hand, that EU citizenship is so heavily tied to free movement rights and yet the status is not granted to a large group of individuals, like EEA nationals, who also have the right to free movement, raises questions about whether the European area in which EU citizenship applies is not too exclusive. On the other hand, the 'differentiated' but comparable citizenship between EU and EEA nationals highlights something questionable about EU citizenship. If the special rights offered by the concept are so easily replicated outside the region of membership, then what exactly can it claim to offer those within its strict territorial bounds? If a regional 'we' is to be meaningful, it should offer

58 Although after some discussion and an explicit declaration on the limits of CRD application in EEA law, Franklin and Fredriksen (n 54) 308; Decision of the EEA Joint Committee No 158/2007 of 7 December 2007 amending Annex V (Free movement of workers) and Annex VIII (Right of establishment) to the EEA Agreement.

59 See Franklin and Fredriksen (n 54) 310–312 citing E-26/13 *Gunnarsson* [2014] EFTA Court Report 254; E-28/15 *Jabbi* [2016] EFTA Court Report 575; E-4/19 Campbell [2020] EFTA Court Report 21.

60 *O and B* (n 41).

61 Franklin and Fredriksen (n 54) 310.

62 Ibid. 310–312.

63 Ibid. 298.

something *more* to those it applies to.[64] Arguably, the right to vote for European Parliament members could offer this, but the political rights offered by EU citizenship are secondary to the much more fleshed out free movement rights, which have always been at the very heart of the concept.[65]

To summarise the above: the tying of citizenship firstly to Member State nationality, and secondly to free movement rights poses a challenge to creating a truly regional citizenship, by tiering belonging and rights for those resident in the jurisdiction of the Union. On the one hand, the Union's 'glue' and demos for membership is likely the rights provided by free movement and the respect of fundamental rights, it is what the region has to offer its people. On the other hand, these rights are significantly limited even within the territory of the Union and larger free movement (EEA) arena, by firstly being allocated almost exclusively in cross-border scenarios, and secondly being differentiated between EU citizens and 'others' who do not enjoy the same fundamental status. EU citizenship is therefore not reflective of the territorial reach of its own key rights, nor of the diverse populations that are a commonality between Member States. The differentiated rights seem to problematize or exceptionalize non-Member State citizens like TCNs and EEA nationals, rather than noting them as a fact of the region as it stands and including them in a broader, post-state membership and giving them a stake in the future of the Union that remains politically relevant to them.

2.4 *The Increasingly Limited Nature of EU Citizenship for Mobile EU Citizens*

As already noted, the focus on free movement rights at the heart of EU citizenship means that there are a limited number of individuals in the Union who are actually enjoying the full range of rights offered by the status. The increasingly limited rights attached to the EU citizenship status prevent it from even being meaningful and relevant to all of the nationals of Member States who *do* find themselves in cross-border scenarios. Not only are the rights mainly aimed at mobile individuals, but they are also generally apportioned based on economic activity and long-term settlement. Overall, this means that 'being European is increasingly a status that is deeply precarious and conditional: a transitory state that is bestowed on rather than inhabited by the European'.[66] One line of case law seems to concretely highlight the

64 Kassoti (n 13) 191.

65 Barnard and Leinarte (n 6).

66 de Witte, F. 'The Liminal European: Subject to the EU Legal Order' (2021) 40 *Yearbook of European Law* 56.

dwindling meaning of EU citizenship: the jurisprudence on welfare access for mobile EU citizens. Scholars have noted how the 'heyday' of EU citizenship jurisprudence saw the Court imposing obligations on Member States to offer some financial solidarity to mobile economically inactive individuals.[67] Over time, this obligation has been whittled down to a general exclusion of such individuals from equal treatment to welfare access and a focus on limits and conditions on their rights,[68] with some tentative assurance that Member States should not contravene the EU charter with their welfare benefits denials.[69] The overarching message from much EU citizenship and free movement jurisprudence is that rights are a general guarantee only for the sufficiently economically active members of European society.[70] This again throws into question the regionalism of EU citizenship in terms of its relevance for the society it claims to have included in its membership. Not only is the status limited in its relevance for much of the population to which it applies, being mainly triggered to provide rights in cross-border scenarios, but its meaning within those scenarios is becoming more limited in nature. The idea that free movement is actually reserved for the economically active or inherently wealthy weakens the idea of the mutual trust and recognition (not to mention solidarity) between Member States when it comes to EU citizens. If such trust is predicated on citizens not coming at any cost to the host Member State, it is a very limited form of trust. Moreover, it again throws into question the idea of EU citizenship standing for common values and ideals, one of the few ways it can create a common identity amongst Member State nationals with otherwise diverse cultural, linguistic and historic backgrounds. If free movement and EU citizenship benefits only the good citizen, the healthy and the wealthy citizen, it is an inherently discriminatory form of citizenship.[71] If EU citizenship's regional flare is its highlighting of a dedication to

67 Paju, J. 'The Charter and Social Security Rights: Time to Stand and Deliver?' (2022) 24 *European Journal of Social Security* 21; Grzelczyk (n 20) para 44.

68 Nic Shuibhne, N. 'Limits Rising, Duties Ascending: the Changing Legal Shape of Union Citizenship' (2015) 52 *Common Market Law Review* 889.

69 C-709/20 *CG v The Department for Communities in Northern Ireland* [2021] ECLI:EU:C:2021:602

70 O'Brien, C. 'Civis Capitalist Sum: Class as the New Guiding Principle of EU Free Movement Rights' (2016) 3 *Common Market Law Review* 937.

71 See generally: Verschueren, H. 'Free Movement of EU Citizens: Including for the Poor?' (2015) 22 *Maastricht Journal of European and Comparative Law* 10; O'Brien, C. 'Unity in Adversity: EU Citizenship, Social Justice and the Cautionary Tale of the UK' (Hart, 2017); Spaventa, E. 'Earned Citizenship – Understanding Union Citizenship through Its Scope' in Kochenov, D. *EU Citizenship and Federalism: the Role of Rights* (CUP, 2017).

fundamental freedoms, rights and values, as well as the mutual recognition flowing between Member States, the reality of current free movement law challenges this. As noted by Strumia, 'while [EU citizenship] enhances and enlarges the sphere of autonomy of European economic actors, it does not trigger truthful reshaping of the community of solidarity that social citizenship relies upon.'[72]

It would therefore appear that, far from creating a regional identity and robust membership of the peoples of Europe, EU citizenship is far too exclusionary to truly reflect the region in which it is otherwise situated. It is not meaningfully relevant to large swathes of the European populace. Quite the opposite, it is only meaningfully relevant for an increasingly limited number of healthy, wealthy, mobile EU citizens, which detracts from its regional relevance and character. Nor is EU citizenship really a reflection of European society, either in terms of its territoriality and geographical relevance, or in terms of the values that it promotes. The differentiated scheme of rights for EU nationals, EEA nationals and third country nationals creates a highly exclusive form of regional citizenship with limited theoretical coherence, and poses a challenge to the idea of common values and respect for fundamental rights and equality making up some of the fabric of this regional concept.

3 The Porosity of the External Borders of EU Citizenship

The external EU border has been described as an 'essential element of its collective identity',[73] albeit an element that can either grow or shrink without impacting the authority or stability of the polity. Yet the fact that EU citizenship now exists and grants a valuable bundle of rights to those included in its membership might prompt a consideration of how jealously the Union should guard those borders, given that (as explored above) EU citizenship hints at the establishment or reflection of a European society shaped by the limited territoriality and nationality of the Member States, thus creating an (albeit minimal) differentiation between EU nationals and non-nationals like EEA citizens or TCNs. The creation and limitation of EU citizenship might, for instance, impact how one judges the process by which other states can accede to the Union, given the need to integrate new members into European soci-

72 Strumia (n 11) 438.

73 Bauböck (n 7) 461.

ety,[74] or perhaps how Member States should account for EU citizenship's effects on their nationality laws or on how their discretion to grant nationality is executed.[75] In the latter cases, the operation of certain nationality laws and the derivative nature of EU citizenship may mean that membership is not limited to those with some geographical (or in some cases even social or cultural) roots within the EU territory itself. Two instances regarding the apportioning of nationality challenge the regionalism of EU citizenship from the perspective of its limited territoriality and broader rights and values. Firstly, the fact that EU citizenship is also granted to Member State nationals in certain Overseas Countries and Territories associated with Member States; and secondly, that certain Member States may continue their practice of citizenship by investment, opening membership up to the wealthy regardless of their country of origin or ties to the Union's territory.

3.1 *EU Citizenship in Overseas Territories of the Member States*

The 'territory' of the EU, most likely imagined as the space existing between the external borders of the Member States in mainland Europe, may represent an oversimplified account of the territorial scope of EU law.[76] The territorial scope of EU citizenship does not actually end at the EU's external border. Due to the *ratione personae* of EU citizenship including all nationals of all Member States, regardless of their country of residence, EU citizenship law partially applies in overseas countries and territories (OCTs) associated with the Union.[77] These territories are largely former colonies of a Member State and reflect their colonial pasts (predominantly France, the Netherlands and the

74 Ibid.

75 This may already be the case, as noted by Strumia (n 11) the Italian Council of State recognised the need to deny naturalisation when it would come with public security concerns, not only for the sake of Italy, but for the sake of the Union since a newly naturalised Italian citizen would be granted the right to free movement, 442.

76 Kochenov, D. 'The Application of EU Law in the EU's Overseas Regions, Countries, and Territories after the Entry into Force of the Treaty of Lisbon' (2012) *Michigan State University College of Law International Law Review* 669, 673–74; Marzal, T., 'The Territorial Reach of European Union Law: a Private International Law Enquiry into the European Union's Spatial Identity' (2024) 73 *International and Comparative Law Quarterly* 29.

77 Kochenov, D. 'The Puzzle of Citizenship and Territory in the EU: On European Rights Overseas' (2010) 17 *Maastricht Journal of European and Comparative Law* 230, 232; Kochenov (n 76) 670. This chapter focuses on OCTs but it is important to note that there are differentiated statuses and legal applications at play in extra-Union territories like the outermost regions, OCTs, and other territories with specific arrangements with the EU. See Broberg, M. 'The EU's legal ties with its former colonies: When old love never dies' (2011) DIIS Working Paper, No. 2011:01.

pre-Brexit United Kingdom).[78] Article 355 of the TFEU[79] lays out how the provisions of the Treaties should apply in overseas (non-EU) territories associated with a Member State. Annex II to the TFEU lays down the OCTs which benefit from 'special arrangements' of association with the Union, and it would appear that this means limited application of the Treaties rather than the full application of EU law.[80] This makes some degree of sense, given that EU law is limited in its territorial scope.[81] According to Article 198 of the TFEU, the purpose of the association is to promote development in these territories and establish 'close economic relations' between them and the Union. This would suggest a mostly economic link between the territories and the Union, rather than a full recognition of any shared belonging, obligations, objectives and values like what is recognised between Member States. Yet despite the limited application of the Treaties to these regions, the nationals of Member States who reside there are EU citizens, unless their Member State actively introduces nationality laws that prohibit this.[82] Most affected Member States do not do this, so some of their nationals – EU citizens – reside far outside the Union. For instance, a Dutch national resident in Aruba or a French national resident in French Polynesia are EU citizens for the purposes of the Treaties. This does not, of course, mean that the territorial scope of EU law is extended to these jurisdictions, but definitely imparts some EU citizenship rights onto the nationals of Member States within them. Most importantly for this chapter, the right to free movement to another Member State will apply to such citizens.[83] Due to the territorial limitations of EU free movement law, free movement between the EU and OCTs would only apply on a one-way basis. EU citizens in OCTs can move to the mainland-Europe territory of another Member State, but not vice versa.[84]

78 Broberg, ibid. Kochenov (n 76) 670.

79 Consolidated version of the Treaty on the Functioning of the European Union [2012] OJ 326.

80 See Kochenov (n 77) 240–41, Broberg (n 77) 8–9.

81 Kochenov (n 77).

82 Such as the UK, which differentiated between different types of British nationalities when EU citizenship was first introduced, see Kochenov (n 77) 237–38.

83 Kochenov (n 77) 244; Kochenov (n 76) 720; the Court has also ruled on the fact that Member States cannot treat their nationals residing abroad differently when it comes to laying down rules for voting eligibility, so that OCT residents should have the right to vote in European Parliament elections if other nationals of that Member State who live in a third country territory are able to do so: see: C-400/04 *Eman and Sevinger* [2006] ECLI:EU:C:2006:545 para 61.

84 Ibid.

Although it is a welcome interpretation of EU law that all Member State nationals are generally treated equally when it comes to the apportioning of EU citizenship rights, so far as they apply within the territory of the Union, it does somewhat challenge the idea of EU citizenship as a regional form of membership. Firstly, by extending the territorial reach of membership into the EU citizenship rubric so far beyond the EU's (presumed) external border, the geographical regionalism of EU citizenship is challenged. It corresponds more to the spatial understandings and interests of individual states than the strict territory of the Union where free movement and the Treaties apply.[85] One may argue the linguistic, historical and cultural ties with the associated Member State could bring these individuals close enough to the broader European society to suggest that the regionalism of EU citizenship is not threatened by this stretching of its reach. However, as noted above, it is questionable if the varied national languages, histories and cultures are what translates to a more supranational feeling of belonging or collectivity. What is more concrete as a basis for the binding of Europeans together is their shared objectives and values in the form of fundamental rights and the mutual trust and recognition that comes with them. Yet the binding of free movement and other fundamental rights is also challenged in the case of OCT-resident EU citizens, due to the non-reciprocity of free movement. As noted above and elsewhere,[86] EU citizenship imparts some obligation for mutual recognition to Member States and all EU citizens alike, by requiring them to recognise other EU citizens' rights to move to their territories and perhaps make demands of their labour markets, or their public systems.[87] The potential for a one-way application of free movement rights between the EU and OCTs challenges the mutuality of that recognition, where Member State nationals from an OCT have their status as EU citizens and rights to intra-EU mobility recognised, but no reciprocal recognition exists in the territory of the OCT. Of course, the Member State associated with an OCT must recognise the belonging of all EU citizens, but that does not retract from the one-way situation relating to their OCTs.

That is not to say that the application of the Treaty to grant EU citizenship to these nationals is not desirable. It fundamentally is, in that it not only respects the Member State ability to set their own nationality laws but also grants economic and social opportunities (free movement) to the Member

---

85 This type of spatial ordering and recognition of individual state interests is nothing new, see Orford, A. 'Regional Orders, Geopolitics, and the Future of International Law' (2021) 74 Current Legal Problems 149.

86 Strumia (n 11) 441; Strumia (n 12) 676.

87 Strumia (n 12) 676–77.

State nationals from these countries.[88] It is also arguably right to have a non-reciprocal form of free movement, so that the autonomy and administration of OCTs do not become impacted by the right to free movement towards their territories.[89] Nevertheless, this particular application of EU citizenship / free movement law to OCTs cannot be said to aid in the construction of a coherent regional form of membership for the EU. Again, one must question whether a more conceptually whole *regional* citizenship would require more control from the EU side, in the form of a membership that is divorced from the nationality of Member States. This may not be as desirable from a social or economic justice standpoint, but would allow the formation of a citizenship with regional territorialism and fully reciprocal values to be entrenched.

3.2 *Citizenship by Investment Schemes: EU Citizenship for Wealthy TCNs?*

An even more topical stretching of the reach of EU citizenship, perhaps again far beyond the EU's borders, are *citizenship by investment* (CBI) schemes. Also known as 'golden passport' schemes,[90] these offer the possibility of gaining a Member State passport (and thus EU citizenship) without any historical, language- or residence-based ties to that jurisdiction, so long as the individual can make a substantial investment, i.e., to the Member States' development fund, or in immovable property. Similar schemes exist, on a larger scale, offering residence by investment, which will not be dealt with in any detail here due to the lack of effect on EU citizenship specifically. Three Member States have so far offered golden passports: Bulgaria, Cyprus, and Malta.[91] The Commission has complained that golden passports are contrary to EU law, and that as they are advertised as a gateway to EU citizenship[92] and the EU territory, they

---

88 Baetens, F. 'European Union, Association of Overseas Countries and Territories' in Max Planck Encyclopaedias of International Law (OUP, 2023) <https://opil.ouplaw.com/display/10.1093/law:epil/9780199231690/law-9780199231690-e626> accessed on 20.11.24.

89 Kochenov (n 77) 246.

90 European Commission, 'Report from the commission to the European Parliament, the Council, the European Economic and Social Committee and the Committee of the Regions: Investor Citizenship and Residence Schemes in the European Union' COM (2019) 12 final.

91 Ibid. 3.

92 Ibid. 1; several CBI consultancies have the EU-access / visa-free travel benefits as the first benefit of the scheme registered on their websites, see: 'Global Citizen Solutions' website <https://www.globalcitizensolutions.com/malta-citizenship-by-investment/>; 'Guide Consultants' Website: <https://www.guideconsultants.com/citizenship-by-investment/malta-citizenship/>; 'Get Golden Visa' Website: <https://getgoldenvisa.com/malta-citizenship-by-investment> (accessed on 29.11.24).

create potential problems for all Member States. As a result, an infringement proceeding was brought against Malta for its CBI naturalisation policy, which allowed naturalisation via investment if one happened to be a TCN with over 750,000 Euros to spare.[93] The concerns raised by the Commission prior to the infringement proceedings were numerous and serious. For instance, the Commission raised concerns that investment by foreign nationals in EU countries selling passports may not be driven by a genuine desire to live and integrate into that Member State, but rather as a means to evade prosecution or law enforcement elsewhere. Another concern was that 'golden passports' would lead to the introduction of organised crime, money laundering or other criminal activities from foreign actors in the EU. Although some security measures and criminal record checks were found in all three countries offering CBI, the Commission suggested that these did not go far enough to protect the other EU Member States from the potential security risks that come with allowing free movement of persons to individuals investing in a Member State passport.[94]

Despite these significant concerns, the case built by the Commission against Malta was criticised[95] for being more concerned with the principle of selling EU citizenship, rather than any concrete infringements of EU law. The Commission challenged Malta on the basis of selling off European values, claiming that the golden passport scheme did not respect the 'fundamental status' of EU citizenship, and that Maltese law should require an individual to have a 'genuine link' with the territory. The Commission based its argument on two Treaty provisions, Art 20 TFEU – the provision establishing EU citizenship – and Art 4(3) TEU[96] on the principle of sincere cooperation. Essentially, the Commission argued that the Maltese policy was contrary to the principle of mutual trust and recognition, as the granting of Member State citizenship also grants EU citizenship and therefore has potential consequences for all Member States. Thus, Member States must take into account the EU law consequences of their naturalisation policies.[97] The Commission relied upon the

93 Incidentally, this is the cheapest of the options available. A Bulgarian passport requires an investment of 1 million Euros, whilst a Cypriot passport would be 2 million.

94 European Commission Report (n 90) 9–10, 12–13.

95 van den Brink, Martijn: *Concise, Clear, and Convincing: The Opinion of Advocate General Collins in Commission v Malta (Citizenship for Sale)*, *VerfBlog*, 2024/10/09, https://verfassungsblog.de/concise-clear-and-convincing/; Weiler, Joseph H. H.: *Citizenship for Sale (Commission v Malta): Who of the Two is Selling European Values?*, *VerfBlog*, 2024/4/14, https://verfassungsblog.de/citizenship-for-sale/.

96 Consolidated Version of the Treaty on European Union [2012] OJ C 326/13

97 C-181/23 *European Commission v Republic of Malta* [2024] ECLI:EU:C:2024:849, Opinion of AG Collins, para 17.

argument that the mutual trust between Member States in recognising each other's nationals is premised on the idea that a genuine link will exist between the individuals and the Member State, and thus all EU citizens within the single EU polity have a common factor (a link to a Member State).[98] This was partly argued on the basis of a judgment from the International Court of Justice in *Nottebohm*,[99] which held that state authorities can refuse to recognise the granting of a nationality to an individual by another state if that individual had no 'genuine link' with the granting state.[100] In *Micheletti* the CJEU held that Member States are obliged to automatically recognise the granting of nationality to individuals by other Member States.[101] Whilst the Maltese authorities saw this as an expression of the absolute sovereignty and competence of Member States to set their naturalisation policies,[102] the EU Commission considered this to be founded upon the idea that there are common standards regarding the granting of nationalities between the Member States, thus allowing room for automatic mutual trust.[103]

AG Collins found the arguments of the Maltese government to be more convincing. He noted how, although EU citizenship is a fundamental status,[104] there is no communal notion or understanding of nationality at the EU level, and that the absence of any indication of this in the Treaties highlights a deliberate choice of the Member States to refrain from setting EU standards for the granting of nationality.[105] According to AG Collins, EU citizens being part of a single political unit does not impact the absolute competence of the Member States to grant nationality on their terms. The principle of mutual trust means that Member States must automatically accept, without question, when an individual has been granted the nationality of another Member State.[106] CJEU jurisprudence setting limits on the loss of citizenship did not indicate to AG Collins that there is an EU law scope or competence to interfere in the acquisition of a Member State nationality.[107]

98 Ibid., para 18
99 *Nottebohm Case (second phase)*, Judgment of April 6th, 1955: ICJ Reports 1955, 4.
100 *Commission v Malta* (n 97), Opinion of AG Collins, para 24.
101 C-369/90 *Micheletti* [1992] ECLI:EU:C:1992:295.
102 *Commission v Malta* (n 97), Opinion of AG Collins, paras 26–27.
103 Ibid. para 24.
104 Ibid. para 43.
105 Ibid. para 45.
106 Ibid. paras 46–47.
107 Ibid. para 52, cf Spieker, who notes that the case law on loss of citizenship has also increasingly begun to refer to acquisition: Spieker, Luke Dimitrios: *Dismissing the Genuine Link by Disregarding Constitutional Principles: Why the Court should not follow Collins'*

The AG was not convinced by the *Nottebohm* argument, stating that the ICJ judgment does not oblige Member States to require a genuine link, it merely allows states not to recognise the granting of nationality to individuals without one. This did not detract, according to AG Collins, from the fact that the requirements of nationality are still a matter for sovereign states and sovereign states alone.[108]

In a somewhat shocking turn of events,[109] the Grand Chamber of the CJEU did *not* follow the Opinion of AG Collins. A full analysis of the Court's judgment in *Commission v Malta*[110] is outside the scope of this chapter. However, the Court's findings offer a potentially important insight into what EU citizenship means for the region. Essentially, the CJEU found that Member State discretion in the granting of their nationality must be exercised in a way that is compatible with EU law.[111] The Court conceptualised an EU understanding of what the 'bond of nationality' entails, claiming it to be a 'special relationship of solidarity and good faith' between a state and its nationals.[112] That 'special relationship' is apparently the basis for the rights and obligations bestowed upon EU citizens by the citizenship provisions in Article 20 TFEU.[113] According to the Court, the respect for the special relationship of solidarity and good faith is a requirement for the 'mutual trust' between Member States that allows for the existence of EU citizenship.[114] Naturalisation laws based on investment – like the Maltese scheme – were found to 'manifestly disregard' the requirement for a special relationship between the state and its nationals, and as a result were considered to have broken the mutual trust that is the basis of EU citizenship.[115] After laying out these guiding principles, the Court went on to assess the investor citizenship scheme in a more detailed manner, to determine if any of the non-financial requirements would take away or blunt its otherwise transactional nature.[116] Having found this not to be the case, Malta

---

Opinion in Commission v Malta, VerfBlog, 2024/10/09, https://verfassungsblog.de/dismissing-the-genuine-link/; see also Spieker, D. and Weber, F. 'Bonds without belonging? The *genuine link* international, union and nationality law' (2024) *Yearbook of European Law* 1.

108 *Commission v Malta* (n 97), Opinion of AG Collins, para 56.

109 Although some may argue that the ruling was foreseeable. For instance, see O'Neill, Ruairi: *The Silent Engine of European Citizenship, VerfBlog,* 2025/5/07, https://verfassungsblog.de/the-silent-engine-of-european-citizenship/.

110 C-181/23 *Commission v Malta* [2025] ECLI:EU:C:2025:283.

111 ibid., para 95.

112 ibid., para 96.

113 ibid., para 97.

114 ibid., para 99.

115 ibid.

116 ibid., paras 104–120.

was held to have commercialised its granting of nationality in a manner that led to a failure in its obligations under Article 20 TFEU and Article 4(3) TEU.[117]

Some scholarship has agreed with the opinion of AG Collins, finding the Commission's case against Malta to be weak,[118] and finding the Court's reasoning to be just as weak,[119] despite the fact that there may be genuine concerns with the results of commodifying citizenship.[120] This is unsurprising, given the lack of detail in the rubric of the Treaty provisions establishing EU citizenship, the absolute nature of the link between Member State nationality and EU citizenship, and the fact that the Court had never yet ruled on the specific matter of citizenship acquisitions and their compatibility with EU law. However, the Commission and Court's concerns about the potential interference with the mutual trust and recognition between Member States when it comes to granting nationality (and with it EU citizenship) seem to have some merit. As Spieker convincingly notes, mutual recognition requires mutual trust, fostered by the faith in the standards of other Member States.[121] He suggests that the 'genuine link' requirement could be a prerequisite for that mutual recognition, which would smooth the current discord between EU citizenship law and international law on the recognition of nationality.[122] Although the 'genuine link' requirement did not really form the basis of the CJEU judgment, the Court did focus on other, related values: solidarity and mutual trust.[123] For the purposes of this chapter, the mutual trust and recognition issue is pertinent. As noted throughout, there is something left to be desired

117 Ibid., para 121.

118 van den Brink (n 95); Weiler (n 95), cf Chamon, Merijn: *A Rejoinder to Citizenship for Sale (Commission v Malta): Some Remarks and Counterarguments, VerfBlog,* 2024/4/15, https://verfassungsblog.de/a-rejoinder-to-citizenship-for-sale/.

119 For a few examples, see: Kochenov, D. *Op-Ed: "Never mind the Law, again: Commission v. Malta (C-181/23)", EU Law Live,* 30/04/2025, https://eulawlive.com/op-ed-never-mind-the-law-again-commission-v-malta-c-181-23/; Peers, S. *Pirates of the Mediterranean meet judges of the Kirchberg: the CJEU rules on Malta's investor citizenship law, EU Law Analysis,* 30/04/2025, https://eulawanalysis.blogspot.com/2025/04/pirates-of-mediterranean-meet-judges-of.html; van den Brink, M. *Why bother with legal reasoning? The CJEU Judgment in Commission v Malta (Citizenship by Investment), EUI Global Citizenship Observatory,* 02/05/2025 https://globalcit.eu/why-bother-with-legal-reasoning-the-cjeu-judgment-in-commission-v-malta-citizenship-by-investment/.

120 Weil, Patrick: *Sale of Nationality as a Violation of Human Dignity, VerfBlog,* 2024/10/02, https://verfassungsblog.de/sale-of-nationality-as-a-violation-human-dignity/; Spieker (n 107).

121 Spieker (n 107).

122 Ibid.

123 Spieker, Luke Dimitrios: *It's solidarity, stupid!: In defence of Commission v Malta, VerfBlog,* 2025/5/07, https://verfassungsblog.de/its-solidarity-stupid/.

in the telos supporting the existence of EU citizenship. If there is to be some clear theory underpinning it, it would be that it represents the mutual trust and recognition offered between the Member States. They are obliged to recognise EU citizens from other Member States, to host them, and to allow them to live, work and retire in their jurisdictions, and perhaps even to access key public resources. The recognition of common standards and values underpinning this mutual trust does seem to strengthen the theoretical foundation of EU citizenship itself:[124] the rights it offers are there precisely because of the ability of Member States to accept the nationals of the others, the solidaristic 'glue' between EU citizens being the common factor of having a 'special relationship of solidarity and good faith' (or even a 'genuine link') to their Member State of nationality. The CJEU has potentially provided some conceptual soundness to what it means to be European, accepting (albeit on thin legal grounds) common standards and 'European' values about the granting of nationality and with it EU citizenship. *Commission v Malta*, in short, might provide for a more comprehensive regional understanding of what ingredients make a European.

Had the opinion of AG Collins been followed, then the CBI dispute would have raised questions about the regionalism of EU citizenship in two ways. Firstly, it would have reaffirmed the porosity of the borders of EU citizenship and its ability to have effects on those even far removed from the Union in terms of geography and cultural and solidaristic integration. Secondly, and related, any permitting of CBI schemes would remind one of the weak grasp that the Union has over the boundaries of EU citizenship. While there is always an element of co-governance at play in defining the parameters of EU citizenship, if the opinions of the Maltese authorities and AG Collins had been correct, there would be no real EU control over the determination of the scope of peoples included in EU citizenship's membership. That undoubtably would have been the sounder legal assessment, but following that path would have meant that the Union could not claim to have created a citizenship born of mutual values and ideas, but that it had rather settled for recognising a political membership of otherwise self-identified, discrete groups stemming from the individual Member States.

124 And vice-versa, the explicit recognition of mutual trust as a principle underpinning EU citizenship solidifies its role as a 'structural constitutional principle' of the EU, see O'Neill (n 109).

4 Conclusion

The concept of EU citizenship reflects a complex interplay between regional aspirations and the practical realities of a fragmented socio-political landscape. While citizenship was established to foster a sense of shared identity and community among the peoples of Europe, its implementation and development reveals inconsistencies that challenge its characterization as a truly regional form of citizenship.

Internally, EU citizenship fails to achieve comprehensive regional inclusivity. Its derivative nature, reliance on the nationality and naturalisation laws of Member States, and concentration on free movement rights stratifies access to and enjoyment or experience of citizenship rights for those residing in the Union. Significant populations within the Union's borders are therefore excluded from or simply not making use of the main rights of EU citizenship, including many (if not most) third country and EEA nationals and the overwhelming number of first-country nationals who do not exercise their mobility rights. These exclusions hinder the Union's ability to reflect the diversity of its territories or to create a cohesive sense of belonging across all its residents. Furthermore, the reliance on mobility as a central feature of citizenship, and the increasing focus on economic activity as the prerequisite for the enjoyment of that feature, again underscores its limitations in addressing the static and less economically privileged members of EU societies.

Externally, the territorial boundaries of EU citizenship blur, again complicating its regional coherence. The extension of free movement rights to Member State nationals resident in overseas territories and the existence of CBI schemes demonstrate the elasticity of EU citizenship, potentially at the cost of its regional identity. The inclusion of overseas territories broadens the geographic scope of EU citizenship, often without reciprocal recognition of mobility rights, while investment-based citizenship may continue to raise questions about what it does or should mean to be a national of a Member State.

Critically, the EU's commitment to mutual recognition – the cornerstone of its internal market – might settle some tensions in the theoretical underpinnings of EU citizenship. While Member States are obliged to recognise the rights of EU citizens from other jurisdictions, the CJEU's newly minted standards for the granting of Member State nationality (based on a 'special relationship of solidarity and good faith') might strengthen the importance of mutual trust in EU citizenship law. Although controversial, the *Commission v Malta* judgment may have opened a way to create a cohesive vision for what it means to be European.

The challenges and inconsistencies in the EU's regional identity that flow from the conceptualization and implementation of EU citizenship are, still, difficult to reconcile. It is hard to imagine how one might explore how EU citizenship could evolve to better reflect regional solidarity while addressing its exclusionary tendencies. Should the Union decouple EU citizenship from national citizenship to create a more inclusive and territorially coherent membership? Can shared values such as fundamental rights, democratic participation, and social integration provide a stronger foundation for regional identity than mobility alone? Additionally, the implications of external factors, such as the role of overseas territories and third country nationals, warrant deeper examination to reconcile the EU's regional and more global characteristics and commitments. Currently, EU citizenship remains territorially and conceptually fragmented, and may do so for the foreseeable future. This fragmentation reflects the competing interests and identities within the Union. While EU citizenship seems to have been a project raised to increase the regional integration of the peoples of Europe, its current form struggles to represent a cohesive, regional European society. Bridging these gaps will require not only substantial legal reform but also a renewed effort to define and concretise the values that underpin EU citizenship, and what they mean for the region.

CHAPTER 9

'Geopoliticization through Law': The European Union and Beyond

Joris E. Larik[1]

Abstract

This chapter investigates the reactions of the European Union (EU) and other regional international organizations (RIOs) – and their laws – to today's more challenging geopolitical environment. This is warranted as the creation of collective strength against outside threats is a prominent rationale in regional integration theories. The chapter first demonstrates that in the EU not only a "geopolitical awakening" in terms of changing political discourse, but also of its legal toolbox can be observed. To illustrate this, a range of new instruments in trade and defence (industry) are surveyed. The chapter subsequently argues that the EU seems to be quite special in that regard compared to other RIOs such as the East African Community (EAC) and the Association of Southeast Asian Nations (ASEAN). In these other RIOs, at most, political discourse acknowledges the new geopolitical landscape, albeit in more general terms. The chapter offers some possible explanations for this discrepancy, focussing on both the difference in demand for new geopolitical tools and the difference in the capacity to supply them. The chapter concludes that the EU's turn to geopolitics may contribute to make it more special (again) compared to other RIOs.

Keywords

Association of Southeast Asian Nations – Comparative regionalism – Defence industry – Defence policy – East African Community – European Union – Geopolitics – Legalization – Strategic autonomy – Trade policy

1 Dr. J. E. Larik is Associate Professor of Comparative, EU and International law at Leiden University.

 DOI:10.1163/9789004700659_011

1 Introduction

The term 'geopolitics' is ubiquitous these days in Western discussions about international politics,[2] not least in Europe. In the 2023 'State of the Union' speech, European Commission President Ursula von der Leyen proclaimed the creation of a 'a geopolitical Union – supporting Ukraine, standing up to Russia's aggression, responding to an assertive China and investing in partnerships'.[3] Previously, the EU High Representative for Foreign Affairs and Security Policy Josep Borrell had already noted that we live in an era of hard power politics, in which everything can be used as a weapon.[4] He then called for the EU's 'geopolitical awakening' to translate into permanent strategic positioning, which makes use of all Union policies and instruments.[5]

This chapter investigates the reactions of regional international organizations (RIOs) to today's more hostile and challenging geopolitical environment. This is merited for two main reasons. First, in theorizing regional integration, one prominent rationale is to create collective strength to be able to better stand up to great powers and other external security threats.[6] Second, as the EU has clearly embraced the notion of geopolitics, and since it continues to serve – sometimes – as a model for other RIOs,[7] it is worthwhile exploring how the EU gave concrete expression to its own 'geopolitical awakening' and whether this reaction can be recognized in other RIOs as well.

Scrutinizing these issues, the chapter argues that one of the main consequences of the EU's 'geopolitical awakening' has been a proliferation of new instruments, including legislation. This proliferation could be described as 'inter arma germinant leges' – times of geopolitical tensions spawn new laws – thus the opposite of Marcus Tullius Cicero's adage 'inter arma silent leges', which can be loosely translated as 'when the weapons speak, the law is

2 C. Nickel, 'What do we talk about when we talk about the "return" of geopolitics?' (2024) 100 *International Affairs* 221.

3 European Commission, '2023 State of the Union Address by President Von der Leyen', Strasbourg, 13 September 2023, <https://neighbourhood-enlargement.ec.europa.eu/news/2023-state-union-address-president-von-der-leyen-2023-09-13_en> (accessed 20 January 2025).

4 European Union, *A Strategic Compass for Security and Defence*, 24 March 2022, <https://www.eeas.europa.eu/sites/default/files/documents/strategic_compass_en3_web.pdf> (accessed 20 January 2025) 4.

5 Ibid.

6 F. Schimmelfennig, 'Regional Integration Theory', in *Oxford Research Encyclopedia of Politics* (26 February 2018), attributing this line of thinking to intergovernmentalism.

7 International Law Association, *The International Law of Regional Organizations: Final Report* (2024), 44–45.

silent'.[8] In the EU, therefore, as much as particularly Russia's full scale invasion of February 2022 is seen as a historic rupture (*Zeitenwende*),[9] there is continuity in the heavy reliance on law as the propellant for taking European integration forward. In other words, after decades of 'integration through law',[10] what can now be observed is the 'geopoliticization through law' in the EU. Meanwhile, considering the examples of two other ambitious regional organizations – the East African Community (EAC) and the Association of Southeast Asian Nations (ASEAN) – it can be concluded that no similar development can be observed. At most, political discourse acknowledges the new geopolitical landscape in these other RIOs. Therefore, as the chapter argues furthermore, the EU's 'geopolitical awakening' and its legal ramifications may thus contribute to make the EU more special (again) compared to other RIOs.

The chapter starts with a brief tracing of the EU's 'geopolitical awakening' as a shift in political rhetoric. Subsequently, the chapter provides an overview (without claiming exhaustiveness) of important new geopolitical instruments adopted by the EU as a legal consequence of this awakening. The analysis then turns to the EAC and ASEAN as comparators, concluding a clear absence of concrete measures. The chapter ends with a conclusion and an outline for a research agenda on the topic of RIOs, geopolitics, and the law.

2 The 'Geopolitical Turn' in the EU

As noted, one major rationale for regional integration is to create collective power vis-à-vis regional or global great powers. However, unlike military alliances such as the North Atlantic Treaty Organization (NATO), the security dimension is mostly not the solely dominant one in RIOs. In addition, RIOs are often set up with the aim of ensuring peace between the member of the RIO and boosting welfare through market integration and its scale effects. The

---

8 J. Klabbers, *International Law* (4th edn, Cambridge University Press, 2024) 218.

9 German Federal Government, 'Regierungserklärung von Bundeskanzler Olaf Scholz am 27. February 2022', 27 February 2022, <https://www.bundesregierung.de/breg-de/aktuelles/regierungserklaerung-von-bundeskanzler-olaf-scholz-am-27-februar-2022-2008356> (accessed 20 January 2025); T. Bunde, 'Zeitenwende as a foreign policy identity crisis: Germany and the travails of adaptation after Russia's invasion of Ukraine' (2025) *British Journal of Politics and International Relations* [online first].

10 M. Cappelletti, M. Seccombe and J.H.H. Weiler, 'Integration Through Law: Europe and the American Federal Experience – A General Introduction' in M. Cappelletti, M. Seccombe and J.H.H. Weiler (eds.), *Integration Through Law: Europe and the American Federal Experience* (Walter de Gruyter, 1986).

economic dimension can be seen as the prime rationale for integration for many RIOs, which is already reflected in their designations, including terms such as 'economic' (e.g., the Economic Community of Western African States, ECOWAS) or 'market' (e.g., the Southern Common Market, Mercosur). This was of course also the case for the EU, which was preceded by the European Economic Community (EEC). It is also reflected in the term 'regional economic integration organization clause' (REIO), which was adapted to 'regional integration organization clause' in newer international agreements.[11] Many RIOs pursue a broader agenda than economic integration, having branched out, such as the EU with its three 'pillars' following the Maastricht Treaty signed in 1992 and the Association of Southeast Asian Nations (ASEAN) with its three communities launched in 2009.[12]

Hence, the EU is certainly not alone in being a RIO that has embraced a wide agenda spanning economics, security, and many other issues. In the last few years, it has embarked on what some scholars term a 'geopolitical turn',[13] which goes hand in hand with a 'geoeconomic turn',[14] a 'unliteral turn',[15] and the quest for 'strategic autonomy'.[16] This section will trace this development, which serves as the conceptual platform from which the new geopolitically inspired instruments were launched.

To better understand the meaning of the EU's 'geopolitical awakening' and its legal ramifications, it is useful to contrast the present with the not-so-distant past. Anecdotally speaking, one could say that a quarter of a century ago one of the most hotly debated issues in the EU's external relations was the import of bananas (the so-called 'banana wars').[17] In 2025, we find ourselves in confronted with debates about scaling up ammunitions production, the pur-

11 R.A. Wessel and J. Odermatt, 'The European Union's engagement with other international institutions Emerging questions of EU and international law' in R.A. Wessel and J. Odermatt (eds.), *Research Handbook on the European Union and International Organizations* (Edward Elgar, 2019) 13.

12 ASEAN, *Roadmap for an ASEAN Community 2009–2015* (2009).

13 K.R. McNamara, 'Transforming Europe? The EU's industrial policy and geopolitical turn' (2024) 31 *Journal of European Public Policy* 2371.

14 S. Bauerle Danzman and S. Meunier, 'The EU's Geoeconomic Turn: From Policy Laggard to Institutional Innovator' (2024) 62 *JCMS: Journal of Common Market Studies* 1097.

15 T. Verellen & A. Hofer, 'The Unilateral Turn in EU Trade and Investment Policy' (2023) 28 *European Foreign Affairs Review* 1.

16 See A. Steinbach, 'The EU's Turn to "Strategic Autonomy": Leeway for Policy Action and Points of Conflict' (2023) 34 *European Journal of International Law* 973, 975.

17 T.G. Taylor & T.E. Josling, *Banana Wars: The Anatomy of a Trade Dispute* (CABI, 2003); H. Kuschel, 'Bananenstreit – und kein Ende?' (1998) 44 *Recht der Internationalen Wirtschaft* 122.

chase of tanks, and where even European nuclear weapons are openly discussed.[18] This shows a remarkable shift in political and scholarly thinking surrounding the EU and its foreign policy.

Originally, the external relations of the European Economic Community focused on trade and development cooperation.[19] The EEC therefore only had civilian instruments, unlike states, which could also rely (to varying degrees) on military might. This gave rise to the characterization of the EEC as a 'civilian power'.[20] At the outset of the integration process in Europe, the main contribution that a united Europe was considered to make to peace and security in the world was to prevent a new war *between* its own Member States, especially Germany and France, as the 1950 Schuman Declaration made clear.[21]

This image of European integration as a mainly inward-looking peace project changed over the course of the 1970s and 1980s, when political leaders wanted to better coordinate their national foreign policies. In the Maastricht Treaty of 1992, this form of cooperation was institutionalized as the 'second pillar' of the European Union, the Common Foreign and Security Policy (CFSP). That the EU was no longer just a 'civilian power' became apparent after the activation of the Common Security and Defence Policy (CSDP), which is part of the CFSP, after the Saint-Malo Declaration in 1998.[22]

While the fall of the Berlin Wall and the enlargement process towards Central and Eastern Europe led to an optimistic sentiment about the role and future of the EU, frustration arose about internal divisions, for example during the Gulf War, the Yugoslavia War, the Kosovo War and the Iraq War.[23] This tension between ambition and reality explains the tone of policy documents from this period. This can best be exemplified by the Laeken

18 J. Hanke Vela & N. Camut, 'As Trump looms, top EU politician calls for European nuclear deterrent', *Politico* (25 January 2024) <https://www.politico.eu/article/europe-nuclear-warfare-detterence-manfred-weber-vladimir-putin-ukraine-russia-war/> (accessed 18 January 2025).

19 Treaty establishing the European Economic Community (1957) art. 110 and 130.

20 F. Duchêne, 'Europe's Role in World Peace' in R. Mayne (ed.), *Europe Tomorrow: Sixteen Europeans Look Ahead* (Fontana, 1972).

21 Schuman Declaration, 9 May 1950, <https://european-union.europa.eu/principles-countries-history/history-eu/1945-59/schuman-declaration-may-1950_nl> (accessed 20 January 2025).

22 S. Keukeleire & T. Delreux, *The Foreign Policy of the European Union* (3rd edn, Bloomsbury Academic, 2022) 190.

23 M. Tocci, 'From the European Security Strategy to the EU Global Strategy: Explaining the Journey' (2017) 54 *International Politics* 487, 488; C. Guicherd, 'The Hour of Europe: Lessons from the Yugoslav Conflict' (1993) 17 *Fletcher Forum of World Affairs* 159.

Declaration from 2001, which provided an outline of the intended new position of the EU:

> Now that the Cold War is over and we are living in a globalized, yet also highly fragmented world, Europe needs to shoulder its responsibilities in the governance of globalization. (…) A power seeking to set globalization within a moral framework, in other words to anchor it in solidarity and sustainable development.[24]

To put it simply, in the eyes of political leaders, Europe should be capable of much more on the global stage than just fighting 'banana wars'. This sentiment was shared and further elaborated by leading scholars. Due to its economic weight,[25] but also through its pioneering role in the field of norms and regulation,[26] the EU could and should become a prominent global player.

This self-confident, and quite non-self-critical, image of the EU as a player on the world stage began to crumble from 2014 onwards with the illegal annexation of Crimea by Russia. In 2016, then High Representative Federica Mogherini released a 'Global Strategy' for the EU. This was, in a sense, the successor to the 2003 European Security Strategy,[27] but characterized by a broad perspective covering the full spectrum of EU policy areas.

On the one hand, emphasis was still placed on the international legal order and multilateralism. On the other, it was now being noted more clearly than before in several places that the EU had its own interests to safeguard, that it must be selective in its external action, and simply cannot achieve all of its ambitions on its own.[28] The central creed of the Global Strategy was therefore 'principled pragmatism'.[29] Furthermore, by prioritizing 'Europe and its surrounding regions',[30] the strategy reflected the 'return' or even 'revenge of ge-

---

24 European Union, Presidency Conclusions – European Council Meeting in Laeken, 14 and 15 December 2001, SN 300/1/01 REV 1, 20.

25 C. Damro, 'Market power Europe' (2012) 19 *Journal of European Public Policy* 682.

26 I. Manners, 'Normative Power Europe: A Contradiction in Terms?' (2002) 40 *Journal of Common Market Studies* 235; A. Bradford, *The Brussels Effect: How the European Union Rules the World* (Oxford University Press, 2020).

27 European Council, *A secure Europe in a better world – European security strategy*, Brussels, 12 December 2003.

28 J. Larik, 'The EU's Global Strategy, Brexit and "America First"' (2018) 23 *European Foreign Affairs Review* 343.

29 European Union, *Shared Vision, Common Action: A Stronger Europe. A Global Strategy for the European Union's Foreign and Security Policy* (June 2016) 16.

30 Ibid., 19.

ography'[31] in thinking about external relations, which is a clear characteristic of a *geo*political approach. In addition, the concept of 'strategic autonomy' was given a prominent place in the strategy.[32] The term 'open' was later added to this, to express, as with 'principled pragmatism', that the EU would still endeavour to adhere to its values – including (economic) openness – as far as possible, while building capacity to safeguard its own values and interests with sufficient independence.[33]

In policy documents from recent years, the call for an 'open but assertive approach' with a focus on European values and interests has only become louder.[34] In a communication on 'rules-based multilateralism', the European Commission and the High Representative stated in 2021 that 'we cannot be multilateralists alone nor only for the sake of it'.[35] Rather multilateralism ought to 'deliver results that serve both EU and global interests and values'.[36] The tone of the discourse on EU foreign policy has thus clearly shifted twenty years after the Laeken Declaration – from optimistic to pessimistic and from fully multilateral to more unilaterally oriented.

The use of the term 'geopolitics' has by now become *de rigueur* in EU policymaking and strategizing. President of the European Commission Ursula von der Leyen stated already in 2019 that she wanted to launch a 'geopolitical Commission'.[37] This was followed in 2023 by the aforementioned observations of the emergence of a 'geopolitical Union'[38] and the EU's 'geopolitical awakening'.[39] This all happened prior to the Russian full-scale invasion of Ukraine,

31 R. Kaplan, *The Revenge of Geography: What the Map Tells Us About Coming Conflicts and the Battle Against Fate* (Random House, 2013).

32 European Union (n 29) 9, 19 and 46.

33 Steinbach (n 16), 974–975.

34 European Commission, *Trade policy review – An open, sustainable and assertive trade policy*, Brussels, 18 February 2021, COM(2021) 66 final, 16, see also European Commission and High Representative of the Union for Foreign Affairs and Security Policy, *EU economic security strategy*, Brussels, 20 June 2023, JOIN(2023) 20 final.

35 European Commission and High Representative of the Union for Foreign Affairs and Security Policy, *Strengthening the EU's contribution to rules-based multilateralism*, Brussels, 17 February 2021, JOIN(2021) 3 final, 1.

36 Ibid.

37 European Commission, 'Speech by President-elect von der Leyen in the European Parliament Plenary on the occasion of the presentation of her College of Commissioners and their programme', Strasbourg, 27 November 2019 <https://ec.europa.eu/commission/presscorner/detail/MT/speech_19_6408> (accessed 20 January 2025).

38 European Commission (n 3).

39 European Union (n 4) 4.

which began in February 2022 and was termed a *Zeitenwende* (historical turning point) by German Chancellor Olaf Scholz.[40]

The *Zeitenwende* caused by Russian aggression was therefore not the starting point of the 'geopoliticization' of EU foreign policy, but it did work as an accelerator of this trend in the field of defence and military capabilities,[41] as well as in other areas. In the Versailles Declaration of 11 March 2022, EU leaders responded collectively to the Russian invasion, which they described as a 'tectonic shift in European history'.[42] The EU response, according to the declaration, would consist of a broader geopolitical repositioning based on three pillars: first, the strengthening of defence capabilities within the EU, including a significant increase in defence budgets; second, the reduction of energy dependence, including gas and oil from Russia; and third, building a more robust economic base, including limiting strategic dependencies such as critical raw materials and semiconductors. These three pillars would thus cover multiple policy areas of the EU, and find their concrete expression in a range of new laws and other instruments.

3 A Growing *Acquis* of 'Geopolitical Law' in the EU

Given that there is a whole range of new instruments adopted by the EU as a tangible expression of its 'geopolitical awakening', there is a need to define them as a group and subsequently to categorize them. It is suggested here that the instruments form an emerging *acquis* of 'geopolitical law', which started to develop already several years before the *Zeitenwende* of February 2022. This *acquis* covers different policy areas and uses different legal bases, among which the CFSP/CSDP, but also other, supranationally characterized Union powers. EU 'geopolitical law' often takes the form of secondary legislation (particularly regulations), but also of other, measures, some of which could potentially be considered 'soft law', such as memoranda and policy documents.

Regardless of this diversity, a common feature of these instruments is that they were adopted with the clear objective of addressing geopolitical risks and threats. Although there is no uniform definition of these risks and threats, a plausible definition from the literature is that they concern, firstly, the rivalry

40 German Federal Government (n 9).

41 R.A. Wessel, 'Ontwikkelingen in het Europees defensiebeleid: bevoegdheden en beperkingen' (2024) nr. 12 *SEW – Tijdschrift voor Europees en economisch recht* 514, 519.

42 Versailles Declaration, 11 March 2022, <https://www.consilium.europa.eu/media/54773/20220311-versailles-declaration-en.pdf> (accessed 20 January 2025) pt. 6.

between and with great powers (United States, China and Russia), secondly, the challenges and disruptions of technological progress, and, thirdly, economic dependencies on countries outside the EU.[43]

The legal instruments, which are part of what is understood here as 'geopolitical law', sometimes explicitly state their underlying geopolitical motivation, for example by referring to the 'current geopolitical situation in the Eastern neighbourhood countries'.[44] Although the term 'geopolitics' is not used in other instruments, the geopolitical dimension is still quite clearly recognizable by implication. This is the case, for example, when an instrument emphasizes the need for 'increasing the Union's resilience in the field of semiconductor technologies' and 'reinforcing the Union's semiconductor ecosystem by reducing dependencies'.[45] Another common feature of these instruments is that they provide the Union with new, unilateral means to expand its options for action in the face of geopolitical risks and threats in the spirit of 'open strategic autonomy'.

These characteristics highlight the inherent geopolitical character of the instruments proposed here, especially if one also takes into account the political context from which they arise. Therefore, this chapter posits that it is possible to adequately define the EU's new 'geopolitical law', even though there will of course always remain borderline cases of instruments that do have a geopolitical dimension, but whose main motivation is different, such as protection of the climate.

Moreover, this chapter proposes to divide the EU's 'geopolitical law' into two main categories. On the one hand, there are security and defence instruments, which are mainly aimed at Russia. On the other hand, there are foreign trade and investment instruments mainly aimed at China, with the United States partly in the background, certainly considering the arrival of the second Trump administration.[46] It must be added, lastly, that instruments of a clearly economic nature are also used to for the purposes of security and defence. Hence, they are grouped here under security and defence instruments. This

43 Steinbach (n 16) 974.

44 Regulation (EU) 2023/2418 of the European Parliament and of the Council of 18 October 2023 establishing an instrument for the strengthening of the European defence industry through joint procurement (EDIRPA) [2023] *OJ* L, recital 11.

45 Regulation (EU) 2023/1781 of the European Parliament and of the Council of 13 September 2023 establishing a framework for measures to strengthen the European semiconductor ecosystem and amending Regulation (EU) 2021/694 [2023] *OJ* L 229/1, recital 2.

46 M. Milanovic, 'Trump's Coercion of America's Allies and the Prohibition of Intervention', *EJIL:Talk!* (13 January 2025), <https://www.ejiltalk.org/trumps-coercion-of-americas-allies-and-the-prohibition-of-intervention/> (accessed 18 January 2025).

includes sanctions and measures to promote European cooperation in the defence industrial domain.

3.1 *'Geopolitical Law' in Security and Defence*

Part of the EU's 'geopolitical law' is aimed at ensuring the security of the European Union, especially against Russian aggression. However, the instruments in this category are not all based on the CFSP/CSDP but also make use of other EU competences such as industrial policy and the internal market.

In 2017, three years after the annexation of Crimea but five years before the Russian invasion of Ukraine, European defence cooperation took three important steps forward. Firstly, the format Permanent Structured Cooperation (PESCO) was launched, promoting closer defence cooperation between EU Member States.[47] Although PESCO was already present in the EU Treaty after the amendments to the Lisbon Treaty, it was only activated in 2017.[48] More than sixty projects are now underway within the framework of PESCO, including military mobility.[49] Secondly, an EU Military Planning and Conduct Capability (MPCC) within the European Union Military Staff.[50] This concerns an operational headquarters that can coordinate small-scale, non-executive military missions such as the EU training missions in Somalia and Ukraine. Both initiatives were most likely made possible by the fact that the United Kingdom had already begun its withdrawal from the EU and had therefore dropped its opposition.[51] Third, although not in the form of EU legislation, in 2017 the Coordinated Annual Review on Defence (CARD) has been launched, which identifies and maps out gaps on an annual basis within the defence plans of the Member States.[52]

---

47 Council Decision (CFSP) 2017/2315 of 11 December 2017 establishing Permanent Structured Cooperation (PESCO) and drawing up the list of participating Member States [2017] *OJ* L 331/57.

48 Consolidated version of the Treaty on European Union [2012] *OJ* C 326/13, art. 42(6), art. 46, and Protocol 10.

49 For an overview of the projects within the framework of PESCO, see: <https://www.pesco.europa.eu/#projects>.

50 Council Decision (EU) 2017/971 of 8 June 2017 laying down the planning and implementation arrangements for EU non-executive military CSDP missions [2017] *OJ* L 146/133.

51 J. Barigazzi, 'EU's small steps toward (whisper it) a military HQ', *Politico* (28 February 2017), <https://www.politico.eu/article/eus-small-steps-toward-whisper-it-a-military-hq-defense-cooperation/> (accessed 20 January 2025).

52 European External Action Service, 'Coordinated Annual Review on Defence (CARD)', 29 March 2024, <https://www.eeas.europa.eu/eeas/coordinated-annual-review-defence-card_en> (accessed 20 January 2025).

The European Defence Fund was then launched in 2021.[53] It was already proposed by the Commission in 2017. It is notable that the fund is part of the regular EU budget within the multiannual financial framework. Nearly €8 billion will be earmarked for this between 2021 and 2027, allowing the European Commission to grant subsidies for cross-border and joint purchase and development of defence technology and capabilities, including PESCO projects.[54]

After the Russian invasion of Ukraine, the development of the EU's geopolitical instruments accelerated further. Firstly, this has led to innovation within the Union's sanctions policy. In addition to economic sanctions against Russia and individuals and entities supporting Putin's regime, the EU also developed new forms of sanctions. These include sanctioning the Russian central bank and disconnecting several Russian and Belarusian banks from the SWIFT financial messaging system. The EU has adopted fourteen such sanctions packages as of early 2025.[55]

Another notable instrument deployed in aid of Ukraine defence against Russian aggression is the European Peace Facility (EPF). It has its origins in the 2003 African Peace Facility, an instrument through which the EU could financially support peace operations and initiatives of the African Union and subregional organizations in Africa.[56] In 2021, it was recast as the 'European Peace Facility', which could also be used outside the African context.[57] After the Russian invasion it was rapidly transformed. The emphasis was now no longer on peacekeeping, but, despite the name *peace* facility, it was used predominantly to support Ukraine's war effort, including by financing the supply of lethal equipment.[58] By the end of 2024, the EU has supported Ukraine with

53 Regulation (EU) 2021/697 of the European Parliament and of the Council of 29 April 2021 establishing the European Defense Fund and repealing Regulation (EU) 2018/1092 [2021] *OJ* L 170/149.

54 S.N. Mengelberg, 'EU en NAVO: concurrerend of complementair? Europese strategische autonomie en de EU-NAVO-relatie' (2022) 3 *Militaire Spectator* 154, 158.

55 Council Regulation (EU) 2024/1745 of 24 June 2024 amending Regulation (EU) No 833/2014 concerning restrictive measures in view of Russia's actions destabilizing the situation in Ukraine [2024] *OJ* L 1745/1.

56 M. Carbone, 'An Uneasy Nexus: Development, Security and the EU's African Peace Facility' (2013) 18 *European Foreign Affairs Review* 103.

57 Council Decision (CFSP) 2021/509 of 22 March 2021 establishing a European Peace Facility and repealing Decision (CFSP) 2015/528 [2021] *OJ* L 102/14. A second purpose of the EPF is to jointly finance certain costs incurred by EU CSDP missions.

58 For example, Decision 2022/338/CFSP of 28 February 2022 on a support measure under the European Peace Facility for the supply to the Ukrainian Armed Forces of military equipment and platforms designed to kill [2022] *OJ* L 60/1.

more than €11 billion through the EPF.[59] The EPF is not part of the regular EU budget, but is a so-called 'off-budget' instrument.[60]

The most recent chapter in this context is a series of new instruments to facilitate the procurement of military equipment within the EU, on the one hand to further support Ukraine in the fight against Russia and on the other hand to ensure the supply of the armed forces of the EU Member States. To be mentioned here is, firstly, the Act in Support of Ammunition Production (ASAP).[61] Through ASAP, €0.5 billion was made available in the period 2023–2025 to financially support EU ammunition producers and the associated supply chains.

Secondly, in October 2023 the European Defence Industry Reinforcement through Common Procurement Act (EDIRPA) was adopted.[62] Through this, €310 million are made available to create financial incentives for coalitions of member states to jointly purchase defence equipment in the period 2024–2025. ASAP and EDIRPA are both part of the regular EU budget.

Given that ASAP and EDIRPA are short-term measures of limited scope, a new strategy for the European defence industry was published by the European Commission and the High Representative in March 2024.[63] On this basis, the European Commission has proposed a European Defence Industry Programme (EDIP).[64] Under this programme, €1.5 billion will be made available during the period 2025–2027 for strengthening the European defence industry, with Ukraine also being closely involved.

As regards the legal basis of these new geopolitical instruments, it is remarkable that some instruments with a clear defence character make use of supranationally established powers of the Union. For example, the legal basis of EDIRPA is Article 173(3) of the Treaty on the Functioning of the European

59 European Council, 'European Peace Facility' <https://www.consilium.europa.eu/en/policies/european-peace-facility/> (accessed 20 January 2025).

60 F. Fabbrini, 'Funding the War in Ukraine: The European Peace Facility, the Macro-Financial Assistance Instrument, and the Slow Rise of an EU Fiscal Capacity' (2023) 11 *Politics and Governance* 53.

61 Regulation (EU) 2023/1525 of the European Parliament and of the Council of 20 July 2023 on support for the production of ammunition [2023] *OJ* L 185/7.

62 Regulation (EU) 2023/2418 (n 44).

63 European Commission and High Representative of the Union for Foreign Affairs and Security Policy, *A new strategy for the European defense industry*, Brussels, March 5, 2024, JOIN(2024) 10 final.

64 European Commission, Proposal for a Regulation of the European Parliament and of the Council establishing the European defence industry program and a framework of measures to ensure the timely availability and delivery of defence products (EDIP Regulation), Brussels, 5 March 2024, COM(2024) 150 final.

Union (TFEU), i.e., the domain of competitiveness of the Union's industry.[65] In ASAP, the legal basis is, in addition to Article 173(3) TFEU, also Article 114 TFEU – the functioning of the internal market.[66] The Commission's proposal for EDIP identifies four different legal bases. In addition to Articles 173 and 114 TFEU, Article 322 TFEU on financial provisions is also mentioned here, as well as Article 212 TFEU on economic, financial and technical cooperation with non-EU countries. This latter legal basis has been added due to the close involvement of Ukraine in this package of measures.[67] What these instruments have in common is that none of them uses the intergovernmental CFSP/CSDP as a legal basis, despite the strong connection with security and defence policy. This can be explained by the prohibition in EU law on combining different legal bases, when the respective procedures are incompatible.[68] Instead, based on the so-called centre of gravity test, the main objective of a measure is identified.[69] Adding the CFSP/CSDP as a legal basis is not permitted under EU law because the intergovernmental way of decision-making is at odds with the supranational *modus operandi* of the other EU policy areas set out in the TFEU.

This use of TFEU powers in the broader context of security and defence means that the role of the European Commission as a 'geopolitical actor'[70] is further strengthened. At the same time, this is a gradual shift rather than a landslide, because the Member States continue to play a prominent role here through the Council. Furthermore, other instruments in this domain, which rely less directly on the internal market, use the CFSP/CSDP as a legal basis, such as PESCO and the European Peace Facility. Here the Member States retain their veto power in decision-making. But also outside of the intergovernmental organized CFSP, EU law has been 'geopoliticized'.

3.2 *'Geopolitical Law' in Trade and Investment*

In the field of foreign trade and investment, the EU already possessed an arsenal of trade defence instruments, including anti-dumping measures and countervailing measures. The EU has actively used this in the past against,

---

65 Regulation (EU) 2023/2418 (n 44); Consolidated version of the Treaty on the Functioning of the European Union [2012] *OJ* C 326/47.

66 Regulation (EU) 2023/1525 (n 61).

67 European Commission (n 64).

68 Case C-300/89 *Titanium Dioxide*, ECLI:EU:C:1991:244.

69 A. Ott, 'EU External Competence' in R.A. Wessel & J. Larik (eds.), *EU External Relations Law: Text, Cases and Materials* (2nd edn, Hart Publishing, 2020) 88.

70 C. Håkansson, 'The Ukraine war and the emergence of the European Commission as a geopolitical actor' (2023) 46 *Journal of European Integration* 25.

among others, the United States, China, and Russia. These existing instruments were thoroughly modernized in 2018.[71]

From 2019 onwards, several new unilateral legal instruments with a clear geopolitical motivation have been added.[72] Here, firstly, the 2019 Foreign Direct Investment Screening Mechanism can be mentioned.[73] It creates a framework for the European Commission and the Member States to ensure that strategic and security interests are not affected by foreign investments. An updated version of this framework was proposed by the European Commission in January 2024.[74] In addition, there are discussions about whether there should additionally be an EU framework for outbound investments.[75]

In 2021, the EU furthermore adopted the Global Gateway. This is a program through which the EU and the Member States intend to invest no less than €300 billion in third countries in the period 2021–2027. The intention is to further develop the infrastructure in these countries, but at the same time it is the European answer to the Chinese Belt and Road Initiative, which has been used as an instrument for increasing China's global influence since 2013.[76]

Greater momentum in terms of producing new geopolitical legislation can be seen from 2022 also in the field of trade and investment. First, the Foreign Subsidies Regulation was adopted in December 2022 and launched in July 2023.[77] Its objective is to combat illegal competition and distortion of the

71 J. Cornelis, 'The EU's Modernization Regulation: Stronger and More Effective Trade Defence Instruments?' (2018) 13 *Global Trade and Customs Journal* 539.

72 Verellen & Hofer (n 15).

73 Regulation (EU) 2019/452 of the European Parliament and of the Council of 19 March 2019 establishing a framework for the screening of foreign direct investments into the Union [2019] OJ L 79I/1.

74 European Commission, Proposal for a Regulation of the European Parliament and of the Council on the screening of foreign investments in the Union and repealing Regulation (EU) 2019/452, Brussels, 24 January 2024, COM(2024) 23 final.

75 European Commission, *White Paper on Outbound Investments*, Brussels, 24 January 2024, COM(2024) 24 final.

76 C.-P. Chu & Z.A. Ferenczy, 'The Shifting Role of the EU's Economic Diplomacy Towards China: The Case of China's Belt and Road Initiative and the EU's Global Gateway' in C.-P. Chu & S.-C. Park (eds.), *Strategies in Changing Global Orders* (Springer, 2023). It should be noted that the foundation for the Global Gateway is not EU legislation, but a policy document: European Commission and High Representative of the Union for Foreign Affairs and Security Policy, *The Global Gateway*, Brussels, 1 December 2021, JOIN(2021) 30 final.

77 Regulation (EU) 2022/2560 of the European Parliament and of the Council of 14 December 2022 on foreign subsidies distorting the internal market [2022] OJ L 330/1.

internal market through state aid from third countries. The European Commission launched the first investigation within this framework in February 2024 against a Chinese state-owned company.[78]

Furthermore, the EU adopted the Anti-Coercion Instrument (ACI) in November 2023.[79] The relevance of such an instrument is highlighted by a dispute between China and Lithuania over the opening of a Taiwanese representative office in Vilnius in 2021. China, which considers Taiwan a renegade province, imposed trade restrictions on Lithuania to put pressure on the country. With the EU ACI, the EU can now formulate collective responses in such cases, including, as a last resort, sanctions.[80] It has already been speculated whether the ACI could be used to counter American coercion against Denmark as part of the Trump administration's stated quest for acquiring Greenland.[81]

Moreover, the European Chips Act of September 2023 can be seen as a geopolitical instrument.[82] Its adoption underlines the strategic importance of semiconductors and associated technologies and aims at developing a European industrial base for semiconductors, making Europe more resilient to future crises and disruptions to supply chains. It is therefore an industrial policy measure aimed at an important aspect of the EU's 'strategic autonomy'. In the same spirit, a regulation was adopted in April 2024 with the aim of better guaranteeing the EU's access to critical raw materials.[83] This goal is to be achieved by strengthening supply chains within the EU on the one hand and by diversifying foreign sources of such raw materials on the other. This turn, propels also the adoption of new bilateral instruments, such as the stra-

78 European Commission, 'Commission opens first in-depth investigation under the Foreign Subsidies Regulation', 16 February 2025, <https://ec.europa.eu/commission/press corner/detail/nl/ip_24_887> (accessed 20 January 2025).

79 Regulation (EU) 2023/2675 of the European Parliament and of the Council of 22 November 2023 on the protection of the Union and its Member States against economic coercion by third countries [2023] OJ L.

80 C. Freudlsperger & S. Meunier, 'When Foreign Policy Becomes Trade Policy: The EU's Anti-Coercion Instrument' (2024) 62 *Journal of Common Market Studies* 1063; L. Schaupp, 'Decoding the Intersection of Trade and Security in the EU's Anti-Coercion Instrument' (2024) 29 *European Foreign Affairs Review* 133.

81 Milanovic (n 46).

82 Regulation (EU) 2023/1781 (n 45). For other EU initiatives aimed at ensuring access to and control over strategic technologies, see Steinbach (n 16) 993.

83 Regulation (EU) 2024/1252 of the European Parliament and of the Council of 11 April 2024 establishing a framework to ensure a secure and sustainable supply of critical raw materials [2024] OJ L.

tegic partnership on raw materials the EU concluded with Serbia in July 2024.[84]

While this list of geopolitical instruments in the field of trade includes the most important examples, one could add others, which may not focus on geopolitics, but which do have a geopolitical dimension attached to them. An example of this is the Carbon Border Adjustment Mechanism (CBAM), which was launched in 2023.[85] Its main objectives are environmental protection and climate action (which is also reflected in the use of Article 192 TFEU as the legal basis for CBAM), as well as protecting the internal market against unfair competition from third countries. Nevertheless, it is also partly about countering competition from China and signalling a pioneering role for the EU on the world stage in the field of regulations. In addition, some internal legislative instruments, such as the Corporate Sustainability Due Diligence (CSDDD) of June 2024 and the Artificial Intelligence (AI) Act of July 2024 and the could be seen as an expression of a geopolitically tinted, long arm of the 'Brussels effect'.[86] These internal instruments allow the EU contribute to setting the global tone in regulation, at least in markets and with actors where the EU exercises such influence.[87] At the same time, such measures can prompt a backlash with clear geopolitical implications, as evidenced by Qatar's threat to halt gas exports to the EU if penalties were imposed under the CSDDD.[88]

The aforementioned trade and investment instruments, as well as certain regulatory instruments, mainly use as legal basis either the common commer-

---

84 Memorandum of Understanding between the European Union and the Republic of Serbia on a strategic partnership on sustainable raw materials, battery value chains and electric vehicles, Belgrade, 19 July 2024.

85 Regulation (EU) 2023/956 of the European Parliament and of the Council of 10 May 2023 establishing a carbon border adjustment mechanism [2023] *OJ* L 130/52. Another example is the legislation on dual-use goods, Regulation (EU) 2021/821 of the European Parliament and of the Council of 20 May 2021 establishing a Union regime for the control of exports, brokering, technical assistance, the transit and transfer of dual-use items (recast) [2021] *OJ* L 206/1.

86 Regulation (EU) 2024/1689 of the European Parliament and of the Council of 13 June 2024 laying down harmonized rules on artificial intelligence (Artificial Intelligence Regulation) [2024] *OJ* L.

87 See, but also with some critical comments, M. Almada & A. Radu, 'The Brussels Side-Effect: How the AI Act Can Reduce the Global Reach of EU Policy' (2024) 25 *German Law Journal* 646.

88 Giedre Peseckyte, 'Qatar warns it will halt gas supplies to Europe if fined under EU due diligence law', *Politico* (22 December 2024), <https://www.politico.eu/article/qatar-warned-to-halt-eu-gas-supplies-if-fined-under-due-diligence-law/> (accessed 20 January 2025).

cial policy (Article 207 TFEU; such as the Anti-Coercive Instrument), or Article 114 TFEU on the functioning of the internal market (such as the Critical Raw Materials Regulation), or a combination of the two (such as the Foreign Subsidies Regulation). This makes sense from an EU law point of view. At the same time, the adoption of these types of geopolitical instruments with an economic character, or 'geo-economic' instruments, can also be seen as an institution shift which strengthens the role of the European Commission through the use of supranational legal bases.[89] The Commission not only has the right of initiative to propose such instruments, but is also responsible for a large part of their implementation.[90] Seeing the wealth of new legal instruments as the most tangible expression of the EU's geopolitical awakening, the analysis now turns to how other RIOs have responded to the rougher international environment.

4 Beyond the EU: Who Else Is Awakening?

Turning now from the EU to other RIOs, the same question can be investigated: Do they show signs of 'geopolitical awakening', and if so, do they translate into any specific measures. To shed light on this, the chapter considers as comparators the East African Community and ASEAN. While this of course cannot claim general findings, this selection brings in two other world regions and two different types of organizations. Both, moreover, have in common that they have wide-ranging ambitions, considering, for example, ASEAN's Political-Security Community and the EAC's recent enlargements (Democratic Republic of Congo in 2022 and Somalia in 2024) and codified aim to establish a common currency and political federation.[91] Therefore, they seem likely candidates for 'geopolitical awakening' as a response to the deteriorating climate in international politics. However, as this section shows, beyond general acknowledgments of this changed climate, no dedicated actions can as of yet

89 C. Weinhardt, K. Mau & J. Hillebrand Pohl, 'The EU as a Geoeconomic Actor? A Review of Recent European Trade and Investment Policies' in M. Babić, A.D. Dixon & I.T. Liu (eds.), *The Political Economy of Geoeconomics: Europe in a Changing World* (Palgrave Macmillan, 2023).

90 F. De Ville, S. Happersberger & H. Kalimo, 'The Unilateral Turn in EU Trade Policy? The Origins and Characteristics of the EU's New Trade Instruments' (2023) 28 *European Foreign Affairs Review* 15.

91 Treaty for the Establishment of the East African Community, signed 30 November 1999, art. 5(2). Note also the East African Community Protocol on Co-operation in Defence Affairs, signed 28 April 2012.

be detected. As explanations, the chapter offers the geographical remoteness of the Russo-Ukrainian war and the lack of the combination of strong institutions and (economic) power in either of them.

As regards for the EAC, its 'EAC Vision 2050', published in 2016, does not use the term geopolitics. It does note under the heading 'Defence, Peace and Security' the ambition to establish an EAC mutual defence pact and to achieve 'self-sufficiency in production of defence hardware for regional security needs and export.'[92] This could be seen as signs of strengthening EAC as a security actor and striving towards its own version of 'strategic autonomy'. However, great power tensions or pressures from such outside powers on the EAC are not made explicit as motivating factors. Specialized bodies such as the EAC Monetary Affairs Committee do occasionally note 'rising geopolitical tensions'.[93] On a ministerial retreat in in July 2024, a call was made for expediting the conclusion of the abovementioned East African Community mutual defence pact and the operationalization of an EAC Council of Ministers on Peace and Security.[94] However, also here there was no explicit mention of a geopolitical necessity or context. The 2024 communiqué of the EAC's highest body, the EAC Summit, does not mention geopolitics, focusing on peace and security issues in the region.[95]

It does not appear that any specific measures, including legislation, have been adopted in the EAC which can clearly be seen to have been prompted by the changed geopolitical environment. It should be added that this includes also measures in the area of trade, which could be used as geopolitical instru-

92 East African Community, *Vision 2050* (EAC Secretariat, 2016) 78.

93 East African Community, *Communiqué of the 25th Ordinary meeting of the East African Community Monetary Affairs Committee, virtual meeting*, 4 March 2022, <https://www.eac.int/press-releases/145-financial-sector/2387-communiqu%C3%A9-25th-ordinary-meeting-of-the-eac-monetary-affairs-committee> (accessed 18 January 2025). See also East African Community, *EAC Monetary Affairs Committee addresses regional economic challenges and progress towards the EA Monetary Union*, 7 May 2024, <https://www.eac.int/press->releases/145-financial-sector/3084-eac-monetary-affairs-committee-addresses-regional-economic-challenges-and-progress-towards-the-ea-monetary-union> (accessed 19 January 2025).

94 East African Community, *Communiqué of the EAC ministerial retreat on peace and security, partner states relations and integration process*, 8 July 2024, <https://www.eac.int/communique/3132-communiqu%C3%A9-of-the-eac-ministerial-retreat-on-peace-and-security,-partner-states-relations-and-integration-process> (accessed 19 January 2025) pt. 5.

95 East African Community, *Communiqué of the 24th ordinary summit of the East African Community Head of State*, 30 November 2024, <https://www.eac.int/communique/3254-communiqu%C3%A9-of-the-24th-ordinary-summit-of-the-east-african-community-heads-of-state> (accessed 19 January 2025).

ments, as is the case for the EU, given that EAC is a customs union, which implies a common trade policy.

As regards ASEAN, the 'Blueprint 2025' for the ASEAN Political-Security Community, published in 2016, remarks on the 'changing strategic and geopolitical landscape'.[96] In this context, it notes the need for a 'common vision for a regional architecture to strengthen ASEAN centrality'[97] and for enhancing 'the role of the ASEAN Foreign Ministers Meeting (AMM) and its Chair' to address geopolitical challenges.[98] Within the ASEAN Political-Security Community, the ASEAN Defence Ministers' meeting recognizes 'the complexity posed by geopolitical and geostrategic dynamics affect regional and global peace and stability',[99] noting also the South China Sea dispute, which implicated the People's Republic of China as a great power. The ASEAN defence ministers, furthermore, stress both the need to 'deepen defence and security cooperation'[100] and commitment to 'a rules-based regional architecture with ASEAN at the centre that upholds international law'[101] in this environment, which is a comparable sentiment to the EU's 'principled pragmatism'. The 2024 Chairman's statement of the ASEAN Summit, the RIO's highest body, also noted 'concern on the intensifying geopolitical tensions in the region' and expressed the leaders' commitment to keep developing the 'regional architecture including through ASEAN-led mechanisms and managing the impact of geopolitical and geostrategic shifts on our region to ensure regional peace and security are not disrupted'.[102]

Thus, compared to the EAC, ASEAN is more explicit about geopolitical tensions, and continues to develop its political-security community, including through various initiatives in the area of defence. However, all this is progressing along the lines of the classic 'ASEAN Way'[103] of consultations, consensus, and a strong reliance of non-binding declarations. Moreover, given that

96 Association of Southeast Asian Nations, *ASEAN Political-Security Blueprint 2025* (ASEAN Secretariat, 2016) 32.

97 Ibid.

98 Ibid., 12.

99 Association of Southeast Asian Nations, *Vientiane Joint Declaration of the ASEAN Defence Ministers' Meeting on ASEAN: Together for Peace, Security and Resilience*, 20 November 2024, 1.

100 Ibid., 3.

101 Ibid., 1.

102 Association of Southeast Asian Nations, *Chairman's Statement of the 44th and 45th ASEAN Summits, Vientiane, Lao PDR*, 9 October 2024, pt. 44.

103 A. Acharya, *Constructing a Security Community in Southeast Asia: ASEAN and the Problem of Regional Order* (3rd edn, Routledge, 2014) 62–68.

ASEAN is a free trade area, there is no common trade policy among its Member States. This is visible, for example, in the example of Singapore, but not other ASEAN countries, imposing unliteral sanctions against Russia due to the latter's aggression against Ukraine.[104]

In sum, it appears that only the EU has 'awakened' geopolitically to such an extent that, first, its general foreign policy outlook changed, and second, it followed suit with a range of new instruments in the areas of trade, defence, and their intersection, which it is already deploying. While the EAC, in its official documents, only shows marginal attention to geopolitics, ASEAN does recognize it more explicitly, though without seeming to pivot its general outlook and adopt new instruments. This leads, then, to the question of why only the EU is showing this clear reaction to the new geopolitical situation and heavy reliance on new legal tools. This chapter suggests two answers: one geographical, one legal and economical.

That geopolitics signifies a 'return' of geography to international politics, is something Europeans became acutely aware of due to the Russian full-scale invasion of Ukraine in 2022. Close proximity to a militarily aggressive great power subsequently caused Sweden and Finland to join NATO, and Denmark to give up its thirty year-long CSDP-opt out and join PESCO.[105] It shattered (misguided) ideas of Europe as a 'garden' of peace compared to a rough 'jungle' outside.[106] While also other developments such as China's growing economic weight and assertiveness and the volatility of U.S. foreign policy contributed to this, it was above all this shock of the *Zeitenwende* which created the political will and momentum in the EU to accelerate down the path described above.

104 Singapore Ministry of Foreign Affairs, *Sanctions and Restrictions against Russia in Response to its Invasion of Ukraine*, 5 March 2022, <https://www.mfa.gov.sg/Newsroom/Press-Statements-Transcripts-and-Photos/2022/03/20220305-sanctions> (accessed 20 January 2025).

105 Council of the EU, *EU defence cooperation: Council welcomes Denmark into PESCO and launches the 5th wave of new PESCO projects*, 23 May 2023, <https://www.consilium.europa.eu/en/press/press-releases/2023/05/23/eu-defence-cooperation-council-welcomes-denmark-into-pesco-and-launches-the-5th-wave-of-new-pesco-projects/> (23 May 2023).

106 European External Action Service, *European Diplomatic Academy: Opening remarks by High Representative Josep Borrell at the inauguration of the pilot programme*, 13 October 2022, <https://www.eeas.europa.eu/eeas/european-diplomatic-academy-opening-remarks-high-representative-josep-borrell-inauguration-pilot_en> (accessed 21 January 2022); see also earlier, R. Cooper, *The Post-modern State and the World Order* (Demos, 2000).

This is not to say that geography does not matter in the other world regions – of course it does. However, to regions like East Africa and Southeast Asia, the Russian invasion of Ukraine was a more distant, and less pivotal event. Aggressive great power behaviour has long been known in Southeast Asia, in particular in the form of the South China Sea dispute, and military interventions by great powers, considering, for example Vietnam's experience with both the United States and the PR China half a century ago. Meanwhile, as becomes evident from the EAC's documents, security concerns and other crises, especially in the DR Congo, are so preoccupying that the Russian invasion represents a remote event. It is certainly an event with ripple effects, as evidenced by the importance of Ukrainian grain exports for food security in the region,[107] but it is not a direct threat. Perhaps this is an obvious point to make, but from a European (or even 'Eurocentric') point of view, it bears making explicit, seeing also the lack of active support for sanctions imposed on Russia by 'Global South' countries.[108] It is also reflective of a broader disagreement or disconnect, including allegations of hypocrisy and double standards.[109] In the words of Indian Foreign Minister S. Jaishankar, there is a need 'to grow out of the mindset that Europe's problems are the world's problems but the world's problems are not Europe's problems'.[110] Hence, Europe's 'geopolitical wake-up call' was not necessarily the world's. While this may be true for the Russian invasion of Ukraine, the geopolitical effects of more assertive Chinese and U.S. foreign policies will be experienced in different world regions, perhaps especially in the Indo-Pacificm, therefore leaving geography only as a partial explanation for the lack of 'awakening' and the equipment with new tools in other RIOs.

Hence, the legal and economic explanation may complete the picture. While there was perhaps less of an immediate and acute demand for new instruments in regions more remote from the Russian aggression against Ukraine, the question is also what other RIOs are capable of offering in

107 S.M. Mwatu, 'Impact of the Russia–Ukraine war on grain and fertilizer supply: Evidence from Kenya' (2023) 9 *World Food Policy* 250.

108 C. Seshadri, 'Western Sanctions on Russia and the Global South's Stance', *RUSI Commentary* (23 November 2023), <https://rusi.org/explore-our-research/publications/commentary/western-sanctions-russia-and-global-souths-stance> (accessed 20 January 2025).

109 C. Alden, 'The Global South and Russia's Invasion of Ukraine' (2023) 3 *LSE Public Policy Review* 1.

110 'Europe Has to Grow Out of Mindset That Its Problems Are World's Problems': Jaishankar', *The Wire* (3 June 2022), <https://thewire.in/government/europe-has-to-grow-out-of-mindset-that-its-problems-are-worlds-problems-jaishankar> (accessed 21 January 2025).

terms of supplying such tools. This requires a combination of both strong institutions embedded in a legal system and economic weight. In the case of the EU, the Commission takes a leading role in the economic instruments, with individual Member States generally not having veto powers to block decisions. In decisions about sanctions and the rest of the CFSP/CSDP, it is true that the unanimity principle in the Council applies.[111] Nevertheless, the political will was there, arguably facilitated by backroom deals and diplomatic pressures, in the wider EU framework, to proceed in expanding and applying the EU's new geopolitical instruments. For example, despite various Hungarian threats of vetoes,[112] the EU had adopted eighteen sanctions packages against Russia as of July 2025.

Moreover, perhaps another obvious but worthwhile point to make is that geopolitical instruments can only work if backed up with the requisite economic weight. This applies to sanctions, including against economic coercion, but also investments, subsidies, and for influencing global standards. In addition, in matters for military aid, procurement, and research and development. Despite the legitimate criticisms of the fragmented EU defence market,[113] which the new measures like EDIP aim to fix, at least the potential of the EU's internal market is there, as is the combined defence spending power of the Member States of now more than 300 billion euro.[114]

It is this combination of strong institutions and legal order and economic weight that makes the EU's geopolitical awakening, and the specific expression it has given to it, possible and meaningful. What the EAC can offer in supranational institutions, it lacks in economic weight. Conversely, what ASEAN can offer in economic potential, it seems to lack in strong common institutions. This is a snapshot of the current situation and could change in the future, including the decline of the EU's relative economic weight and competitiveness, but it contributes to explaining why the EU's geopolitical awakening has taken shape the way it did, and not in other RIOs.

---

111 Treaty on European Union (n 48) art. 24(1).

112 G. Gavin, V. Jack and C. Gijs, 'Hungary teases veto over new EU Russian gas sanctions', *Politico* (13 May 2023), <https://www.politico.eu/article/hungary-veto-eu-russia-gas-sanctions/> (accessed 20 January 2024).

113 T. Mueller, 'Strategic options for the European defence industry in the 2020s' (2024) 41 *Defense & Security Analysis* 49.

114 Joshua Posaner, 'EU defense spending projected to boom to €326B', *Politico* (4 December 2024), <https://www.politico.eu/article/eu-defense-spending-projected-boom-326b-european-defence-agency-russia-war-security/> (accessed 21 January 2025).

5 Conclusion and RIO Research for the Future

As this chapter has shown, the turn to geopolitics has met with very different responses from RIOs. The EU's 'geopolitical awakening' is not only expressed in the form of a more sombre and assertive political rhetoric, but has led to a range of new legal instruments, of which key examples were presented. These instruments can be considered as a growing *acquis* of 'geopolitical law', whereby regardless of the use of different legal bases, the coverage of different policy areas and whether Russia or China is the main target, the geopolitical motivation is clearly recognizable. While this trend already started several years before the full-scale Russian invasion of Ukraine, that latter development has been the major driver and accelerator of this trend for the EU.

By contrast, other RIOs, namely the East African Community and ASEAN, show no similar development of 'geopoliticization through law'. This is so despite the high ambitions of both organizations, including in the field of security and defence. Geopolitics are mentioned in some policy documents, but a clear rhetoric shift, let alone the adoption of a new toolkit of instruments, cannot be detected so far. The chapter offered a dual explanation of geographical remoteness from the Russo-Ukrainian war and the lack of a combination of strong institutions and economic weight.

Since many of the EU's new instruments have only recently been adopted, and RIOs will continue to evolve and adapt around the world, a research agenda for comparative regionalism and the legal aspects of RIOs emerges. In closing this chapter, the following core research questions are proposed for this agenda:

- *Rule of law*: What remedies are available to persons targeted or otherwise adversely affected by the Union's new geopolitical instruments? This includes, for example, (legal) persons who are affected by EU sanctions, but also companies that experience negative consequences due to investigations into foreign subsidies, or that do not agree with the outcomes of tender procedures in the field of defence equipment. At the same time, as both people and companies in other world regions will be affected by geopolitical tensions, the question there arises if they would not benefit from regional measures to protect them. For both these aspects, legal research is essential.
- *Effectiveness*: To what extent will the EU's new instruments be able to achieve their respective objectives, and the overarching goal of a more resilient and decisive Union? The adoption of laws and their analysis alone still say very little about whether they will actually make the EU an effective geopolitical force. Hence, tackling this question will require an

approach that combines law, economics, political science, and other disciplines. These findings, in turn, will serve as valuable evidence for other RIOs that may consider going down the path of 'geopoliticization through law'.

- *Interinstitutional relations and reform*: To what extent are the new geopolitical instruments shifting the balance of power between the EU institutions? In particular, do they lead to a (creeping) power transfer towards supranational institutions such as the European Commission? This article noted a slight move towards supranationalization through the use of legal bases from the TFEU for some of the new instruments in the field of security and defence. This will form an important part of the broader discussion on decision-making processes within the EU, and could serve as inspiration – or cautionary tales – for other RIOs.

It is expected that further instruments that can be considered part of the EU's 'geopolitical law' will be adopted in the coming years. At the same time, it will become clear how existing instruments are applied in practice – including in the context of the foreign policy of the second Trump administration in the U.S. – and in which cases this will lead to legal disputes. Other RIOs will also continue to develop and adapt to internal and external challenges. The need for rigorous legal and interdisciplinary research on the subject of RIOs, geopolitics, and the law will therefore only increase.

Acknowledgements

The author would like to express his sincere gratitude to Santiago Dresen and Susanna Koppe for the assistance in completing this chapter. The chapter builds on an earlier, shorter publication in Dutch, J. E. Larik 'Geopolitiek recht' in de EU: inter arma germinant leges' (2024) nr. 12 *SEW – Tijdschrift voor Europees en economisch recht* 523.

CHAPTER 10

Latin America Regional International Organizations and Climate Change: Managerialism and Judicialization

*Andrés Delgado Casteleiro**

Abstract

This chapter explores the legal dynamics of Latin American RIOs and their impact on the region's approach to climate change regulation. By examining these legal dynamics, this contribution brings forward an alternative way of regional ordering other than the EU. It illustrates that, like any other strategy for RIOs, the Latin American approach has strengths and weaknesses, offering valuable insight into the heterogeneous nature of RIOs as a single category. From that starting point, the chapter examines how Latin American RIOs have addressed the fight against climate change and argues that the region's dynamics oscillate between managerial coordination and judicial strategies. Thus, climate change would be tackled from two opposing perspectives: a managerial one in which Latin America's RIOs would be, at best, venues to share best practices and a judicial perspective where regional litigation advances common legal standards regarding climate change in the region.

Keywords

Regional International Organisations – Climate Change – Latin America – Managerialism – Judicialization – Legal Formalism – Soft Law – Climate Change Litigation – Human Rights – Environment

1 Introduction

A contribution about Regional International Organizations (RIOs) in Latin America in a volume about the European Union (EU) as a Regional Interna-

* Andrés Delgado Casteleiro is affiliated with CUNEF Universidad, Madrid, Spain.

 | DOI:10.1163/9789004700659_012

tional Organization may suggest that the EU serves as a model for Latin American RIOs.[1] Comparative analyses of regionalism have traditionally focused on whether the EU could serve as a model for other RIOs, especially the Latin American ones.[2] The achievement of European unity (whatever that might mean) through economic and political integration has influenced the thought of many Latin American scholars.[3] Underpinning these comparisons is the notion of the EU as the highest evolved RIO:[4] the RIO every other RIO copies. For instance, the Andean Community was designed with the European experience in mind.[5] Besides the colonial undertones of such analyses,[6] they often miss the different legal dynamics that inform RIOs.[7] For instance, the discussions in the 50s and '60s regarding establishing a Latin American Common Market were not conceptualized as a precursor to deeper political integration as the familiar narratives for the EU go. Instead, the common market was seen as a necessary step towards development.[8]

Considering that the underpinning rationale of RIOs in Latin America differs from the EU's underpinning, the comparison might not be an adequate methodology to reflect on Latin American RIOs vis-à-vis the EU. Instead, the analysis of the Latin American RIOs' practices on themselves shows alternative approaches to regional cooperation beyond the EU method. The reasons for the difference with the EU might be multifaceted, not only legal, political,

1 Marise Cremona, 'The Union as a Global Actor: Roles, Models and Identity' (2004) 41 *Common Market Law Review* 553, 554.

2 See most notably: Ernst B. Haas, 'The Uniting of Europe and the Uniting of Latin America' (1967) 5 *JCMS: Journal of Common Market Studies* 315.

3 Horacio H. Godoy, 'La integración de América Latina y el proceso del poder mundial' (1968) Estudios Internacionales 368 Felipe Herrera, 'La tarea inconclusa: América Latina integrada' (1973) ibid. 3 Gordon Mace, 'Regional Integration in Latin America: A Long and Winding Road' (1988) 43 *International Journal* 404 Francisco Orrego Vicuña, *La integración política: su realidad, su necesidad* (Editorial Jurídica de Chile, 1966).

4 Jan Klabbers, 'The European Union in the law of international organizations' in Ramses A Wessel and Jed Odermatt (eds.), *Research Handbook on the European Union and International Organizations* (Edward Elgar Publishing, 2019) 27.

5 E.g., Karen J. Alter and Laurence R. Helfer, 'Legal Integration in the Andes: Law-Making by the Andean Tribunal of Justice' (2011) 17 *European Law Journal* 701.

6 The colonial underpinnings of International Institutional Law are well established: Jan Klabbers, 'The Emergence of Functionalism in International Institutional Law: Colonial Inspirations' (2014) 25 *European Journal of International Law* 645.

7 Philippe De Lombaerde, Frank Mattheis and Charlotte Vanfraechem, 'Mercosur Compared' in Toscano Franca Filho and others (eds.), *The Law of Mercosur* (2010) 167.

8 The Latin American Common Market. Prepared by the Secretariat of the Economic Commission for Latin America. UNITED NATIONS. Department of Economic and Social Affairs, 1959. E/CN.12/531, p. 1. Available at: https://repositorio.cepal.org/handle/11362/29176.

or economic, but also due to more profound undercurrents like history or geography. Not aligning with the EU model reflects diverse regional political and legal dynamics, which is not a sign of RIO's underdevelopment. Thus, by bringing forward the Latin American experience regarding RIOs and climate change, this contribution sheds light on how other regional orderings tackle climate change, not as a way to critique them as they are not following the EU model or by trying to draw common lines with, but by showing other possibilities as to how to conceptualize RIOs.

This contribution explores the legal dynamics of Latin American RIOs and their impact on the region's approach to climate change regulation. The chapter examines how Latin American RIOs have addressed the fight against climate change and argues that the region's dynamics oscillate between managerial coordination and judicial strategies. Thus, climate change would be tackled from two opposing perspectives: a managerial one in which Latin America's RIOs would be, at best, venues to share best practices and a judicial perspective where regional litigation advances common legal standards regarding climate change in the region.[9]

This chapter is structured in three parts to comprehensively understand the unique political and legal dynamics that inform Latin American RIOs regarding climate change regulation. It begins by discussing the distinct approach to RIOs in Latin America, characterized by the prevalent role of law and unstable politics. The chapter then explores specific examples of Latin American RIOs and their approaches to climate change regulation, followed by an analysis of the judicialization of climate change in the region. Finally, the chapter concludes with insights into the role of Latin American RIOs in addressing climate change.

2 Latin American RIOs, Regionalism, Politics and the Law

The heterogeneous nature of RIOs may challenge the value of any inquiry that conceptualizes them as a single category.[10] It is not only the institutions, competences, or system of sources that can differ widely but also their approach to the concept of region and their relations with other RIOs (significantly when they territorially overlap) that limits the worth of a comparative endeavour.

9 On the role of judges in relation to climate change policy see: Laura Burgers, 'Should Judges Make Climate Change Law?' (2020) 9 *Transnational Environmental Law* 55.

10 Eva Kassoti, 'The European Union and Other Regional International Organizations: Tales of Solidarity' (2024) 21 *International Organizations Law Review* 190, 192.

This section analyses them in two parts. First, it focuses on the idea of region and its impact on the way Latin American regionalism has evolved. Second, it discusses how the Latin American legal tradition has influenced the development of RIOs within Latin America.

2.1 *The Region Is a Political Concept*

At first glance, the concept of a region should be considered neutral, a descriptive term that defines the geographical scope of an international organization.[11] As Carvalho critiques, this notion of the region would conceptualize it as '*a depoliticised legal space*.'[12] However, in Latin America, the idea of the region is eminently political: the region is a legal space determined by politics. In this regard, it is more beneficial to approach the concept of the region by taking Boisson de Chazournes's definition. For her, the region would consist of two elements: a geographical one (the idea of geographical proximity) and a political one (the presence of some shared values or interests).[13]

Regarding Latin American RIOs, the practice shows how the political element is more prevalent than the geographic one. The overlap of regional projects in Latin America is evidence of the political nature of the region and how shared values or interests play a more prominent role in the delimitation of the region than geography. The dichotomy between Latin Americanism and Pan-Americanism would be the perfect example of how the region entails a specific notion of ordering with politics embedded within it.[14] Whilst Latin Americanism saw Latin America as the relevant geographical space (excluding the United States),[15] Pan-Americanism, an all-American movement (including the United States) with regional cooperation as its primary objective, saw all the continent as the relevant region.[16] These regional projects have

---

11 Antony Anghie, 'Identifying Regions in the History of International Law' in Bardo Fassbender and Anne Peters (eds.), *The Oxford Handbook of the History of International Law* (Oxford Academic, Oxford University Press, 2012) 1060.

12 Fabia Fernandes Carvalho, 'Regional International Organizations and Regionalism in the Theory of International Law' (2024) 21 *International Organizations Law Review* 115, 119.

13 Laurence Boisson de Chazournes, *Interactions between Regional and Universal Organizations: A Legal Perspective* (Brill | Nijhoff, 2016) 8.

14 Gordon Mace, 'Regional Integration in Latin America: A Long and Winding Road' (1988) 43 *International Journal* 404, 407. Liliana Obregón, 'Regionalism Constructed: A Short History of 'Latin American International Law'' (2012) European Society of International Law Conference Paper Series.

15 José María Torres Caicedo, *Union latino-americana, pensamiento de Bolivar para formar una liga americana.* (Rosa y Bouret, 1865).

16 Juan Pablo Scarfi, *The Hidden History of International Law in the Americas: Empire and Legal Networks* (Oxford University Press, 2017) 6.

been regarded as contradictory, and each of them gained some momentum in different periods.[17] Thus, the prevalence of Pan-Americanism in the 1930s and 1940s culminated in the creation of the Organization of American States (OAS), or the failed Free Trade of the Americas. Likewise, a Latin Americanist approach influenced the creation of the Latin American Free Trade Association (LAFTA) in the 1960s, the Mercosur in the 1990s, and the Union of South American Nations (UNASUR) in the 2000s.[18] For instance, the UNASUR was the paradigm of the so-called post-hegemonic regionalism[19] whereby 'regional structures characterized by hybrid practices as a result of partial displacement of dominant forms of US-led neo-liberal governance in the acknowledgment of other political forms of organization and management of regional (common) goods.'[20]

Furthermore, the rise of new Latin American RIOs would be linked to political shifts in the Latin American States.[21] The political element would even delineate the relevant region independently of the geographical component. Some Latin American RIOs have flexible concepts of membership. For instance, the Bolivarian Alliance for the Peoples of Our America (ALBA in its Spanish acronym) and Mercosur, in addition to Member States, also provide for the existence of observer states that are closely aligned with the politics underpinning the respective RIO.[22] As a result, since politics define the Latin American region, RIOs proliferates, shifting their membership over time and rendering them unstable organizations. Therefore, Latin American RIOs tend to have a short life span linked to contingent politics. For instance, UNASUR was created in 2008; by 2018, most members had withdrawn and the organization became a RIO in name only. Similarly, ALBA only functioned for ten years and is nowadays considered defunct.[23]

---

17 Ibid.

18 José Briceño-Ruiz and Isidro Morales, 'Post-hegemonic regionalism in the Americas' (2017) Toward a Pacific-Atlantic Divide, 1.

19 José Briceño-Ruiz and Andrea Ribeiro Hoffmann, 'Post-hegemonic regionalism, UNASUR, and the reconfiguration of regional cooperation in South America' (2015) 40 *Canadian Journal of Latin American and Caribbean Studies* 48.

20 Pia Riggirozzi and Diana Tussie, 'Post-hegemonic regionalism' in *Oxford Research Encyclopedia of International Studies* (2021) 12. Briceño-Ruiz and Morales Thomas Legler, 'Post-hegemonic regionalism and sovereignty in Latin America: optimists, skeptics, and an emerging research agenda' (2013) 35 Contexto internacional 325.

21 Briceño-Ruiz and Morales, n 18, 6.

22 Iran and Syria in ALBA, New Zealand, and Mexico in Mercosur.

23 Rafael A. Porrata-Doria Jr., 'ALBA and UNASUR: Back to the Future?' (2021–2022) 20 *Santa Clara Journal of International Law* 1, 17.

Member States' withdrawal from Latin American RIOs is also a recurring fact. In addition to Argentina, Brazil, Colombia, Ecuador and Uruguay withdrawing from UNASUR, Chile and Venezuela withdrew from the Andean Community in 1974 and 2006, respectively. Moreover, Venezuela withdrew from the Inter-American Convention on Human Rights in 2012. All these withdrawals respond to the political shifts in the region: the disappearance of common interest due to changes in a State's government translates into its withdrawal.[24]

In Latin America, the concept of region goes beyond geography, with shared values and interests playing a significant role in its definition. The rise, fall, shifts and withdrawals would mirror the pendular nature of Latin American politics.[25] This results in the proliferation of RIOs with short lifespans, which makes cooperation on long-term issues like climate change difficult.

2.2 *The Role of Law in Latin American RIOs*

As a reaction to the political element in Latin America, be it because of its counter-hegemonic potential against imperialism[26] or the formalist tradition of legal actors,[27] law plays a central role in structuring the region.[28] Regarding Latin American RIOs, the prevalence of law as the vehicle driving regional cooperation creates a conundrum. On the one hand, any form of regional cooperation needs to be structured through legal instruments. On the other hand, Latin America's legal formalism embraces a concept of sover-

24 Rafael Vargas-Hidalgo, 'La Crisis del Pacto Andino' (1977) 112 Boletín de Información, 101.

25 Olivier Dabène, 'Introduction: Electoral Cycles, Continuity, and Change in Latin American Politics: A Framework for Analysis' in Olivier Dabène (ed.), *Latin America's Pendular Politics: Electoral Cycles and Alternations* (Springer International Publishing, 2023) 2.

26 Nicole Jenne, 'The Origins of Regional Ideas: International Law, External Legitimization and Latin America's 'legalismo'' (2022) 24 *Journal of the History of International Law / Revue d'histoire du droit international* 500, 511.

27 Juny Montoya, 'The Current State of Legal Education Reform in Latin America: A Critical Appraisal' (2010) 59 *Journal of Legal Education* 545, 547. Jorge Contesse, 'International Law Scholarship in Latin America' (2024) 64 Virginia Journal of International Law, 3. For an overview of the evolution of formalism in Latin America, see: Diego Eduardo López Medina, *Teoría impura del derecho: la transformación de la cultura jurídica latinoamericana* (Legis 2009).

28 Juan Pablo Scarfi, 'Denaturalizing the Monroe Doctrine: The rise of Latin American legal anti-imperialism in the face of the modern US and hemispheric redefinition of the Monroe Doctrine' (2020) *Leiden Journal of International Law* 1.

eignty that emphasises equality between nations and the principle of non-intervention in domestic affairs,[29] diminishing the potential for rules-based cooperation.

2.2.1 Law and Sovereignty

Under the legalist paradigm, new regional cooperation initiatives are channelled through international treaties.[30] However, a robust understanding of sovereignty restricts the mandate of Latin American RIOS. The OAS Charter illustrates this point when Article 1 makes a clear connection between the principle of conferral and the principle of non-intervention:

> The Organization of American States has no powers other than those expressly conferred upon it by this Charter, none of whose provisions authorises it to intervene in matters that are within the internal jurisdiction of the Member States.

The tension between the RIO's mandate and the Member States' interests might manifest in two ways. First, the principal-agent theory, typical of international organizations theory,[31] combined with the strong notion of sovereignty that characterizes Latin American International Law, leads to close monitoring by member states to ensure strict adherence to the mandate of Latin American RIOS. For instance, in 2018, Argentina, Brazil, Chile, Colombia and Paraguay penned a joint letter complaining about how the Inter-American Court of Human Rights (IACtHR) applied the Inter-American Convention on Human Rights (IACHR).[32] More specifically, they argued that the Court was not 'respecting the legitimate space of autonomy available to

29 Arnulf Becker Lorca, *Mestizo International Law* (Cambridge University Press, 2014) 62.

30 Jenne, n 24, 518

31 Andrew Guzman, 'International Organizations and the Frankenstein Problem' (2013) 24 *European Journal of International Law* 999. On the functionalist theory underpinning the relationship between Latin American RIOS and its Member States, see: Guy Fiti Sinclair, 'Between Functionalism and Hegemony: Regional International Organizations in the History of International Law' (2024) 21 *International Organizations Law Review* 65. Jan Klabbers, 'Contending approaches to international organizations: between functionalism and constitutionalism' in Jan Klabbers and Asa Wallendahl (eds.), *Research Handbook on the Law of International Organizations* (Edward Elgar, 2011).

32 República Argentina, la República Federativa del Brasil, la República de Chile, la República de Colombia y la República del Paraguay. Declaración Sobre el Sistema Interamericano de Derechos Humanos (2019), available at. https://repositorio.uca.edu.ar/bitstream/123456789/8628/1/declaracion-sobre-sistema-interamericano.pdf. Last accessed: 12 September 2024.

States', i.e., sovereignty, and that the Court was not following its mandate insofar as it was not strictly applying the sources of International Human Rights Law.[33] Thus, these States noticed that the Inter-American Court of Human Rights did not strictly adhere to its treaty. Instead, it used teleological interpretation to maximize the effectiveness of the Inter-American Commission on Human Rights. This was seen as a deviation from its mandate and interference with their sovereign space. This strong notion of sovereignty is so prevalent that even sectoral Latin American RIOs, like the Latin American Organization for Fisheries Development (OLDEPESCA), provide as its basic principles:

> The principles of equality, sovereignty, independence of the States, solidarity, non-intervention in domestic affairs and respect for the different political, economic and social systems, ..., and respect for the sovereignty of States over their fishery resources.[34]

Second, the tension between a RIO's mandate and the interests of the member states can also account for the limited presence of law-making powers within the organization. A feature sometimes present in a RIO's competence is the possibility of being conferred law-making powers.[35] RIOs can adopt legal instruments that would bind its Member States. Given the importance of the legal form in the region, it would be understandable to assume that Latin American RIOs would have those law-making powers. However, only a few Latin American RIOs would them powers. For instance, the different institutions of the Andean Community can adopt Decisions and Regulations. Andean decisions are binding for its Member States as soon as they are approved and are generally applied directly in the Member States.[36] Similarly, the Ouro Preto Protocol outlines a system of sources that grants normative powers to Mercosur's bodies, constitutive treaties and protocols.[37] Yet, the rest of the RIOs in Latin America lack those law-making powers.

---

33 Ibid.

34 Article 3 Agreement instituting the Latin American Organization for Fisheries Development (OLDEPESCA).

35 Damian Chalmers, 'The Distinctiveness of Regional International Organization Law' (2024) 21 *International Organizations Law Review* 43, 53.

36 Articles 2 and 3 Treaty Creating the Court of Justice of the Cartagena Agreement. For an analysis of the Andean Community's system of sources, see: Jorge Antonio Quindimil López, *Instituciones y Derecho de la Comunidad Andina* (Tirant lo Blanch, 2006) 190.

37 Article 41 Protocol of Ouro Preto. See: Belén Olmos Giupponi, 'Sources of Law in MERCOSUR' in Marcílio Toscano Franca Filho, Lucas Lixinski and Belén Olmos Giupponi (eds.), *The Law of MERCOSUR* (Bloomsbury Publishing, 2010).

In addition, the limited reach of law within Latin American RIOs is also present in their limited role in fostering treaty-making. International organizations, regardless of whether they are universal or regional, have traditionally been forums where international conventions have been negotiated.[38] RIOs would foster cooperation that would result in the adoption of regional international instruments. The OAS would be an example of a Latin American RIO that, besides adopting resolutions binding on its Member States, also serves as a forum for treaty negotiation. However, the role of the OAS as a treaty forum has had some mixed results.[39] On the one hand, significant treaties like the American Convention on Human Rights have been negotiated and signed under OAS' auspices. On the other hand, it is worth noting that only a small number of Inter-American treaties have received ratification from all OAS Member States.[40]

To a certain extent, Latin American RIOs' legal form would not permeate into its internal structure. Latin American RIOs are more focused on coordinating its members' actions than on establishing an autonomous system of legal sources.[41] As a result, their main instruments would be political, taking the form of declarations, resolutions and action plans rather than legally binding instruments. The political nature of most Latin American RIOs' instruments reduces the scope for collective action and, at best, fosters coordinated approaches.

Latin American States' concern for their policy space translates into narrow RIO mandates and soft law instruments. The compliance problems characterising Latin American RIOs and legal processes explain these instruments.[42] Since Latin American States struggle with compliance, a broader mandate increases the possibility of infringing said mandate.

---

38 José E Alvarez, *International Organizations as Law-makers* (Oxford University Press, 2005) 317.

39 Jean-Michel Arrighi, 'Some Recent Contributions of the Inter-American System to International Law' in Jorge E Viñuales and others (eds.), *The International Legal Order in the XXIst Century/L'ordre juridique international au XXIeme siècle/El órden jurídico internacional en el siglo XXI* (Brill Nijhoff 2023) 1018.

40 Ibid.

41 Chalmers, n 33, 53.

42 Jorge L. Esquirol, *Ruling the Law: Legitimacy and Failure in Latin American Legal Systems* (Cambridge University Press, 2019).

2.2.2 Dispute Settlement and Latin America

The prevalence of the law as a structural element would also explain the central role that dispute settlement plays in the region.[43] The Bogotá Pact usually exemplifies the significant role of dispute settlement in Latin America. Concluded under the auspices of the OAS, the Bogotá Pact would provide for compulsory jurisdiction of the International Court of Justice on

a) The interpretation of a treaty;
b) Any question of international law;
c) The existence of any fact which, if established, would constitute the breach of an international obligation;
d) The nature or extent of the reparation to be made for the breach of an international obligation.[44]

Latin American countries are the most frequent users of the International Court of Justice. Most cases involve essential aspects of sovereignty, such as territorial and maritime disputes, or relate to the principle of non-intervention. Similarly, the compulsory jurisdiction of dispute settlements is also a defining feature of the courts established under Latin American RIOs.[45]

As with law in general, the functioning of these dispute settlement mechanisms has had mixed results.[46] The IACtHR is a noteworthy example. On the one hand, it has become a success story as regards regional courts of human rights and is even considered a guiding light of the transformative constitutionalism movement.[47]

On the other hand, the IACtHR replicates the same compliance problems that haunt Latin America.[48] As Cavallaro and Brewer show:

---

43 On the role of international dispute settlement in Latin America, see: Ximena Fuentes, 'Latin American states and the International Court of Justice' in Natalie Klein (ed.), *Litigating International Law Disputes: Weighing the Options* (Cambridge University Press, 2014) 79. Cf. Juan José Quintana, 'The Latin American Contribution to International Adjudication: The Case of the International Court of Justice' (1992) 39 *Netherlands International Law Review* 127.

44 Article XXXI Bogotá Pact.

45 E.g., Central American Court of Justice, Caribbean Court of Justice, the Andean Tribunal of Justice, Mercosur Permanent Review Court.

46 Salvatore Caserta, *International Courts in Latin America and the Caribbean: Foundations and Authority* (Oxford University Press, 2020), 12.

47 Armin von Bogdandy and René Urueña, 'International Transformative Constitutionalism in Latin America' (2020) 114 *American Journal of International Law* 403.

48 Damián González-Salzberg, 'Complying (Partially) with the Compulsory Judgments of the Inter-American Court of Human Rights' in Pedro Fortes and others (eds.), *Law and Policy in Latin America: Transforming Courts, Institutions, and Rights* (Palgrave, 2017) 39.

> A review of the Inter-American Court's past cases demonstrates that the Court does face frequent non-implementation of its judgments. Governments may openly reject certain orders, but even more commonly they assert that they will comply or are in the process of complying, yet fail to take the steps necessary to bring their practices into line with the requirements of the Court's judgment.[49]

Likewise, engagement with dispute settlements has also led to a backlash against Latin American RIOS, with some Latin American States withdrawing from the Bogotá Pact (El Salvador and Colombia) and the IACtHR (Venezuela and the Dominican Republic) and other States expressing their discomfort with how the IACtHR was interpreting human rights law.[50]

Operating in the same pendular fashion that informs the concept of region, the prevalence of the legal form also oscillates. Nowadays, the most recent Latin American RIOS are characterized by their open-ended nature and informality. For instance, in the aftermath of UNASUR's collapse, Argentina, Brazil, Chile, Colombia, Ecuador, Guyana, Paraguay and Peru established the Forum for the Progress and Integration of South America (PROSUR) through a political declaration[51] and provided for the coordination through summits rather than creating an institution that would support its objectives. The political declaration does not even mention the term organization; instead, it favours the creation of a space that 'should be implemented gradually, have a flexible structure, be lightweight, inexpensive, with clear operating rules, and have an agile decision-making mechanism.'[52] The notion of flexibility, as opposed to a fixed structure established by a treaty, is also mentioned in other parts of the

49 James L. Cavallaro and Stephanie Erin Brewer, 'Reevaluating Regional Human Rights Litigation in the Twenty-First Century: The Case of the Inter-American Court' (2008) 102 *American Journal of International Law* 768, 785.

50 República Argentina, la República Federativa del Brasil, la República de Chile, la República de Colombia y la República del Paraguay. Declaración Sobre el Sistema Interamericano de Derechos Humanos (2019), available at. https://repositorio.uca.edu.ar/bitstream/123456789/8628/1/declaracion-sobre-sistema-interamericano.pdf. Last accessed: 12 September 2024.

51 PROSUR. Declaración de Santiago para la renovación y el fortalecimiento de América del Sur. https://foroprosur.org/wp-content/uploads/2020/09/Declaracion-de-Ministros-de-RREE-1.pdf. Last accessed: 12 September 2024.

52 PROSUR. Article 3 Declaración de Santiago para la renovación y el fortalecimiento de América del Sur. https://foroprosur.org/wp-content/uploads/2020/09/Declaracion-de-Ministros-de-RREE-1.pdf. Last accessed: 12 September 2024.

declaration.[53] While this flexibility might allow for faster decision-making, it also limits the depth of the cooperation: it rarely fosters the cooperation that would be in the lasting interest of all its members.[54]

3 Latin American RIOs and Climate Change

Given the panorama described in the previous section, three possible scenarios arise regarding how Latin American RIOs tackle global challenges like climate change. A new Latin American RIO would be established in the first scenario so that Latin American States could cooperate on climate change issues on a regional basis. In the second scenario, that cooperation is channelled through existing Latin American RIOs, which adopt instruments to tackle the challenges of climate change. In the third scenario, climate change cooperation is structured through the existing Latin American RIOs, albeit in a limited fashion, mainly through litigation on climate change channelled through a Latin American RIO's dispute settlement mechanism.

3.1 *A Latin American RIO to Cooperate on Climate Change?*

The potential for Latin American RIOs to have a specific policy focus is not a novelty. Besides the obvious Latin American RIOs focused on trade policy, like Mercosur or ALADI, other Latin American RIOs take a sectoral approach unrelated to trade. For instance, the Pan-American Health Organization, before becoming a regional agency of the World Health Organization,[55] had as mandate: 'to promote and coordinate efforts of the countries of the Western Hemisphere to combat disease, lengthen life, and promote the physical and mental health of the people.'[56] Likewise, OLDPESCA focuses on 'the correct use and protection of fishery resources within its maritime jurisdiction zones of each

53 PROSUR. Article 4 Declaración de Santiago para la renovación y el fortalecimiento de América del Sur. https://foroprosur.org/wp-content/uploads/2020/09/Declaracion-de-Ministros-de-RREE-1.pdf. Last accessed: 12 September 2024.

54 Why Prosur is not the way to unite South America. https://www.economist.com/the-americas/2019/03/21/why-prosur-is-not-the-way-to-unite-south-america?fsrc=scn%2Ftw%2Fte%2Fbl%2Fed%2Fwhyprosurisnotthewaytounitesouthamericabello. Last accessed: 12 September 2024.

55 Article 54 WHO Constitution.

56 Organization Pan American Health and Organization Pan American Health, *The Constitution of the Pan American Health Organization* (1991) art 1.

State whilst preserving the marine and freshwater environment and applying rational conservation policies.'[57]

Thus, under the first possible scenario, the region's politics would have coalesced to advance deeper cooperation on climate change. Since cooperation in the region is usually structured through an international legal instrument, following the same reasoning, a regional cooperation initiative on climate change could exist, provided that the political element is present. However, that is not the case. The region's politics have not seen the merits of a regional approach to climate change.[58]

3.2 *Climate Change within Latin American RIOs' Mandate*

An examination of how the current Latin American RIOs might approach climate change can be conducted from three perspectives. First, from a constitutional point of view, what does Latin American RIOs' primary law say about climate change? Second, from a material point of view, how do Latin American RIOs tackle climate change in practice? Third, from a formal point of view, i.e., what kind of instruments have been used by Latin American RIOs to tackle climate change?

3.2.1 The Constitutional Nature of Climate Change Policy

UNASUR was the only Latin American RIO that expressly mentioned the fight against climate change in its mandate. Article 3 of UNASUR lists its specific objectives: 'The protection of biodiversity, water resources, and ecosystems, as well as cooperation in disaster prevention, and in combating the causes and effects of climate change.' Thus, there was an opportunity for cooperation on ambitious fashion. Yet, UNASUR reproduced Latin American RIOs' common characteristics of a lack of a solid internal structure, which could support climate change action in this case. UNASUR's structure responded to the traditional intergovernmental characteristics. It consisted of three councils (Heads of State and Government, Ministers of Foreign Affairs and Delegates), which a General Secretariat supported.[59] The UNASUR Treaty recognized the possibility of creating additional sectoral councils be-

57 OLDEPESCA. Preamble of the Agreement instituting the Latin American Organization for Fisheries Development (OLDEPESCA). chrome- https://treaties.un.org/doc/Publication/UNTS/Volume%201427/volume-1427-I-24116-English.pdf. Last accessed: 12 September 2024.

58 On the fragmented politics of climate change in Latin America, see: Guy Edwards and J Timmons Roberts, *A fragmented continent: Latin America and the global politics of climate change* (MIT Press, 2015).

59 Art 4 UNASUR Treaty.

sides these bodies.[60] However, regardless of the constitutional recognition of the fight against climate change, it was not prioritized without UNASUR's structure.[61] No sectoral council or other institutional mechanism was set up on the issue.[62]

Moreover, the few instruments UNASUR adopted were guidelines or declarations, but it did not propose any joint instrument to tackle climate change.[63] Given UNASUR's demise, its potential impact on setting the agenda has wholly diminished, rendering it irrelevant in the current discussions on climate change.

Another interesting example of how climate change is recognized in the constitutional law of the Latin American RIO is the OAS. Even though the OAS Charter does not mention climate change, the subsequent Summits of the Americas have incorporated it as part of the OAS mandate. Given that these summits, although carried out outside of the OAS' framework but with the full support of the OAS secretariat, gather the Heads of State and Government of the OAS Member States, their declarations are seen as mandates for the RIO.[64] The Summit's declarations establish a mandate for addressing climate change in the region. Initially, it just encouraged the OAS States 'to ratify and begin implementation of the provisions of the Framework Convention on Climate Change'[65] back in 1994. Nowadays, the declarations take a more complex stance. The IX Summit of the Americas, Los Angeles, held in 2022, encouraged the OAS States 'To accelerate measures on climate change adaptation, taking into account different national circumstances,' and among the ways to strike that balance between cooperation and the sovereign space so prevalent in the region,[66] the declaration lists mechanisms that should play a role in that

60 Art 5 UNASUR Treaty.

61 Andrea Ribeiro Hoffmann, 'Climate Change Cooperation in Latin American Regionalism' in Andrea Ribeiro Hoffmann, Paula Sandrin and Yannis E. Doukas (eds.), *Climate Change in Regional Perspective: European Union and Latin American Initiatives, Challenges, and Solutions* (Springer, 2024) 29.

62 Diego Vera Piñeros, Paula Prieto Ararat and Daniela Garzón Amórtegui, 'De Unasur a Prosur: una gobernanza ambiental reducida y un legado de desaciertos para la Amazonia' in Eduardo Pastrana Buelvas and Nicole Stopfer (eds.), *Gobernanza multinivel de la Amazonia* (Fundación Konrad Adenauer, 2020) 128.

63 Ribeiro Hoffmann, n 59, 32

64 Lourdes M Regueiro Bello and Claudia Marín Suárez, 'Cumbre de las Américas: alter ego de la OEA: Summit of the Americas: alter-ego of the OAS' (2022) 04 Cuadernos de Nuestra América 178.

65 Summit of the Americas Plan of Action, Miami 1994, p. 16. Available at https://summit-americas.org/i_summit/i_summit_poa_en.pdf. Last accessed: 12 September 2024.

66 See supra section 2.2.

accelerating process.[67] The flexible relationship between the OAS and the Summit of the Americas allowed climate change policy to become part of the OAS constitutional mandate.

3.2.2 The Substance of Climate Change Regulation: Between Environment, Human Rights and Disaster Prevention

The lack of express mention of climate change in the constituent instrument of most Latin American RIOs raises the issue of whether there might be some implied power that can be derived from other legal bases. As anyone familiar with international institutional law, implied powers are a common feature of international organizations, and Latin American RIOs are no exception.

A cursory view identifies that Latin American RIOs often implicitly derive their climate change initiatives from three policy areas: disaster management environment and human rights. These are not exclusive, meaning that climate change issues might arise from more than one of these legal bases.

3.2.2.1 *Disaster Management*

Climate change policy nowadays is usually articulated from two policy perspectives: mitigation and adaptation.[68] An analysis of the practice of Latin

67 IX Summit of the Americas, Los Angeles, 2022 'Continue to scale up and enhance finance and investments in climate action from a wide variety of sources and to work towards enhancing capacity to access and benefit from these investments and finance flows, particularly by the most vulnerable countries;

c. Enhance environmental education, through research and active and inclusive participation from all stakeholders to build capacities for climate change adaptation and mitigation for current and future generations, including youth, indigenous peoples, persons of African descent, civil society, women's organizations, the private sector, policymakers, practitioners and persons working in related industries;

d. Redouble efforts to incorporate climate risks in plans, policies, operations and sectoral budgets in order to generate resilience in strategic sectors and reduce vulnerability to climate change;

e. Develop efficient, transparent, exact, coherent and comparable systems for monitoring and evaluating climate change adaptation and mitigation actions;

f. Enhance and promote delivery of climate information services, decision-making support tools, and early warning systems to improve understanding and response to climate impacts and minimize loss and damage associated with the adverse effects of climate change across sectors and different scales.' Available at: https://www.summit-americas.org/sisca/env_climate.html. Last accessed: 12 September 2024.

68 Andrea Lucas Garín, 'Cambio climático y acuerdos comerciales regionales' (2017) Una mirada desde el Sistema Multilateral de Comercio, Santiago de Chile: Ediciones Universidad Finis Terrae 39, 25.

American RIOs shows that adaptation measures prevail over mitigation. More specifically, adaptation measures are taken within the context of disaster management. Underpinning this approach is that natural disasters, be it extreme weather events, earthquakes, or even volcanic eruptions, are part of the region's day-to-day lives. Consequently, inasmuch as climate change has increased the frequency and strength of extreme weather events as one of its consequences, Latin American RIOs would approach adaptation measures from that angle. For instance, Resolutions from the Association of Caribbean States (ACS) and the Andean Community show how climate change affects disaster management policies.[69] Likewise, the OAS practice is an excellent example of the link between climate change and disaster management. Its Department of Sustainable Development lists 'Risk Management and Adaptation to Climate Change' within its programmatic areas.[70] The OAS conceptualizes climate change policy as a factor in increasing natural disasters.

Consequently, the instruments focus on adapting to and mitigating natural disasters resulting from climate change rather than explicitly mentioning it.[71]

---

69 ACS. Declaración de Merida. Sexta Cumbre De Jefes De Estado Y/O Gobierno De Los Estados, Países Y Territorios De La Asociación De Estados Del Caribe, 30 April 2014, para 9. Andean Community. DECISIÓN N° 860 Aprobación de la 'Guía para la Coordinación de la Asistencia Humanitaria entre los Países Miembros de la Comunidad Andina' https://www.comunidadandina.org/DocOficialesFiles/Gacetas/Gaceta%204017.pdf Last accessed: 12 September 2024; Andean Community. Decisión 529 – 'Creación del Comité Andino para la Prevención y Atención de Desastres CAPRADE' https://www.comunidadandina.org/DocOficialesFiles/Gacetas/GACE3017.pdf. Last accessed: 12 September 2024.

70 https://www.oas.org/en/sedi/dsd//RiskManagement/default.asp. Last accessed: 12 September 2024.

71 See: AG/RES. 2750 (XLII-O-12) Existing Mechanisms for Disaster Prevention and Response and Humanitarian Assistance Among the Member States (Adopted at the second plenary session, held on 4 June, 2012); AG/RES. 2647 (XLI-O-11) Existing Mechanisms for Disaster Prevention and Response and Humanitarian Assistance among the Member States (adopted at the fourth plenary session, held on 7 June, 2011); AG/RES. 2610 (XL-O-10) Existing Mechanisms for Disaster Prevention And Response and Humanitarian Assistance Among the Member States (adopted at the fourth plenary session, held on 8 June, 2010); AG/RES. 2492 (XXXIX-O-09) Existing Mechanisms for Disaster Prevention and Response and Humanitarian Assistance among the Member States (adopted at the fourth plenary session, held on 4 June, 2009); AG/RES. 2314 (XXXVII-O-07) Existing Mechanisms for Disaster Prevention and Response and Humanitarian Assistance among the Member States (adopted at the fourth plenary session, held on 5 June, 2007); AG/RES. 2182 (XXXVI-O-06) Adoption of the Amended Statutes of the Inter-American Committee on Natural Disaster Reduction (adopted at the fourth plenary session, held on 6 June, 2006); AG/RES. 2184 (XXXVI-O-06) Natural Disaster Reduction, Risk Management, and Assistance in Natural and other Disaster Situations (adopted at the fourth plenary session, held on 6 June, 2006); AG/RES. 2114 (XXXV-O-

For instance, the 2012 Resolution does not mention climate change. Still, it is designed to adapt to 'the new realities and complexities of disasters and to the new framework for action in the international arena.'[72]

Mercosur also has a 'Climate Change Adaptation and Risk Management Commission,' yet no information is available on the Mercosur system concerning this commission's meetings, begging the question of whether the commission has even met. In any case, there is a Meeting of Ministers and High Authorities on Comprehensive Disaster Risk Management within Mercosur, which follows the same pattern as the previous examples, in which climate change is seen as an element that increases natural disasters.[73]

3.2.2.2 *Environment*

A logical entry point for the discussions on climate change would be via environmental policy. The practice shows that the environmental policy aspect would allow Latin American RIOs to adopt measures dealing with mitigation rather than solely with adaptation as the disaster management competence. This is the case of the Central American Integration System (SICA), which created the Central American Commission on Environment and Development.[74] This Commission has published a Regional Strategy on Climate Change,[75] which takes a broader focus than just disaster management and establishes other strategic areas like capacity building, education, awareness,

05) Natural Disaster Reduction And Risk Management (Adopted at the fourth plenary session, held on June 7, 2005); AG/RES. 2024 (XXXIV-O-04) Natural Disaster Reduction (adopted at the fourth plenary session, held on 8 June, 2004); AG/RES. 1955 (XXXIII-O-03) Natural Disaster Reduction (resolution adopted at the fourth plenary session, held on 10 June, 2003); AG/RES. 1885 (XXXII-O-02) Natural Disaster Reduction (adopted at the fourth plenary session held on 4 June, 2002); AG/RES. 1682 (XXIX O 99) OAS Natural Disaster Reduction and Response Mechanisms (resolution adopted at the first plenary session, held on 7 June, 1999). Available at: https://www.oas.org/en/sedi/dsd/RiskManagement/Mandates.asp. Last accessed: 12 September 2024.

72 Ibid, p. 1.

73 Mercosur. XXXI Reunión de Ministros y Altas Autoridades de Gestión Integral de Riesgos de Desastres, Foz de Iguazú, 19 September 2023, p. 4. https://documentos.mercosur.int/simfiles/docreuniones/97548_RMAGIR_2023_ACTA03_PT.pdf. Last accessed: 12 September 2024.

74 Constitutive Agreement of the Central American Commission on Environment and Development, 30 March 2012, https://www.sica.int/documentos/convenio-constitutivo-de-la-comision-centroamericana-de-ambiente-y-desarrollo-ccad_1_96566.html. Last accessed: 12 September 2024.

75 SICA. Estrategia Regional de Cambio Climatico – ERCC. 01 November 2010. https://www.sica.int/documentos/estrategia-regional-de-cambio-climatico-ercc_1_96568.html. Last accessed: 12 September 2024.

communication, citizen participation, technology transfer, negotiations and international management.[76]

Likewise, in CARICOM, Article 65 of the Revised Treaty of Chaguaramas focused on environmental protection. Although it did not mention climate change, CARICOM established the Caribbean Community Climate Change Centre. Though initially focused on adaptation to climate change,[77] it also focused on mitigation policies.[78]

3.2.2.3 *Human Rights*

The interconnectedness of human rights and climate change policy significantly shapes the approach to addressing the latter in Latin America. In 2008, the OAS General Assembly adopted a resolution recognising that 'climate change is a shared concern of all humankind, and that its effects have an impact on sustainable development and could have consequences for the full enjoyment of human rights.'[79] As a result, the Assembly requested the Inter-American Commission of Human Rights (IACHR) to investigate the potential connection between the adverse effects of climate change and the full enjoyment of human rights. Yet it was not until 2021 that the IACHRs adopted a resolution on how climate change affects the human rights obligations of Latin American states.[80]

Though, as Lucas and Ossandón have argued, the link between the human right to health and climate change is a given,[81] the IACHR goes beyond that linkage. The resolution adopts a comprehensive approach to human rights,

---

76 Ibid, p. 47.

77 CARICOM. ACC Project (2003): Caribbean Risk Management Guidelines for Climate Change Adaptation Decision Making. Caribbean Community (CARICOM) and South Pacific Regional Environment Programme (SPREP), Barbados. http://dms.caribbeanclimate.bz/M-Files/openfile.aspx?objtype=0&docid=2879. Last accessed: 12 September 2024.

78 See Small Island Developing States (SIDS) Sustainable Energy Initiative (SIDS DOCK). https://www.caribbeanclimate.bz/blog/2017/07/27/2012-2016-sids-dock/. Last accessed: 12 September 2024.

79 AG/RES. 2429 (XXXVIII-O/08) Human Rights and Climate Change in The Americas (adopted at the fourth plenary session, held on 3 June, 2008). https://www.acnur.org/fileadmin/Documentos/BDL/2009/6977.pdf.

80 IACHR. Resolution No. 3/2021 Climate Emergency: Scope of Inter-American Human Rights Obligations (adopted by the IACHR on 31 December, 2021). https://www.oas.org/en/iachr/decisions/pdf/2021/resolucion_3-21_ENG.pdf. Last accessed: 12 September 2024.

81 Andrea Lucas Garín and Marco Ossandón Chávez, 'Climate Change and the Right to Health in the Inter-American System of Human Rights' (2023) 1 *Global Health Law Journal* 31, 53.

focusing on outlining nine dimensions that systematize the human rights obligations of States in the context of the climate crisis. This approach aims to guide public policy decisions under a rights-based framework rather than just listing how human rights are affected.

Notably, the resolution puts human rights at the centre of Latin American States' climate change policies by setting a negative obligation as a starting point. More specifically, States must ensure that climate norms, policies and actions are developed to avoid negatively impacting human rights.[82] Also, the centrality of human rights leads to establishing positive climate change obligations with a wide-ranging impact. More specifically, the resolution establishes that: 'for the effective protection of human rights, States must take appropriate measures to mitigate greenhouse gases, implement adaptation measures and remedy the resulting damages.'[83] Latin American States would have a human rights obligation to adopt mitigation and adaptation measures. That human rights obligation would have a similar nature to economic, social and cultural rights, which means that it must be guaranteed 'to the maximum of the resources available to the State to progressively achieve their full effectiveness by all appropriate means'.[84] The IACHR would be configuring the human right to a healthy environment as a basis for adopting climate change policies in Latin America.

3.2.3 The Managerial Form of Climate Change Regulation

One consistent approach to regulating climate change in Latin American RIOs is the use of managerial tools rather than legal ones. Regardless of the substantive approach or the RIO, there is a clear preference for managerial techniques. In Latin American RIOs, a prevalence of instruments like action plans or strategies and other documents not legally binding can be observed. Even a powerful substantive statement like the IACHR resolution does not have binding force. These managerial tools are more associated with corporate governance and management than the law itself.[85] This phenomenon responds to the legal and political dynamics previously described.

82 IACHR. Resolution No. 3/2021 Climate Emergency: Scope of Inter-American Human Rights Obligations (adopted by the IACHR on 31 December, 2021), para 5.

83 Ibid, para 15.

84 Ibid.

85 Yet in recent years, there has been managerial turn in international organizations practices: Dimitri Van Den Meerssche, *The World Bank's Lawyers: The Life of International Law as Institutional Practice* (Oxford University Press, 2022)

On the one hand, in recent years, regional cooperation has been channelled through political and informal gatherings. Thus, it is coherent that the instruments that this more informal RIOs adopts are of a political and/or managerial nature. This pattern is prevalent in Latin American RIOs of a more informal nature, like the Community of Latin American and Caribbean States (CELAC). The declarations enshrining the results of the Heads of Government and Presidents summits contain some paragraphs about climate change policy. For instance, the latest summit's declaration stressed the necessity of coordinating regional action without giving that much substance.[86] Also, CELAC adopted the managerial approach by adopting action plans. In its latest one, it established that one of its objectives is promoting the evaluation and monitoring of regional reality based on the monitoring framework of the Sustainable Development Goals of the 2030 Agenda. This objective then translates into a series of strategies based chiefly on promoting dialogues to exchange best practices.[87]

On the other hand, when it comes to formal RIOs, the use of managerial tools responds to the concerns over competence creep and Latin American States' concern for safeguarding the policy space. Even in those Latin American RIOs with a more formal structure, most of the instruments dealing with climate change take a managerial approach. Thus, SICA has a regional climate change strategy, including a 5-year action plan with objectives, implementation axes and strategic guidelines. For instance, the strategic objective: 'Strengthen and generate regional actions to promote the mitigation and reduction of greenhouse gas emissions and the transition to low-carbon economies in the SICA countries' is pursued through different implementation axes, with 'Institutional Strengthening' being one of them. Within this axis, there are strategic guidelines such as: 'Promote policy dialogue on the environment and energy, and revive the Regional Alliance on Energy and Environment programme to support the achievement of energy targets and Nationally Determined Contributions (NDCs) for CO_2 emission reduction commitments made by the region's countries.' This intricate array of goals, implementation frameworks, and strategic directives resembles corporate governance more than International Institutional Law. Similarly, CARICOM, UNASUR and the

86 CELAC. Declaration of Kingstown VIII Summit of Heads of State and Government of the Community of Latin American and Caribbean States (Celac) Kingstown, 1 March, 2024. https://onenewsstvincent.com/wp-content/uploads/2024/03/final-declaration-of-kingstown.pdf. Last accessed: 12 September 2024.

87 CELAC. Plan de Trabajo Presidencia Pro-Tempore Argentina, 2022 a https://www.sela.org/media/3225726/plan_de_trabajo_celac_2022.pdf. Last accessed: 12 September 2024.

Andean Community have established guidelines to enhance coordination among their Member States regarding climate change.[88] Consequently, even in those RIOs with a formal structure, rather than regulation or cooperation, coordinating initiatives through informal instruments are favoured.

The prevalence of managerial techniques rather than legal instruments could be seen as a sign of our times or the logical consequence of Latin American States' concern for safeguarding the policy space. In that sense, Latin American RIOs' climate change policies seem to foster coordination and exchange of better practices and information, leaving States the policy space and autonomy to establish their policies.[89]

3.3 *The Judicialization of Climate Change*

With the prevalence of judicialization in Latin American law, it should come as no surprise that the region is no exception to the increasing trend of climate change litigation. There are 164 cases in the region, with Brazil taking the lead with 85.[90] However, this judicialization does not extend to the tribunals set up in the different RIOs, except for the Inter-American Human Rights System. This fact might be due to the unstable nature of the RIOs that host them. For instance, the Mercosur dispute settlement bodies have had little activity for over a decade. The Permanent Review Tribunal has yet to issue an award since 2012.[91]

---

88 CARICOM. ACC Project (2003): Caribbean Risk Management Guidelines for Climate Change Adaptation Decision Making. Caribbean Community (CARICOM) and South Pacific Regional Environment Programme (SPREP), Barbados. http://dms.caribbeanclimate.bz/M-Files/openfile.aspx?objtype=0&docid=2879. Last accessed: 12 September 2024. UNASUR. 'Guidelines for the elaboration of a regional agenda for the sovereign management of natural resources and their use for the integral development of South America. Andean Community. DECISIÓN N° 860 Aprobación de la 'Guía para la Coordinación de la Asistencia Humanitaria entre los Países Miembros de la Comunidad Andina' https://www.comunidadandina.org/DocOficialesFiles/Gacetas/Gaceta%204017.pdf. Last accessed: 12 September 2024.

89 Erika Pires Ramos and Fernanda de Salles Cavedon-Capdeville, 'Regional responses to climate change and migration in Latin America. In Benoît Mayer and François Crépeau (eds.), *Research Handbook on Climate Change, Migration and the Law* (Edward Elgar Publishing, 2017) 281.

90 These numbers have been built from Climate Case Chart: https://climatecasechart.com/search-non-us/. Last accessed: 12 September 2024.

91 Laudo del Tribunal Permanente de Revisión en el asunto N° 01/2012 «Procedimiento Excepcional de Urgencia solicitado por la República del Paraguay en relación con la suspensión de su participación en los Órganos del Mercado Común del Sur (MERCOSUR) y la incorporación de Venezuela como Miembro Pleno».

There is minimal practice regarding the Inter-American Human Rights System: only three petitions to the IACHR and two advisory opinions to the IACtHR. Petitions are actions brought by individuals against a State party and can eventually become cases before the IACtHR.[92] Of the three petitions concerning climate change issues, one petition has been denied, and two are pending. The first petition addressed the Inuit Circumpolar Conference's request for relief from human rights violations resulting from the impacts of climate change caused by acts and omissions of the United States. This petition was dismissed because the petitioners had failed to determine how such acts and omissions amounted to human rights violations protected by the Inter-American System of Human Rights.[93] The second petition, which was filed in 2013 and is still pending, concerns the impact of Canada's carbon emissions on the human rights of the Athabaskan people.[94] This petition is similar to the denied Inuit's petition against the US.[95] However, unlike the Inuit's action, which was rejected within a year, this one has been pending for over a decade. The third petition, filed in 2021, concerning the long-term health harms to children by toxic trash disposal in Haiti, is also pending.

With one petition denied on admissibility and the other two pending, it is impossible to articulate a general theory of the petition system's role in climate change policy. When examining the IACHR's role in addressing climate change, the lack of contentious cases on the issue suggests a diminished role for the IACHR by civil society bringing the petitions, especially when compared with the amount of domestic litigation on the issue.

Regarding how states perceive the IACtHR's role in addressing climate change, the picture is more optimistic for those who favour human rights litigation to advance climate change policy. Traditionally, environmental issues arose as part of the case law on the rights of indigenous peoples.[96] In those

---

92 Article 61 American Convention on Human Rights.

93 IACHR. *Petition to the Inter-American Commission on Human Rights Seeking Relief from Violations Resulting from Global Warming Caused by Acts and Omissions of the United States.* Petition P-1413-05. https://climatecasechart.com/wp-content/uploads/non-us-case-documents/2006/20061116_na_decision.pdf

94 IACHR. *Petition to the Inter-American Commission on Human Rights Seeking Relief from Violations of the Rights of Arctic Athabaskan Peoples Resulting from Rapid Arctic Warming and Melting Caused by Emissions of Black Carbon by Canada.*

95 Juan Auz, "So, this is permanence': The inter-American human rights system as a liminal space for climate justice' (2021) 22 *Melbourne Journal of International Law* 187, 20.

96 ICtHR. *Case of the Kaliña and Lokono Peoples V. Suriname.* Merits, Reparations and Costs Judgment of 25 November, 2015, para. 173. Available at https://corteidh.or.cr/docs/casos/articulos/seriec_309_ing.pdf. Last accessed: 12 September 2024.

judgments, the IACtHR established a link between the rights of those communities and environmental protection.

This trend of linking human rights and the environment expanded outside the realm of indigenous peoples' rights in *Advisory Opinion OC-23/17*. Colombia asked the IACtHR about the environmental obligations in the American Convention on Human Rights context. The IACtHR, building on previous obiter dicta,[97] recognized that 'there is an undeniable link between the protection of the environment and the enjoyment of other human rights.'[98] From this starting point, the American Convention on Human Rights recognizes three types of environmental obligations:

1) an obligation to prevent environmental damages, which involves a duty to regulate, a duty to supervise and monitor, a duty to require and approve environmental impact assessments, a duty to prepare a contingency plan, and a duty to mitigate if environmental damage occurs;[99]
2) an obligation to cooperate;[100] and
3) an obligation to provide information, justice and public participation.[101]

Against this backdrop, Chile and Colombia requested a second advisory opinion on climate change in 2023. It concerns the scope of the State's obligations to respond to the climate emergency.[102] The request seeks to clarify Advisory Opinion OC-23/17 further, and specially:

> The scope of the human rights affected by the climate emergency, and the State obligations to address this, individually and collectively, addressing its causes and consequences urgently and taking into account considerations of equity, justice, prudence and sustainability.[103]

---

97 ICtHR. *Case of Kawas Fernández v. Honduras*. Merits, reparations, and costs. Judgment of 3 April, 2009. Series C No. 196. para. 148. This case concerned the unsolved murder of an environmental activist. Available at: https://corteidh.or.cr/docs/casos/articulos/seriec_196_ing.pdf. Last accessed: 12 September 2024.

98 ICtHR. Advisory Opinion OC-23/17 of November 15, 2017, requested by the Republic of Colombia. The Environment and Human Rights. Available at: https://climatecasechart.com/wp-content/uploads/non-us-case-documents/2017/20171115_oc-2317_opinion-4.pdf. Last accessed: 12 September 2024.

99 Ibid. para 123–174.

100 Ibid. Para 181–210.

101 Ibid. 210–241.

102 ICtHR. Request for an advisory opinion on the Climate Emergency and Human Rights submitted to the Inter-American Court of Human Rights by the Republic of Colombia and the Republic of Chile. Pending. Available at: https://corteidh.or.cr/docs/opiniones/soc_1_2023_en.pdf. Last accessed: 12 September 2024.

103 Ibid.p. 6.

Even though two advisory opinions might not be enough to conclude the role of the IACtHR in relation to climate change, they signal how the region portrayed climate change policy in recent years. Human rights seem to be the language through which the law at the regional level articulates climate change obligations. Climate change would be a human rights issue. Moreover, given that Advisory Opinions are binding in the same terms as the ICtHR judgments,[104] adopting climate change policies necessarily needs to consider the environmental obligations recognized by the American Convention on Human Rights as declared by the ICtHR in its opinions.

This approach would be following Latin America's legalist tradition. On the one hand, it is noteworthy that it is through advisory opinions lodged by States and not through contentious cases brought by individuals that the IACtHR establishes far-reaching climate change obligations. The acquiescence of the States could be seen as the factor that explains the difference between the approaches of the IACtHR and the IACHR. On the other hand, the advisory opinions show how, although in a limited fashion, the law plays a key role regarding the cooperation on climate change in Latin America. In contrast to the actions carried out in the other Latin American RIOs, where rather than cooperation, coordination and sharing best practices prevail, within the ICtHR, cooperation is legal in nature.

4 Conclusion

This chapter explored how Latin American RIOs have approached the question of climate change policy and examined how the region's legal dynamics have influenced its response to climate change. By reviewing these legal dynamics, this contribution brought forward an alternative way of regional ordering other than the EU. It sought to illustrate that, like any other strategy for RIOs, the Latin American approach has both strengths and weaknesses. The Latin American perspective on RIOs offers valuable insight into the diversity within this category. To a certain extent, it would challenge the usefulness of that category. How can sectoral regional organizations like OLDEPESCA be analysed from the same point of view as more 'general' RIOs like the OAS?

104 ICtHR. Advisory Opinion Oc-21/14 Of August 19, 2014, Requested by the Argentine Republic, The Federative Republic of Brazil, The Republic of Paraguay and the Oriental Republic of Uruguay Rights and Guarantees of Children in the Context of Migration and/ or in Need of International Protection. Available at: https://corteidh.or.cr/docs/opiniones/seriea_21_eng.pdf. Last accessed: 12 September 2024.

Nevertheless, as products of a certain region, they share some commonalities.[105]

The chapter began by exploring how law and politics shape the creation, design, success and failures of Latin American RIOS. Unlike the European Union, where the doctrines of implied powers and the teleological interpretation are an integral part of its identity, when it comes to Latin American RIOS, the formalist tradition sees with suspicion those doctrines. In turn, Latin American formalism triggers contradictory processes regarding RIOS. The prevalence of the law as a way of ordering regional cooperation would give certainty and some degree of control to the Member States. They are indeed the masters of their treaties.

Yet, that control transforms into instability and informality. As a result, the proliferation of RIOS summed up with a concern over the place of the law within them, resulted in the proliferation of initiatives that, rather than fostering cooperation on climate change in the region, advance some coordination. Paradoxically, a region that is very vulnerable to the impacts of climate change has not failed to take a more proactive cooperation stance regarding climate change.

Moreover, those coordination initiatives are characterized by their informal nature. More than legal instruments, they are managerial tools that also limit their impact in their reach to advance climate change policy beyond what each State might internally decide. The chapter has shown that the only exception where the region has established some climate change rules has happened through reconceptualising climate change as a human rights issue and judicializing it. While this approach might foster some cooperation between the States in the region, it is still unclear whether it will be effective, especially if an account is taken of the compliance problems that beset Latin American States.

105 On the issue of the common law of RIOS, see: ILA: The International Law of Regional Organizations Final Report. (2024). Available at: https://www.ila-hq.org/en_GB/documents/ila-study-group-regional-organisations-final-report-may-24. Last accessed 25 October 2024.

Index

Action plans
Managerial use 32, 250, 252, 268–270, 274
Adaptation 266–270
Disaster management 264–267
Advisory opinions
Inter-American Court of Human Rights 271–273
African Union (AU) 31, 70, 120, 130–131, 144, 236
Andean Community 10, 57, 251, 255, 257, 265, 270
Disaster management policies 265
Legal instruments 270
Anti-Coercion Instrument 170–197
Arab League (AL) 144, 167
Arctic Council 27–28
Argentinian crisis 59–60
Articles on Responsibility of International Organizations (ARIO) 8, 144, 162–163
Articles on Responsibility of Internationally Wrongful Acts (ARSIWA) 144, 155
Association of Southeast Asian Nations (ASEAN)
Charter 61–62
Geopolitical awakening 242–245
Economic community 62
Plus three (+3) 43, 62–63
Political-Security Community 245
Regional integration 61–65
Way 244
Asian crisis 61

Bologna
Declaration 81
Process 78–88

Caribbean Community Climate Change Centre 267
China 28–29, 43, 62–65, 171, 193, 227, 234, 239–241, 244–246, 248
Citizenship
By investment 202, 216, 219–224
EU 84, 119, 201–225
Climate change
Judicialization 252, 270–273
Managerial strategies 252, 268–269
Regional cooperation challenges 261
Regional litigation 261, 270–272
Sectoral approaches 261, 263, 274
Committee procedure, or comitology 179
Common commercial policy, or CCP 177–179, 188, 194
Common foreign and security policy, or CFSP 176, 188, 194, 230, 233, 235, 238, 247
Competence sharing 221–223
Compliance problems 49, 258–260, 274
Conceptual pluralism 32
Countermeasures 8, 14, 16, 144–145, 155, 162–167, 176–181, 186–191, 194–196

Dispute settlement 35, 37, 42–43, 49, 51, 56–59, 61, 170, 181, 191, 193, 196, 259–261, 270

East African Community (EAC) 57, 226, 228, 242–243, 248
East Asia 43, 46, 62–63
Economic coercion 170–197, 247
Economic interdependence 42–44, 47, 50–59, 63–65
EEA. *See also* EU Education Area 69, 78
EEA Nationals 205, 211–215, 224
Effectiveness 179–180, 248, 257
EGD. *See* European Green Deal 72
EHEA. *See also* European Higher Education Area 68, 78, 80–84, 88
Environmental policy
Central American Integration System 266
Mercosur 261, 266, 270
Erga omnes (obligations) 16, 142–145, 150, 154–158, 155, 163, 164–167, 169, 187, 189, 196
European Commission 53, 68, 72–78, 81–84, 106–108, 128–129, 172, 202, 227, 232, 236–240, 242, 249
European Council 73, 82
European Defence Fund 236
European Defence Industry Programme 237

European organizations 24–27
European Peace Facility 237, 238
European education policy 78–80

Flexibility
 Regional structures 254, 261
Foreign Direct Investment (FDI) 46, 59, 174, 180, 239
Foreign Subsidies Regulation 174, 239–240, 242
Free movement 80, 119–141
Functional organizations 23
Fundamental rights 204–205, 210, 213, 215, 218, 225

General interest 14, 16, 143, 144–146, 153–158, 160–163, 166–169
Geopolitics/geopolitical
 Geopolitical awakening 16, 226–229, 232–234, 241–249
Global Gateway 240
Global South 43–44, 46, 59–60, 65, 246
Global Strategy 231
Golden passport 206, 219–220

Hegemony 47, 50, 58
Hierarchy 144, 149, 152
Human rights
 Climate change and human rights 250, 267–268
 Inter-American Court of Human Rights 255–257, 259–260, 270–273
 Right to health 101, 109, 111, 268
 Right to science 99–100, 109, 113

Institut de droit international 163
Integration through law 228
Inter-American Convention on Human Rights
 Application and interpretation 255–256, 258, 271–273
Interinstitutional Relations 249
International Court of Justice (ICJ) 24, 26, 33, 150, 154–155, 164, 183, 221–222, 259
International Law Association (ILA) 2, 119, 175, 203, 227
International Law Commission (ILC) 5–6, 8–9, 25, 34, 36, 97, 143, 154, 158, 163, 184–185, 187
International responsibility 181, 186–188
Intraregional trade 42–43, 46–47, 51, 53–61, 63–64
Investment screening 174, 239

JTF. *See also* Just Transition Fund 72–77
JTM. *See also* Just Transition Mechanism 68, 71–73, 76, 89
JTTP. *See also* Just Territorial Transition Plan 74–77
Judicialization
 Climate change cases 252, 270–272
 Human rights focus 272–273

Laeken Declaration 232
Law of treaties 38, 165
Legal formalism
 Impact on cooperation 255–256
 Regional governance 274

Mercosur
 Disaster management 266
 Legal sources 257
Mixity 35–36
Mutual trust 205, 214, 218, 220–222, 224
Mutual recognition 205–206, 215, 218, 222–224

North American Free Trade Agreement (NAFTA) 42, 55–58, 63–64
Nationality 80, 202–203, 207–208, 213, 215–219, 221–224
Neofunctionalism 40, 51
Non-intervention 176, 181–185, 187, 190, 193, 195, 256–257
Non-state actors 28, 117
North Atlantic Treaty Organization (NATO) 27–28, 228, 245
Nomenclature of Territorial Units for Statistics (NUTS) 69, 75, 77

Organization of American States (OAS)
 Climate Change mandates 263–264

Disaster management policies 265
Overseas countries and territories 216, 219

Permanent Structured Cooperation (PESCO) 235–236, 238, 245
Phenomenology 3, 20, 22
Political organizations 23
Principled pragmatism 231–232, 244
Procurement
Defence/military 234, 237
Health 106–107, 110–111, 117
Professional practices 22

Realism 48
Region
Definition 4, 11, 25–26, 69–72, 119, 143–144, 253–255
Regional Citizenship 10, 119–120,124, 201–202, 205–206, 213, 215, 219, 224
Regional economic integration organizations (REIOS) 7–9, 24, 30–31, 229
Regional identity 11–12, 16–17, 205, 210–211, 215, 224–225
Regional international actor 71
Regional international law 143, 146–148
Regional international organization(s), RIO(s)
Definition 3, 26–27
Discussions in the ILC 5, 7–9
EU as a RIO 7, 15, 28–29, 32–38, 66, 69, 71, 89, 96–97, 99, 112, 117, 175, 188–189, 194–195, 197
Latin American RIOS 252–274
Regional thinking 68–72, 74, 77, 89–90
Regionalism
Comparative 41
Hegemonic 42, 44, 47–54, 57–58, 60–65, 145, 156–158, 167, 169
New 45, 70
Response measures 175–177, 179–181, 183–184, 186ff
Retorsion 161–162
Rule of Law 11, 103, 121, 127–128, 156–157, 159, 161, 248
Russia 12, 17, 27, 166, 175, 187, 227, 228, 232ff

Southern African Development Community (SADC) 43, 57–61, 64–65, 120–121
Sanctions 16, 144–146, 150–153, 159ff, 174–175, 189, 236, 240, 245, 246–247
Securitization 123, 136, 140, 173–175
Societal demands 45, 47, 51
Solidarity 3, 12, 205, 214–215, 224–225
Sovereignty
Constraints on regional law-making 43–44, 67–68, 71–72, 178, 185–186, 220–222, 256–257, 259
Space
Legal space 6, 67, 69, 85, 87–88, 90
Territorial space 6, 69–70, 216
Spatial. *See also* spatially 12, 39, 67, 69, 71, 89, 216, 218
Strategic autonomy 229, 232, 234, 240, 243
Subnational 69, 71–72, 89–90
Summit of the Americas
Climate change declarations 263–264
Supranational
Bodies and institutions 49–54, 56, 61, 65, 247, 249
Organizations 29–31, 68, 194

Taxonomy
International organizations 23
Trade, Development, and Cooperation Agreement (TDCA) 60, 65
Territory 6, 12, 25, 66–68, 74, 120, 202, 208, 210, 213, 216–220
Third country nationals 120, 125–126, 128, 133–134, 208, 215, 225

Union of South American Nations (UNASUR)
Climate change mandate 262
Institutional structure 262–263
United Nations
Charter 95–96, 99–100, 103, 112, 121, 143, 146–153, 185
Framework Convention on Climate Change 263
Security Council (UNSC) 146, 150–153, 162, 167
United States 55, 183, 234, 239, 246, 253, 271

Universal organizations 1, 6, 68, 143, 253
Unilateral turn/unilateralism 173, 229, 234, 239, 242
USMCA (United States–Mexico–Canada Agreement) 42

Values
EU values 12, 14, 103–104, 121, 159–160, 165–166, 204, 211, 215–217, 220, 223–225, 232
Pertaining to RIOS 3, 11, 12, 143, 169, 203, 206, 214, 253, 255
Verwaltungszweck 29

WTO Dispute Settlement Mechanism, WTO DSM 56, 176–177, 181, 190–196

www.ingramcontent.com/pod-product-compliance
Lightning Source LLC
LaVergne TN
LVHW020653300926
849161LV00004B/933